ArtMARC
Sourcebook

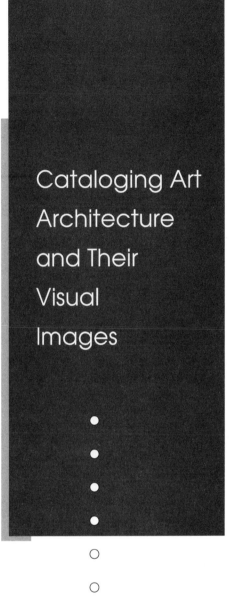

Cataloging Art
Architecture
and Their
Visual
Images

Linda McRae and Lynda S. White

E d i t o r s

On behalf of the
Art Libraries Society of North America

AMERICAN LIBRARY ASSOCIATION
Chicago and London   1998

Text design by Dianne Rooney

Composition by the dotted i in Berkeley on Xyvision

The paper used in this publication meets the minimum
requirements of American National Standard for Information Sciences—Permanence of Paper for Printed
Library Materials, ANSI Z39.48-1992. ∞

Library of Congress Cataloging-in-Publication Data
ArtMARC sourcebook : cataloging art, architecture, and
   their visual images / Linda McRae and Lynda S. White,
   editors.
        p.   cm.
      "On behalf of the Art Libraries Society of North America."
      Includes bibliographical references and index.
      ISBN 0-8389-0723-7
      1. Cataloging of art—United States. 2. MARC formats
   —United States. I. McRae, Linda. II. White, Lynda S.
   N440.A78   1997
   025.3′4—dc21   97-39441

Printed in the United States of America.

02 01 00 99 98   5 4 3 2 1

Contents

iii

Foreword

Sherman Clarke

Over the past thirty years, the MARC formats for bibliographic and authority records have become more and more the foundation for cataloging data at individual libraries and for cooperation between libraries. The formats for individual types of publications (for example, printed books, printed serials, maps, music, computer files, graphic materials) have been integrated over the past five years. While the MARC formats are principally the means of communicating the records to users or from system to system, the database structure used does affect the data, sometimes directly and other times indirectly. As libraries have lived in a machine-readable environment, common elements of cataloging records have become increasingly similar from institution to institution.

In general, visual resources collections have automated more recently than libraries. As these collections consider how to structure their data in an automated environment, it is beneficial to look at how other cataloging communities have done the task. Especially for those visual resources collections that are aligned with universities or other institutions that use MARC, a database structure based on MARC can be expedient in that it allows for access to the visual resources across the institution and allows the visual resources collection to benefit from the expertise in automation and other tools across the institution. This *Sourcebook,* by laying out the issues and discussing case studies using MARC in visual resources collections, can further significantly the debate surrounding, and progress of database structures for, art materials and visual documents thereof.

As a thirty-year-old but evolving language, MARC has some characteristics that reflect its age. The weight of millions of bibliographic records seems to preclude at present changing the formats in fundamental ways to newer technology. Theorists and practitioners are regularly at work adapting MARC to changing technology. HTML (hypertext markup language) and SGML (standard generalized markup language), at the moment, are being used for sharing information over the Internet; mapping of MARC data for readability by SGML-compliant browsers proceeds. Of course, the technology does not remain constant and already one hears of XML (extensible markup language), which will provide considerably more flexibility than HTML while being easier to code than documents in SGML.

If MARC is an "old" language for communicating data, why consider it against others? The most compelling reason for using the same database structure as other collections of similar or disparate materials is the potential for sharing the expense and time of cataloging and access thereto. Those visual resources collections now using MARC are mostly driven by this potential. The use of bibliographic and authority records by libraries has shown that cataloging can be shared by diverse institutions. The cataloging practices of art libraries have changed considerably as they discovered the benefits of this sharing. For example, subject heading practice is more likely to follow a standard vocabulary, such as *Library of Congress Subject Headings* or *Art and Architecture Thesaurus* (with only minor variations if any), than was the practice at many art libraries before they started using a bibliographic utility, such as RLIN or OCLC. And names are usually taken from such authority files as the Name Authority File maintained by the Library of Congress.

Similar to libraries using the same library system, visual resources collections using the same database vendor have user groups that meet during the meetings of professional organizations, such as the Visual Resources Association, or independently, as well as having electronic discussions via e-mail lists. As groups share databases, records, and database structures, they discover that much of their data can be dealt with in the same way and that individual catalogers can emphasize description and access that is of special importance to their particular collections.

The sharing of cataloging data is enhanced by the sharing of authority data. Because an authority record for a work of art could provide much of the context for that work of art, an interactive authority file will expedite the indexing of visual resources. For example, rather than repeating "German Renaissance Crucifixion panel from the Isenheim Altarpiece by Matthias Grünewald," the authority record for the work could carry this data as well as the painting's variant titles, dates, medium, dimensions, and repository. An individual descriptive record would only need to have a link to the authority record. In this scenario, the authority record serves as a sort of object record.

Whether the final choice for an individual collection of works of art, visual documents, or both is MARC or another database structure, this *Sourcebook* addresses the fundamental issues and suggests solutions that will allow for significantly increased sharing of information among visual resources collections, between these collections and other purveyors of information, and to the user. MARC's use by libraries has provided for great sharing among libraries. Standard markup languages allow disparate data to be viewed and used on the Internet. There is not one answer for all, but the use of a standard significantly enhances the potential for effective sharing of cataloging data.

One of MARC's strong points in the United States is the governance structure for USMARC. Although the formats are maintained at the Library of Congress, the Library is advised by the USMARC Advisory Group, which includes the Machine-Readable Bibliographic Information (MARBI) Committee of the American Library Association and representatives from the principal library vendors and professional information associations in the United States and Canada. Efforts are now underway to harmonize the USMARC formats with those of Canada (CanMARC) and the United Kingdom (UKMARC). The professional associations on the Advisory Group have significant input into the evolution of the formats. As cataloging communities beyond the library world use MARC, the evolution of the formats is enriched by their participation. It is my fervent hope that this *Sourcebook* will encourage use of the MARC formats by visual resources collections and that such use will enrich how the formats serve the entire art information community. The evolution of access to information is breaking down the traditional barriers between libraries, slide collections, and museums, and their cataloging communities. By sharing information using common descriptive and access languages, we increase the potential usefulness of all our collections.

Preface

The *Sourcebook* contains chapters representing a rich and complex array of institutions, collections, and object types. Chapters are about evenly divided between surrogate image collections (visual images in the form of slides and microfiche) and collections of art and cultural objects. Both create records for the art object. Surrogate image collections, typically referred to as visual resources collections, add a second layer of information describing the visual document.

Part I reviews the development of the MARC format and its adaptation for art, architecture, and visual document records. It examines the complexities inherent in documenting one-of-a-kind art objects and their visual images, and it describes the differences between art object and book cataloging. Drawing from the data compiled in tables 1 through 3, the authors analyze MARC records from twenty-three institutions, including the sixteen examples in the *Sourcebook*. Elements needed to describe art objects and their visual images are mapped to fields in the MARC record using the Visual Resources Association (VRA) *Core Categories for Visual Resources,* version 2.0. An adaptation of the *Categories for the Description of Works of Art* (CDWA), published by the Getty Information Institute for the description of museum objects, the VRA *Core* contains data elements not only for art objects and cultural artifacts, but also for architecture and site-specific structures. A full description of the VRA *Core Categories* is included in the *Sourcebook* as appendix A.

Because of the added complexity of surrogate records, the special issues regarding these documents have been treated separately in both the Introduction and the body of the book. Visual resource collections are grouped together and presented in Part II in chronological order. Surrogate collections can be further divided into those containing primarily images of built works (Rensselaer Polytechnic Institute, Clemson University, the University of Illinois–Chicago, the University of Virginia, and the University of Nebraska–Lincoln) and those containing primarily images of art and cultural objects (Cleveland Museum of Art, Florida International University, the National Gallery of Art, and the University of Montreal).

The first chapter introduces a pioneering project begun over a decade ago. Jeanne Keefe describes in some depth the initial and subsequent choices made in preparation for the project at Rensselaer Polytechnic Institute, and her discussion of collection- versus item-level cataloging continues to be a very relevant issue. Articles about the Rensselaer project have appeared in several publications, and the *Sourcebook* chapter updates the project to the present and considers future options.

In the second chapter Vesna Blazina and Ginette Melançon-Bolduc describe a unique example of a three-way mapping project, necessitated by the use of commercial software for the slide collection at the Bibliothèque de l'Aménagement, Université de Montréal. The project involves mapping from a locally defined set of data elements to field names in a commercial database to MARC tag equivalents. Complications that occur from the use of commercial software are further developed in the next chapter that follows by Ann Abid, Eleanor Scheifele, Sara Jane Pearman, and Elizabeth Lantz of the Cleveland Museum of Art Library. CMA's experiences, particularly regarding indexing limitations in the software and the subsequent effect on the way information is sorted and presented on public access screens, are a reminder that systems issues as well as format issues go into planning most conversion projects.

By using NOTIS, a popular software designed for library applications, the Clemson University Architecture Slide Library was able to make a smoother transition to the MARC format. This project described in chapter 4 was first published in the *VRA Bulletin* in 1990. Updated for the *Sourcebook,* the chapter by Phyllis Pivorun is noteworthy for its discussion of the types of issues that go into the planning phases for such a project. It also acts as a reminder not only that the MARC format continues to be adjusted to the needs of the user communities, but also that projects such as Clemson's, initiated nearly ten years ago, continue to adjust the format as they learn what works and what does not.

One of the early applications influenced by the Clemson project is described in chapter 5 by Mayra Nemeth of Florida International University (FIU). The project at FIU differs from that at Clemson in that it represents a bare-bones record structure scaled down to minimize cataloging time and maximize the use of keyword searching. Although such an approach has its limitations, it is well worth considering for institutions with limited funds and staff looking for a quick solution. The Clemson project was also a model for the project at the University of Nebraska–Lincoln, described in the chapter by Margaret Emons. Emons' chapter highlights issues of visual image documentation with regard to the use of the imprint and physical description fields.

Lynda White of the University of Virginia introduces the concept of cataloging levels and makes an intriguing proposition that includes scholars in the third level of the cataloging process. White's chapter also takes up the issue of collection- versus item-level cataloging. Taking the opposite approach from Rensselaer Polytechnic, White makes some convincing arguments for the extra work, particularly involving subject indexing, required for item-level cataloging.

More recent projects include those at the University of Illinois–Chicago and at the National Gallery of Art, Washington, D.C. The chapter by David Austin describing the Conway Microfiche Collection purchased by the University of Illinois–Chicago is especially enlightening in its discussion of the nonrelational structure inherent in the MARC format and the consequent whole/part issues particularly relevant to cataloging architecture. The following extremely instructive chapter describes a recent project undertaken at the National Gallery of Art Slide Library. Gregory Most carefully highlights deviations from standard MARC tagging for printed materials, indicating which tags have been adapted for local usage and explaining the adaptation as it applies to works of art.

Part III contains chapters describing object collections representing a wide variety of institution types—historical archives (the California Historical Society), museums (the National Museum of American Art, the Milwaukee Public Museum, and the Metropolitan Museum of Art), and libraries (the Pierpont Morgan Library, the National Art Library at the Victoria and Albert Museum, and the Prints and Photographs Division of the Library of Congress). Objects cataloged by these institutions include architectural drawings and other materials representing built works, paintings, cylinder seals, prints, photographs, site-specific sculpture, and artists' books.

The chapters on object collections are also organized chronologically, beginning with the Inventories of American Painting and Sculpture at the National Museum of American Art (NMAA). The Inventory of American Sculpture is one of the earliest examples of object documentation using the MARC format. Christine Hennessey's chapter includes the more recent project begun in 1991, which, by adding the Inventory of American Painting to the database, brought the number to over 300,000 works of art in public and private collections worldwide—all the more amazing considering that each work is cataloged at the item level, necessary because the original object is being cataloged. The uniqueness of this project makes it relevant to both image and object collections. Because most of the works included are not owned by the NMAA, issues of ownership and location are similar to those for visual image collections. Because the Inventories include condition assessment, their solutions are especially applicable to museum collections. Hennessey's chapter also contains a discussion of variant titles for art works and the use of in-house authority files and term lists.

The second chapter in Part III describes a MARC project at the National Art Library (NAL) in the United Kingdom. The National Art Library has permanent quarters in the Victoria and Albert Museum, and its physical affinity with the museum is reflected in a collection that includes a complex array of text documents, art works, and numerous items that bridge the gap between object and text, such as artists' books. Although the National Art Library is in the United Kingdom, its close links to the United States can be seen not only in its choice of USMARC rather than UKMARC, but also in its collaborative work with one of the vocabulary projects of the Getty Information Institute, the *Art and Architecture Thesaurus* (AAT). Jane Savidge's chapter describes at some length the NAL's use of AAT terms as faceted strings in the 654 field. One of the more innovative features of the NAL project is the use of special indexes linked to codes in the 049 field. Such indexes make it possible for users to conduct atypical and highly specialized searches on unique aspects of particular object types or collections, such as searching binding collections by type of binding or manuscript collections by manuscript number. Particularly intriguing is Savidge's account of NAL's use of the 773 field and a machine-generated obverse used to link parent/child records. The 773 field was originally used for archival collections and other traditional library materials but is also being used with other types of grouped works, such as drawings in a portfolio and studies for a finished work of art.

The Library of Congress Prints and Photographs Division's Washingtoniana II project described in the chapter by Karen Chittenden provides access to over forty thousand architecture design and engineering drawings related to the Washington, D.C., metropolitan area. The ongoing project, begun in 1989, includes the preservation, conservation, and storage of the drawings in addition to their documentation using both the MARC format and additional finding aids. This project provides an excellent example of the complexity encountered in documenting architecture and the need to link parts in a hierarchical structure. Utilizing a three-tier approach, the project began by capturing the data with collection-level records created for archives of architects or architectural firms. The second tier captures data at the group or unit level with records pertaining to a single building or design project. The third tier contains data about each drawing within a unit and was initially documented in

finding aids. Included with the project is a data dictionary that documents field content and tagging in detail. The Library of Congress Prints and Photographs Division Data Dictionary is included in the *Sourcebook* as appendix B.

The next chapter, by Susan Otto, describes several photograph collections at the Milwaukee Public Museum, including a collection of original photographs taken by Sumner W. Matteson. Like his better-known counterpart, Edward Curtis, Matteson traveled the country documenting its changing frontier. The Matteson photographs owned by the Milwaukee Public Museum, which concentrates on Native American culture, are a valuable research tool in a museum whose significant collections include North American Indian ethnology. Because the photographs are treated as primary objects rather than visual documents, the chapter is included in the section on object collections. However, while two of the collections described in the chapter treat photographs as works of art, the third example describes a collection of photographs as surrogates that document some of the artifacts in the museum's ethnology collection. Otto does not discuss the possible conflict inherent in this mixture of photographs as original objects and photographs as visual documents, but the project is new and it may be too soon to tell whether it will lead to problems of access for the user.

The chapter by Patricia Keats, describing some of the objects in the California Historical Society's collections, confirms the view that, more so than libraries or museums, archives are notorious for the complexity of their collections. The chapter includes not only records for traditional museum objects (including prints, drawings, photographs, and items more typically associated with archival materials, such as broadsides and advertising illustrations), but also extremely unique items, such as money belts and other cultural artifacts. In addition to the great variety of object types, the chapter also describes the Society's accompanying imaging project, and is the only chapter in the *Sourcebook* that describes scanning images and linking them to the text record.

The chapter by Elizabeth O'Keefe describes the development of a MARC database designed to document the Pierpont Morgan Library's collection of ancient Near Eastern cylinder seals. Although cylinder seals seem to be unique objects, issues brought to light in their documentation are far from unique to object collections. O'Keefe's description of the difficulties of composing a title for unnamed items and her discussion of subject analysis are particularly enlightening and applicable to a wide variety of art objects. Special characteristics of the Morgan project include the nonstandard usage of several fields and the modification of subfields to provide detailed description of the narrative scenes on the seals.

In the final chapter, Judith Jaroker and Constance Old describe plans for a project at the Metropolitan Museum of Art. Known as the Performing Arts Index, the project documents and indexes museum objects whose content or subject matter is relevant to the performing arts—dance, theater, and music. The project calls for the use of specialized thesauri, such as the *Répertoire International d'Iconographie Musicale* composed by the Research Center for Musical Iconogra-

phy. As might be expected, issues of subject access are emphasized in this chapter with suggestions that include the expanded use of the 6XX subject access subfields in a way that would distinguish subject access to images depicted on the objects from subject access to the objects themselves.

All these institutions have in common a willingness to improvise and to modify the MARC format to meet the specialized needs of cataloging art and architecture images and objects. Lacking both descriptive cataloging rules and a format with tags specifically designated for art and architecture data, these institutions have not achieved uniform results, but they have put the formats to the test and have proven they can be made to work.

Acknowledgments

In 1986, at a Visual Resources Association conference in San Francisco, an ad hoc committee was formed to investigate the potential of the MARC format for cataloging and documenting art objects and their visual documents. The committee located eleven institutions that were doing MARC projects, but a comparison of tag usage proved to be virtually impossible because there was no common vocabulary with which to describe art objects. Consequently, not only did MARC tag usage vary among institutions, no two institutions used exactly the same terminology to describe the local data fields being tagged.

A decade has made all the difference. In 1996, the Getty Information Institute, formerly the Getty Art History Information Program, published a document known as the *Categories for the Description of Works of Art* (CDWA), which is a very thorough set of data elements that can be used to document art objects in museum collections. At the same time, more and more institutions were trying out the MARC format on image and object collections. Between 1986 and 1994, when plans for the *Sourcebook* began, we had identified over sixty institutions that were either using or considering the use of MARC.

Also during this time, the VRA Data Standards Committee was conducting an extensive review of data elements used in visual resources collections. As they developed their own Core elements, they used the CDWA, mapping to the CDWA whenever possible, and adding categories not included in the CDWA. Recognizing the importance of the MARC format, the committee also attempted to map the Core elements to MARC tags.

As we write, the VRA *Core*, version 2.0, is being released with revisions based on the comments of many outside reviewers. The authors were fortunate to take part in these initiatives and to have had access to both the data and to the many talented and knowledgeable individuals who offered their expertise. We especially want to thank our colleagues on the VRA Data Standards Committee, our colleagues in the visual resources profession, and those many individuals in both the museum and library fields who lent their expert advice in critiquing the VRA *Core*.

In seeking an appropriate venue for publishing the *Sourcebook*, we thought first of the Art Libraries Society of North America (ARLIS/NA). We are especially indebted to ARLIS/NA and to the ARLIS/NA Publications Committee, both for initially accepting our proposal for publication and, recognizing the extent of the project, for arranging for the American Library Association (ALA) to publish the manuscript. For this we are particularly indebted to Jack Robertson, 1996–97 president of ARLIS/NA, and Jeanne Brown, 1996–97 chairperson of the ARLIS Publications Committee. We would also like to thank Marlene Chamberlain, Mary Huchting, and Dianne Rooney at ALA for their guidance in preparing the manuscript.

Organizations and individuals who were instrumental in providing financial support include Elizabeth O'Keefe from the Pierpont Morgan Library who suggested we contact Sydney Babcock, trustee of the Rosen Foundation, who arranged a Rosen Foundation grant; the University of Virginia Library Faculty Research Committee for approving research leave for Lynda White; and the University of South Florida Professional Development Committee for awarding Linda McRae professional development leave to complete the book.

Although we cannot name everyone who indirectly made our job a little easier, many individuals who assisted us directly need to be acknowledged. With apologies in advance for the inevitable egregious omissions, herewith in no particular order: for technical assistance, Kathleen Lynch, Christie Stephenson, Leslie Rahuba, Suzanne Bombard, Kaylyn Hipps, and Diana Liang; for ideological and editorial feedback, Ann Burns, Sherman Clarke, Sara Shatford Layne, Edward Gaynor, Christie Stephenson, and Chris Kiefer; and for assistance with the bibliography, Leslie Ann Bell, Robert Baron, Douglas Dodds, Elisa Lanzi, and the University of Virginia LEO Interlibrary Loan staff (especially Lew Purifoy).

Above all, we want to thank those who contributed to this book by being willing to share their less than perfect and certainly not standard MARC records. To our friends, colleagues, and especially our spouses, David Burke and Chris Kiefer, for their patience, moral support, and ever-present sense of humor, we are sincerely grateful.

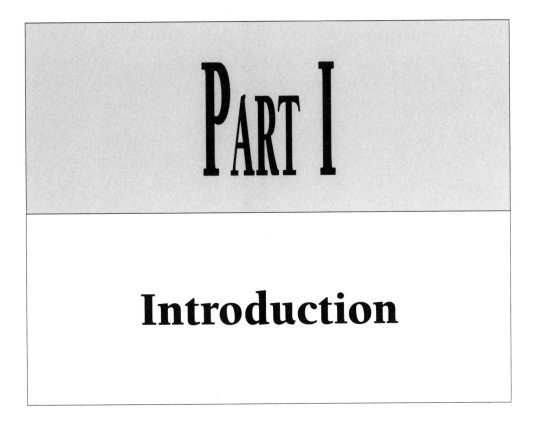

PART I

Introduction

Beginning with a machine-readable format designed primarily for cataloging books (MARC), the Library of Congress added formats for serials, maps, and music in the 1970s and for archives and manuscripts (AMC), visual materials (VIM), and moving images in the 1980s.[1] The AMC and VIM formats in particular attracted the attention of catalogers who previously had been unable to use traditional library formats (archivists, visual resources librarians, and museum personnel)—catalogers working with a variety of unique image and object collections.

Motivated not only by the introduction in the 1980s of the AMC and VIM formats, but also in the 1990s by the development of sophisticated databases and technology capable of image capture and storage, institutions began to look for existing record structures that would quickly put their collections online and make them accessible to the public. The prospect of being able to share cataloging was an important incentive for using existing formats that could be distributed over bibliographic utilities. Before widespread use of the Internet and the introduction of the World Wide Web, bibliographic utilities seemed to be the only viable option for the distribution of such records. Integrating visual document and object records within a central catalog of other materials such as books, maps, moving pictures, and sound recordings, thereby making it possible to conduct a search on a single subject across collections, also proved to be an inducement for using the MARC format.

By the end of the 1980s a number of institutions, usually affiliated with large research libraries, had begun to experiment with the new formats, making local modifications. In the early 1980s the AVIADOR project at Columbia University's Avery Architecture and Fine Arts Library received much attention as one of the first examples of architectural records cataloged in the new VIM format. In 1985, Rensselaer Polytechnic Institute also began to adapt the VIM format for use in the Architecture Slide Collection, and the Smithsonian's National Museum of American Art began cataloging the Inventory of American Sculpture using a modified MARC format. Shortly afterward, the Getty Information Institute (formerly the Getty Art History Information Program) began a MARC-mapping project with its Photo Study Collection. Projects at the Syracuse University Art Collection (SUART), the Cleveland Museum of Art, and Clemson's Gunnin Architecture Library followed. More recently, many other institutions have joined their ranks, including the Pierpont Morgan Library, the California Historical Society, and, in the United Kingdom, the National Art Library at the Victoria and Albert Museum.

Defining the Differences

An underlying premise in all the projects in the *Sourcebook* is that the attributes or elements needed to describe a text document are the same as or similar to those needed to describe a visual document or object.

Although many of the elements may be similar or at least equatable, many differences remain. For example, the subjective analysis inherent in the process of translating visual information into words depends on a number of factors, not the least of which are the experience, knowledge, and tools the translator brings to the task. Although this has always been the case, with traditional book cataloging the potential for inconsistencies has been greatly minimized by controlled vocabularies, name authorities, formats that include appropriate and well-defined data elements designed specifically for the medium, and rules that provide guidance in the application of data content. The absence of equivalent tools for cataloging art objects and visual documents does not present insurmountable obstacles, but it does help to account for the lack of consistency in current MARC records used to describe art objects and images.

Although there has been no united effort by the art and library communities to overcome these obstacles, major steps have been taken over the past decade, particularly by the Getty Information Institute, to develop tools that will produce a more standard approach to the description of art objects. Vocabulary tools published by the Getty include the *Art and Architecture Thesaurus* (AAT), first published in 1990 and periodically updated, most recently in 1996 with the electronic version, *Authority Reference Tool* 2.1; the *Union List of Artist Names* (ULAN), published in both paper and electronic versions in 1994; and the *Categories for the Description of Works of Art* (CDWA), published in electronic form in 1996.[2] The CDWA consists of a very thorough set of categories covering virtually every element of information needed to describe a work of art. Although many of the *Sourcebook* projects were begun before the publication of these tools, project updates indicate that virtually all now use the AAT. The CDWA is relatively new, but its value as a mapping tool is attested to in the *Sourcebook* analysis.

While new vocabulary and authority tools were being introduced into the art community, the MARC format was undergoing changes of its own. Between 1994 and 1996, in order to implement format integration, the Library of Congress introduced changes to some of the field tags. Unfortunately, these changes did very little to make it easier to catalog art objects and visual documents, but in the twenty years since the MARC format was first introduced it has undergone many adjustments and continues to evolve to meet the needs of a growing community of users.

As one of the new community of MARC users, art object catalogers bring a new perspective to standard bibliographic cataloging practices, a perspective based partially upon their experiences with relational database design and partially upon some fundamental differences between cataloging an art object and cataloging a published document. The concepts behind the design of the MARC format (notwithstanding its acronym) are based upon pre-automated principles of organization, namely the card catalog. The card catalog provided access through a limited number of entries—a primary or main entry heading and as many added entry headings as the document seemed to warrant, generally three or four. These concepts of main and added entry headings followed cataloging into the machine age, affecting the structure, arrangement, and indexing of tags in the MARC format.[3]

The design of the format is also associated with cataloging concepts based on a limited number of "objects" to catalog, referred to as the "object in hand." These objects are books, serials, maps, music, manuscripts, archival materials, graphic materials, and moving images, each with its own format (before format integration), rules for describing content, and, for graphic materials, its own subject thesauri. Although the intellectual content or subject matter can be vast, the number of object types and physical descriptions has been relatively small and reasonably manageable. The approach to cataloging nonbook materials has been to make adjustments to the book format by adding or more carefully delineating fields specifically designed for a particular type of object description.

In the case of graphic materials, specialized vocabulary was introduced to make it easier to describe the physical form or object type. Although discipline-based vocabularies pertaining to content or subject matter have been developed for such disciplines as art and medicine, it has traditionally been the object's form rather than its intellectual content that has driven cataloging rules and formats. This approach works reasonably well as long as the number of forms is limited. Archival objects, moving pictures, and particularly graphic materials, with their potential for representing numerous object types, not only have required special formats and vocabulary, but also have opened the door to the infinite world of objects in general and art objects in particular, intruding upon a once stable environment and challenging some long-held concepts of information access and retrieval. As more and more of these objects are captured in digital form and added to online catalogs, the challenge of providing intellectual access to them will grow.

Most works of art and architecture are one-of-a-kind objects, which offer very different cataloging challenges. For example, book catalogers dealing with the object in hand are cataloging an object of which there are many, many identical copies. Each has an identical title page that presents in readable form most of the information needed to describe the work, if not delineate its subject. Art object catalogers are also trying to catalog an object, but it is a unique object often not "in hand," and it does not have a title page to provide descriptive information. The subject is sometimes obvious simply from looking at the object, but more often the subject is open to widely varying interpretations by scholars. Some of the basic information that book catalogers take for granted (creator, title, date, object type) must be painstakingly researched before an art object can even begin to be cataloged. And often, knowing where to begin the search is a product of the cataloger's knowledge of the discipline—and not of his or her cataloging skills. The visual resources cataloger must first be able to *read* the image or object, just as a book cataloger must know French or German to catalog books in those languages. But the language of art and architecture is very subjective, so this, too, can lead to inconsistencies in how the same object is cataloged from one collection to the next.

Bridging the Gap

To describe any object, some basic questions must be answered. They include the well-known journalistic questions of who, what, where, and when. "Who" answers questions about individuals or entities and their relationship to the object. "What" answers questions about the object itself, including both its physical and intellectual description. "Where" and "when" answer spatial or geographical and temporal questions relating to the object. Applied to an art object, these interrogatives typically ask the following: Who created this object? Who altered it? Who commissioned it? Who owns or owned it? Who does it depict? What type of object is it? What is its name? What is it made of? What is it about? Where and when was it made? Where is it now and where has it been? When was it altered? When was it bought or sold? The MARC format asks questions pertaining to who, what, where, and when, but those same questions asked about books or published items often cover issues that either do not apply at all or do not apply in the same way to a work of art.

The abundance of information on the Internet has underscored the need to create bridges among user groups, collections of materials, and interchange formats, and has demonstrated the need to discover a mechanism for sorting out the avalanche of information now available on the World Wide Web. Traditional information providers such as OCLC have understandably begun to question how this will affect, replace, or preferably complement and be exchangeable with existing systems. In 1995, to meet the challenge, OCLC, in collaboration with the Coalition for Networked Information, proposed a set of "metadata" elements now referred to as the *Dublin Core Metadata*.[4] The *Dublin Core* is intended to describe the essential features of electronic documents needed to support resource discovery, in effect to bridge the gap among diverse collections. Underlying the concept of the *Dublin Core* is the notion that a top layer of very general information can be used to describe any number of document-like objects, referred to as DLO's, and be extensible in such a way as to link to more detailed categories of information for domain-specific retrieval. Over the last two and a half years, the framers of the *Dublin Core* have met in four subsequent workshops to refine the elements and to identify mechanisms for extending the element set to a wider group of collections and user communities. As these different communities begin to analyze the *Dublin Core* and recommend ways to make it extensible to meet their particular needs, the difficulty in bridging this gap becomes ever more apparent, and some of the issues are similar to those encountered in the examples from the *Sourcebook*.

Proposals for extending the *Dublin Core* elements include adding subelements or qualifiers that could be used to expand a concept by either type or scheme. One issue of particular relevance to the arts community is the need to distinguish between the record for the original object and the record for its visual document or image surrogate. A suggestion has been made to add qualifiers such as "original" or "surrogate" to source content elements to make this distinction. A second issue is the need to distinguish between an item-level record and a collection-level record. Referred to as "granularity," the various levels of access needed to discover museum, visual arts, and cultural heritage materials on the Web require the implementation of finding mechanisms that have greater specificity than the simple, unqualified *Dublin Core* elements provide. A report from the arts community suggests using hierarchical terms such as *parent of, child of,* or *member of* with the *Dublin Core* Relation element.[5]

Another obstacle to bridging the gap between diverse collections is language itself. Different user communities attach special meaning to concepts that can only be understood within the semantic context. For example, the date element in the first version of the *Dublin Core* was defined as the date of publication, reflecting the intellectual context or bias of the original framers who were primarily affiliated with the library community. The wording in the new date element has been revised to take into account the great variety of potential objects to which it may apply, but the example demonstrates the context-sensitive nature of language.

When the *Dublin Core* elements were mapped to the MARC format in MARBI Discussion Paper No. 86, some of the elements were so ambiguously defined that they appeared to have no clear purpose for book cataloging. The author, Rebecca Guenther, commented that the Coverage element (defined as describing the spatial and temporal characteristics of the object) was "generally not applicable."[6]

From the limited perspective of cataloging text documents, it is true that most of the temporal and spatial characteristics of the object are covered in the imprint fields where the date and place of publication are recorded. But such a statement illustrates some of the limitations of the MARC format for describing art objects, where temporal and spatial designations have nothing to do with the time and place of publication but can be crucial to identifying an object that not only has no publication date, but also does not have a title or known author.

Notwithstanding these limitations, the MARC format is continually undergoing revision, and as a result of her initial analysis of the *Dublin Core* elements, Guenther proposed the addition of a new tag that was approved in December 1996. Guenther has been actively involved in the *Dublin Core* workshops and, while representing the library community, has had the opportunity to come into contact with individuals with vastly different documentation needs and perspectives. Her analysis of the *Dublin Core* and its ability to be mapped to the MARC format has led to an important addition to the format, a tag that will be especially useful for catalogers of art and architecture. Discussion Paper No. 86 noted an important difference between book and object cataloging—the concept of main entry. In the days of the card catalog, it may have been necessary to determine one point of access as the main entry heading. That point of access was often the author. Today, AACR2 rules still link the author information to either a tag for main entry or added entry headings, and because the concept of main entry implies singularity, it is not a repeatable field. Up until very recently, if the MARC format was used to catalog an art object or any object for which there is more than one individual responsible for its creation, an arbitrary decision was forced concerning the main entry heading. The new 720 tag is a repeatable, uncontrolled name field for recording creator names on records that do not use standard cataloging rules.[7] Although this is a relatively simple accommodation to the needs of catalogers outside the library community, it seems to signify a new philosophy toward diverse collections. Every kind of collection, object, and visual surrogate has found its way to the Web. One of the positive consequences of this retrieval chaos, and the primary purpose of the development of the *Dublin Core* elements, is that it may have begun a long overdue and fruitful dialogue between traditional information providers and managers of the kinds of collections described in the *Sourcebook*.

A seminar on cataloging digital documents held at the Library of Congress in October 1994 highlighted the difference between text and image cataloging. One of the exercises "engaged the participants in . . . cataloging an electronic image, with many present discovering to their chagrin that the task was more difficult than they imagined. Numerous choices for main entry led some to question the value of adhering to this practice for electronic materials. Should a photograph of a Palladian villa be entered under Palladio, the photographer, the creator of the digital image, or the villa? The problem confounded the group and underscored the need for more documentation and training."[8] Whether the object being cataloged is represented by a digital or an analog visual document makes little difference; to the visual resources cataloger, it is the original, unique object that is of interest rather than its various manifestations in surrogate form.

The MARC format does not easily accommodate the different layers of information necessary to describe a visual document in any format, as well as the original that is of primary interest to the user. This has been evident in the debate that has been waged for some time in the cataloging community about how to handle microforms, which are typically surrogates of books or serials. Should there be a separate record for each format or can the microform copy be listed in the same MARC record as the original hard copy? The proliferation of separate records for each format has proven confusing to users, but the MARC format does not yet have an effective means of accommodating information about original works and their surrogates. This may be because the means one might employ in one's own database are at odds with the transfer of records from one database to another, particularly to multi-institutional databases where the original and the surrogate may vary.

The Issues of Surrogacy

The issues of surrogacy are particularly relevant to a discussion of the chapters in the *Sourcebook* because over half the chapters represent surrogate collections. Visual documents or surrogates can take several forms—primarily slides, but also photographs, negatives, microfiche, digital images, drawings, engravings, posters, and so forth. As surrogates, their physical form is generally noted, but it is the object depicted (the work of art or architecture), not the visual document itself (the slide or photograph), that is of primary significance. Notwithstanding, some surrogate forms may also be original objects, and, to add to the complexity, they could conceivably represent both a surrogate image on the one hand and an original object on the other, even in the same collection.[9]

The value of the visual document should not be overlooked. Image surrogates do not just stand for or represent an original object; they document an original object at a particular moment in time and from a particular point of view. The visual document contains its own temporal and spatial characteristics. It may define a particular time period—a view of Cologne Cathedral in the winter of 1943 or a view of the Sistine ceiling before or after restoration; or it may define a particular vantage point—an exterior view of Cologne Cathedral from the northeast or a detail view of the central panel of the Sistine ceiling. The visual image not only provides information about an object from a particular vantage point, but sometimes it also can be the only visual record of an object that has been lost, stolen, or destroyed. It can also provide a record of the object over time. Through models and reconstructions, the visual image can pull together objects (e.g., altarpiece panels) that once existed as a single unit but have since been dispersed and no longer physically reside in the same place.

The complex issues brought to light in cataloging visual documents or surrogates could be instructive for those attempting to design a core electronic record mappable to a wide variety of object and collection types, since many electronic records have the potential for being surrogates themselves. For those who have not worked with surrogates, one of the most difficult issues to grasp is the idea of the "layered" record. In cataloging any surrogate, whether it is a slide depicting a work of art or a digital hypertext record of a book, such as *Moby Dick* originally published in 1851, there are at least two layers of information—the layer for the original object, and, attached to that, the layer for one or more surrogate objects. Each layer may contain data elements for the same type of information—creator, date of creation, physical description—but if a clear distinction between the data elements describing the surrogate and the data elements describing the original object is not maintained, they can become confusingly intertwined.[10]

Although some tags—title and creator—within a MARC record have been applied in a fairly straightforward manner to the original object, other elements pertaining to the physical description become muddied in the confusion between visual document data and original object data. Most visual resources catalogers take a leap of faith and simply translate the imprint field—date and place of publication—to mean date and place of creation for the original object, but data pertaining to physical dimensions and medium often end up in fields that are clearly intended to describe the object in hand, not the object depicted in the object in hand.[11] What is needed is a kind of parallel format in which both the work in hand and the represented work could be described either within the same record or through a mechanism that would link the record for the object to the record for its visual documents.

Vertical and Parallel Linking

The issue of record linking for surrogate data also applies to original work data when the work is composed of parts. Many objects exist as a single unit composed of several parts—a silver place setting, an altarpiece, an architectural complex. In some cases, those parts may have been created by separate artists, designers, or architects over different periods of time, and even manufactured in different geographic locations. In other circumstances, an object such as an altarpiece may have been designed by a single individual but over time its parts may have been separated and dispersed, coming to reside in several different collections. The data for each part may therefore be quite different from the data for the whole.

In addition to a hierarchical (whole/part, host/unit) link, it may also be necessary to designate a parallel link. For example, in a work such as Michelangelo's *Creation,* the *Creation* could be the primary object, with details of the hands or heads linked as parts, but the *Creation* is just one of many panels in the *Sistine Ceiling,* which in turn is part of the *Sistine Chapel,* which is part of the *Vatican.* Which is the primary object? Such issues are beyond the scope of this analysis, but they illustrate the need for developing linking mechanisms in the MARC format to account for complex relationships typically found with many art objects and built works.

Architecture presents particularly instructive examples both in the complexity of the whole/part relationships and the importance of record linking or nesting. It is quite common for an architecture collection to contain the actual plans and models, sometimes designed by several different architects for single or multiple firms; visual documents of the plans and models; and photographs or slides of the building—under construction, completed, and from many different points of view. All of the objects and images refer to the same architectural structure, but each contains information unique to itself. Until recently, the MARC format only partially addressed linking issues, but the capacity to enumerate smaller units in larger entities in a MARC record has recently been added. A new field, 774 (constituent item entry) has recently been defined in the past year, based on the RLIN 789 field developed for the AVIADOR project. Also the 773 field (host item entry) has been generalized for links to host items. Although most of the examples in the *Sourcebook* come from projects begun before these fields were defined and generalized, both the National Art Library at the Victoria and Albert Museum and the Library of Congress Prints and Photographs Division use the 773 field to link component parts.

Mapping to MARC

Data from the record samples supplied by the sixteen chapters in the *Sourcebook* are recorded in tables 1 through 3 (see the Tables of MARC Mapping section). A careful comparison of the tables with the lists of categories found in the various chapters will appear to reveal some missing data. In an attempt to compress the material into table form and at the same time be as concise as possible, it was necessary to omit data elements rarely used. Elements used by fewer than five institu-

tions are omitted from the tables. The tables also contain data from MARC projects not included in the *Sourcebook,* such as the SUART and AVIADOR projects. Terminology used in the tables to describe data elements is taken from both the CDWA and the Visual Resources Association *Core Categories for Visual Resources,* version 2.0 (an adaptation of the CDWA for visual document collections).[12] The CDWA was designed to describe art objects in museum collections, although it also includes a category called "related visual documentation" intended to describe surrogate data. The Visual Resources Association Data Standards Committee selected elements from the CDWA to create its own core categories and added two new categories for describing the geographic location of objects in the environment, such as architecture and site-specific sculpture (Current Site and Original Site).

The CDWA was published in 1996 and the VRA *Core Categories* were first released in fall 1996. Therefore, these documents were not available to the institutions whose records are included in this analysis. The CDWA was developed for the very purpose for which it is being used here—to provide a standard set of categories for describing works of art. Had it been available to those institutions when they began mapping to MARC, at least one layer of subjective analysis could have been eliminated. Because the CDWA was not available, each institution had to interpret the MARC tags according to its own local definitions so that a term intended to describe a concept such as "creator" may have been called one thing in one collection and something quite different in another.

For the sake of clarity and consistency, it was decided to use terminology taken from the CDWA and VRA *Core Categories* to analyze MARC usage among the projects in the *Sourcebook.* The first step, therefore, was to analyze each institution's local definitions and equate them to categories in the CDWA and VRA *Core,* and then map the CDWA and VRA *Core Categories* to MARC tags. Such a procedure implies a one-to-one relationship between a data element in the CDWA and a tag or subfield in the MARC format. If each data structure supplied only one place for each item of information, such a one-to-one relationship might be possible. Unfortunately, this is not the case.

The mapping exercise proved to be very difficult. It was done on several separate occasions with no reference to the previous mapping, and resulted in as many slightly different mappings. Each time, our thinking became more refined and, by the sixth mapping, we felt it was the best we could do given the subjectivity inherent in the process.

Definitions for each institution's data elements are fuzzy at best and nonexistent at worst, and are sensitive to subjective interpretation as well. Some of the institutions' lists of MARC tags were inadequate for explaining exactly what data element or category of information was equated with a particular tag so that sample records and text in the chapters had to be consulted to infer meaning.

Deciding on the primary object being cataloged was also fraught with questions that muddied the mapping. If collection-level records were being used, the primary object could be very different from that of an item-level record, and yet be the same entity. For example, if one were cataloging Michelangelo's *Creation* panel from the *Sistine Ceiling* as the primary object in an item-level record, the *Creation* might be the title and the specific view, for example, *Adam,* might be recorded in the 520 tag. A collection-level record might consider the *Sistine Ceiling* to be the primary object and include the *Creation* panel along with all the *Sybils* and *Prophets* to be specific views listed in a 505 tag. This confusion made it difficult to determine precisely whether the 520 or 505 should be considered the title of the object or the view description of the visual document.

In addition, the mapping exercise was difficult because it required mapping very different organizational concepts. The CDWA, which was never intended as an exchange format, has a structure based on organizational principles very different from those of the MARC format. While the CDWA has only one element for each concept, many tags in the MARC format can accommodate the same element of information. For example, the concept for the date of creation as it pertains to a work of art is described in the CDWA category Creation-Date as "any date or range of dates associated with the creation, design or production of the work of art or its components." In the MARC format, this concept could be recorded in a number of different places. Among the examples of date tags taken from twenty-three institutions documented in table 2, creation date has been recorded in seventeen different fields in the MARC record. Although the imprint area (260c) is by far the most popular choice, creation date is also recorded in several title statement subfields, in several note fields, in several fixed fields, and in several added entry fields—all seemingly legitimate based on field definitions for the MARC format.

In addition to there being too many choices for some types of information, the reverse is also true. Some data elements used to describe a work of art or its surrogate have no appropriate MARC tags. In that case, the note fields are typically pressed into service.

Table 3 illustrates the heavy use of the 5XX fields, particularly the summary note field (520) used for twelve different CDWA categories.

Some of the inconsistencies could be resolved by making adjustments to the guidelines for content designators in certain fields. The *USMARC Format for Bibliographic Data* is periodically updated. One update could be devoted to changes that would affect the cataloging of cultural objects. Because content designation is actually based on cataloging principles outside the MARC field descriptions—namely the rules outlined in AACR2 and the policies in the *Subject Cataloging Manual*—changes in these documents would also have to be made. The *Anglo-American Cataloguing Rules*, second edition, was last revised and published in 1988. Although chapter 8 (graphic materials) refers to surrogate forms, it does not address the issue of surrogacy as it applies to a visual document of a work of art. For the most part, visual resources catalogers in image collections using the MARC format simply disregard the "object in hand" concept on which so much else hinges, but that rule has had an effect on the structure of the MARC format, making it difficult to distinguish between information describing the visual document and information describing the work of art.

An initiative in the United Kingdom begun in 1991 by an ARLIS/UK and Ireland Cataloging and Classification Committee resulted in a discussion paper that makes recommendations for revisions to AACR2 to accommodate cataloging art reproductions.[13] Since 1991, following acceptance of the need for revision by the British Library Association and the British Library, this paper has been revised and expanded to form a set of draft rule revisions. These rule revisions were to be resubmitted during 1997. If these recommendations were adopted by the Joint Steering Committee for Revision of AACR in conjunction with a few changes in the current MARC format, many of the issues and problems highlighted in the *Sourcebook* could be resolved.

Analysis

Information is arranged and tagged numerically in the MARC format. Excluding the fixed fields and early variable fields (01X–09X for numbers and codes), there are ten general areas based partially upon the older concepts of access through main entry, added entry, and subject, and partially upon other types of data typically used in describing a published item, such as imprint, edition, and series information. The format numbering for description and access begins with main entry fields whose numbers range from 100 to 130. The 100 and 110 tags are the most relevant to art object cataloging as they contain the concept of personal and corporate authorship as linked to main entry. There are actually three primary areas in the format that answer the question "who created it" and that may be equivalent to the Creator category. They are tags 100/110 (main entry—personal/corporate names), 700/710 (added entry—personal/corporate names), and 720 (uncontrolled name field).

Among the twenty-three projects in table 2, nearly all used either 1XX or 7XX fields to record Creator information. Two institutions used a 600 field (subject added entry—personal name). Other choices included adding the information to a Note field or to the 245 field (title and statement of responsibility), but in each case, these choices were in addition to using the 1XX or 7XX fields, based on AACR2's rules for main and added entry. The format does not utilize all the available numbers so the range from 13X to 19X is undesignated and could be used for new categories of information.

The title fields begin in the 200s and range from 210 to 247; they are equivalent to the Title category. There are title fields for uniform title, translated title, variant title, and title proper. Even though works of art generally do not have official titles, the 245 field (title proper or title statement) is the field typically used. Until recently, the concept of uniform title as applied to a work of art was dealt with according to subject cataloging principles at the Library of Congress, with an emphasis on English-language headings. A proposal from the Works of Art Group of the Cataloging Advisory Committee of the Art Libraries Society of North America (ARLIS/NA) has recently been presented to the Library of Congress; this proposal addresses only named works of art but begins a more discipline-based discussion of the concept of uniform title.

In the examples analyzed for the *Sourcebook*, there is a high level of agreement in the use of the 245 field to record title or name information. All twenty-three institutions used the 245 tag, although other title fields (240, 242, 246, 247) are also used as well as 130 (main entry—uniform title), 630 (subject added entry—uniform title), and 740 (added entry—uncontrolled related/analytical title). An exception to this practice is the use of the 520 (summary note) field by the Milwaukee Public Library and the Pierpont Morgan Library to describe titles for parts.

There seems to be a schism or, more mildly, some confusion regarding titles for works of art that are structures. Although architects and architectural historians consider building names to be titles, librarians who catalog drawings and photographs of structures consider building names to be subjects or names of corporate bodies; they are cataloging the representation rather than the building. Visual resources catalogers, on the other hand, are generally cataloging the work, in this case a building, rather than the slide, photograph, or architectural drawing, and thus the title is the name of the building. A prototype MARC record developed for an ARLIS/NA workshop in 1987 used the 610 for titles of buildings but the 245 for other works of art. The AVIADOR project at the Avery Library also uses a subject field for the names of buildings (697) in addition to the 240, but uses both the 245 and the 789 for titles of specific drawings; in other words, they are using the title fields for the work in hand, the architectural drawing, which is considered to be the primary object of interest rather than the building itself. The National Gallery of Art Photographic Archives uses the 110b and 110p for titles and parts of works of architecture, but has an authority record for each building.

Numbers ranging from 250 to 265 generally cover aspects of publication, including edition and imprint information. This is an area that would require some changes as well as some further field definition to accommodate object/image data. The only category typically assigned to the imprint/edition area is Date. Based on field description, the 260 tag (subfield c) is probably appropriate for Date data (fifteen of the twenty-three projects use the 260 and all twenty-three use a Date category), but some comments should be added to the field definition to make this clearer and to admonish the cataloger to distinguish original work data from visual document data. Because temporal data are very important for the description and retrieval of cultural objects, the date field needs to be an indexed field.

There may be reasons for selecting fields other than 260c for date information having to do with the way the local system displays information or searches some tags and not others, but the 260c tag seems to make the most sense based on the field definition, which is actually broad enough to include not only the concept of "publication and distribution," but also "production," suggesting that the object being described could be a manufactured object instead of a published document. Regarding unpublished documents, this idea is clarified in an additional note in the field definition that states "for unpublished items . . . this field may not be used or may contain only subfield c."[14] The statement does not mean that the 260 field cannot be used, only that it may not be, and if it is, the date will be recorded under subfield c. But it also implies that the date may be recorded elsewhere—a statement supported by our findings.

The physical description area is covered in the 300 to 359 number range. Categories that tend to occur in the 3XX fields include Materials, Techniques, Inscriptions, and Object/Work Type categories that answer such questions as "What is it made of?" and "What is it?" Of the nineteen institutions in table 2 that document materials information, the 300 field and the 340 field are most typically used to record information about materials, suggesting that there is a fair consensus for use of the 3XX fields for this type of data. The 340 field seems to be the most appropriate based on the USMARC field definition. Although it is labeled "medium," its subfields include techniques and dimensions. Only a few changes, including adding a subfield for the categories Inscriptions and Object/Work Type, and possibly renaming 340 with a more inclusive name, would be needed to make the field entirely adequate to accommodate physical description data pertaining to the art work. One of the biggest problems with the 3XX fields is their use for both original work and visual document data, but if a separate area were created for visual document data, the problem would be eliminated. The number of surrogates is generally recorded in the 300 field.

The 4XX fields contain series information. These fields do not appear to be used extensively by visual resources catalogers. When they are used, they generally seem to be used in a reasonably straightforward manner to describe series type data. For example, the 4XX fields may be used either to record the name of a slide set containing many works of art (as is the practice at Florida International University) or to link related works, such as studies, models, and sketches, or dispersed parts, such as polyptichs and architectural decoration (as is the practice at the National Gallery of Art Slide Library). The 4XX fields also can be used for series intended as such by the creator, for example, Goya's *Los Caprichos*.

Numbers between 500 and 59X are the notes fields. Unlike the series fields, the notes fields are used extensively by image/object catalogers and consequently present many issues. They are used for a variety of reasons, but primarily because many categories

are needed to describe works of art that simply have no other logical place in the MARC format. A few of the 5XX fields seem truly appropriate. For example, the 561 field is defined as a provenance note field and can be used for the category Ownership—Collecting History. The 585 field is reserved for exhibitions information and could equate to the category Exhibition/Loan History. Most of the 5XX tags, however, are not so easily adaptable to art object data, and the 500 (general note) and 520 (summary note) fields are used indiscriminately for practically everything. The 545 biographical or historical note is reserved for historical and biographical information about the main entry (creator), but in some cases is being used for historical information about the original object.

The categories that lack well-defined fields in the MARC format and that are consequently relegated to various notes fields are Owner's Name and Number, Nationality/Culture, Inscriptions, Conservation, and Object/Work Type. Although it might be argued that Object/Work Type does have an appropriate place in the 655 (genre/form subject access) field, art object catalogers view this information as part of the physical description, not as an aspect of the subject matter. This perception explains expansions to MARC already suggested for Object/Work Type and Inscriptions in the 3XX fields. With some adjustment to the field description, ownership data could be recorded in the 535 field (location of original/duplicates). Nationality/Culture data are more typically recorded in the 6XX subject fields. Although this is not entirely satisfactory, it may be the most logical choice. As might be expected, the notes area has also been used extensively for surrogate data, including Visual Document View Description, Visual Document Source, Visual Document Owner, and Visual Document Type.

Two other categories that lack a home in MARC but are needed for visual resources cataloging are Current Site (the location of a built work, sculpture, garden, performance, and so on) and Original Site (the original location of an object that has been moved and may reside in a repository). Current Site is different from Repository where a work of art may be deposited; it delineates the geographic location, sometimes including the street address, which distinguishes one building of the same name from another (e.g., Notre Dame). Subfield 245b has been used for Current Site to distinguish by place any structures that have the same title, and the 651 (subject added entry—geographical name) tag has also been used to designate site when it is the subject of a document. Seventeen of the projects in the tables use Current Site information but in thirteen different MARC tags. Geographic site is a critical category for architecture, archaeological sites, site-specific sculpture, environmental sculpture, and performance art, but particularly for architecture for which a creator may not be known or where the title is identical (e.g., Notre Dame).

Numbers 600 to 69X are subject access fields. Although subject access (from the bibliographic perspective) and Subject Matter (as defined in the CDWA) do not necessarily equate, several of the 6XX fields are typically used to contain terminology applied to the subject content of a work of art. The 600 to 630 field tags refer to persons, corporations, or titles that are subjects of a work. The 64X fields are undesignated. Subject access fields 650 (topical term) and 654 (faceted topical terms) equate most closely to the CDWA category Subject Matter, but both 650 and 654 have also been used to record other data that would typically fall into the CDWA categories Object Type, Materials, Techniques, and Styles/Periods/Groups/Movements. Subject access field 651 (geographical name) is used most often to record information about the Current Site or about the location of the repository, answering the questions "Where was it made?" or "Where is it now?" Based on the field definition for 655 (genre/form), this tag should probably be used to describe the physical form of the work that equates most closely to the CDWA category Object Type, but, like 650 and 654, it has been used to record information about both Object Type and Subject Matter.

A significant distinction between the two cataloging cultures can be seen in the use of the 6XX fields as documented in table 3. Bibliographic catalogers think of subject matter in much broader terms, using such concepts as "topical term" and "genre/form" often qualified with spatial and temporal concepts. Practically everything that can't be recorded under the author, title, physical description, or imprint fields is considered a subject or an added entry. Art object catalogers, on the other hand, tend to limit subject matter to the narrative content or iconographic subject depicted on or by the art work. Terms describing the work's form, geographic location, or association with a particular period or style are considered separate concepts and are not recorded in fields reserved for subject content.

Catalogers of architecture, who seldom have to document narrative content or iconographic subjects, consider the subject matter to be the structural elements as well as the materials and techniques used in the construction. This approach conflicts with the CDWA definitions, in which Materials, Techniques, and Subject Matter are considered separate categories. In this respect, architecture catalogers would find the broader bibliographic interpretation of subject matter more consistent with their approach to subject indexing. However, where the actual terminology for subject indexing is concerned, the AAT, not LCSH, is the preferred thesaurus. For example, while LCSH does have terms for "Architecture, domestic" that encompass all kinds of houses, the terminology in the AAT is much richer and more specific.

Keyword searching in bibliographic databases could make such distinctions inconsequential, but the desire to refine a search by combining specific concepts requires the very distinction between such categories as subject matter, work type, materials, and style/period that are currently blurred in the 6XX fields.

Like the 5XX notes fields and the 6XX subject access fields, the 7XX added entry fields are often used for information that does not fit neatly anywhere else. For example, the 710 (corporate name) tag has been used to record Repository Name, Place, and Number information, and the 752 (hierarchical place name) tag has been used for Context—Architecture Site and Place information. The fields between 76X and 78X are Linking Entry fields and have the potential for resolving some of the whole/part and object/surrogate relationships that are currently unresolved in the MARC format. Field tag 773 (host item entry) has been used to link the unit work to its host work, while the 774 (constituent unit entry) can be used to list unit items in a record for the host. Field 789 was used by the AVIADOR project for linking item works to the host work but has recently been defined in MARC as 774.

Numbers 800 to 830, which are for added entry/series data, are seldom used by art object catalogers. The 850 to 859 field tags are for holdings information and have been used primarily to denote Repository. Repository information has been recorded about equally in either tag 852 (holdings—location) or tag 535 (location of originals). As currently defined, either would probably be adequate but designating one, probably the 535 field, for repository information pertaining to art works would help to maintain consistency. The 900 tags are mostly undefined or defined for local, nonstandard use. In the *Sourcebook* analysis, the 900 area is used in only one instance to record data about the source of the visual document.

Mapping to MARC: Visual Document Data

Currently, there is no appropriate place in the MARC format for visual document data, but there are a number of possible solutions. Visual document data could be added as a specially designated subfield under each appropriate field in the record for the work. For example, in the 3XX physical description area, one subfield could be reserved for data covering the physical description of the visual document. A second option would be to keep all the visual document data together by assigning a new area in the MARC format for visual document data. A third option would be to expand the 533 field, which is used by catalogers to hold information about photocopied or microfilmed reproductions. A fourth alternative would be to create a collection-level record (defined as an umbrella record for the cultural work, not unlike a cover record for analytics) for the work, using 76X–77X linking entry tags to link the record for the visual document to the record for its work.[15] A fifth alternative would be to create a collection-level record for the work to which could be appended any number of related item-level records for the visual documents. The item-level records could each have the same information categories as the collection-level record for the work, though the content of the categories would be different; the item records would need to be equally searchable.[16] This would accommodate many views of a work or varied relationships among the visual documents that reflect relationships among parts of the original work. Or, last, MARC could be redefined as an "object-oriented" database structure in which the record for each visual document would be linked to authority files for various aspects of the original work—creator, object type, subject, repository, site, and so forth—so that information relevant to each visual document would not need to be rekeyed for each item record.[17] These last two options would entail a major change in the structure of the MARC record and, though probably the best solutions for recording visual documents and the intricacies of relationships among cultural objects, would likely be prohibitive in terms of the cost of software changes for the bibliographic utilities.

Examples from the *Sourcebook* of categories for surrogate data found in various tags in the MARC format include the following types of information for the visual document: view description, type, format, owner, owner number, source, date, classification,

measurements, color, number of images, and series/sets. The *Sourcebook* examples tend to take one of two approaches to recording information about the view. One approach tends to be used for collection-level cataloging, the other for item-level cataloging. The information about the view is generally recorded either in a subfield of the title statement area (240, 245, subfield b or p) or in a note area (500, 505, 520). Collection-level records (such as those at the University of Nebraska, Florida International University, and Clemson) use the 505 (formatted contents note) to record view data. Field 505 is a notes field designed to "contain the titles of separate works or parts of an item."[18] Based on this definition, various views of a single structure or item could qualify as parts of the item pertaining to the record for the whole. Item-level records (such as those at the University of Virginia and the University of Chicago) use a subfield in the title statement area, 240 or 245, subfield p or b. Subfield p is for a description of a part, while subfield b is designated to be used for either the remainder of the title or other title information. The University of Chicago makes an interesting distinction between the point of view, or "aspect," and the object part by assigning the aspect to subfield b and the part to subfield p. The University of Virginia uses subfield p to designate and group together the types of views of a structure (plan, exterior, interior, etc.) while using the 520 to describe more fully the view of each image.

Visual Document Type is defined as the generic identification of the medium of the document (e.g., photograph, slide, CD-ROM). In the examples in table 2, Visual Document Type data are recorded in twelve different areas of the MARC format and, in some cases, appear in two separate places in the same record. Most typically, these data are recorded in either the 245h subfield or the 300 physical description field, both of which can be indexed. For integrated collections, users must be able to make distinctions between format types, and for libraries doing collection-level cataloging, users need to know that a single record may refer to a number of different objects. Montreal and the University of Virginia, for example, include Visual Document Type information in the 245h field (245 = title; h = general material designation). On the OPAC screen, the title information is followed by the word "slide" in brackets. Rensselaer Polytechnic uses the 949 field, a locally designated field, to indicate more detailed information about the number or types of slides pertaining to a set. Several institutions (the University of Nebraska, the University of Virginia, Florida

International University, and Clemson) also use the 300 field (physical description) for this information.

Visual Document Source is defined as the name and location of the agency, individual, or repository from which the visual document may be obtained, or a bibliographic citation in the case of copy photography. A surrogate image may come from one of several different sources. It may be purchased from a commercial vendor. It may be photographically copied from a printed source and consequently may be linked to a bibliographic citation. It may be photographed by an individual or by the owning agency and donated to a visual resource collection or archived by the owning institution. Although the 260 field (imprint) has been used (particularly in the case of commercial images), once again, use of the 260 field to describe data pertaining to the visual document muddies the distinction between visual document and original object data. Because there is no truly appropriate place in the MARC format for this information, most institutions have used one of the 5XX fields (note), with 590 (local note) being the most popular. The citation note field (510) has also been used as well as the general note field (500), the source of acquisition field (541), and the action note field (583).

Other visual document categories, such as Measurements and Color, fall into the broader category of physical description and generally end up in one of three areas in the MARC format—300 (physical description), coded 007 (physical description), or 5XX (notes). The number of images being cataloged in a single record is also typically recorded in the 300 field. The listing of a purchased set or series of images in the 400 field fosters confusion about whether the series name was intended by the creator or by the publisher. Classification information, because it is typically locally defined, usually is recorded in the 099 or 059 tags.

Conclusion

Many things could be done to make the MARC format more compatible with the descriptive requirements of art works and visual documents of art and architecture. Some of these changes would be relatively easy to make. They would include minor adjustments to existing MARC tags and commensurate changes in the field descriptions. Other changes would require either the expansion of existing areas within the format or the addition of new tags. For example, the concepts of time, place, and physical description exist in the MARC format, but their definitions and configurations present special challenges for catalogers of art objects and visual documents of art and architecture.

Along with the title of a published document, time and place (date and place of publication) are nearly always a given and consequently play a different role in records for traditional library materials. The equivalent type of information for an art work—the period and place associated with its manufacture and its physical description, particularly the type of object it is—may be the only clues to its identity. Because art objects and built works are unique objects often lacking a title or even a known creator, temporal and geographic designations, along with a general physical description of the object, can be essential not only for description, but also for access. Time and place are particularly important, for example, in locating the records for a building with no known architect. The fact that visual resources catalogers have established categories for the site or location of the work in the environment indicates the importance they place on geographic description.

Another important distinction between these concepts applied to a work of art as opposed to a book is that although they are important elements used in the object's description, they are equally crucial elements used in its access. However, they do not describe what the work is about and consequently, from the visual document cataloger's point of view, they do not belong in the subject access fields. An expansion of both the imprint and physical description areas in the MARC format, providing clearly defined and indexable fields for temporal, geographic, and physical description data as they pertain to works of art and architecture, would greatly improve the format for documenting this type of material.

A cluster of issues is connected with the concept of surrogacy as it relates to visual documents of art and architecture, and no single area in the MARC format can be simply expanded to accommodate all these issues. In its least complex form, the surrogate might be compared to the bibliographic concept of a reproduction, where the original item is described in the main portion of the bibliographic record and data relevant to the reproduction are recorded in a note field, such as 533 (reproduction note). In such a case, where a slide depicts a two-dimensional painting, for example, the record for the original would carry most of the data for description and access, and the description of the visual document might be recorded in an appropriate field, much as the reproduction is noted in the 533 field as a copy in a different form.

Many visual documents, however, are not copies. With a three-dimensional work of art, vantage point alone turns the visual document into something other than just a copy in another form. In the case of a complex work of art, vantage point may also isolate individual elements, making the subject indexing for a single visual document somewhat different from the subject indexing of other visual documents of the same work taken from different vantage points. The need to be able to access a single image that carries a specific subject content has forced some institutions to create separate records for each visual document, thereby duplicating much of the information pertaining to the work.

Built works in particular demonstrate yet another level of complexity in that the visual document not only documents vantage point, it also typically documents parts of the whole structure. To complicate matters, some architectural complexes, such as *St. Peter's* in Rome, may be built over an extended period of time and by a number of different architects and designers. The visual document record must capture this information and also contend with the order or relationship of each part to the whole structure. Certainly there should be a single record for the complex as a whole, but researchers need to be able to move from one level to another and quickly locate the specific image that demonstrates a particular aspect of a particular section of a part of the larger architectural structure.

Can the MARC format handle this type of complexity? Can the new 7XX linking fields be made to work with the same kind of ease as SGML records? None of the examples in the *Sourcebook*, with the exception of the National Library in the United Kingdom, begins to work out solutions to such complex issues of linking, but these issues will need to be resolved if art works, and particularly visual documents of art and architecture, are to find their way into bibliographic databases and at the same time provide the kind of access to images that researchers require.

In addition to structural aspects of the MARC format that would need some alterations, there are issues of data content as outlined in AACR2 that are beyond the scope of this book and exist outside the MARC format, but that will also ultimately need to be resolved before art works and their visual documents can find a comfortable home in bibliographic databases.

The MARC format has proven to be a flexible structure, adaptable to the changing needs of a growing community of users, if only unofficially. It is currently the only widely accepted documentation format that is also easily shareable. Although the Internet has great potential, it does not yet provide quick and easy access to consistently presented or formatted information. Notwithstanding its current chaotic characteristics, the Internet will inevitably have its effect on information providers such as OCLC, and that effect may result in solutions to the issues of linking crucial to visual document collections.

It is hoped that the *Sourcebook* not only will provide examples of actual projects that can be used as guidelines for developing new projects but also will generate discussion on the wider issues of cataloging visual documents and works of art, architecture, and material culture that can lead to refinements in the MARC format, refinements that will make MARC a truly useful tool not only for those who catalog our cultural heritage but for those who study it.

NOTES

1. In the *Sourcebook*, the term *MARC* refers to the implementation in the United States, also known as US-MARC. MARC implementations in other countries may vary and some comments may refer to MARC tags outside the United States.

2. Getty Information Institute, *Art and Architecture Thesaurus*, 2nd ed. (New York: Oxford University Press, on behalf of the Getty Art History Information Program, 1994); Getty Information Institute, *Art and Architecture Thesaurus: The Authority Reference Tool*, version 2.1 (New York: Oxford University Press, 1994); *Union List of Artist Names* (New York: G. K. Hall, 1994); Getty Information Institute, *Categories for the Description of Works of Art* (Santa Monica: Getty Information Institute, 1996).

3. Esther Green Bierbaum, "A Modest Proposal: No More Main Entry," *American Libraries* 25, no. 1 (January 1994): 81–84.

4. Stuart Weibel, Jean Godby, Eric Miller, et al., "OCLC/NCSA Metadata Workshop Report," March 1995; Web site at: <http://www.oclc.org:5046/oclc/research/conferences/metadata/dublin_core_report.html>. See also <http://purl.oclc.org/metadata/dublin_core/>.

5. Catherine Grout and Tony Gill, "Visual Arts, Museums, and Cultural Heritage Metadata Workshop Report," August 6, 1997. Web site at: <http://vads.ahds.ac.uk/metadataf2.html#2> (The Status of the Edinburgh Recommendations).

6. Rebecca Guenther, "Mapping the Dublin Core Metadata Elements to USMARC," MARBI Discussion Paper No. 86 (1995); Web site at: <http://lcweb.loc.gov/marc/>.

7. Rebecca Guenther, "Defining a Generic Author Field in USMARC," MARBI Discussion Paper No. 88 (May 1995). Web site at: <http://lcweb.loc.gov/marc/>.

8. Sarah E. Thomas, "Summary: Seminar on Cataloging Digital Documents," October 1994, p. 2; Web site at: <http://lcweb.loc.gov/catdir/> or <http://lcweb.loc.gov/catdir/semdigdocs/summary.html>.

9. Sherman Clarke, "Illustrated Books and Book Illustrations at the Amon Carter Museum Library," *Art Documentation* 14, no. 4 (winter 1995): 21–23.

10. Sara Shatford, "Describing a Picture: A Thousand Words Are Seldom Cost Effective," *Cataloging & Classification Quarterly* 4, no. 4 (summer 1984): 13–30.

11. Maryly Snow, "Visual Depictions and the Use of MARC: A View from the Trenches of Slide Librarianship," *Art Documentation* 8, no. 4 (winter 1989): 186–190.

12. For a complete list of categories and definitions in the CDWA, see Getty Information Institute, *Categories for the Description of Works of Art* at <http://www.ahip.getty.edu/gii/index/cdwa.html/>; for a complete list of categories and definitions contained in the VRA *Core,* see appendix A at the end of this book; brief definitions of additional noncore categories mapped are also in appendix A.

13. Roy McKeown and Jane Savidge, "ARLIS/UK and EIRE Joint Working Group Revision of AACR2 to Accommodate Cataloging of Art Reproductions: A Document for Discussion by LABL," *VRA Bulletin* 20 (winter 1993): 19–27.

14. *USMARC Format for Bibliographic Data Including Guidelines for Content Designation,* 1994 ed. Prepared by Network Development and MARC Standards Office (Washington, D.C.: Cataloging Distribution Service, Library of Congress, 1994), 260–261.

15. This approach, though not for surrogate records, was pioneered at Columbia University for the AVIADOR project and was documented by Jeffrey J. Ross in *Cataloging Architectural Drawings: A Guide to the Fields of the RLIN Visual Materials (VIM) Format as Applied to the Cataloging Practices of the Avery Architectural and Fine Arts Library, Columbia University, Developed for Project AVIADOR,* Topical Papers, no. 1 (Tucson: Art Libraries Society of North America, 1992).

16. A prototype for this structure is outlined in Stephen Paul Davis, "Digital Image Collections: Cataloging Data Model and Network Access" (New York: Columbia University Libraries, 1995), <http://www.columbia.edu/cu/libraries/inside/projects/diap/paper.html>.

17. For a thorough discussion of this concept, see Michael Heaney, "Object-Oriented Cataloging," *Information Technology and Libraries* 14, no. 3 (September 1995): 135–153.

18. *Bibliographic Formats and Standards,* 2nd ed. (Dublin, Ohio: OCLC Online Computer Library Center, 1996), 5:11.

Tables of
MARC Mapping

Using the Tables

The following tables compile data taken from the project documentation of twenty-three institutions including the sixteen examples represented in the *Sourcebook.* Data are presented in three tables organized by institution, table 1; by categories used to describe the work and the visual document, table 2; and by MARC tag number, table 3.

Table 1 (MARC Mapping by Institution) lists projects by an abbreviated name for the institution or project. These names appear in the first row across the top of the table.[1] Projects are ordered chronologically from left to right beginning with the earliest. Institutions creating MARC records for visual documents come first, followed by institutions creating MARC records for original works. The lefthand column lists categories describing the work followed by categories describing the visual document. Categories taken from the VRA *Core Categories for Visual Resources,* version 2.0, are given first and are labeled "CORE." Miscellaneous categories not found in the VRA *Core* follow and are labeled "OTHER CATEGORIES."[2] MARC tag numbers applying to the categories in the lefthand column are documented for each institution, e.g., institution RPI 1985 (Rensselaer Polytechnic Institute, project begun 1985) uses MARC tags 650, 653, and 654 for information describing the Work Type.

Table 2 (MARC Mapping by Categories) compiles the data from table 1 and lists MARC tag numbers and usage numbers for each category. As in table 1, the lefthand column contains category labels describing the work followed by category labels describing the visual document. MARC tag numbers for each category are listed by usage in descending order. Next to each category label is the number of projects documenting the category (in parentheses) and the number of different MARC tags used for the category [in brackets], e.g., sixteen different MARC tags were used for the category Work Type in twenty projects employing at least one MARC tag for information describing this category.

Table 3 (MARC Mapping by Tag Number) compiles the data from table 2 ordered by MARC tag number. The lefthand column lists tag numbers in ascending order. Each row includes the tag number, the tag label, and corresponding category labels. The following chart gives a broad outline of MARC tags and their functions.[3]

Tag Group	Function
0XX	Bibliographic control numbers and coded information
1XX	Main entries
2XX	Titles and title paragraph (title, edition, imprint)
3XX	Physical description, etc.
4XX	Series statements
5XX	Notes
6XX	Subject access entries
7XX	Added entries other than subject or series; linking fields
8XX	Series added entries and holdings
9XX	Local use fields

NOTES

1. VISUAL DOCUMENT PROJECTS

RPI 1985: Rensselaer Polytechnic Institute, Architecture Library, Troy, N.Y. (Jeanne M. Keefe, "The Rensselaer Slide Database in Retrospect").

NGA 1986 (photos): National Gallery of Art, Photographic Archives, Washington, D.C. (Andrea Gibbs and Pat Stevens, "MARC and the Computerization of the National Gallery of Art Photographic Archives," *Visual Resources* 3 [1986]: 185–208).

ARLIS 1987: Art Libraries Society of North America, Washington Conference Workshop, 1987 (Toni Petersen, "Subject Control in Visual Collections," *Art Documentation* 7, no. 4 [winter 1988]: 131–135).

Montreal 1988: Université de Montréal, Bibliothèque de l'Aménagement, Montréal (V. Blazina and Ginette Melançon-Bolduc, "Mapping to MARC at the Bibliothèque de l'Aménagement Université de Montréal," *Visual Resources Association Bulletin* 18, no. 3 [fall 1991]: 14–21).

Cleveland 1988: Cleveland Museum of Art, Slide and Photograph Collections, Cleveland (Ann Abid, Eleanor Scheifele, Sara J. Pearman, et al., "Planning for Automation of the Slide and Photograph Collections at the Cleveland Museum of Art: A Draft MARC/Visual Materials Record," *Visual Resources Association Bulletin* 19, no. 2 [summer 1992]: 17–21).

Clemson 1989/95: Clemson University, Gunnin Architectural Library, Clemson, S.C. (Phyllis Pivorun, "Why and How MARC Is Being Used for Automating the Architecture Slide Collection at Clemson University," *Visual Resources Association Bulletin* 18, no. 2 [summer 1991]: 18–21; updated 1995).

FIU 1991/95: Florida International University, Audio-Visual Library, Miami (Mayra Nemeth, "Cataloging for Art's Sake at Florida International University," *Visual Resources Association Bulletin* 20, no. 2 [summer 1993]: 25–31; updated 1995).

Nebraska 1993: University of Nebraska–Lincoln, Architecture Library (Margaret L. Emons, "Cataloging Architecture Slides at the University of Nebraska–Lincoln," *Visual Resources Association Bulletin* 20, no. 3 [fall 1993]: 24–28).

UVa 1993: University of Virginia, Fiske Kimball Fine Arts Library, Charlottesville (Lynda S. White, "Image Cataloging in MARC at the University of Virginia," *Visual Resources Association Bulletin* 21, no. 3 [fall 1994]: 23–31).

Illinois 1993: University of Illinois–Chicago, Architecture and Art Library (David Austin, "MARCing Architecture," 1996).

NGA 1993 (slides): National Gallery of Art, Slide Library, Washington, D.C. (Gregory P. J. Most, "National Gallery of Art Slide Library, Washington, D.C.," 1995).

CCA 1994: Centre Canadien d'Architecture, Montreal (Toni Petersen and Patricia J. Barnett, eds., *Guide to Indexing and Cataloging with the Art and Architecture*

Thesaurus [New York: Oxford University Press, 1994]: 363–365).

DSC 1997 ver. 2.0: Visual Resources Association Data Standards Committee, *Core Categories*, 1997.

OBJECT PROJECTS

NMAA 1985: National Museum of American Art, Inventory of American Sculpture, Washington, D.C. (Christine Hennessey, "The Inventories of American Painting and Sculpture: Cataloging in MARC," 1995).

Avery 1985: Columbia University, Avery Architectural and Fine Arts Library, New York (Jeffrey J. Ross, *Cataloging Architectural Drawings: A Guide to the Fields of the RLIN Visual Materials (VIM) Format as Applied to the Cataloging Practices of the Avery Architectural and Fine Arts Library, Columbia University, Developed for Project AVIADOR,* Topical Papers, no. 1 [Tucson: Art Libraries Society of North America, 1992]).

Auburn 1986: Studio 218, Auburn, Ala. (Carolyn Havens, "Cataloging a Special Art Collection," *Cataloging & Classification Quarterly* 9, no. 4 [1989]: 27–49).

V&A 1987: Victoria and Albert Museum, Library, London (Jane Savidge, "The National Art Library, Victoria and Albert Museum, London," 1996).

SUART 1989: Syracuse University, Art Collection, Syracuse, N.Y. (Deirdre C. Stam and Ruth Palmquist, *SUART: A MARC-based Information Structure and Data Dictionary for the Syracuse University Art Collection* [Syracuse: Museum Computer Network, 1989]).

LC P&P 1989: Library of Congress, Prints and Photographs Division, Washington, D.C. (Karen Chittenden, "Washingtoniana II: Cataloging Architectural, Design, and Engineering Collections in the Prints and Photographs Division of the Library of Congress," 1996).

Milw 1991: Milwaukee Public Museum, Milwaukee (Susan Otto, "MARC Format for the Photograph Collection at the Milwaukee Public Museum," 1995).

CalHist 1994: California Historical Society, San Francisco (Patricia L. Keats, "Cataloging Images in MARC at the California Historical Society," *Visual Resources Association Bulletin* 22, no. 4 [winter 1995]: 19–35).

Morgan 1994: Pierpont Morgan Library, New York (Elizabeth O'Keefe, "From Cuneiform to MARC: A Database for Ancient Near Eastern Cylinder Seals Owned by the Pierpont Morgan Library," 1995).

PerfArts 1994: Metropolitan Museum of Art, Performing Arts Index, New York (Judith Jaroker and Constance Old, "The Performing Arts Index at the Metropolitan Museum of Art," 1995).

2. The data elements are from the Visual Resources Association's *Core Categories for Visual Resources,* version 2.0, and from the *Categories for the Description of Works of Art.* See appendix A for term definitions.

3. *Bibliographic Formats and Standards,* 2nd ed. (Dublin, Ohio: OCLC Online Computer Library Center, 1996), 3.

Table 1 | MARC Mapping by Institution

MARC MAPPING VISUAL DOCUMENT PROJECTS			
	RPI 1985	*NGA 1986*	*ARLIS 1987*
Work Categories			
CORE			
Work Type	650,653,654	100x,130ag,630ag	650,655
Title	240,245ab	110b,245a	245,610
Measurements	653a	300c	300
Material	653a	300a	650
Technique		300a	650
Creator	100,110,111,260b,700,710,711	100,110,700,710	100,110,700,710
Role		100e,110e,700e,710e	
Date	260c,653a	260c,008cd	245f
Repository Name		710b	
Repository Place		099a,710a	
Repository Number			
Current Site	650z,651a	110a,710a,610ab	651
Original Site			
Style/Period	650ay	245f	650
Nationality/Culture			
Subject	600,650,653,654	100x.2,600abc,650a	600,650,651,653
Related Work		240ap	
Relationship Type		240p	
Notes	500	500a	500
OTHER CATEGORIES			
Variant Title		740a	
Translated Title		740a	
Creator's Series/Edition			
Location Produced	260a		
Provenance		700x	561
Physical Description		300ih	650
Documentation		510a	
Exhibitions	711		
Inscriptions		591a	
Source of Acquisition			
Conservation			
Visual Document Categories			
CORE			
Type	740a,007b		
Format			
Measurements	740a,007h		007h
Date			
Owner			
Owner Number	099a		059
View Description	245p,949a-k,740a	110p,130p	245gp
Subject			
Source	583j	590a	260
OTHER CATEGORIES			
Classification	059dfglnprtvz		059
Color	007d		007d
Number of Images	949		
Series/Set			

(Continued)

Table 1 | MARC Mapping by Institution—VISUAL DOCUMENT PROJECTS (Continued)

	Montreal 1988	Cleveland 1988	Clemson 1989/95
Work Categories			
CORE			
Work Type	695,630g	655	
Title	245a,630a	245ab	245,440,830
Measurements		340	
Material	695	340	
Technique		340	
Creator	700,710	100,110,111,700,710,711	100,110,111,700,710,711
Role			
Date	630f	759	245
Repository Name		859	
Repository Place		859	
Repository Number		023	
Current Site	043		245
Original Site			
Style/Period	695		
Nationality/Culture			
Subject	695	520,600,611,650,651,654,659	520,600,610,611,650,651,654
Related Work		503,779	440
Relationship Type			
Notes	500	500	500,520
OTHER CATEGORIES			
Variant Title		246,247	740
Translated Title	740	242	
Creator's Series/Edition		250,440	440
Location Produced		260	
Provenance		561	
Physical Description		340	
Documentation		510	
Exhibitions		111,711	111
Inscriptions		562	
Source of Acquisition			
Conservation		359	
Visual Document Categories			
CORE			
Type	1024,245h	Holdings	
Format			
Measurements			
Date			
Owner	090a	Holdings	
Owner Number	090a	Holdings,099	502
View Description	630g	Holdings	505
Subject			
Source	500	Holdings	590,927
OTHER CATEGORIES			
Classification			
Color	500		
Number of Images	090c,500		300
Series/Set	500	440	

	FIU 1991/95	Nebraska 1993	UVa 1993
Work Categories			
CORE			
Work Type			654,655
Title	245ab,740	245	240,245a
Measurements			340b
Material	520		340,654
Technique			
Creator	100,245c,700,710,711	100,600,610,700,710	100,110,111,700,710,711
Role			700e,710e,711e
Date	520	500	046,260c
Repository Name			535
Repository Place	520		
Repository Number			510
Current Site		043,651	245b,851
Original Site			
Style/Period			
Nationality/Culture			
Subject	653	650,651,654	600,610,611,650,651,654,690
Related Work			500,740,773
Relationship Type			
Notes			500,545
OTHER CATEGORIES			
Variant Title	246,500		740
Translated Title	500		242
Creator's Series/Edition			440
Location Produced			
Provenance			561
Physical Description			755ayz,340
Documentation			500,581
Exhibitions	590,711		111,711
Inscriptions			500
Source of Acquisition			
Conservation			
Visual Document Categories			
CORE			
Type	245h	007,245h	300,245h
Format			
Measurements			300
Date			
Owner		049	040
Owner Number			099
View Description	505	505	245p,505,520
Subject			
Source	260,590	260	510
OTHER CATEGORIES			
Classification		099	099
Color	300	300	
Number of Images	300	300	300
Series/Set	440	440,490	

(Continued)

Table 1 | MARC Mapping by Institution—VISUAL DOCUMENT PROJECTS (Continued)

	Illinois 1993	NGA 1993	CCA 1994	DSC 1997 ver. 2.0
Work Categories				
CORE				
Work Type	654	690	654	655
Title	240,245,740	245	245	24X
Measurements		300c		340b
Material	240h,300/3	300		340ace
Technique				340d
Creator	100,110,700	100,110,700	600	1XX,7XX
Role	100e,110e,700e	100e,110e,700e		1XXe,7XXe
Date	240f,243f,245fg	260cg	260c	260c
Repository Name	852e	710		535a
Repository Place	852acd	710		535bc
Repository Number		710n		035
Current Site	752, 852	710/1	043,245,651,654bz	651,752
Original Site	752, 852			651,752
Style/Period		690y	654by	655y
Nationality/Culture		690z		650
Subject	600,654,655	600,610,650,651,695	651	084,6XX
Related Work		440		787
Relationship Type		440		787g
Notes	500	500		5XX
OTHER CATEGORIES				
Variant Title	246			
Translated Title	243	245b		
Creator's Series/Edition		250		
Location Produced		260e		
Provenance				
Physical Description				
Documentation		585,590		
Exhibitions		711	711	
Inscriptions		591		
Source of Acquisition				
Conservation				
Visual Document Categories				
CORE				
Type	007,300b		300,655,245h	533a
Format				533e
Measurements			300c	533e
Date				533d
Owner		035	040	533c
Owner Number	099			533n
View Description	240bp,243bp,245bp, 246bp,740bp	245bp	500	245p,505,520
Subject				084,6XX
Source	503,581			541
OTHER CATEGORIES				
Classification		099		
Color			300b	
Number of Images	300a		300a	
Series/Set		440		

MARC MAPPING WORK PROJECTS

	NMAA 1985	Avery 1985	Auburn 1986	V&A 1987
Work Categories				
CORE				
Work Type	245h,340h,655,740h	650	245h	007dhj,049,245h,655
Title	245	240,245,697	245	130,240,243,245
Measurements	300		300c,500	300c
Material	340		300b	004,005,300b,340,755
Technique				300b,755
Creator	100,110,700,710	100,110,245c,700,710,789c	100,710	100,110,111,700,710,711
Role	100e,110e,700e,710e			100e,110e,111e,700e, 710e,711e
Date	260c	240f,260c,789d	260,500	260c
Repository Name	591			
Repository Place	591cdefghi			
Repository Number	591l		035	
Current Site	591cdeghi	043,691		
Original Site				
Style/Period				
Nationality/Culture				
Subject	650	600,610,650,654,690	650,690	600,610,611,630,654, 690,691
Related Work	595	130,799		243,773
Relationship Type	595			774
Notes	520,594	500,545,590	500	500,502,504,520,590
OTHER CATEGORIES				
Variant Title	740	740		740,500
Translated Title				
Creator's Series/Edition				440,490,250
Location Produced				
Provenance	593	561		561
Physical Description			300a,500	003,300,755
Documentation	510,530b	510		510
Exhibitions	585		500	585
Inscriptions	562			500
Source of Acquisition				
Conservation	596,597,598,599	590		583
Visual Document Categories				
CORE				
Type	530	300b,245h,520,655,755,789p		583
Format				
Measurements		300c		
Date				
Owner		040		
Owner Number		789i		
View Description		245b,655,789t		
Subject				
Source				
OTHER CATEGORIES				
Classification				
Color		300a,520,789p		
Number of Images		300a,520,789l		
Series/Set				

(Continued)

Table 1 | MARC Mapping by Institution—WORK PROJECTS (Continued)

	SUART 1989	LC P&P 1989	Milw 1991
Work Categories			
CORE			
Work Type	655	007,245h,650,655	300
Title	245	245,505,610ab,650,651a	245,520
Measurements	300cg	300c	
Material	340ce	300b	300
Technique	300h		
Creator	100,110,545,700,710	100,110,700,711	100
Role		100e,110e,700e,711e	
Date	260c	260c,610y,650y,651y	033,260,518
Repository Name		040,852a	260b
Repository Place	851	852e	260a
Repository Number	099a	541e	035,518
Current Site		245a,610z,650z,651a	
Original Site			500
Style/Period		610y,650y,651y	
Nationality/Culture	545		500,650
Subject	650,655,657	600,610	650,690,752
Related Work	245b	773,580	245,503
Relationship Type		580	
Notes	500,520	500,520	
OTHER CATEGORIES			
Variant Title	246		
Translated Title			
Creator's Series/Edition	250		
Location Produced			440,518,752
Provenance	561a		
Physical Description			
Documentation	510a,581a		
Exhibitions	561e		
Inscriptions	300n,500	500	
Source of Acquisition	541	541a	
Conservation	590bc		
Visual Document Categories			
CORE			
Type		530	
Format			
Measurements			
Date			
Owner			260b
Owner Number			035,050,080,530,533
View Description			
Subject			
Source			
OTHER CATEGORIES			
Classification			
Color			
Number of Images			
Series/Set			

	CalHist 1994	Morgan 1994	PerfArts 1994
Work Categories			
CORE			
Work Type	245h,300,655,755	245h,300a,654O	007,300
Title	245	245a,520ABC	245,240,630
Measurements	300c	300c	300
Material	300b	300b,654M	300,340
Technique			
Creator	100,110,260b,700,711		100,110,111,700
Role			
Date	260c	046abde,260c	033,518
Repository Name	040	040,535,852a	040,850
Repository Place		852e	
Repository Number		035a,524a,797a	852
Current Site			
Original Site			
Style/Period		654PY	045
Nationality/Culture		654P	
Subject	600,610,650,651,653, 654,691	653,655a	600,610,611,650,651,655, 656,657,690
Related Work		544	500
Relationship Type			
Notes	500,505,590	500	500,502,511,545
OTHER CATEGORIES			
Variant Title			500
Translated Title			
Creator's Series/Edition	440		440
Location Produced	260a	654Z	044
Provenance		561	561
Physical Description		654L,654S	
Documentation		510ac,581a	510,581
Exhibitions		585a	585
Inscriptions		546ab,562ab	518
Source of Acquisition	590	561	561
Conservation		590a	
Visual Document Categories			
CORE			
Type		530a	530
Format			
Measurements			
Date			
Owner	590		
Owner Number		530d	530,856
View Description			
Subject			
Source		530b	
OTHER CATEGORIES			
Classification			
Color			
Number of Images			
Series/Set			

Table 2 | MARC Mapping by Categories

Work Categories	MARC Tag	Number Used	MARC Tag	Number Used	MARC Tag	Number Used
Work Type (20)[16]	655	9	630	2	690	1
	245	6	049	1	695	1
	654	5	100	1	740	1
	650	4	130	1	755	1
	300	4	340	1		
	007	3	653	1		
Technique (6)[4]	300	3	650	1		
	340	2	755	1		
Material (19)[11]	300	10	004	1	650	1
	340	7	005	1	653	1
	654	2	240	1	695	1
	755	1	520	1		
Measurements (15)[4]	300	11	500	1		
	340	3	653	1		
Title (23)[16]	245	22	110	1	650	1
	240	6	130	1	651	1
	520	2	24x	1	697	1
	610	2	243	1	830	1
	630	2	440	1		
	740	2	505	1		
Related Work (11)[15]	773	3	130	1	740	1
	245	2	240	1	779	1
	440	2	243	1	787	1
	500	2	580	1	799	1
	503	2	595	1	544	1
Date (23)[17]	260	15	518	2	650	1
	245	3	008	1	651	1
	033	2	243	1	653	1
	046	2	520	1	759	1
	240	2	610	1	789	1
	500	2	630	1		

( ) Number of projects using category
[ ] Number of MARC tags used for category

Work Categories	MARC Tag	Number Used	MARC Tag	Number Used	MARC Tag	Number Used
Subject (23)[19]	650	15	653	5	100x.2	1
	600	13	655	4	6xx	1
	651	9	520	2	630	1
	654	9	657	2	656	1
	610	8	691	2	659	1
	690	6	695	2		
	611	5	084	1		
Repository Name (12)[8]	040	4	710	2	850	1
	535	3	260	1	859	1
	852	3	591	1		
Repository Place (11)[9]	852	3	260	1	591	1
	710	2	520	1	851	1
	099	1	535	1	859	1
Repository Number (11)[11]	035	4	518	1	710	1
	023	1	524	1	797	1
	099	1	541	1	852	1
	510	1	591	1		
Current Site (17)[13]	651	6	650	2	654	1
	043	4	710	2	691	1
	245	4	110	1	752	1
	610	2	591	1	851	1
					852	1
Original Site (4)[4]	752	2	500	1	651	1
					852	1
Notes (19)[10]	500	17	502	2	511	1
	520	5	5xx	1	594	1
	545	3	504	1		
	590	3	505	1		
Creator (22)[14]	100	19	111	6	545	1
	700	18	245	2	610	1
	110	15	260	2	7xx	1
	710	14	600	2	789	1
	711	8	1xx	1		
Nationality/Culture (5)[5]	650	2	545	1	690	1
	500	1	654	1		
Variant Title (11)[4]	740	6	500	3		
	246	4	247	1		

(Continued)

Table 2 | MARC Mapping by Categories (Continued)

Work Categories	MARC Tag	Number Used	MARC Tag	Number Used	MARC Tag	Number Used
Translated Title (7)[5]	242	2	243	1	500	1
	740	2	245	1		
Series/Edition (8)[3]	440	6	250	4	490	1
Style/Period (10)[9]	650	3	245	1	655	1
	654	2	610	1	690	1
	045	1	651	1	695	1
Location Produced (7)[6]	260	4	440	1	654	1
	044	1	518	1	752	1
Provenance (10)[3]	561	8	593	1	700	1
Physical Description (7)[7]	300	3	003	1	654	1
	340	2	500	1		
	755	2	650	1		
Documentation (10)[6]	510	8	500	1	585	1
	581	4	530	1	590	1
Exhibitions (13)[6]	711	6	111	3	561	1
	585	4	500	1	590	1
Inscriptions (10)[6]	500	4	591	2	518	1
	562	3	300	1	546	1
Source of Acquisition (5)[3]	541	2	561	2	590	1
Conservation (6)[7]	590	3	596	1	599	1
	359	1	597	1		
	583	1	598	1		
Relationship Type (6)[6]	240	1	580	1	774	1
	440	1	595	1	787	1

( ) Number of projects using category
[ ] Number of MARC tags used for category

Visual Document Categories	MARC Tag	Number Used	MARC Tag	Number Used	MARC Tag	Number Used
Vis Doc View Description (13)[14]	245	7	130	1	630	1
	505	5	240	1	655	1
	520	2	243	1	789	1
	740	2	246	1	949	1
	110	1	500	1		
Vis Doc Type (14)[12]	245	6	655	2	740	1
	300	4	520	1	755	1
	530	4	533	1	789	1
	007	3	583	1	1024	1
Vis Doc Owner (9)[7]	040	3	090	1	590	1
	035	1	260	1		
	049	1	533	1		
Vis Doc Owner Number (12)[11]	099	4	050	1	502	1
	530	3	059	1	789	1
	533	2	080	1	856	1
	035	1	090	1		
Vis Doc Source (11)[10]	260	3	510	1	583	1
	590	3	530	1	927	1
	500	1	541	1		
	503	1	581	1		
Classification (5)[2]	099	3	059	2		
Vis Doc Measurements (6)[4]	300	3	533	1		
	007	2	740	1		
Vis Doc Format (1)[1]	533e	1				
Color (7)[5]	300	4	500	1	789	1
	007	2	520	1		
Number of Images (9)[6]	300	7	500	1	789	1
	090	1	520	1	949	1
Vis Doc Series/Set (5)[3]	440	4	490	1	500	1

Table 3 | MARC Mapping by Tag Number

Tag Number	Tag Label	Categories
007	Physical Description	Work Type Vis Doc Type Vis Doc Measurements Color
008	Fixed Length Data Element	Date
023	Other Standard Identification	Repository Number
033	Date-Time-Place of an Event	Date
035	System Control Number	Repository Number Vis Doc Owner Vis Doc Owner Number
043	Geographical Area Code	Current Site
044	Country of Publishing/ Producing Entity Code	Location Produced
045	Time Period of Content	Style/Period
049	Local Holdings	Work Type Vis Doc Owner
050	LC Call Number	Vis Doc Owner Number
059	Undefined	Vis Doc Owner Number
090	Local Call Number	Vis Doc Owner Number Number of Images
099	Local Call Number	Repository Place Repository Number Vis Doc Owner Number Vis Doc Classification
100	Main Entry/Personal Name	Creator Subject Work Type
110	Main Entry/Corporate Name	Current Site Title Creator Vis Doc View Description
130	Main Entry/Uniform Titles	Title Related Work Work Type Vis Doc View Description

Tag Number	Tag Label	Categories
240	Title/Uniform Titles	Date Material Vis Doc View Description Title Related Work
242	Title/Translated Titles	Translated Title
243	Title/Collective Uniform Titles	Related Work Date Vis Doc View Description
245	Title/Title Statement or Title Proper-name by Which Material Is Known	Title Translated Title Related Work Work Type Creator Date Current Site Style/Period Vis Doc View Description Vis Doc Type
246	Title/Varying Form of Title	Vis Doc View Description Variant Title
247	Title/Former or Title Variations	Variant Title
250	Edition/Imprint/Statement	Series
260	Edition/Imprint/Publication, Imprint	Date Creator Location Produced Vis Doc Source Vis Doc Owner Repository Name Repository Place
300	Physical Description/General	Vis Doc Measurements Inscriptions Color Vis Doc Type Material Technique Work Type Physical Description Measurements Number of Images

(Continued)

Table 3 | MARC Mapping by Tag Number (Continued)

Tag Number	Tag Label	Categories
340	Physical Description/Medium	Material Technique Work Type Physical Description Measurements
359	Physical Description/Undefined	Conservation
440	Series Statement/Added Entry Title	Related Work Series/Edition Location Produced Title Vis Doc Series/Set
490	Series Statement/Traced Differently	Series/Edition Vis Doc Series/Set
500	Notes/General Note	Vis Doc View Description Vis Doc Source Measurements Color Vis Doc Series/Set Number of Images Exhibitions Inscriptions Related Work Documentation Physical Description Translated Title Variant Title Nationality/Culture Notes Original Site Date
503	Notes/Undefined	Related Work Vis Doc Source
504	Notes/Bibliography Note	Notes
505	Notes/Formatted Contents Note	Notes Vis Doc View Description Title
510	Notes/Citation, Reference Note	Documentation Vis Doc Source Repository Number
518	Notes/Date-time and Place of an Event Note	Date Location Produced Inscriptions Repository Number

Tag Number	Tag Label	Categories
520	Notes/Summary Note	Notes Material Title Date Repository Place Subject Vis Doc Type Number of Images Color Vis Doc View Description
524	Notes/Undefined	Repository Number
530	Notes/Additional Physical Form Available Note	Vis Doc Source Documentation Vis Doc Type Vis Doc Owner Number
533	Notes/Reproduction Note	Vis Doc Owner Number Vis Doc Type Vis Doc Format Vis Doc Measurements Vis Doc Date
535	Notes/Location of Original/ Duplicates Note	Repository Name Repository Place
541	Notes/Source of Acquisitions Note	Source of Acquisition Vis Doc Source Repository Number
544	Notes/Location of Associated Archival Material Note	Related Work
545	Notes/Biographical or Historical Note	Creator Nationality/Culture Notes
546	Notes/Language Note	Inscriptions
561	Notes/Provenance Note	Provenance Exhibitions Source of Acquisition
562	Notes/Copy and Version Identification Note	Inscriptions
580	Notes/Linking Entry-Complexity Note	Related Work
581	Notes/Publications about Described Material Note	Documentation Vis Doc Source

(Continued)

Table 3 | MARC Mapping by Tag Number (Continued)

Tag Number	Tag Label	Categories
583	Notes/Action Note	Conservation Vis Doc Type Vis Doc Source
585	Notes/Exhibitions Note	Exhibitions Documentation
590	Notes/Local Note	Documentation Notes Conservation Exhibitions Source of Acquisition Vis Doc Owner Vis Doc Source
591	Notes/Undefined	Current Site Inscriptions Repository Name Repository Place Repository Number
593	Notes/Undefined	Provenance
594	Notes/Undefined	Notes
595	Notes/Undefined	Related Work
596	Notes/Undefined	Conservation
597	Notes/Undefined	Conservation
598	Notes/Undefined	Conservation
599	Notes/Undefined	Conservation
600	Subject Access/Subject Added Entry Personal Name	Subject Creator
610	Subject Access/Subject Added Entry Corporate Name	Title Date Current Site Creator Style/Period Subject
630	Subject Access/Subject Added Entry Uniform Title	Date Title Work Type Subject Vis Doc View Description

Tag Number	Tag Label	Categories
650	Subject Access/Subject Added Entry Topical Term	Work Type Nationality/Culture Style/Period Material Technique Subject Title Date Current Site Physical Description
651	Subject Access/Subject Added Entry Geographical Name	Current Site Original Site Style/Period Title Date Subject
653	Subject Access/Index Term Uncontrolled	Subject Date Measurements Material Work Type
654	Subject Access/Subject Added Entry Faceted Topical Terms	Work Type Subject Physical Description Material Location Produced Style/Period Current Site Nationality/Culture
655	Subject Access/Genre Form	Work Type Vis Doc Type Subject Vis Doc View Description
657	Subject Access/Index Term Function	Subject
659	Subject Access/Undefined	Subject
690	Subject Access/Local Subject Access	Subject Nationality/Culture Style/Period Work Type
691	Subject Access/Local Subject Access	Subject Current Site

(Continued)

Table 3 | MARC Mapping by Tag Number (Continued)

Tag Number	Tag Label	Categories
695	Subject Access/Local Subject Access	Subject Style/Period Material Work Type
697	Subject Access/Local Subject Access	Title
700	Added Entry/Personal Name	Creator
710	Added Entry/Corporate Name	Current Site Repository Number Repository Name Repository Place Creator
711	Added Entry/Meeting Name	Exhibitions Creator
740	Added Entry/Uncontrolled Related Analytical Title	Vis Doc Type Title Work Type Related Work Variant Title Translated Title Vis Doc View Description Vis Doc Measurements
752	Added Entry/Hierarchical Place Name	Current Site Original Site
755	Added Entry/Obsolete	Work Type Physical Description Vis Doc Type Material Technique
759	Added Entry/Undefined	Date
773	Linking Entry/Host Item Entry	Related Work
774	Linking Entry/Component Item Entry	Relationship Type
779	Linking Entry/Undefined	Related Work
789	Linking Entry/Undefined	Creator Date Vis Doc View Description Vis Doc Type Vis Doc Owner Number Color Number of Images

Tag Number	Tag Label	Categories
797	Undefined	Repository Number
830	Series Added Entry/Uniform Title	Title
850	Holdings/ALT Graphics/Holding Institution	Repository Name
851	Holdings/ALT Graphics/Obsolete	Repository Place Current Site
852	Holdings/ALT Graphics/Location	Current Site Original Site Repository Name Repository Place Repository Number
856	Holdings/ALT Graphics/Electronic Location Address	Vis Doc Owner Number
859	Holdings/ALT Graphics/Undefined	Repository Name Repository Place
927	Undefined	Vis Doc Source
949	Local Processing Information	Number of Images Vis Doc View Description

PART II

MARC Projects:
Visual Documents

The Rensselaer Slide Database in Retrospect

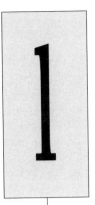

Jeanne M. Keefe

In 1985, the Rensselaer Polytechnic Institute's Graphics Curator used funding from the National Endowment for the Arts to investigate and test the applicability of the *Art and Architecture Thesaurus* (AAT) to the organization and cataloging of the Architecture Library's slide collection. This coincided with the administration's decision to convert the library's card catalog to an online public access system and to eventually integrate the slide catalog into that database. It was during the initial stage in the conversion process that we were asked to consider several questions:

Is AAT terminology useful to both cataloger and patron?

What problems are encountered when we apply AAT terminology to an established slide collection?

What level of expertise would be needed for a cataloger or an indexer to use the AAT to its fullest advantage?

What amount of time is involved in converting just a small part of a slide collection to the online catalog format?

How much time would it take to convert fifty thousand slides?

These were not the last of our questions, by any means. We encountered many problems before the final implementation of the system and several more afterward. This is a brief account of that evolutionary process, including an update on the changes that have occurred in the past ten years and the issues that are still left unresolved after all this time.

The Slide Library

The Rensselaer Architecture Library's slide collection was established in 1932 and at the time of this project contained approximately fifty thousand slides, as well as smaller collections of maps, drawings, models, microfiche, microfilm, records, tapes, and films. In 1995, the collection still contains all the above, except that the slides number just over ninety thousand and we now collect videotapes and CD-ROMs. Staffing at the time of the project was limited: one full-time slide curator, one half-time temporary research clerk, and two

41

or three part-time student assistants. Today the slide library is staffed by one three-quarter-time curator and one or two part-time student workers. In 1985 the staff was responsible for all the normal reference, cataloging, accessioning, circulation, in-house photography, and general housekeeping duties along with the added conversion responsibilities of research, worksheet completion, and data entry. These responsibilities remain the same today.

Although it is currently housed in the Architecture Library, the slide collection developed as a separate entity to support the curriculum and faculty of the school of architecture. The original classification system was based on medium (painting, architecture, etc.) and was arranged according to a very loose combination of historical, geographical, chronological, and stylistic determinants that were redefined over the years to resemble an imprecise synthesis of the "University of California at Santa Cruz (Tansey)" system for categorizing visual content and the "Metropolitan Museum of Art" classification listing for styles and periods.

Slides about architecture were arranged chronologically and art slides were arranged alphabetically by artist's name. Certain subject areas, such as planning, architectural design, and building construction, were classified according to the Architecture Library's Vertical Filing System. By 1985, over thirty separate subject categories had evolved, each with its own distinct classification scheme. Some were arranged numerically, others alphabetically, and still others were arranged by subject heading. A card index and authority file had been developed and maintained to aid the user. Despite this fact, slide retrieval developed into a true art form with only the most veteran and sophisticated patrons able to locate the slides they needed in any reasonable amount of time.

Identifying the Problems and Anticipating the Requirements

Through careful monitoring of collection usage and the solicitation of patron commentary, we were able to isolate several serious problem areas that needed to be addressed before we could proceed with the conversion project.

- The existing system was limited with regard to accommodating new or expanded subject areas. Integrating new materials required redefining the beginning or end of an existing area. As an example, slides of an excavation of a Viking fishing village had to be squeezed to fit between English Norman and Gothic if we wanted to keep them in order.

- Little or no accommodation was made for non-Western cultures or their artifacts, and space for new technological subject areas had not been designed into the system. These areas were now needed to support the changing faculty and curriculum of the school.

- Severe fragmentation had occurred in some of the larger and more important architectural subject areas, such as *St. Peter's* in Rome. In the collection, slides of *St. Peter's* could be found in as many as nine different locations, ranging from Early Christianity through the twentieth century to maps and architectural practice. It was a retrieval nightmare.

- Finally, and maybe more important, no professional curator or librarian had been in charge of the collection since its inception. Staffed by student workers and the occasional clerk, the collection suffered from inconsistent and often erroneous cataloging practices. Patron complaints centered on the lack of thorough cross-referencing, the time it took to retrieve slides because of subject fragmentation, and the difficulty of browsing the collection because two-inch-by-two-inch and the larger glass lantern slides were filed together in the same drawer.

Obviously, these problems had to be dealt with during the planning process along with identifying special requirements we might have in order to meet our main objective of developing and implementing a system that would serve our patrons more efficiently and effectively. Several distinct areas of consideration were identified:

- The need to devise a new call number system that would allow the entire collection to be integrated into only three distinct headings (art, architecture, and reference/generic) and at the same time be flexible enough to accommodate new or different subject areas within that three-heading framework.

- The need to develop new subject areas and expand existing ones in order to keep pace with the demands of our faculty and changes in our curricula, as well as the needs of patrons from both inside and outside the Institute.

- The need to standardize our use of descriptive terminology and to regulate our cataloging practices in order to improve consistency to the greatest extent possible. Extensive cross-referencing was needed to reduce retrieval times and to facilitate the compilation of topical lectures (e.g., daylighting or precast concrete buildings).

- Labor-saving devices also needed to be built into the new system, and particular attention needed to be paid to the automatic printing of slide labels and accession lists.

- It was also our goal to build in compatibility with videodisc and CD-ROM technologies so that we could incorporate them in the future.

In an effort to accommodate these new considerations we decided to approach our materials in a different way. Conventionally, art and architecture slides were viewed and cataloged as surrogates of works of art. As compositions they have focal points and those focal points become the primary subjects described by the cataloger. However, we decided that it would be more appropriate to our needs to view the slide as a document, similar to a manuscript that contains much more information than simply the title page and the author. Although the title (e.g., Sydney Opera House) remained the primary denotation, the slide document itself contained visual information that covered a variety of subjects (Ridge beams, Glass curtain walls, Shell vaulting, Precast concrete ribs, Tiles, Concert Halls, etc.). By incorporating each of these different points into our cross-referencing system, this site is now quickly available to patrons needing examples of certain types of materials, structures, or designs. This means that a slide of a statue inside a fifteenth-century Gothic cathedral is now readily available to the patron looking for examples of medieval armor or dress. Viewing a slide as a document instead of a composition significantly increases its usefulness as a visual resource. A single image can now be approached along several different subject paths, eliminating the need for duplicate slides for filing into the various subject categories and, ultimately, producing a savings in terms of storage space and collection development.

The Development Stage

Once we had identified our needs and reviewed our various options it was decided that we should utilize the computer technologies and expertise available to

us at Rensselaer. In 1984, the library replaced its card catalog with an online information system called InfoTrax™. The system used the Stanford Public Information Retrieval System (SPIRES) database management system operating under the Michigan Terminal System (MTS). Our patrons were already familiar with the system because the holdings of the Architecture Library were on it. We felt that the new slide database needed to be compatible with the existing system in order to allow for future integration.

It was also our intention to test the usefulness of the AAT's terminology in a working slide library. The different ways in which we decided to use the AAT hierarchies will become clear once the composition of the data entry worksheet is understood. The structure of the AAT Styles and Periods hierarchy was used as the basis for devising a new classification scheme, and we used the entire AAT as our authority file.

The first cataloging worksheet we designed had twenty-one fields that were easily manipulated to meet data entry, printing, and display requirements and also to create multiple indexes. After completing and testing the original worksheet, we became aware of the new OCLC Audiovisual Media format, which was, at that time, consistent with *USMARC Format for Bibliographic Data,* and we decided to redesign the worksheet accordingly in order to make the slide database more compatible with Rensselaer's online information system. This decision required us to expand the worksheet's fields and subfields.

This revision stage lasted for over a year and a half and was the most time-consuming and difficult step in the entire process. With generous help from the staff of Rensselaer's cataloging department, we attempted to match and merge the fields from our first worksheet with the fields and subfields defined by MARC. Difficulties arose during this process because the vast majority of the slides in our collection were produced in-house or locally or were purchased before 1935 (lanterns) and we lacked the bibliographic documentation needed to develop a standardized MARC record. Unfortunately, our slide collection did not fit neatly into the criteria used by MARC to define its fields and subfields. This was a dilemma soon to be faced by many others trying to accomplish the same feat, some with greater success and others with less.

This situation inevitably led us to reinterpret and expand the current MARC field and subfield definitions in a very open-ended and self-serving manner. We did not strictly adhere to the criteria set down by MARC; instead we expanded and reinterpreted several of the definitions to meet our particular needs.

For example, architectural slides do not usually have a uniform title as do some paintings, so they were divided and put into the 245 field (title statement), and our generic/reference slides were put into field 242 (translation of title by catalog agency).

During the course of this reinterpretation process four different worksheets evolved as we attempted not only to accommodate MARC definitions but to predict the direction of the collection's future development. Fields that appeared to be not very useful in the immediate future were included in anticipation of future needs. In deciding to use MARC field codes and definitions, we gained a fair amount of consistency and compatibility; however, we also gave up some flexibility and a measure of control over our own work process. In addition, using MARC multiplied the number of necessary fields and subfields, nearly doubling the size and complexity of the first worksheet.

In retrospect, we attempted to accomplish too many tasks at once. We were not able to second-guess the future and provide for every alternative. Who would have guessed that we would move from a mainframe to a PC environment in just a few short years? In order to keep the worksheet logical and useful to both cataloging and data entry personnel, we had to postpone our plans to incorporate the printing formats and accession lists. Although our design for the first worksheet was straightforward and very collection specific at the time, it would have eventually ended up being just another stopgap solution. On the other hand, the next worksheet design was so complicated and confusing it hardly seemed worth the effort.

After abandoning the printing format, we tried to streamline the second worksheet design down to the most basic components, purposely leaving out exact field numbers and subfield codes. The second- and third-generation worksheet designs required the cataloger to provide the basic bibliographic information (title, subject, location, descriptors, etc.), and to essentially ignore the delimiters of MARC fields and subfields. The accurate field delimiters were then left to be determined by the curator and added to the worksheet during the editing phase just before data entry. This meant that nonprofessional staff could be used to fill in the worksheets by copying the information gathered from books, articles, labels, and accession records. Then the curator could check this information for errors and fill in the appropriate field numbers and subfield codes. In March 1986, using our third version of the worksheet, we began to convert the slide collection.

Implementation

After completing about three months' worth of worksheets, we began to enter the data into the database. Online, the worksheet form was simply a list of all the necessary MARC fields in numeric sequence. When we began it took about twenty minutes to enter the record for one slide. It soon became obvious that our third worksheet was not very efficient in terms of data entry and that we would have to devise yet another. The last worksheet design, as seen in figure 1-1, once again includes all the necessary fields and subfields, thereby making it easier for untrained staff to move between the paper worksheet and the online entry form. This last worksheet appears to be complicated and overworked, but it substantially reduced errors in both cataloging and data entry because it approached the process in a very straightforward and logical manner.

Because the Rensselaer slide library had been designated as a test site for the AAT, a device was needed with which we could monitor its usefulness. Toward that end we decided to place all non-AAT terms in field 653 and all AAT terms in the 650 field (the 654 had not yet been adopted). By making this distinction we could monitor user terminology by means of transaction logs, an unobtrusive way to monitor user activity.

As we became more familiar with the various field definitions it took less and less time to fill in the paper worksheets. However, the initial research required for each site or particular building varied according to the resources available. Our conversion began with the Prehistoric section for two reasons: first, we felt that the subject would be a good test area as far as our research procedures were concerned; and second, it was one of the smallest sections in the collection and we felt it would serve as a good gauge of time requirements. By the time we reached Stonehenge it became obvious that we were not working very efficiently. Because we were entering one record for each slide, most of the worksheets pertaining to a particular site or building contained almost identical information with only minor variations concerning details. In order to save work we began to photocopy the first complete worksheet on the subject and then just add the variable information pertaining to accession number and view to the copied sheets. The basic information was constant, but the particulars had to be appended and, with a subject such as the caves at Lascaux, France, which contained as many as forty slides, we saved a lot of conversion time by adopting this method.

• = blank space	Page 1

TYPE "G" PROJECTED GRAPHICS	; GMT "SLIDES"	;007 PHYSICAL DESC. "••| bs (slide) || HJ (2X2″) || HZ (3½X4″) || IZ (other)"	RECORD (IRN) #

CALL NUMBERS: ARCHITECTURE
;059
"••| d _____ (AAT List 2) | p ___ (Country)
| far | r _____ (State)
| g _____ (AAT List 1) | t ___._ (Title)
| L _____ (Site) | v _____ (AAT List 3)
| n ___._ (City) | z _____" (Detail #)

FINE ARTS
;059
"••| ffa
| n ___._ (Name)
| t ___._ (Title)
| v _____ (AAT #4)
| z _____" (Detail #)

GENERIC
;059
"••| frf
| v _____
_____"
(AAT List #5)

LOCAL USE NUMBERS
;099 CATALOGING AND ACCESSION NUMBERS
"•9| a _____ / _____ (Accession/Catalog #s)
| a _____ (List of Acc. numbers
_____" in the slide set)

PERSONAL NAMES:
;100   Artist-Architect-Designer, etc.
"0•| a _____ (Single name)
"1•| a _____ (Last, First)
"2•| a _____ - _____ (Hyphenated)
| c _____ (Title) | d _____" (Dates)

;110   Corporation-Partnership-Firm-Organization
"0•| a _____ (Surname, inverted)
"1•| a _____ (Place name)
| b _____ (Dept, Agency)
"2•| a _____" (Corporation name)

;111   Event-Exhibition-Competition-Project
"0•| a _____ (Personal name)
"1•| a _____ (Place name)
"2•| a _____ (Type name)
| n _____ (# in a series) | d _____ (Dates)
| c _____" (Site of event)

TITLES:
;240   UNIFORM TITLES - FINE ARTS SLIDES
"00| a _____ (No article)
02| a _____ (1 letter article)
03| a _____ (2 letter article)
04| a _____ (3 letter article)
| p _____" (View of Part)

;245   ARCHITECTURE OR GENERIC-REFERENCE SLIDE TITLES
"00| a _____ (Proper Title)
| b _____ (Part of Title)
| p _____" (Section)

IMPRINT
;260   PRODUCTION INFO
"••| a _____ (Place of Production)
| b _____ (Name of Producer)
| c _____" (Date of Production)

Figure 1-1 | Data Entry Worksheet for the Slide Collection   (Continued)

GENERAL FIELD NOTES: Page 2
;500   NOTES
"•• | a _____
          _____ "

LIBRARY ACTION INFORMATION:
;583
"•• | a _____ (Action needed) | c _____ (Date accessioned)
    | h _____ (Requested By) | j _____ (Source of slide)
    | k _____ " (Library notes)

SUBJECT ENTRIES
;600   SUBJECT OF THE WORK OF ART OR PHOTOGRAPH
"04 | a _____ (Single Name)
"14 | a _____ , _____ (Last, First)
"24 | a _____ - _____ (Hypenated)
    | c _____ (Title) | d _____ " (Dates)
;650   LIBRARY OF CONGRESS SUBJECT HEADINGS FOR GENERIC SLIDES | y _____ (Time Period)
"•0 | a _____ (Subject Title) | x _____ (Part) | z _____ " (Place)
;651   GEOGRAPHIC TERMS
"•4 | a _____ (Site) | a _____ (City) | a _____ (State or Province)
    | a _____ (Country) | a _____ " (Alternate spellings)
;653   NON-AAT TERMS, FREE-FORM TERMS AND DESCRIPTIONS
"2• | a _____
    | a _____
    | a _____
    | a _____ (Medium) | a _____ (Dimensions of work)
    | a _____ " (Dates of Production, Manufacture or Construction)

;654   ART AND ARCHITECTURE THESAURUS TERMINOLOGY
"1• | a _____ (Primary AAT Terms)
    | a _____
    | a _____
    | a _____
    | a _____
    | a _____
    | a _____ "
    | 2 AAT

ASSOCIATED NAMES
;700   ASSOCIATED ARCHITECTS, ARTISTS, DESIGNERS, PERSON'S NAMES
"0• | a _____ (Single name)
"1• | a _____ , _____ (First, Last)
"2• | a _____ - _____ (Hyphenated)
    | c _____ (Title) | d _____ " (Dates)
;710   ASSOCIATED CORPORATION-PARTNERSHIP-FIRM-ORGANIZATION
"0• | a _____ (Personal Names)
"1• | a _____ (Place Name) | b _____ (Dept or Agency)
"2• | a _____ " (Corporation name)
;711   ASSOCIATED EVENT-EXHIBITION-COMPETITION-PROJECT
"0• | a _____ (Personal Names)
"1• | a _____ (Place Name)
"2• | a _____ (Type name) | d _____ (Dates)
    | n _____ (# in a series) | c _____ " (Site of event)

HOLDINGS - SETS OF SLIDES - LOCAL USE INFO
;949   NUMBER OF VIEWS IN EACH TITLE
"01 | a _____ (Plans) | b _____ (Sections) | c _____ (Drawings) | d _____ (Models) | e _____ (Aerials)
    | f _____ (Exteriors) | g _____ (Interior Views) | h _____ (Details) | l _____ (Garden Views)
    | j _____ (Paintings & Frescoes) | k _____ " (Furnishings and Utilitarian Items)

Figure 1-1 | Data Entry Worksheet for the Slide Collection (Continued)

As a result of the increase in worksheet production, a backlog of data entry occurred. In addition, data entry became a very repetitive and boring task because the exact same information was being entered over and over again. In order to alleviate this problem our systems analyst created a *clone* command so that we could duplicate a single entry record as many times as needed. The data entry person could then access each of these cloned records to change or add the pertinent information that distinguished that particular slide from all the others with the same title.

The next logical step was to stop photocopying the worksheets and just make out a primary worksheet, simply filling in the distinctive information on all subsequent sheets (different size, color, source, view, accession number, etc.). At each of these learning stages we were able to save time on the conversion.

The Stratagem

Once all these implementation problems were identified and successfully solved, our conversion process began to proceed at a slow yet steady pace. By the end of 1986, we had managed to convert two entire sections of the architecture collection, Prehistoric and Egyptian, and we began to convert the section on twentieth-century architecture. It had taken eight months for two half-time employees to convert and enter records for approximately 1,300 slides. At that rate it would take us over fifteen years to convert the entire collection! The grant from the National Endowment for the Arts was due to conclude at the end of February 1987, and at that point we would lose our temporary staff. It was impossible to imagine how we would ever be able to continue this conversion to an online database, let alone complete it. We needed to devise a new strategy.

While trying to formulate a solution to our problem we realized that we had overlooked one very important element in the search strategy: *A computer display or printout of a textual record would never replace the visual image itself.* Because our patrons were actually looking for visual images, we surmised that they would never choose to use a slide based on a written record alone. Until image storage technology advanced to the point where we could link our records database to an image database and be able to present the materials remotely, our patrons were still going to have to physically go to the drawers and pull out the image they were looking for to be sure it contained the visual information they required. All the database could provide, in its present form, was a listing of what we had and where it was stored. Furthermore, because all slides with the same title (e.g., the Robie House) are stored together in the same drawer under the same call number in view sequence, what was really needed was for us to simply consider all slides having the same title as a *set*. This supposition provided us with our new strategy.

Our new system called for us to store only one entry record per *set*, meaning a group of slides relating to the same work, having the same title. That one record would contain all the appropriate information pertaining to the building, the accession numbers of all the slides in the set, and a holdings field listing the number and types of views contained in the set. (See sample catalog entries in figure 1-2.)

As new slides were added in the future, or damaged ones removed, updating the record would require only adding or removing the relevant information from the fields containing the accession numbers and the views. By changing to this new strategy we would no longer have to store over seventy thousand records; we could reduce that number to about twenty-five thousand. In addition, the slide search was facilitated greatly by the fact that now the patron was presented with only one record per set, instead of fifty, and that one record contained all the information necessary for the patron to decide if it was worth going to the slide cabinets at all.

The Public Display

In 1986, Rensselaer's InfoTrax information system was an integrated set of databases that provided information about the different types of resources available in both the Folsom Library and the Architecture Library. The library's catalog database contained a general listing of books, journals, Rensselaer theses, art prints, audiocassettes, phonograph records, and audiovisual items. During the past ten years those resources have expanded to include an electronic reserves, homework, government documents, technical reports, scores, computer software, audiovisual media, manuscript collections, and the Institute's archives, as well as providing access to other research databases not owned by the library and access to the Internet. InfoTrax was designed so that all fields and subfields were searchable in data entry mode. By using the simple FIND command the staff was allowed to search fields not available to the patron, such as

IRN - 13102;
DATE-ADDED = 02/10/87;
DATE-UPDATED = 05/31/89;
TYPE = G;
GMT = Slides;
007 = " |hz|hj|db|dc";
059 = " |d4|far|gf|np232|pfr|tp232|vg";
100 = 1 |aGarnier, Jean-Louis-Charles|d1825 - 1898;
245 = 00 |aParis Opera House|pcutaway perspective job;
500 = " |aCeiling painted by Marc Chagall in 1964. Sculptural groups by J. B. Carpeaux ";
583 = " |anone|c1986|hlibrary";
590 = " |ac2l841/19:FR:P:OH,2";
590 = " |al660/19:FR:P:OH:6|a6l36|a6l47|al741|al662|al8l4|al13O4|aCl5631|al0942
650 = " 7 |a0pera houses perspective drawings|aBeaux art|amodern European|aBaroque revival
            |amosaics|aloggias|aarcades|acaryatids|abird's eye perspectives|aaxial building|avaulted ceilings
            |aauditoriums|aconcert halls|aperforming arts buildings";
650 = " 7 |astages|astaircases|astairways|astairs|amarble|aRococo revival|aorchestras|arotundas |adomes|a,metal
            domes|acopper|acolonnades|avestibules|agabled towers|afoyers|adressing rooms";
651 = " 0 |aParis, France";
653 = " |al862 - 1875|acandelabras|achandeliers|aescalier d' honneur|agilt|agabled flytowers|alateral domes|alateral
            pavilions";
740 = 0l |a2in by 2in slides: 2 perspectives (1 color), 4 exteriors (1 col), 2 interiors (1 col), and 6 3in by 4in slides
            (I plan, 1 section, 2 interiors, 2 exteriors);

IRN = 13285;
DATE-ADDED = 02/25/87;
DATE-UPDATED = 06/05/89;
TYPE = G;
GMT = slides;
007 = " |hj|db";
059 = " |d4|far|gf|nv662.l|pau|ts822.6,vg";
100 = 1 |aLoos, Adolf|dl870 - 1933;
245 = 00 |aSteiner House|pview from the garden, an early photograph;
500 = " |aThe facade on St. Veitgasse has been radically tampered with, that the original curved & plated roof
            having been replaced by a pitched roof. The interior has also been subjected to substantial alterations";
583 = " |anone|cNovember 1979|jRowland: A History of the Modern Movement";
590 = " |a2l3O2/20:AU:VI:STH:6|al4985|al4986|al4987|al4988|al4989|al4990";
650 = " 7 |aArchitect-designed houses|ahouses|adwellings|adomestic architecture|aresidences|aresidential|adetached
            houses|aroofs|ametal|alaminated|aflat roofs|abalconies|awindows|aplaster|alime mortar";
651 = " 0 |aVienna|aAustria|aWien";
653 = " |al9l0|acurved roof|awood cement|abays";
740 = 0l |al plan, 1 section, 1 elevation, 3 exteriors, 1 interior;

Figure 1-2 | Catalog Entry Samples

medium, action needed (condition of the slide), requestor (the name of the person who requested the slide be produced or purchased), IRN number (record number), and source (the source from which we acquired the slide).

Although access was limited, the patron could search the database in several ways. Slides could be searched and identified by subject, title, name, geographic location, call number, accession number, source, date of completion, and/or descriptors, both non-AAT and AAT. SPIRES allowed the user to search by single words or strings beginning with the command FIND and expanding the search with the word OR and narrowing it with the word AND. By combining several search terms (e.g., FIND about *Houses* AND *Pennsylvania* AND by *Frank Lloyd Wright*) the user could zero in very quickly on exactly what was needed. The commands used in the visual display format for the public models are as follows:

- The BRIEF command displays title, architect/artist/designer, and site on the same line.

- The CALL and PRINT commands display and print the information provided in the BRIEF format along with the call number, accession number, and size of the slide.

- The DETAIL command gives the user all the information seen in the CALL command plus a truncated listing of the descriptor/subject fields, dates, notes, and a list of the current holdings in the set (see figure 1-3).

Future changes to the display format could be planned as we received feedback from our users about what other information they would like to have displayed.

Project Summary

At the end of the original project a report was written that covered many of the considerations, conclusions,

---

TITLE : Sydney Opera House; post-1945, aerial view
BY : Utzon, Jorn
SUBJECT : Opera houses, auditoria, auditoriums, ceramic tiles, performing arts buildings, concrete halls, music halls, music auditoria, symphony halls, movie theaters, theatres, cinemas, restaurant, ribbed vaults, ribbed arches
concrete beams, concrete paint, podium, roof trusses, roofing, roofing tile, ribs, vaulted roofs, shell roofs, reinforced concrete, lattice roofs, shell structures, shell vaults, towers, steel trusses, ceremonial ways
workspaces, workshops, wood walls, wood ceiling, wooden ceilings, concrete vaults, concrete structures, concrete pilings, concrete joints, glass, glass walls, laminated materials, cables, cable roofs, cable-stayed structures, ridge boards, precast concrete, granite
granite powder cement, bronze window mullions, ridge beams
SITE : Australia, Sydney, New South Wales. Benelong Point
DATES : 1957 - 1973
SIZE : 2×2 in. color
HOLDINGS : 3 Plans, 11 sections/drawings, 2 aerial views, 29 exterior views, 3 interior views, 3 details
CALL NO : 20:AUS:SY:SOH:6

TITLE : The Crystal Cathedral. Garden Grove Community Church: General view, exterior.
BY : Johnson, Philip
Johnson/Burgee
SUBJECT : Glass, buildings, glass doors, glass roofs, glass windows, glass walls, curtain walls, non-bearing walls, enclosure walls, window walls, heat-resisting glass, space frames, gussets, web members
plates, structural frames, steel trusses, chords, pipe, concrete, concrete columns, concrete pilings, mechanically operated doors, horizontal sliding doors, girders, marble pools, fountains
clerestories, porticoes, space trusses, hangar doors, neo-fundamentalist church architecture
SITE : United States, Garden Grove, California, USA
DATES : 1983
SIZE : 2×2 in b&w, color
HOLDINGS : 1 plan, 1 section, 1 aerial view, 6 exterior views (4 in color), 3 interior views (2 in color)
NOTES : Designed for the Reverend Dr. Robert Schuller
CALL NO : 20:US:CA:GA:CC:6

Figure 1-3 | Detail Display Samples

and predictions for the future we had made during that period. We realized that fine-tuning would continue to be necessary as new problems surfaced and more refined technologies came into use. We had hoped at the time that we would be able to link the database to a videodisc of the slide images as soon as it was economically feasible. This proposal seemed the logical next step because it would cut down on the general wear and tear on the collection by reducing refiling, handling, and breakage. Access to the Internet was not even a consideration at that time. We thought that if we could store and display our images online we could eliminate the need for browsing in the drawers and eventually do away with the use of call numbers entirely. This would also allow us to store the slides in accession number order, thereby solving our storage and drawer-shifting problems; at the same time we could eliminate interfiling by simply adding all new slides to the end of the accession number sequence.

The strategy of cataloging a series of same-title/subject slides as a set not only proved to be a significant labor and timesaving device but also cut down on our database storage needs and facilitated the information retrieval process. Rather than hamper our patron's ability to retrieve relevant material, it abbreviated the search process considerably. At the time we felt that it served as an optimal compromise, especially since the set method of cataloging had precedence in both the cataloging of monographs under a series entry and the cataloging of sets of materials by archivists. We felt that, by extension, one could even look on the cataloging of a monograph as a single record representing a collection of chapters and sections on a single topic. Museums have long used this approach when cataloging such items as sets of silverware, dishes, jewelry, and dresser sets. We felt that this set method of cataloging would put online conversion within the reach of the many slide libraries suffering from both staff and budgetary restrictions.

As for the answers to the questions proposed at the beginning of the project (and the beginning of this chapter), the following is a summary of our conclusions.

- *Is AAT terminology useful for catalogers and patrons?*

The catalogers found the AAT terminology to be very useful, especially the Styles and Periods hierarchy. In this area, any attempt at standardizing the terminology is bound to be helpful. The breakdown by culture and reign was espe-

cially useful when categorizing historical periods during which several distinctive styles were in evidence. This hierarchy served both as our authority file and as a comprehensive guide for cross-referencing terminology. By using the AAT, both the cataloger and the patron are led to terms that they previously would not have thought of using. In addition, the AAT details particular components to such an extent that there can be little room for confusion. The use of this terminology allows our users to quickly pull together lectures on such diverse topics as lighting techniques, concrete construction, or stylistic revivals. These options are invaluable to patrons using a collection that is classified according to artistic styles, medium, or historical periods.

- *What problems were encountered when AAT terminology was applied to an established slide collection?*

We didn't encounter any problems applying the terminology itself. Most of our problems using the AAT had to do with the form it was in while we were using it. This test was conducted before the AAT was published so we worked with computer printouts that were unwieldy. In addition, because a merged alphabetical listing of the twenty-two completed hierarchies did not yet exist, each had to be searched individually, which was time-consuming. The published edition and the computer edition definitely make the AAT easier to use.

- *What level of expertise is necessary for an indexer or cataloger to use the AAT to its fullest extent?*

This is basically a collection-specific question because the required expertise would change depending on the scope of the individual collection and the level of specificity required. Whether a cataloger was creating a MARC record would also affect the level of expertise needed. Generally, a cataloger would need a basic knowledge of art and architectural history along with good clerical and research skills. Indexers need an initial training period of at least three months to reach an acceptable level of competence and efficiency, but this period might be shortened if the indexer had previous experience with MARC-based cataloging of nonbook materials.

- *How much time would be involved in converting a small part of a collection to the online catalog for-*

mat? How much time would it take to convert an entire collection of approximately fifty thousand slides?

After we completed the training period and stopped making out one record for every slide, it took two half-time employees (or one full-time employee) one month to research and re-catalog approximately 520 slides and to enter them into the database. At that rate it would take less than two years to convert ten thousand slides and nearly eight years to convert fifty thousand. The only way to cut that time is to employ more people. The major advantage to this strategy is that once a subject section has been converted, updating the records to include additional slides is simple. New titles, however, would still require research and worksheets.

We believed that the larger the slide collection the greater the need for an online catalog. In the three years between 1986 and 1989 we came to appreciate the fact that we had a lot less busywork to do in order to keep our records up-to-date. To add a new slide to an existing set, all we had to do was update the record, add the new accession number, and add the view to the holdings field. Because the majority of our new accessions were different or better views of converted titles, we could cut the time we needed to add new slides by 75 percent. Although we still had to complete worksheets to add new titles, these were limited to selected contemporary buildings and new works of art. Devising a format for printing labels and accession records could only further reduce the time it takes to process a new slide into the collection.

We understood that the use of the *MARC Audiovisual Materials Format* had both its detractors and its supporters. We encountered firsthand what kind of problems can occur when one tries to apply it to a working collection. This is especially relevant when you are dealing with the field definition limitations and the original cataloging of unpublished nonbook materials. As long as MARC can be reinterpreted and redefined beyond its existing parameters to meet the distinct needs of these specialized collections, it will continue to be a useful tool. We also recognized that consistency and standardization of descriptive terminology should be pursued and encouraged within the profession. The use of both MARC cataloging and AAT terminology promotes standardization and consistency. This interest, however, should not put unnecessary restrictions on our ability to comprehensively catalog unpublished nonbook materials, thereby limiting user access to those materials. Subject-specific collections, such as architecture slides that have been produced in-house, are very difficult to catalog using MARC "by the book" and without using some open interpretation of the field and subfield definitions. When we designed the Rensselaer Online Catalog for Slides, we decided to forgo some of the standardization we desired in order to ensure greater access to the collection. We considered this to be an acceptable compromise.

In Retrospect

When this project was begun we were navigating through relatively uncharted waters. Personal computers, records management software, CD-ROM players, and the Internet were either still products of the future or so expensive we couldn't begin to think of incorporating them at that time. I remember getting an estimate of $62,000 to transfer eighty thousand slides onto a master disc that we could then run off the mainframe and link to our database. At the time it was more than we could afford. Today imaging seems to have become imperative, even though it is still beyond our budget.

The years between 1987 and 1997 have not been kind to libraries and museums alike. Downsizing, budget cuts, staff reductions, and shrinking grants have hit us quite hard. The ever-increasing belief that visual resource collections all will be digitized and available over the Web to anyone, anywhere, anytime has strengthened the conviction that slides are mastodons waiting to tumble into the tar pits. And maybe they are. Institutions are wary of investing in what they consider to be obsolete (or at the very least mature) media and technologies such as slides, especially during these financially uncertain times. Words like *interactive learning, multimedia, workstations,* and *remote access* have practically replaced such terms as *audiovisual, projection, computer terminal,* and *collection.* As the technological barriers that previously existed between operating systems and software programs begin to blur and then disappear, the operating and records management systems of ten years ago do indeed take on the qualities of a stumbling mastodon.

During these years our staff hours have been cut back from one full-time professional, two half-time workers, and several part-time student workers to one three-quarter-time professional and a few part-time student workers. During the same time period the production of new slides and the circulation rate have increased by one-third over the previous rate. There is no longer any time or staff to continue the conversion process. This situation has been further influenced by the administration's decision to transfer all the library's records and databases from the SPIRES database management system on the mainframe to a commercially available system. We will lose much of the flexibility we had with a system that had been created in-house and, as a result, all our less-than-picture-perfect MARC records for slides may not survive the transfer process. The slide database will probably have to be a stand-alone database because of the difficulties in integrating it and this will add to the expense. The decision on whether we will transfer is still pending.

Does this mean that I think all our work was in vain? Emphatically, *no!* As with all experimentation it was a learning process and in several ways it set the stage for the decisions we were going to have to make in the future. Our struggle to create comprehensive MARC records that could be accessed through as many points as possible taught us that big isn't necessarily better. The more comprehensive the descriptive field, the better the chance that it would be similar to other records in the same subject area. Therefore, the harder it became to locate an individual record without a well-defined search strategy. I find a touch of irony in the fact that if and when we do set up a Web site or change over to a stand-alone system, I will probably end up using a record very similar to the very first worksheet we designed. That will depend on whether the idea of shared cataloging really becomes feasible. Furthermore, I'm not sure how many visual resources managers have a firm grasp of the extent to which digitalization and the Internet will change how we organize and access our collections. What further changes will be necessary? Will we be able to maintain or increase our current level of standardization? Will any of this even be possible during this fast-paced time of transition? None of these questions can be answered satisfactorily until we decide whether we are going to jump on the CD-ROM/Internet bandwagon now or wait until the verdict is in. Most of us cannot afford to do anything but wait.

However, while we wait we might be asking ourselves some very basic questions, such as:

- What is the purpose of our collection and is that purpose likely to change in the next ten years?

- Who are our primary patrons and do we have a responsibility to any groups outside those to whom we are currently held accountable? Given the copyright problems inherent in putting images on the Web, what percentage of our collection could realistically be used without incurring liability?

- Who would really be served by putting those images on a homepage or making them available through the online catalog?

- Do we actually have any images that are so unique that they could not be found in any other architecture slide collection?

- What proportion of our patrons will not be served by these actions because they lack the technology necessary to access the databases or CD-ROMs?

- Are these above-mentioned options really the best use of our already limited resources?

You need to answer these questions to your own satisfaction before you can even begin to formulate your next step. In my opinion it would be imprudent to proceed until you have.

BIBLIOGRAPHY

Art and Architecture Thesaurus. New York: Oxford University Press, 1990.

Keefe, Jeanne M. "The Image as Document: Descriptive Programs at Rensselaer." *Library Trends* 38, no. 4 (spring 1990): 659–681.

The Metropolitan Museum of Art. "Photograph and Slide Library." *The Metropolitan Museum of Modern Art Slide Library,* 1968.

Michigan Terminal Systems Ver. 6.0 (MTS 6.0). Ann Arbor: Regents of the University of Michigan, 1988.

Petersen, Toni, and Pat Molholt, eds. *Beyond the Book: Extending MARC for Subject Access.* Boston: G. K. Hall, 1990.

Simons, Wendell W., and Luraine C. Tansey. *A Slide Classification System for the Organization and Automatic Indexing of Interdisciplinary Collections of Slides and Pictures.* Santa Cruz, Calif.: University of California, 1970.

Stanford Public Information Retrieval System Ver. 87.04 (SPIRES 87.04). Palo Alto, Calif.: Stanford University, 1987.

Mapping to MARC at the Bibliothèque de l'Aménagement, Université de Montréal

*Vesna Blazina and
Ginette Melançon-Bolduc*

Collection

The Bibliothèque de l'Aménagement, one of twenty-three branch libraries of the Université de Montréal Library System, provides documentation services for the Faculté de l'Aménagement, which can be translated as School of Environmental Design. It has four departments: Architecture, Industrial Design, Landscape Architecture, and Urban Studies. The school, which offers both undergraduate and graduate programs, has a teaching staff of 147 and 1,053 students. The primary mission of the library is to support the teaching and research needs of its users. The general public also has access to library services.

The Diathèque, or Slide Library of the Bibliothèque de l'Aménagement, Université de Montréal, which was established in the early 1970s, is part of the library and has a collection of forty thousand slides.

Before automation there was a card catalog arranged by author, location, and subject while the slides were filed, and still are, by accession number.

Project

From the very beginning our goal has been to create a database which will offer search strategies (Boolean logic operators, truncation, adjacence) as sophisticated as those used by major bibliographic utilities. Our priority has been the use of natural language for subject retrieval and standardized descriptive cataloging.

In 1987, when we first conceived the project, we had to face the crucial problem of the cataloging format for our slides. The faculty was consulted as to their needs and expectations, literature was examined, and several automation projects, such as those

---

Reprinted with permission of the *Visual Resources Association Bulletin,* Vesna Blazina, and Ginette Melançon-Bolduc from "Mapping to MARC at the Bibliothèque de l'Aménagement, Université de Montréal," *Visual Resources Association Bulletin* 18, no. 3 (fall 1991): 14–21.

at the University of Texas at Austin and Rensselaer Polytechnic Institute in Troy, New York, were visited. The record format and the record size were discussed with the computer center of the university before ordering the hardware which in 1987 included a Zenith AT 248 microcomputer with 512K of RAM and a 40MB hard disk, monitor, and printer. We chose the EDIBASE software package developed by Inform 2 of Montréal as the most appropriate for our needs. Its main features are sophisticated retrieval strategies, automatic generation of thesauri, and the fact that it operates in French although an English version is also available.

Slide librarians have often grappled with the problem of collection-level versus item-level cataloging. By item-level we mean creating a record for each slide or image rather than creating one record for a set of slides or images. Even before we started automating we had opted for item-level cataloging. The desire to have a record for each slide was actually one of the main reasons for computerizing. Although we considered it essential, it seems that consensus regarding this issue has only recently been reached among slide curators.

Like most librarians trying to use AACR2 to catalog slides, we stumbled on the question of authorship. Who is the author of the slide? The photographer who took the picture of the object or the artist who created the object? After all, what do we want to catalog, the slide as the photographer's creation or the slide as a representation of the artist's work? In the beginning we tried to do both and ended up with thirty-six fields per slide record. During our long evolutionary process we came to the conclusion that cataloging the slide as a representation of the artist's work is what really counts. Having resolved this basic conflict we were able to substantially reduce the size of our slide record, but it was still too large. The longer the record the greater the cost of both storage and data entry. Through experimentation we were able to further trim the record and arrived at a format that was both realistic and satisfactory. While being short and simple, it contained all the basic information needed to retrieve a slide.

Mapping to MARC

Just as we started implementing the computerization project in 1988, a new problem surfaced. The possibility of acquiring a local online public catalog for our

library system was being seriously considered by the university. The online public catalog would be part of an integrated mainframe system encompassing virtually all library activities. We had been told at the very outset of our project that the cost of adding our slide records to the existing microfiche catalog produced by UTLAS (University of Toronto Library Automation System) would be prohibitive. But with the introduction of the OPAC, we felt compelled to explore the possibility of using the MARC format for cataloging the slide collection as MARC was the standard cataloging format for the other collections in our library. After several months of consulting both our EDIBASE supplier and our cataloging department to see how the two formats could be brought together and adapted to our needs, a solution was worked out which was very similar to the original format that we had chosen, and which needed minimal conversion to become compatible with the UTLAS MARC (LHF4). We can now produce diskettes with our slide records ready to be loaded into the university database as soon as it becomes available. In the meantime, the records are being loaded into the Diathèque microcomputer database.

Slide libraries in three other Montréal universities —Concordia, McGill, and Université de Québec à Montréal—started thinking about automation at about the same time as we did. We formed the Image Group and met regularly to discuss our problems and to exchange information. It is significant that we needed each other's support more often during the initial stages of the project when all the basic decisions about software and hardware lay ahead of us. We thought at the beginning that the four institutions might adopt the same software and the same cataloging format but eventually each slide library chose the system which was compatible with the resources already available on its campus. The Concordia Fine Arts Slide Library decided to use EDIBASE, the same software package that we use, but did not consider using MARC.

Examples

Figure 2-1 is an example of a slide cataloging record in its EDIBASE format as loaded in the Diathèque microcomputer. The tags, the field names, the definition, and the content of each field are described in figure 2-2.

```
-NO-     DIA8811007
-MED-    031
-AC1-    AMEN 032639
-AC2-
-TI-     Pavillon au poisson du marché de Hungerford à Londres
-TA-     Hungerford Fish Market
-DA-     1835
-PV-     Dessin d'architecture
-GE-     Angleterre * Royaume-Uni * Europe
-GEO-    e-uk-eu
-AEP-    Fowler, Charles, |d 1792-1867
-AEC-
-DE-     Marché couvert * couverture en verre * Charpente en métal
-TR-     Halle * Verrière
-SO-     Diapositive faisant partie d'Ouvrages d'ingénieurs aux 19e et 20e siècles: de 1775 au Crystal Palace =
         Structural Architectures by Engineers 19th-20th Centuries: from 1775 to the Crystal Palace/conception
         Sylvie Deswarte, Raymond Guidot; textes Raymond Guidot; traduction Alberto R.M. Rosa; réalisation CCI
         Edition: Huguette LeBot assistée de Marie de Besombes. -- Paris: Centre Georges Pompidou/CCI, c1976. --
         Jeu de (24 diap. couleur 2x2 po.) + livret de commentaires bilingue (français-anglais). -- (Urbanisme
         et architecture = Urbanism + Architecture; 4, t.1.15)
-NT-     Partie inférieure de la diapositive -- Gravure tirée du Supplément au Traité théorique et pratique de l'art de
         bâtir de Jean Rondelet/G.A. Blouet. Paris: Didot, 1847
-FIN-

*Indexed terms
```

Figure 2-1 | Slide Cataloging Record in EDIBASE Format

The MED (physical medium of the work) and the GEO (geographic area code) fields are concessions to MARC. They remain in the record but are not searchable by default (e.g., without specifying the field).

Our labels are generated by the computer. They contain the identifiers for the university (UM) and the library (AMEN) as well as the accession number.

The copy with the MARC code intact can be transferred onto a diskette and forwarded to the cataloging department for conversion into UTLAS MARC records.

Figure 2-3 illustrates what the slide record shown in figure 2-1 looks like in its MARC format, while figure 2-4 establishes the corresponding fields of the EDIBASE and MARC formats.

MARC fields 1019 (cataloging source code), 1032 (encoding level), and 1083 (local interest code) have no equivalent in our EDIBASE record. For each keyword in the EDIBASE field DE (descriptors) and TR (related term), MARC creates a separate 695 field while data from TI (title), DA (date), and PV (point of view) EDIBASE fields are merged in MARC field 630. The first 630 subfield is identical with 245|a, the second contains the dates, while the third contains the

point of view. MARC field 500 merges information from two EDIBASE fields—SO (source) and NT (notes). The first 500 note identifies the kit to which the slide belongs, the second locates the image on the slide (lower part), and the third indicates the source of the image (figure 2-3).

The most important fields of the MARC record are those which are used to generate the four sections of the Université de Montréal Libraries' COM catalog:

Field 245 and the field group 7XX generate the author-title section.

Field 630 generates the subject headings section.

Field 695 generates the KWIC index.

Field 090 generates the topographical section.

We decided to use the title, field 245, as the main entry heading. The artist's name or names are entered in the 7XX field group as added entries.

There are three basic reasons why we do not load MARC records into our database. Firstly, EDIBASE is unable to search properly through the whole record when fields are identified with numeric tags only.

Tags	Field Name	Definition and Content
-NO-	Record Number	Unique identification number assigned to each record. Our record shows: DIA8811007 DIA = for DIAME, name of database 88 = cataloging year 11 = cataloging month 007 = cataloging rank of the record Entry validated by format.
-MED-	Unicat/Telecat Code	Physical medium of the work. Our record shows: 031 Code reserved for black and white 2x2 slides. Entry validated by format.
-AC1-	Classification Number	Contains local inventory data. Our record shows: AMEN 032639 AMEN = Aménagement, name of the library 032639 = accession number of the slide Entry validated by format.
-AC2-	Number of Copies	Number of copies in the collection. Field used only when there is more than one copy.
-TI-	Title	Designates work depicted on the slide. Our record shows: Pavillon au poisson du marché de Hungerford à Londres Name of building controlled by BABEL thesaurus.
-TA-	Alternate Title	Title different from -TI- Our record shows: Hungerford Fish Market Here English form of the title. Entry generated by the system. Different names in various languages stored in BABEL thesaurus are automatically added to this field.
-DA-	Date(s) of Execution	Year when built. Our record shows: 1835
-PV-	Point of View or Form	Point of view from which the building is seen and/or form of architectural representation. Our record shows: Dessin d'architecture Entry controlled by CYCLOPE thesaurus.
-GE-	Geographic Area Code	Location of the building. Natural language is used to formulate the statement. Our record shows: Angleterre * Royaume-Uni * Europe Entry controlled by ULYSSE thesaurus.
-GEO-	Geographic Area Code	Country where building is located. We use a list based on Appendix II.B of MARC formats for bibliographic data. Our record shows: e-uk-eu Code used for England. Entry controlled by ULYSSE thesaurus.
-AEP-	Author/Personal Name	Architect(s) responsible for the work depicted. Our record shows: Fowler, Charles, |d 1792-1867 The first subfield contains the surname and the forename(s). The second subfield contains the dates of birth and death. Entry controlled by CYBELE thesaurus.

Figure 2-2 | Format Specifications for Slide Cataloging Records

-AEC-	Author/Corp. Name	Name of firm, business, company, or partnership responsible for the design of the work depicted.
		Entry controlled by CYBELE thesaurus.
-DE-	Descriptors	Keyword(s) desired in the record which do not occur in the other fields that are indexed.
		Our record shows: Marché couvert * Couverture en verre * Charpente en métal
		Entry controlled by PANDORE thesaurus.
-TR-	Related Terms	Keywords desired in the record but which do not occur in the other fields that are indexed.
		Our record shows: Halle * Verrière
		Keywords generated by the system.
		Synonyms and broader terms found in PANDORE thesaurus are added automatically to this field.
-SO-	Note/Specific to Kit	Describes the kit to which the slide belongs.
		Our record shows: Diapositive faisant partie de...
-NT-	Notes/Miscellaneous	Contains additional information not found elsewhere in the record.
		Our record shows 2 notes:
		The first one locates the image on the slide (lower part). The second one indicates the source of the image.
-FIN-	End of Record	

*Indexed terms

Figure 2-2 | (Continued)

Tags	Field Content
1019	x
1024	031
1032	k
1083	???
U035	‖aDIA8811007
043	‖ae-uk-eu
090 1	‖aAMEN 032639‖ bAM‖ fDIA
245 00	‖aPavillon au poisson du marché de Hungerford‖ h[Diapositive]
500	‖aDiapositive faisant partie d'Ouvrages d'ingénieurs aux 19e et 20e siècles: de 1775 au Crystal Palace = Structural Architectures by Engineers 19th-20th Centuries: from 1775 to the Crystal Palace/conception Sylvie Deswarte, Raymond Guidot; textes Raymond Guidot; traduction Alberto R.M. Rosa; réalisation CCI Edition: Huguette LeBot assistée de Marie de Besombes. -- Paris: Centre Georges Pompidou/CCI, c1976. -- Jeu de (24 diap. couleur 2x2 po.) + livret de commentaires bilingue (français-anglais). -- (Urbanisme et architecture = Urbanism + Architecture; 4, t.1.15)
500	‖aPartie inférieure de la diapositive
500	‖aGravure tirée du Supplément au Traité théorique et pratique de l'art de bâtir de Jean Rondelet/G.A. Blouet. Paris: Didot, 1847
630 9	‖aPavillon au poisson du marché de Hungerford‖ f1835‖ gDessin d'architecture
695	‖aMarché couvert
695	‖aVerrière
695	‖aToiture en verre
695	‖aCharpente en métal
695	‖aHalle
700 10	‖aFowler, Charles, ‖ d1792-1867
740 00	‖aHungerford Fish Market

Figure 2-3 | MARC Record for the Slide in Figure 2-1

```
-NO-        =MARC field U035
-MED-       =MARC field 1024
-AC1-       =MARC field 090| a
-AC2-       =MARC field 090| c, not used in our example
-TI-        =MARC fields 245| a and 630| a, repeated twice in the MARC record
-TA-        =MARC field 740
-DA-        =MARC field 630| f
-PV-        =MARC field 630| g
-GE-        =no equivalent in MARC record, EDIBASE field for geographical names in natural language
-GEO-       =MARC field 043
-AEP-       =MARC field 700
-AEC-       =MARC field 710, not used in our example
-DE-        =MARC field 695, repeatable
-TR-        =MARC field 695, repeatable
-SO-        =first MARC field 500
-NT-        =two separate MARC fields 500
```

Figure 2-4 | Equivalent Fields of EDIBASE and MARC Formats

That is why we use alphabetical tags, for example, field 700 is AEP in our database. Secondly, EDIBASE is unable to hide the MARC codes and indicators in the fields. Thirdly, while we were warned by our supplier that it is not advisable to repeat any fields in the EDIBASE records, some MARC fields, such as the 500 and the 695, have to be repeated for each information element they contain.

Authority control in EDIBASE records is provided by five locally generated thesauri: CYBELE for architects' names, BABEL for building names, ULYSSE for geographical names, PANDORE for subject headings, and CYCLOPE for points of view.

The Université de Montréal Libraries' COM catalog entries are used as authority for the names of the architects. When they are not available, other major reference sources are used and cross-references are established for alternate forms of a name.

Uniform title entries are established by following local policies. However, establishing those local policies was not easy because it was necessary to solve the problem of the correspondence between the title and the image. Early on we realized that possessing a lot of information about an image tempted us to go beyond the image, to describe what "we knew was there" rather than what we could see. In other words, by being overzealous, we were running the risk of confusing the user. As we all know most slides do not have a title nor do most buildings have a name, which means that the cataloger has to come up with an adequate descriptive title. How general or how detailed should that title be? We wanted to "cram" as much information as possible into the title to make it meaningful. We were trying to make sure that we would not have to enrich other fields of the record, such as GE, DE, and NT, because of insufficient information in the title. We, therefore, established fairly strict rules about the content and the syntax of the title.

Geographical names are automatically added to the ULYSSE thesaurus which establishes links between names of provinces, states, and continents. For example, if there is an entry for London, the thesaurus automatically adds entries for England and the United Kingdom, provided the entry is not London, Ontario, which requires Ontario, Canada, and North America as added entries.

All the subject headings are locally generated and standardized by the PANDORE thesaurus. The French version of the *Library of Congress Subject Headings* produced by Université Laval is the main inspiration of subject entries. Other reference sources, *Art and Architecture Thesaurus* among them, are also consulted, but unfortunately cannot be used because they have to be translated into French. The French version of the *Art and Architecture Thesaurus* is eagerly awaited.

In order to save time we try not to put more than three subject headings (descriptors) per record: function of the building, style, and materials, if these are not obvious from the title entry. Since all the fields of the record are searchable we want to avoid duplicating information from field to field.

Personnel

In the last three years two employees, a special projects librarian and a library technician, have worked on this project full-time, while the head librarian participated in the planning and orientation of the project as necessary. Several computer specialists and library administrators contributed their ideas in the initial stages. Clerical services have also been available intermittently.

Hardware Update

We have recently doubled the memory of the microcomputer by adding another 40MB hard disk for a total of 80MB while RAM has been expanded to 1MB. Parallel with the automation project, a special effort was made to renew our collection—ten thousand slides have been ordered within the last year. So far we have been able to catalog six thousand of those slides and hope to be able to double our inputting capacity when a second computer arrives.

At that time we also plan to let our users do their own searching in the database. For our users' benefit we have developed a report with a special layout which is given with the slides. For example, in the case of a search concerning the architecture of the French régime in Montréal, seventy-one entries have been retrieved. Our report-generating program establishes a list of seventy-one slides and numbers them from one to seventy-one in the accession number order citing author, firm, title, point of view, date, and subject headings for each slide (figure 2-5), followed by an author index (figure 2-6), and a subject index (figure 2-7). The numbers in the index refer to the sequential number that the report-generating program has attributed to each record in the file. The indices become especially useful when a large number of slides are retrieved. In this way information about the slides remains available to the user once the slide itself is in the projector.

Liste de Diapositives

70		71	
Cote:	AMEN 102516	Cote:	AMEN 102517
Auteur(s):	Meloche, F. Edouard,1855-1914 * Perron, J. Eugène	Auteur(s):	Meloche, F. Edouard,1855-1914 * Perron, J. Eugène
Firme(s):	Perrault & Mesnard, 1880-1894	Firme(s):	Perrault & Mesnard, 1880-1894
Titre:	Eglise Notre-Dame-de Bonsecours, 400 rue Saint-Paul est, Montréal	Titre:	Eglise Notre-Dame-de Bonsecours, 400 rue Saint-Paul est, Montréal
Vue:	Extérieur	Vue:	Extérieur
Date:	1771	Date:	1771
Sujet(s):	Architecture régime français * Construction en pierre * Façade ouest	Sujet(s):	Architecture régime français * Construction en pierre * Façade sud Chevet

*Indexed terms

Figure 2-5 | Architecture of the French Régime in Montréal, Records Generated by the Report Layout Program

Index des Auteurs

Figure 2-6 | Architecture of the French Régime in Montréal, Author Index Generated by the Report Layout Program

Index des Sujets

Figure 2-7 | Architecture of the French Régime in Montréal, Subject Index Generated by the Report Layout Program

Conclusion

Use of the MARC format has been successfully implemented at the Diathèque of the Bibliothèque de l'Aménagement, Université de Montréal. For the time being, slide records are loaded into the local microcomputer and are then ready to be loaded into the library system mainframe network. It has been our deepest conviction from the start that, if possible, MARC should be used because it is the only universally shared descriptive standard which will permit us to exchange bibliographic information. Museum curators who share with slide curators the problem of cataloging art objects are also thinking of using MARC for their needs. Furthermore, slide librarians applying for grants to computerize their collections have often been asked by the subsidizing institutions whether they were going to use MARC. Thus more and more slides cataloged in machine-readable form are joining the ranks of many other documents both print and nonprint.

People involved in automation are usually forced to think about standards. Several decades ago this phenomenon happened in print media. Today automation is forcing slide librarians to think about cataloging standards which could be shared by the whole community. By opening new possibilities, automation has created new responsibilities for sharing and exchanging bibliographic information. It is our duty to make the visual media as accessible as the print media and eventually establish a link between them.

3 Planning for Automation of the Slide and Photograph Collections at the Cleveland Museum of Art: A Draft MARC/ Visual Materials Record

Ann Abid, Eleanor Scheifele, Sara Jane Pearman, and Elizabeth Lantz

Automating the book collection of the Ingalls Library at the Cleveland Museum of Art in 1988 offered the opportunity to begin thinking about the automation of the Library's vast holdings of slides and photographs. The contract that was negotiated with Dynix, Inc. included the following statement:

> The vendor shall provide ten days of analyst and programmer time to review the library's photographs and slides database requirements and modify the software purchases by the library to accommodate a pilot database of these materials and to permit printing of slide labels. . . . The record format to be used shall conform to the draft MARC standards and shall be capable of being reformatted to the finished MARC standard.

This article briefly presents the background of the slide and photograph libraries, details the CMA Library's MARC/VM format and the corresponding indexes designed to be used in the Dynix online system, and discusses the major problems encountered with the enumeration of holdings.

The slide and photograph collections of the Cleveland Museum of Art number approximately 710,000 images (370,000 slides; 340,000 photographs). The two collections have historically been maintained as totally separate manual systems with different staffs, cataloging procedures, and classification schemes. The library's visual collections are a vital aspect of the museum's resources and reflect the needs of its staff researchers.

The visual collections of the CMA far outnumber the book collection of 167,000 volumes. Separation of the visual materials database from the bibliographic database was considered essential in reducing patron confusion in searching. The plan is to present an initial search menu from which the patron will select either the bibliographic or the visual materials catalog.

Reprinted with permission of the *Visual Resources Association Bulletin* and Ann Abid, Eleanor Scheifele, Sara Jane Pearman, and Elizabeth Lantz from "Planning for Automation of the Slide and Photograph Collections at the Cleveland Museum of Art: A Draft MARC/Visual Materials Record," *Visual Resources Association Bulletin* 19, no. 2 (summer 1992): 17–21.

A committee comprised of Ann Abid, Head Librarian; Eleanor Scheifele, Photograph Librarian; Sara Jane Pearman, Slide Librarian; and Elizabeth Lantz, Assistant Librarian for Technical Services, was formed to design a Dynix-compatible MARC/VM format in order to convert existing cataloging information for slides and photographs into machine-readable records. Ann Abid provided an overview of the Dynix system while Pearman and Scheifele provided specialized information about the content and needs of visual collections. Lantz explained the standard use of the various MARC fields. The combination of expertise worked well in tailoring the MARC format for use in creating machine-readable records for visual materials.

The resultant MARC format was based heavily on three specific MARC formats: books, film, and visual materials.[1] Other projects were examined for usage of fields, including the Smithsonian Institution's Inventory of American Sculpture.[2] A listing of the CMA-selected MARC tags with an explanation of standard and local use is provided in figure 3-1.

In designing the CMA MARC format it was decided that existing MARC fields should be used in a standard manner when possible. For example, an effort was made to accommodate free text informational needs in fields already specified for inputting in free text form, and to use fields and subfields designated as repeatable for repeatable information. With the exception of four, all field tags are currently used in US-MARC. The four exceptions were introduced in order to accommodate information critical to the curatorial aspects of museum research: conservation information (359); creation date (759); linking information such as model for, copy after (779); and the location of object (859).[3]

Once the MARC format was designed, discussion revolved around the indexes needed to provide access to the slide and photograph collections, keeping in mind the manner in which museum staff and other patrons utilize the two collections.

In spite of the decision to separate the bibliographic and visual materials databases as far as searching is concerned, it is hoped that the visual materials database will be able to utilize the more than 220,000 authority records already online in the bibliographic database. Library of Congress Name Authority File and *Library of Congress Subject Headings* will constitute the primary authorities, with standards developed for creating authority headings not found online.

Dynix has indexes in place for author, artist, institution, and subject, and the various title indexes extant are suitable to the newly developed CMA MARC/VM format. Field 520 (narrative description of subject) will be indexed and searchable as contents keyword in the manner of the existing 505 field in the MARC Books format. The field tags incorporating numbers (010, 020, 023) are already mapped and indexed on Dynix but adjustments need to be made to accommodate the variety and format of the numbers to be used in the cataloging of slides and photographs. The only new index necessitated by the format was a provenance or location index. Mapped from fields 111, 561, 711, and 859, the provenance or location index makes it possible to search current and previous owners, collectors, museums, and sites, as well as the location of works on extended loan to other institutions, or works at auction or for which no other location can be determined.

The practicalities of searching were examined based on the format and indexes created. As a result of the vast holdings of the slide and photograph collections, a major searching problem surfaced immediately. Artist authority searches for well-known artists such as Picasso or Rembrandt resulted in thousands of hits. To modify this situation, a hard-coded subfield |n (medium) was added to field 340 (physical description). After searching artist authority for Picasso, the 340 |n would allow the search to be further limited by medium, thus resulting in a more manageable search.

Additionally, the committee adapted the Dynix holdings screen for use with the slide and photograph collections. Once again, problems arose because there are works with hundreds of views, parts, and details. As the holdings screen documents the number of holdings and their locations, this produced holdings information too lengthy and cumbersome to be useful to the patron. A decision was made to handle such works by creating multiple cataloging records, distinguishing among them by the use of a subtitle. For instance, the title would be the name of an illuminated manuscript and the subtitle would correspond to an individual page or folio. This reduces the number of holdings for each cataloging record to a more manageable number. Figures 3-2 and 3-3 are examples for *The Hours of Queen Isabella the Catholic of Spain*, a manuscript in the CMA collection.

MARC Field Tag Number	Standard Use/Local Use
010	LCCN/Gernsheim Number[4]
020	ISBN/Bartsch Number[5]
023	STANDARD FILM NUMBER/Documentation numbers—including museum accession number, print catalog numbers (Hollstein, Hind, Lehrs), manuscript numbers
040	CATALOGING SOURCE/Cataloging Source
099	LOCAL CALL NUMBER/Free Text Call Number or Location Code
100	MAIN ENTRY—PERSONAL NAME/Main Entry-Artist/Creator Name
110	MAIN ENTRY—CORPORATE NAME/Main Entry-Name of corporation/firm/factory/workshop/museum or museum department
111	MAIN ENTRY—MEETING NAME/Main Entry-Name of conference/Exposition/Exhibition
242	TRANSLATION OF TITLE BY CATALOGING AGENCY/Translation of title by cataloging agency
245	TITLE STATEMENT/ǀa=Main title or description; ǀb=Name of specific part/area/building
246	VARYING FORM OF TITLE/Varying form of title
247	FORMER TITLE OR TITLE VARIATIONS/Former title
250	EDITION STATEMENT/Numerical edition of prints/sculptures
260	PUBLICATION, DISTRIBUTION (IMPRINT)/Place, name and dates for Fabricator (enabler as opposed to creator)
340	MEDIUM/Physical description consisting of medium, dimensions, production technique, frame, unit type (shape) and hard-coded subfield to be used in limiting searches by medium
359*	Conservation information
440	SERIES STATEMENT/ADDED ENTRY-TITLE/Series title
500	GENERAL NOTE/General notes
503	BIBLIOGRAPHIC HISTORY NOTE/History note indicating relationship to other objects, or editions
510	CITATION/REFERENCES NOTE/ Citation/References note
520	SUMMARY, ABSTRACT, ANNOTATION, SCOPE, NOTE/Narrative description of subject
561	PROVENANCE NOTE/Provenance
562	COPY AND VERSION IDENTIFICATION NOTE/Information on marks associated with object
590	LOCAL NOTES/Special notes relating to actual slide or photograph
600	SUBJECT ADDED ENTRY—PERSONAL NAME/Subject Added Entry-Artist/Creator Name
610	SUBJECT ADDED ENTRY—CORPORATE NAME/Subject Added Entry-Name of corporation/firm/factory/workshop/museum or museum department
611	SUBJECT ADDED ENTRY—MEETING NAME/Subject Added Entry-Name of conference/Exposition/Exhibition
650	SUBJECT ADDED ENTRY—TOPICAL TERM/Subject Added Entry-Topical Term
651	SUBJECT ADDED ENTRY—GEOGRAPHIC NAME/Subject Added Entry-Geographic Name
654	SUBJECT ADDED ENTRY—FACETED TOPICAL TERMS/AAT
655	INDEX TERM—GENRE/FORM/Subject term for form (e.g., mask, altar)
659*	Iconclass
700	ADDED ENTRY—PERSONAL NAME/Added Entry-Personal name
710	ADDED ENTRY—CORPORATE NAME/Added Entry-Name of corporation/firm/factory/workshop/museum or museum department
711	ADDED ENTRY—MEETING NAME/Added Entry-Name of conference/Exposition/Exhibition
759*	Creation date
779*	See also (descriptive linking note; e.g. copy after, model for)—provides capability to track an altarpiece or manuscript whose component panels or folios are now dispersed in various collections
859*	Owner/Location of object

*Field tags not currently used in USMARC. Field 359 adapted from the Dynix Film format. Fields 659, 759, and 779 adapted from the MARC fields used in the Smithsonian Institution's Inventory of American Sculpture.

Figure 3-1 | Dynix MARC Format for Visual Materials

04 FEB 92	Cleveland Museum of Art PUBLIC ACCESS CATALOG	10:36AM

Call Number Photograph Library   Status: IN
              C Neth MSS   9 other copies

AUTHOR   1) Master of the Older Prayerbook of Maximilian I, c. 1444-1519 and workshop
(ARTIST)   2) Horenbout, Gerard, c. 1452-1541
             3) Master of the Dresden Prayerbook, act. c. 1470-1500
             4) Master of the Prayerbook of 1500, act. c. 1480-1490

TITLE   Hours of Queen Isabella the Catholic of Spain: Calendar.
IMPRINT   Ghent, ca. 1492-1497 (MARC TAGS 260, 759) (PLACE, CREATION DATE)
SUBJECTS   1) Labors of months
             2) Flowers--15th century--Netherlandish

----More on Next Screen----

Press <Enter> to see next screen:
Commands: SO=Start Over, B=Back, RW=Related Works, C=Copy status, S=Select for reserve,
<Enter>=Next Screen, ?=Help

04 FEB 92	Cleveland Museum of Art PUBLIC ACCESS CATALOG	10:36AM

Call Number Photograph Library   Status: IN
              C Neth MSS   9 other copies
Continued...
             3) Insects--15th century--Netherlandish
             4) Landscapes--15th century--Netherlandish
             5) Ghent-Bruges School

NOTES   1) Ink tempera and gold on vellum, 22.5 x 15.6 cm. (MARC TAG 340)
             2) CMA Bulletin (DEC 81) (MARC TAG 510)
             3) Cleveland Museum of Art, Leonard C. Hanna Jr. Fund, Cleveland, Ohio USA
             (MARC TAG 859)
             4) Book of Hours (MARC TAG 655)

---End of Title Info---

Press <Enter> to see Copy status:
Commands: SO=Start Over, B=Back, RW=Related Works, S=Select for reserve, P=Previous Screen,
?=Help

Figure 3-2 | Sample OPAC Screens

```
04 FEB 92                        Cleveland Museum of Art                        10:37AM
                                 PUBLIC ACCESS CATALOG

Author     Master of the Older Prayerbook of Maximilian I, c.
Title      Hours of Queen Isabella the Catholic of Spain... Holds: 0

CALL NUMBER                                    STATUS              LIBRARY
   1.   PHOTOGRAPH LIBRARY                      IN                 Cleveland Museum of Art
        C Neth MSS f. 2r January (Feast)

   2.   PHOTOGRAPH LIBRARY                      IN                 Cleveland Museum of Art
        C Neth MSS f. 2v January (Snow Landscape)

   3.   PHOTOGRAPH LIBRARY                      IN                 Cleveland Museum of Art
        C Neth MSS f. 3r February

   4.   PHOTOGRAPH LIBRARY                      IN                 Cleveland Museum of Art
        C Neth MSS f. 5r April (Squire and Damsel)

   5.   PHOTOGRAPH LIBRARY                      IN                 Cleveland Museum of Art
        C Neth MSS f. 5v April

   6.   SLIDE LIBRARY                           IN                 Cleveland Museum of Art
        41 Mss. 15th c. f.11v-12r October-November

                        ----10 copies, More on Next Screen----

Choose a command:
Commands: SO=Start Over, B=Back, <Enter>=Next Screen, S=Select for reserve, P=Previous Screen, ?=Help
```

```
04 FEB 92                        Cleveland Museum of Art                        10:37AM
                                 PUBLIC ACCESS CATALOG

Author     Master of the Older Prayerbook of Maximilian I, c.
Title      Hours of Queen Isabella the Catholic of Spain... Holds: 0

CALL NUMBER                                    STATUS              LIBRARY
   7.   SLIDE LIBRARY                           IN                 Cleveland Museum of Art
        41 Mss. 15th c. f.5r April

   8.   SLIDE LIBRARY                           IN                 Cleveland Museum of Art
        41 Mss. 15th c. f.5v April, 2

   9.   SLIDE LIBRARY                           IN                 Cleveland Museum of Art
        41 Mss. 15th c. f.6r May

  10.   SLIDE LIBRARY                           IN                 Cleveland Museum of Art
        41 Mss. 15th c. f.6v May, 2

                        ----10 copies, More on Previous Screen----

Choose a command:
Commands: SO=Start Over, B=Back, S=Select for reserve, P=Previous Screen, ?=Help
```

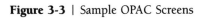

Figure 3-3 | Sample OPAC Screens

The current Dynix holdings record contains a variety of item-specific information. The fields were adapted to the acquisition needs of the slide and photograph collections, providing a place for vendor information, order numbers, source information, and information on gifts and exchanges, as seen in figure 3-4. Each individual holdings record is also linked to a unique barcode, thus providing circulation control.

A small pilot database utilizing the CMA MARC/VM record will be mounted on the library's Dynix system. The future of the larger project remains in question because of the limitations of current hardware capacity and the enormity of the task of inputting records for all slides and photographs in the collection.

The average length of the visual materials records appears longer than those of bibliographical records. The CMA Library's online bibliographical records were predicted at an average of one thousand characters for contractual purposes. In actuality, the average length of bibliographical records on the system is about five hundred characters. A test group of cataloged slides and photographs revealed that records of twenty thousand characters were present. Even disregarding the length of the test group records, the

hardware capacity required for a joint bibliographical and visual online database at the Cleveland Museum of Art Library would require a minimum of three times the capacity of its present system.[6]

Additionally, the absence of an international, unified database of cataloged information on works of art means inputting of records for so many individual objects will take many years even if adequate staff were to be made available.

The experience of automating the CMA visual collections seems at this time to be the antithesis of that experienced earlier in automating library book collections—whereas, large book collections moved ahead with automation, the enormity of the Cleveland Museum of Art Library's visual holdings has assumed a prominent role in slowing the speed with which automation will be achieved.

```
 *   BIBKEY
       Dynix system number
 2   COLLECTION
       Slides or Photographs
 3   CALL #
       Location or filing code
 4   DESCRIPTION
       Details, sections, exterior
 5   VENDOR #
       Vendor #, order #, neg. #
 6   SOURCE
       Vendor name and address
 7   ACCESSION #
       Old numbers on photographs or slides
 8   ITYPE
       Slides, photographs, or videotapes
```

Figure 3-4 | Holdings Record

NOTES

1. Dynix encouraged the use of the MARC Film format already installed on the system.

2. Projects from the Syracuse University Art Collection, National Gallery of Art Photography Archive, Rensselaer Polytechnic Institute Architecture Slide Library, and the MARC Manuscript and Archive format were also examined.

3. Field 759 accommodates the date of creation. Field 260 accommodates the date(s) of fabrication as opposed to creation. Both fields may be used.

4. The Gernsheim number relates to the *Corpus Photographicum of Drawings*, an ongoing photographic subscription providing standardized documentation for drawings (currently over 130,000 items) whose primary access is by assigned consecutive number.

5. The Bartsch number refers to a photographic subscription (c. 18,000 items) initiated by the Warburg Institute and enumerated according to Bartsch's numerical system in *Le Peintre graveur* (1803–1821). It is distinct from the published *Illustrated Bartsch*.

6. The original Library Dynix system was mounted on an Ultimate 3025 minicomputer with 2 megabytes of memory and one 510-megabyte disk using the Pick operating system.

Why and How MARC Is Being Used for Automating the Architecture Slide Collection at Clemson University

Phyllis Pivorun

Background of Collection

The Architecture Slide Collection was established in the early 1960s by the faculty of the College of Architecture. Steady growth of the cataloged collection, with a constantly increasing backlog, has been documented over the last fifteen years. The collection is located in the Gunnin Architectural Library which operates as a branch of Clemson University Libraries. The branch library is situated in the College of Architecture; and its resources, including the slide collection, support the undergraduate and graduate programs in architecture, landscape architecture, construction science and management, city and regional planning, and visual arts. The primary mission of the library is to serve the classroom and research needs of the sixty-five faculty and 650 students in the college while simultaneously serving the university in general, as well as accommodating area community users. There is an open door policy for the slide collection. Clemson University Libraries has jurisdiction over the slide collection, but the College of Architecture provides a notable portion of the operational funds.

The slide collection currently has over eighty thousand slides in the cataloged collection and a backlog of more than twenty thousand slides. Following local weeding policies, poor quality slides and images of questionable value are continually subject to withdrawal; 2,380 slides were withdrawn over the last five years. The cataloged slides are organized according to a natural language, local classification system which is generally arranged according to art form (file category) and then subdivided respectively by period, architect or artist, and location. In addition, there are related topical categories. Before automation, an accession number was assigned to each slide providing

Reprinted with permission of the *Visual Resources Association Bulletin* and Phyllis Pivorun from "Why and How MARC Is Being Used for Automating the Architecture Slide Collection at Clemson University," *Visual Resources Association Bulletin* 18, no. 2 (summer 1991): 18–21.

a unique identifier used for circulation control. For authority control, a card catalog served as a subject shelf list with cross-reference files by personal name, by location, and by building type only for twentieth-century architecture. The card catalog included a complete record of the cataloged collection by accession number. No back-up cards are filed with the slides. Slide labels and catalog cards are produced with two IBM electronic memory typewriters.

Planning Phase

The need to automate the Architecture Slide Collection was first recognized in 1982. A study of microcomputer hardware and software systems was initiated and a list of requirements for a system, along with goals for improving the organization of the collection, were documented. Working with the library administration and an automation task force, the goals and objectives were prioritized with the other needs in the library.

With the onset of the computer age in libraries, the development of NOTIS (Northwestern Online Totally Integrated System) began in 1970 at Northwestern University Library in Evanston, Illinois. Having made the decision to automate, Clemson University Libraries purchased the system in 1983, began installing it in 1984, and introduced LUIS (Library User Information Service—the main online public catalog) in 1985. Each year the system has been further developed and refined. As an integrated mainframe system, its functions encompass virtually all library activities. The NOTIS system at Clemson is designed to provide users with a single access tool for locating and determining availability of a variety of library materials, regardless of format or medium, and users are able to access materials online not only from the library, but also from remote areas via terminals and personal computers.

Since the NOTIS system was well in place at Clemson and met the major requirements of an automated system for the Architecture Slide Collection, the decision was made in fall 1987 to use NOTIS to automate the collection. Points of consideration and NOTIS justifications were:

Requirements	*NOTIS Justifications*
1. Extensive storage capacity	1. Mainframe
2. Broad public access	2. Mainframe networks and remote access
3. Separate slide database	3. Separate institutions capability within the NOTIS system
4. Standard "cataloging" format	4. MARC format
5. Authority control	5. Separate institutions capability within the NOTIS system
6. Enhanced title access	6. Keyword and Boolean searching capabilities
7. Subject access	7. Standard subject headings and keyword and Boolean searching capabilities
8. Call number system	8. Twenty plus alpha-numeric characters in the holdings record
9. Collection shelf list	9. Call number
10. Slide label production	10. Fields downloaded via the mainframe file to a microcomputer system (proposed)
11. Circulation control	11. Item records created in the system and slides bar coded
12. Cataloging and user statistics	12. Local record management capabilities using statistical programs (SAS)

The philosophical aspects of the basic design of the database were established by the library administration and faculty. Based on the cost and time that would be necessary to "catalog" the slides in the system following AACR2 (*Anglo-American Cataloguing Rules,* 2nd ed.) cataloging rules, the decision was made to "index" the slides as individual sets on an item or image-depicted level. Clemson University Libraries is a participating member of the OCLC (Ohio College Library Center, now Online Computer Library Center) bibliographic utility. "Cataloging" in

NOTIS would require each record to be searched and loaded in OCLC, which would involve extensive time and a substantial amount of money for user fees. The cataloging process would also require that each slide would have to be cataloged individually and cataloged according to AACR2 rules for slides. Following the rules for uniform title, all nonuniform titles would be placed in brackets. Nonuniform titles for slides would include all locally produced or locally established-titles. Only commercially produced slide titles and any titles produced locally for original slides would be considered uniform titles. For indexing the slides in NOTIS, uniform titles are established by following local policies and authorities, and brackets are not used.

Following the philosophical decision for the basic design of the database, commitments were made for equipment, supplies, cataloging tools, and staff, including other units within the library. Nine different individuals have been involved in the project, including the library administration, unit heads, and support staff. Use of the system was limited at first to an extensively used NOTIS test file. Then permission was granted to input a small number of test slide records into the LUIS database. These records were later transferred into the separate slide database which was established in May 1989.

Implementation

The first priority of the study phase of the project was to establish local NOTIS MARC (Machine-Readable

Cataloging) format standards for creating image-depicted level bibliographic records. The Rensselaer Polytechnic Institute, Troy, New York, slide automation project in the College of Architecture (a slide automation project applying the OCLC MARC II Audiovisual Media Format and testing the applicability of the *Art and Architecture Thesaurus* [AAT]) was consulted for reference.

At Clemson, the NOTIS MARC Visual Materials Format (VMF) was adapted to meet the needs for a machine-readable slide bibliographic record. Terminology for coding machine-readable records includes field tags, indicators, and subfields or delimiters. A listing of the selected MARC field tags including designated use and specified local use is displayed in figure 4-1.

Note that the decision was made that a slide bibliographic record would document the set of slides on a subject (a project or an artwork). The number of slides for the record is entered in the 300 field. The 1XX field group is the Main Entry for input of an architect or artist's name; any additional names are en-

MARC Field Tag Number	Designated Use/Specified Local Use
100	Main entry—Personal name/Architect or artist's name
110	Main entry—Corporate name/Firm, partnership, or corporate name
111	Main entry—Meeting name/Exhibition or competition
245	Title statement/Name of project or artwork, location of project, date of work
300	Physical description/Number of slides for record
440	Series statement/Added entry—Title/Title for project complex or artwork series
830	Series added entry—Uniform title/Use for locally established uniform titles
500	General note
505	Formatted contents note/View code and descriptive view of each slide
520	Summary, abstract, annotation, scope, etc. note/Summary note or scope note for the subject
600	Subject added entry—Personal name
610	Subject added entry—Corporate name
611	Subject added entry—Meeting or conference
650	Subject added entry—Topical term/Library of Congress descriptors (indicator 0), local authorities (indicator 4), AAT descriptors (indicator 7)
651	Subject added entry—Geographic name
654	Subject added entry—Faceted topical terms/AAT descriptors
700	Added entry—Personal name
710	Added entry—Corporate name
711	Added entry—Meeting name
740	Added entry—Variant title
590	Local note/Source of acquisition displayed—Originals, duplicates, purchased
927	Source for acquisition/Source of acquisition not displayed—Copywork, purchase price, local notes

Figure 4-1 | NOTIS MARC Visual Materials Format (VMF)

tered in the 7XX field group as added entries. The 245 field is the Title Statement which includes the name of the project or artwork, location of project, and date of work; added entries for title are entered in the 7XX field group. A series field, the 440 field, was designated to input the title of a project complex or an artwork series (for example: Cathedral Group, Pisa) while the specific subject (Campanile) is input in the 245 field. The 520 field, the Summary Note, was designated for documenting a scope note for the record or the subject. The description of the individual slide views for a record, including the physical description of individual slides, if not standard two-by-two-inch color slides, is entered in free-text form in the repeatable 505 field, the Contents Note.

Testing of the MARC fields included considerations on how the individual record would appear to the public and also how records and fields would index. Special features of selected MARC fields were determining factors including the use of: (1) fields specified for inputting in free-text form, (2) field length and repeatable field—which were locally changed in two NOTIS MARC fields, (3) field keyword indexed—for public access (this is the reason the call number appears in the bibliographic record in the 502 field), (4) field displays to the public versus nondisplay to public—this was the factor for designating the 590 and 927 fields for documenting source of acquisition, and (5) fields that can be stripped from the system providing the capability of keeping information confidential—this is true for 900 fields in the NOTIS MARC VMF format.

The inclusion of standard subject headings in the bibliographic record provides subject searching capabilities through indexing for public access. Guidelines for local standard subject headings for slides were developed along with a checklist for determining subject headings including art form, medium, style, period, type, structure, materials, and so forth. After studying authorities and considering the indexing capabilities, the decision was made to use LCSH (*Library of Congress Subject Headings*) as the primary authority for establishing subject headings with one Library of Congress subject heading required for each record. The AAT (*Art and Architecture Thesaurus*) is used as a secondary authority. The 650 field with an indicator 0 is used to input a Library of Congress topical subject heading, while an indicator 4 is used to enter a local authority topical subject heading. The 650 field with an indicator 7 is the tag to input an AAT faceted topical subject heading in Library of Congress standard format, and the 654 is the field tag to enter AAT fac-

eted topical terms in a string. The 6XX field group is used to input a name as a subject heading.

In addition to the bibliographic record, holdings and item records are also created in the NOTIS system. Holdings records document the number of holdings and their location. The item records provide online circulation control, and each slide is bar coded linking the slide to its item record.

Checking for consistency of record creation, authority control, and building of an online slide database authority file is handled by the Clemson University Libraries cataloging unit and is the designated responsibility of the Special Formats Cataloger. Forms for requesting an authority record creation or amendment were developed by the cataloging unit.

The importance of consistency and documentation were emphasized during the study phase of this automation project. The complete cataloging process was documented, including policies and tools. A NOTIS slide cataloging worksheet and a NOTIS slide inputting form were developed, and detailed procedures for creating records in NOTIS were written.

The main obstacle of this project was not the establishment of local NOTIS MARC format standards for creating slide bibliographic records, but the development of a call number system for the slide collection. Over a year was spent developing and documenting a system and reorganizing the slide collection to establish consistency within the system while maintaining the integrity of the classification scheme for browsers.

In spring 1995 the automated slide label production system was established. Labels are laser printed via submitting a SAS batch program which pulls the specified data from the NOTIS bibliographic, holdings, and item records. The data file is then captured from the mainframe via Fetch and downloaded into a local custom-designed FileMaker Pro Macintosh program. If needed, the data fields are then edited, and the labels printed.

Conclusion

The situation and commitments at Clemson have contributed to the success of the project. Money, time, and staff have been principal considerations. A major monetary factor is the benefit of free computer time and services at Clemson. The library administration and staff have been very supportive of this project especially in allocating time and personnel, as well as in providing education and guidance on a one-to-one basis.

The philosophy of the NOTIS slide database at Clemson allows for "shared information" and not for "shared cataloging" since the records are not to be loaded into a bibliographic utility. But the database is accessible through mainframe networks, and any of the information may be procured without charge. However, because of local decision-making policies and the use of nonstandard slide classification schemes, one may need to ask: Will it ever be possible to "share cataloging," to actually share records when individuals have generally created local titles for the slides in their collections? It is our hope at Clemson that the use of the MARC format will certainly be an important first step in the quest for shared information.

Cataloging for Art's Sake at Florida International University

Mayra F. Nemeth

Florida International University in Miami, one of nine universities in the state university system of Florida, is a comprehensive, doctoral granting, public, multi-campus institution offering a broad array of undergraduate, graduate, and professional programs for over 23,300 students. The art and architecture slide collection resides in the audiovisual section of the library at the University Park campus. The collection's primary function is to support the teaching of visual arts and architecture classes, but it is open to all faculty and students at the university.

The collection consists of approximately sixty-five thousand slides. From its beginnings in the early 1970s, it has been cataloged according to the classification system developed at the University of California–Santa Cruz. One of the reasons for choosing this system was that it offered the possibilities of automation. One of the basic requirements set by the system's originators was that it should allow for the collection (in the words of Simons and Tansey) "to be fully cataloged or indexed, preferably by automated means."[1]

Background

The first attempt at automating the slide collection was made in the early 1980s with the purchase of a PC and the dBase III–based program, ImageRun/SlideRun. The project was abandoned after an unrecoverable crash and the departure of the trained student assistant who did data entry. In the mid-1980s NOTIS was selected to be the online integrated catalog system for the State University System of Florida. NOTIS and its OPAC "LUIS" (Library User Information Service) encompass all library activities and include most of the library's collections in all formats. Access is possible from remote locations as well as in the library.

Reprinted with permission of the *Visual Resources Association Bulletin* and Mayra F. Nemeth from "Cataloging for Art's Sake at Florida International University," *VRA Bulletin* 20, no. 2 (summer 1993): 25–31.

From the beginning of the project, MARC-based records for all materials in the audiovisual collections were loaded from OCLC archival tapes with the exception of art slides. The possibility of entering MARC-based records for art slides was explored at the time of the conversion to NOTIS but it was not until 1991 that several factors came together which convinced the cataloging department to consider including the slide collection in the NOTIS database. One of those factors was an article by Phyllis Pivorun published in the *Visual Resources Association Bulletin* describing the development of a MARC-based record format used to catalog the architecture slide collection at Clemson University.[2] This article was the catalytic agent needed to jump-start the FIU project, which has finally fulfilled and even surpassed the vision of the curators who had chosen Simons and Tansey's Santa Cruz classification system twenty years before.

Because Clemson also uses NOTIS software, the article answered many of the concerns of the cataloging department at FIU. Clemson's cataloging department graciously shared their expertise by answering questions and sending sample records, copies of their worksheets, and instructions. The Clemson project proved that it could be done, and, with their help, we did not have to begin from scratch. This made all the difference.

Getting Started

FIU's cataloging staff must also be credited for its willingness to allow the audiovisual staff to take on such a unique project. After documents from other universities were consulted, it was decided in a series of meetings with the administration and the cataloging department that the main goals would be twofold, based on the needs of a wide range of patrons in a general library setting. Those goals would be to design a database which would allow for multiple access points through keyword searching, and to automate the circulation control system. At the same time, the data entry process needed to be simplified since the additional staff allocated for the project would be only one student assistant working fifteen hours a week. The need to simplify the process also played a part in the decision to begin the project by starting with twentieth-century art (painting, sculpture, graphics, and drawing).

Since 1991, over sixteen thousand records have been entered into the LUIS database, mostly of nineteenth- and twentieth-century painting, drawing, graphics, sculpture, and architecture. Initially, there were four basic ways to search a record in LUIS—by author/artist, by title, by Library of Congress subject headings, and by keyword. Recently, the system has been enhanced to include proximity, location, format, and date searching. The slide records have been modified to include a 007 field tag to make possible format searching. Field tag 653 is being used for free stringing of AAT terms. Although we now include these AAT subject terms, for a variety of reasons, it was decided to omit Library of Congress subject headings. This was done partially to save time but also because we felt a keyword search drawing from other elements in the record, such as title, would be adequate to meet the needs of our users.

Omitting subject headings also meant that the library did not contribute slide records to OCLC. In addition to the requirement to use Library of Congress subject headings, OCLC expects the kind of strict adherence to descriptive cataloging practices that presents a problem when making such decisions as how to formulate uniform titles. In all other respects, however, FIU developed a record which conforms to standard library cataloging rules and formats. The visual materials cataloger, head of the special materials cataloging section, developed a basic format for slides based on *Anglo-American Cataloguing Rules,* 2nd ed. (AACR2), chapter 8, and the OCLC/MARC format for audiovisual media.

FIU's abbreviated format is designed to use existing fields (tags and subfields) in a standard manner without deviating from the appropriate and intended use. The record describes the original artwork and a note identifies it as a slide reproduction. The date of completion of the artwork is entered in the publication date fixed field, an adaptation that makes more sense to the user, as these dates appear in the artist and title indexes. Physical measurements of the work are not entered since that information is not considered an access point. Call number access is obtained through the holding record information.

Field Tags and Usage

The complete list of MARC tags used in a record are displayed in figure 5-1. Field tag 100 (main entry—personal name) is used for the artist's name. Field tag 700 (added entry—personal name) is used to accommodate additional artists when the work represents a

Field Tag Number	Designated Use/Specified Local Use
* 100	Main entry—Personal name/Artist's name
* 245	Title statement/Title of art work, building name
	subfields: |b for subtitle, parallel title; and |c for statement of responsibility (artist's name)
*+ 246	Variant title/Variant or parallel title (can be used more than once)
260	Imprint/Publisher and date of purchase
300	Physical description/Number of slides and color
* 440	Series statement/Title for series or sets of slides
500	General note/Information on translated, added, supplied, or variant titles, etc.
* 520	Summary, abstract or annotation note/Artist nationality, art work medium and date, location, etc.
* 505	Contents note (formatted)/Titles in sets or series, views, details
590	Local note/Source of acquisition—exhibits, etc.
*+ 653	Index term—Uncontrolled/AAT terms
* 700	Added entry—Personal name/Collaborating artists
* 710	Added entry—Corporate name
* 711	Added entry—Conference or meeting name/ Exhibit name
* 740	Added entry—Title analytics/Second work title

* Indexed and/or keyword indexed
\+ Integrated format fields

Figure 5-1 | FIU's Abbreviated MARC Format

collaboration. The complete Library of Congress authority files are being regularly loaded in FCLA (Florida Center for Library Automation) databases, so it is possible to search them directly and to derive name authority records into the LUIS database. Artists' names not in the Name Authority Files are searched in the *Union List of Artist Names,* and authority records are created.[3]

Field tag 245 is the title statement field. The title is taken from the chief source of information according to the rules for cataloging graphic materials (AACR2, 8.1B). Lacking a chief source, the information can come from secondary sources. If no title can

be found in any source, the rules instruct the cataloger to "devise a brief descriptive title."[4]

Format integration is being introduced in stages. The 246 field is now used for variant and parallel titles. The 740 field is now used for the title of a second work on the same slide. Architectural works are being entered using the building name, and the city and country where it is located, as a title main entry in the field tag 245. The name of the building is searched in the Library of Congress authority file. The architects, corporate names, and other persons associated with the building are entered in 700 and 710 field tags. Field tag 500 (general note) provides an explanation of translated, added, supplied, or variant titles.

Field tag 440 (series statement) is used for a title when work is done in series, such as Joseph Alber's "Homage to the Square," or for a title of a set of slides. Field tag 505 (contents note) lists views, description of details, or individual titles in sets or series. Whenever possible, collection-level cataloging is done. Field tag 300 (physical description) lists the number of slides cataloged under one record while field tag 505 lists each slide-view or detail separately.

Most of FIU's slide collection is purchased from slide vendors. Field tag 260 (imprint) is used for the name of the publisher or vendor. When a slide is acquired locally as from an exhibition, that information is explained in field tag 590 (local note) and the name of the exhibition is designated in field tag 711 (added entry—conference or meeting name). FIU does not do copy photography from books and, therefore, does not designate a field for this information.

You will notice that the 520 summary note field, which is an indexed field for keyword searches, holds a number of discrete pieces of information. Included in this field are the location of the art work (entered only when a work is attached permanently to a location), the medium, and other information usually associated with how the work would be classified (e.g., American sculpture). According to AACR2 chapter 8.7, which deals with the note area, it is entirely within the rules to use the field in this way.

Keyword Searching

A patron may formulate a keyword search by requesting k=American wood sculpture (see figure 5-2). Selecting item 20 ("Mother and Child" by Elizabeth Catlett) will bring up the individual record (see figure 5-3). This record includes the artist, the title, the

Search Request: K = Slide Wood Sculpture American   Keyword
Index
Search Results: 42 Entries Found   Florida International University

	Date	Title	Author
10	1965	Long Beach contract (visual)	Kohn, Gabriel
11	1960	Acrotere (visual)	Kohn, Gabriel
12	1970	Gauge (visual)	Kipp, Lyman
13	1963	Inside out (visual)	Hudson, Robert
14	1944	White anxiety (visual)	Greene, Gertrude
15	1938	Construction (visual)	Diller, Burgoyne
16	1974	Figure (visual)	Catlett, Elizabeth
17	1971	Magic mask (visual)	Catlett, Elizabeth
18	1975	Singing head (visual)	Catlett, Elizabeth
19	1968	Black unity (visual)	Catlett, Elizabeth
20	1972	Mother and child (visual)	Catlett, Elizabeth
21	1935	Wood mobile (visual)	Calder, Alexander
22	1928	Standing woman (visual)	Calder, Alexander
23	1928	The horse (visual)	Calder, Alexander

_____ Continued on next screen

Commands: Type line # to see individual record
            E Introduction   F Forward   H Help
            O Other Options   B Back   Menu More databases

Figure 5-2 | Keyword Search

Search Request: K = Slide Wood Sculpture American   Long View
Visual Material - Record 20 of 42 Entries Found   Florida International University
                                    Screen 1 of 1

Title:	Mother and child <slide> / Elizabeth Catlett.
Distribution:	Chicago, IL : Rosenthal, 1979
Description:	2 slides : col.
Series:	Two centuries of Black American art
Contents:	1. Front view -- 2. Side view.
Summary:	Slide reproduction of an American artist's pecan wood sculpture, 1972.
Authors/Artists:	Catlett, Elizabeth, 1919-

Location:	Call Number:	Status:
1. Univ. Park AV Slide	P630D C3651 M918	Enter HO for holdings

Commands: HO Holdings   P Previous Record   Menu More databases
            E Introduction   BR Brief View   I Index
            O Other Options   N Next Record   H Help

Figure 5-3 | Keyword Search Single Record

Search Request: T = Mother and Child
Visual Material - Record 7 of 21 Entries Found

Holdings Detail
Florida International University

Title: Mother and child

Location 1

Location: Univ. Park AV Slide coll. - 1st fl.
Call number: P630D C3651 M918

Library Has: 1-2

Commands: V View Record   P Previous databases   Menu More databases
            E Introduction   BR Brief View
            I Index   O Other Options
            N Next Record   H Help

Figure 5-4 | Keyword Search Single Record/Holdings Screen

017/1:	|a HAVE YOU DERI? IF YES ERASE THIS LINE; USE EOF key
035/1:	|a (FMFI)AVUP slide EG
100:1	|a Last Name, First, |d BIRTH-DEATH dates. CHECK AUTHORITY
245:10:	|a Title of work |h slide: |b subtitle/ |c Artist name. (FIRST LAST)
260:	|a Place, ST : |b Publisher, |c date.
300/1:	|a 1slide : |b col.
440/1:0:	|a Series title (no period)
520/1:	|a Slide reproduction of (NATIONALITY) i.e., an American artist's (medium) oil painting, DATE OF WORK.
5005/2:0	|a Contents note -- 1. enumerate items.
590/3:	|a Acquired as part of the exhibit "NAME OF EXHIBIT," Place, Date.
590/4:	|a DID YOU ENTER DT/1? (Date of work), DOES IT MATCH DATE in summary (520)? DID YOU ERASE 017? IF ALL IS OKAY, ERASE THIS LINE (590).
599/1:	|a eg
711/1:21:	|a Name of exhibit. CHECK AUTHORITY.

Figure 5-5 | Prompting Template

source of the slide, a description of the physical format, series information, views, and a summary which tells the patron this is a slide of an American artist's wood sculpture. The date of the work, 1972, is included. The holdings screen provides the call number and location (see figure 5-4) and is linked to a screen which indicates the availability of the item. A patron could also retrieve the record through an author/artist search under Catlett, Elizabeth, or a title search under "Mother and Child." Since titles can vary, keyword searching generally yields the most productive results.

Data Entry Template

Rather than work from a worksheet, a "template" derived from the OCLC audiovisual format was created in the database. This template has required fixed fields and delimiters already in place (see figure 5-5). It prompts the student assistant doing data entry with helpful hints on how to enter the information. Since FIU is converting an existing collection, the information is taken directly from the slide label. At this time, labels are not being generated from the records.

The information appearing on the slide label is entered and a new record is created. This record is then derived or copied and serves as the template for the next slide by the same artist. By altering that which is different (title, views, etc.) it is possible to enter many works of an artist easily since many of the fields will remain constant. The NOTIS system also allows for the programming of function keys to facilitate input of constant data in certain fields, for example, imprint, series title, notes, etc.

Name Authorities

Name authority searching for all artists not already established in the database is done in the OCLC NAF (name authority file). A number of other sources are used as well, including the *Index to Artistic Biography,* to verify and create entries for artists that do not appear in the OCLC name authority file.[5] Series and exhibits titles are established by the head of special materials cataloging following AACR2. The *Art and Architecture Thesaurus* is used as the source to establish terms for the summary and contents notes.[6]

In addition to the bibliographic record, two other records are associated with each entry: a copy holdings record where information on location, call number, and copies is entered; and an item record where the bar code on the slide is linked for circulation control. A MARC holdings record is also created for works in sets, parts, and pieces.

Conclusion

Several test records were entered in August 1991 to determine how a bibliographic record would appear in the OPAC and how circulation would proceed. This helped us decide to integrate the slide database with other materials—books, journals, audiovisuals, etc.; for example, the field labels for name entry in LUIS display as author/artist. The records have been available to the public from the beginning of the project. Access to the collection on the OPAC has not only increased the public's awareness of the existence of the collection, it has also increased usage.[7]

Student assistants have come and gone and the rate of progress fluctuates accordingly. Training a student assistant is a major task with varying degrees of success. By limiting data entry/record creation to a specific period within the general collection, a reasonable expectation of completeness and achievement is created. It is still a work in progress. As we begin to tackle other time periods and more difficult areas of the collection, modifications to the record structure will need to be undertaken. We believe that with the advent of format integration, which permits the use of any field from any of the formats to be used in a single record, MARC will be flexible enough to allow this. As new tools, such as the *Thesaurus of Geographic Names,* become available, they will be incorporated into our authorities. ICON-CLASS is also under consideration, but the constraints of money, time, and staff have necessarily kept the project from becoming too complicated in these early stages. Although we are aware that much remains to be done, there is now an administrative commitment to this project where there was none before.

NOTES

1. Wendell W. Simons and Luraine C. Tansey, *A Slide Classification System for the Organization and Automatic Indexing of Interdisciplinary Collections of Slides and Pictures* (Santa Cruz: University of California, 1970), 2.

2. Phyllis Pivorun, "Why and How MARC Is Being Used for Automating the Architecture Slide Collection at Clemson University," *Visual Resources Association Bulletin* 18, no. 2 (summer 1991): 18–21.

3. *Union List of Artist Names* (New York: G. K. Hall, 1994).

4. *Anglo-American Cataloguing Rules,* 2nd ed. Prepared by the American Library Association, the British Library, the Canadian Committee on Cataloguing, the Library Association, and the Library of Congress, ed. Michael Gorman and Paul Winkler (Chicago: American Library Association and Canadian Library Association, 1978), 19.

5. Patricia Pate Havlice, *Index to Artistic Biography* (Metuchen, N.J.: Scarecrow Press, 1973).

6. *Art and Architecture Thesaurus* (New York: Oxford University Press, on behalf of the Getty Art History Information Program, 1990).

7. Access to FIU's slide records is also available through the Internet at http://www.fiu.edu/~library. Select WebLUIS.

Cataloging Architecture Slides at the University of Nebraska–Lincoln

Margaret L. Emons

The University of Nebraska–Lincoln (UNL) is the flagship campus of the University of Nebraska system. The UNL College of Architecture is the only architecture degree-granting program in Nebraska. Degrees granted at UNL are the BSAS (Bachelor of Science in Architectural Studies), MARCH (Master of Architecture) and MCRP (Master of Community and Regional Planning), and BA and MA in Interior Design. The College of Architecture employs thirty-two faculty and has over 750 students enrolled.

Background

The Architecture Slide Library, which is part of the University Library System, is housed within the Architecture Library. The position of slide curator is administered under the art and architecture librarian. The slide library contains over forty thousand slides, approximately one thousand photographs, and lantern slides. The slide library primarily supports the curriculum of the Architecture College. Images represent all types of built environments: buildings and building interiors, city plans and views, landscapes, and decorative arts and furnishings. As a branch of the University Libraries, the Architecture Slide Library is open to the entire campus and serves not only architecture faculty and students, but also faculty and students from other programs and disciplines, local architects, and the general public.

The College of Architecture provides the materials budget for the slide library, which covers the purchase of new slides, equipment, and supplies. The University Libraries fund the slide curator's salary and provide support for cataloging and automation.

The Architecture Slide Library has been in existence since 1984. In 1987, the slide library was automated on a PC using INMAGIC, a commercial software

Reprinted with permission of the *Visual Resources Association Bulletin* and Margaret L. Emons from "Cataloging Architecture Slides at the University of Nebraska–Lincoln," *VRA Bulletin* 20, no. 3 (fall 1993): 24–28.

package, the University of California–Santa Cruz classification system, *Library of Congress Subject Headings* (LCSH), and the *Art and Architecture Thesaurus* (AAT). UNL was a test site for the development of the AAT. In the spring of 1991, the hard drive used for the slide database reached capacity. As part of the purchase process for a high-cost item such as a new computer, the art and architecture librarian was asked by the library administration to write a long-range plan and subsequent proposal for continued automation of the Architecture Slide Library. Goals for the automation of the slide library were identified, and included automated circulation functions, wide-range patron access, large growth potential for records, and the transportability of data.

Getting Started

In the process of preparing the long-range automation plan, the slide curator and the architecture librarian made the decision to use the MARC format as a basis for the slide record. Articles such as "Visual Depictions and the Use of MARC: A View from the Trenches of Slide Librarianship" by Maryly Snow, "Sharing the Wealth: Software for MARC-based Cataloging of Visual Materials" by James Bower, and "Why and How MARC Is Being Used for Automating the Architecture Slide Collection at Clemson University" by Phyllis Pivorun suggested that other slide libraries were also using MARC to catalog slides.[1]

After the initial decision to use a MARC format was made, the use of the University Library's Innovative Interface System (IRIS), which incorporates the MARC formats into its technical modules, became the logical choice. (IRIS is a turnkey system designed for libraries.) The Automated Systems Officer and the Chair of Technical Services were consulted, and both agreed that the IRIS system would meet all of the automation goals for the slide library. It was proposed that the slide library's database would be converted to the MARC format; that cataloging would be done with collection-level records; that records would be cataloged using Online Computer Library Center (OCLC) standards; that LCSH and the AAT would be used for subject access; and that the University of California–Santa Cruz system would be used for classification. After a lengthy review process, the proposal was approved by the Dean of Libraries in January 1993.

In designing and preparing a MARC record which could be used for slides, the essays in *Beyond the Book,*

the article by Sara Shatford in *Cataloging and Classification Quarterly,* and in particular the article by Phyllis Pivorun in the *Visual Resources Association Bulletin* proved to be most helpful.[2] The MARC record developed by the slide curator was reworked by the head cataloger, then reworked again by the slide curator and the architecture librarian. After some negotiation and compromise, the MARC record for slide cataloging was finalized in April 1993.

The Project

The full OCLC MARC record and a table of MARC fields and their descriptions can be seen in figures 6-1 and 6-2. Field tag 043 (geographical area code) is used when warranted by the subject matter, and helps to identify the geographic location of a work. This allows patrons to limit searches by geographic area. In figure 6-1, "e--fi" stands for Europe, Finland. The code is taken from OCLC's codes for countries. Field tag 007 (physical description) is used to identify projected graphics, in this case, a slide. Field tag 099 (local free text call number) is used for the University of California–Santa Cruz Classification Number. This field is searchable. Because it is a locally generated classification number, it does not appear on the record.

Field tag 100 (main entry—personal name) is used for "the person chiefly responsible for the creation of the intellectual or artistic content of a work" (AACR2R, p. 312).[3] This field is searchable. Field tag 245 (title statement) is used for the title proper and the remainder of title information. This field is searchable. The title is taken from the chief source of information, "the item itself including any labels, etc. that are permanently affixed to the item or a container that is an integral part of the item" (AACR2R, p. 202).[4] If title information is not available from the chief source then it is taken from the container, accompanying textual material, or other reference sources. If the title is taken from accompanying material, which must be identified, no brackets are used. If the title information is supplied by the cataloger, square brackets are used.

Field tag 260 (imprint) is used for the place of publication, name of publisher, and date of publication. This field created the most controversy. For commercially published items, this field works well, but for nonpublished items it may be confusing. The slide curator and the architecture librarian believe that this field should reflect the date of creation of the original

```
HELD BY LDL - NO OTHER HOLDINGS
        OCLC: 28084051        Rec stat: c
        Entered: 19930510     Replaced: 19930629     Used: 19930510
        Type:          g      Bib lvl: m      Source: d      Lang: N/A
        Type mat:      s      Enc lvl: I      Govt pub:      Ctry: xx
        Int lvl:       e      Mod rec:        Tech:  n       Leng: nnn
        Desc:          a      Accomp:         Dat tp: q      Dates: 1900, 1993
   1    040            LDL | c LDL
   2    007            g |b s|d c |e j |h j |I c
   3    043            e -- fi --
   4    090            |b
   5    049            LDLL
   6    100     1      Aalto, Alvar, |d 1898-1976.
   7    245     10  *  [Aalto Studio, Munkkiniemi, Finland] |h slide / |c [Alvar Aalto, architect].
   8    260            |c [19--]
   9    300            6 slides : |b col.
  10    500            Built 1955.
  11    505     0      A.A. Exterior, view from street, privacy wall -- B.A. Exterior, facade seen from
                       corner of wall -- E.A. Exterior, general view from side entrance -- I.A. Exterior,
                       detail of window and facade -- K.A.-K.B. Interior, studio, plants on wall.
  12    600     10     Aalto, Alvar, |d 1898-1976.
  13    610     20     Aalto Studio (Munkkiniemi, Finland)
  14    650     0      Windows |z Finland |z Munkkiniemi |x Slides.
  15    651     0      Munkkiniemi (Finland) |x Buildings, structures, etc. |x Slides.
  16    654     1      |c h |a Studios (Work spaces) |2 aat
  17    654     1      |c r |a Architects' houses |c f |b Modern Movement. |2 aat
  18    654     2      |c r |a Entrances. |2 aat
  19    654     2      |c r |a Boundary walls. |2 aat
```

Figure 6-1 | Technical Screen/Holdings Record

object. Articles published in *Cataloging and Classification Quarterly* by Sara Shatford were used as the basis for this argument. After much debate the head cataloger rejected these arguments for several reasons. Lack of documentation by visual resources professionals concerning the use of MARC and lack of published standards were two important reasons. Also, no slide records could be found in OCLC which used the 260 field this way. The head cataloger also made valid arguments, stating that this field should be used uniformly for published and nonpublished materials. It should serve as an explanation for the creation of the physical format of the material. Perhaps a solution would be for a companion field for the 260 to be used to describe the creation of the original artistic object. We chose to use field tag 500 (general note) for the date or dates associated with a work. This field is also used for any additional information needed.

Field tag 300 (physical description) is used for the number of slides and physical detail of color. Field tag 440 or 490 (series statement—title) is used when the slides cataloged are part of a series or set. This field is searchable. Field tag 505 (contents note) is used to describe the different views of a work. This field tag was chosen over field tag 520 (summary) because the field tag 505 in the IRIS system is keyword searchable. The head cataloger developed the form of input for this information, thus linking the contents and the item records.

Field tag 600 (subject added entry—personal name) is used for the architect's name. The names of designers and builders are always used as a subject access point. This field is searchable. Field tag 610 (subject added entry—corporate name) is used for firm names and building names. This field is searchable. Field tag 650 (topical subject) is used for Library

Field Tag Number	Designated Use/Specified Local Use
007	Physical description/Code for slide
040	Cataloging source/Code for cataloger
043	Geographical area code/Code for geographic location
049	Local holdings/Code for institution
099	Local free text call number
100	Main entry—personal name/Architect, builder, designer
245	Title statement/Title proper
260	Imprint/Source (for vendor)
300	Physical description/Number of slides/color/b&w
440	Series satement—title (traced)/Series information when applicable
490	Series statement—title traced differently/Series information when applicable
500	General note/Date of work
505	Contents note/Views
600	Subject added entry—personal name/Architect, builder, designer
610	Subject added entry—corporate name/Corporate name
650	Subject added entry—topical term/Library of Congress Subject Headings
651	Subject added entry—geographic/Specific location
654	Subject added entry—faceted topical/AAT
700	Added entry—personal name/Additional names
710	Added entry—corporate name/Additional names

Figure 6-2 | MARC Fields and Descriptions

of Congress subject headings. This field is searchable. Field tag 651 (geographic subject) is used for geographic subject headings. This field is searchable and as a general rule is linked to buildings, structures, etc., so that they can be searched by location. Field tag 654 (faceted topical subject) is used for the AAT terms. This field is searchable.

Field tag 700 (added entry—personal name) is used for architects or designers other than the main entry. This field is searchable. Field tag 710 (added entry—corporate name) is used for firms other than the main entry. This field is searchable.

Because slide records would be added to OCLC and the University's Online Public Access Catalog (OPAC), the cataloging manual used was from the cataloging department with some adaptations for slide cataloging.

Labels are not generated from the record but are produced separately in the slide library using LABELware, a software program specially designed to produce 35mm slide labels. Each slide is bar coded, a process that is also completed in the slide library. This allows each item to circulate individually. Bar coding information is linked to the record; thus, the status of each item appears on the record (see figure 6-3).

Title: aalto studio   UNL Libraries & Schmid Library

Title	[Aalto Studio, Munkkiniemi, Finland] [slide] / [Alvar Aalto, architect]
Author	Aalto, Alvar, 1898-1976.
Publisher	[19-]
Descript.	6 slides : col.
Contents	A.A. Exterior, view from street, privacy wall -- B.A. Exterior, facade seen from corner of wall -- E.A. Exterior, general view from side entrance -- I.A. Exterior, detail of window and facade -- K.A.-K.B. Interior, studio, plants on wall.

Location	Call no.	Status
1 > Arch Slide	P392B A247C.C A247 A.A	Available
2 > Arch Slide	P392B A247C.C A247 B.A	Available
3 > Arch Slide	P392B A247C.C A247 E.A	Available
4 > Arch Slide	P392B A247C.C A247 I.A	Available
5 > Arch Slide	P392B A247C.C A247 K.A	Available
6 > Arch Slide	P392B A247C.C A247 K.B	Available

V > Find Specific Volume/Copy	A > Another Search by Title
M > More Bibliographic Record	I > More Items
R > Browse Nearby Entries	Z > Show Items Nearby on Shelf
N > New Search	O > Other Options

Choose one (V, M, R, N, A, I, Z, S, T, O)

Figure 6-3 | User Screen/Search by Title

Conclusion

In conclusion, this project has worked very well for UNL. However, I would not recommend a project like this to every slide library. The primary goals for this library were automated circulation functions and greater access to slide records. OCLC and an integrated automation system are very expensive and time-consuming. As part of a large academic library system, the slide library had access to OCLC and an OPAC already in place. We were also fortunate to have great technical support on all levels and at all points in the project.

NOTES

1. Maryly Snow, "Visual Depictions and the Use of MARC: A View from the Trenches of Slide Librarianship," *Art Documentation* 8, no. 4 (winter 1989): 186–190; James Bower, "Sharing the Wealth: Software for MARC-based Cataloging of Visual Materials," *Visual Resources Association Bulletin* 17, no. 3 (fall 1990): 23–26; Phyllis Pivorun, "Why and How MARC Is Being Used for Automating the Architecture Slide Collection at Clemson University," *Visual Resources Association Bulletin* 18, no. 2 (summer 1991): 18–21.

2. Toni Petersen and Pat Molholt, eds., *Beyond the Book: Extending MARC for Subject Access* (Boston: G. K. Hall, 1990); Sara Shatford, "Analyzing the Subject of a Picture: A Theoretical Approach," *Cataloging and Classification Quarterly* 6, no. 3 (spring 1986): 39–62; Pivorun, "Why and How MARC Is Being Used."

3. Michael Gorman and Paul W. Winkler, eds., *Anglo-American Cataloguing Rules,* 2nd ed., 1988 revision (Chicago: American Library Association, 1988).

4. Ibid.

Image Cataloging in MARC at the University of Virginia

Lynda S. White

Setting

The Fiske Kimball Fine Arts Library of the University of Virginia (UVa) is a physically separate unit of the University Library serving the needs of the Departments of Art and Drama, and the School of Architecture, but administratively separate from them. Its image collection primarily serves the faculty and students of the School of Architecture. The school is comprised of the Departments of Architectural History, Architecture, Landscape Architecture, and Urban Planning. There are seventy-six faculty, and 185 graduate along with 350 undergraduate students currently enrolled in the school. The collection was organized in the 1960s to support the architectural history program which began offering a doctorate in 1988. The collection's emphasis, therefore, is on architectural history and the organizational scheme is based upon the needs of an architectural history program. Consequently, the images supporting the other three departments, as well as other programs such as Drama, often do not fit into the major classification scheme of the collection. Since the image collection is part of the university's library system and is supported by state tax revenues, we must serve not only the School of Architecture but the university, the surrounding community, and whoever else may need our assistance.

The image needs of the Art Department are met by their departmental slide collection located across a parking lot from the library. The curators of the two image collections attempt to maintain contact regarding collection development and services, but are administratively separate. Nevertheless, there is some overlap between the collections; e.g., the library maintains a small, basic collection of art slides, while the Art Department is stronger in ancient architecture which is not emphasized in the curriculum of the School of Architecture.

Reprinted with permission of the *Visual Resources Association Bulletin* and Lynda S. White from "Image Cataloging in MARC at the University of Virginia," *VRA Bulletin* 21, no. 3 (fall 1994): 23–31.

The library's image collection is comprised of around 170,000 slides and photographs of several design-related fields. Of these, 135,000 slides are fully cataloged. Complete card sets are filed in a dictionary catalog separate from the image files. The sets include cards for the designer(s), title(s), location, building type(s) and use(s), and any other subject or name entries that will facilitate finding the images. Each card displays all of this information in addition to the call number which leads to the filing location. For each building or structure there is also a separately maintained shelf list card(s) which lists and describes each image classified under a specific call number along with the source of the image. This source has always proved to be a valuable reference tool (e.g., for design students searching for floor plans or elevations of specific buildings) and is essential information should the image need to be replaced. Our primary means of acquisition is copy photography; we do not allow duplication of any images in the collection.

The classification scheme was developed by architectural historian William Bainter O'Neill sometime in the mid- to late 1960s. The cataloged images are organized by country, within country by century, then by architect or artist (or title if there is no designer), and lastly by title, so that all images relating to a structure or entity are filed together. For example, the call number A-(18-19)-Je-4.1-1 refers to the first slide of Monticello cataloged into the collection: A = America, 18-19 = 18th–19th centuries (era in which Jefferson lived), Je = Jefferson, 4.1 = Monticello.plans, 1 = first slide cataloged. Generic images of paving patterns and construction techniques do not fit into this model. However, it works very well for historians who often bypass the catalog and consult the image files directly.

The remainder of the collection is organized in two ways. Images that do not fit the above scheme (they lack an architect and title) are arranged in notebooks of slide pages by broad subject areas. They have no card sets but instead have cursory coding which indicates that they are of domestic architecture, religious architecture, transportation, technology, decorative arts, urban views, landscape elements, etc. These are usually subdivided by country if that information can be discovered. The determining factor for adding an image to these notebooks is that there is simply not enough information available to construct a formal call number. Images which can fit the formal scheme constitute the backlog; they are arranged in drawers by country and then designer and will require enough additional research to catalog that they have to be dealt with as time permits.

Goals and Groundwork

It was because of the continued growth of the collection of "uncatalogable" images in the notebooks that we determined it was time to automate. With the collection staffing level at less than half-time, and acquisitions averaging six thousand to eight thousand images per year, it became increasingly difficult to remember where any particular incompletely identified image might be stored. Locating these images is particularly problematic when the patron's description is also incomplete or muddled.

We had been considering various means to automate since 1985, usually stand-alone systems where we would have to develop our own database. But we were reluctant to invent a new structure when MARC would suffice and was more "share-able"; and we were stymied by lack of the necessary equipment and staff to develop our own system. Thus we simply waited until the technology (NOTIS) had developed, the Library had purchased it, and the need for special equipment and software was negated.

Around the fall of 1991 other factors conspired to push us onward: First, the Library's integrated online catalog, *VIRGO* (using NOTIS software), had been running successfully for two years and the University Library had just decided that it should include records for *all* materials owned by the Library, not just print materials; this meant that we had a ready-made vehicle for an automation project. Second, the Fine Arts staff had virtually completed the correction of Fine Arts' book holdings in the *VIRGO* database, freeing already trained staff for a new project; and third, a renegade group began meeting to work on the Digital Image Study Project (DISP). All of these factors provided the additional justification and impetus for meeting the more far-ranging need for intellectual access to images that transcended the architecture image collection.

The groundwork for the MARC project was laid over many years through attending Southeast College Art Conference and Art Libraries Society of North America conferences and workshops, as well as through reading and networking.[1] Our greatest debt is to Phyllis Pivorun who not only uses the MARC format but also NOTIS software. Her project at Clemson University's Gunnin Architectural Library is the most direct model for UVa's project. Nonetheless, there are differences between the two projects: (1) The MARC fields used are, perhaps unfortunately, not identical; (2) UVa chose to use item-level rather than collection-level records for most of our records; and (3) we chose to use a processing unit rather than an institution group (NO-TIS database conventions), which means that our image records are interfiled with records for books, manuscripts, scores, videos, etc., and are not a separate catalog. Thus far we are pleased with that choice as it brings together, for the same structure, records for books, manuscripts, and images on one OPAC (Online Public Access Catalog) search screen; the downside is the sometimes very lengthy OPAC index for a single built work. We also chose to display our records in the OPAC from the beginning. Consultants in our Systems Office pointed out that there would be very few records for a very long time and that the chances of anyone finding one would be remote—although, happily, patrons have already found and enthusiastically used these new records. We are thus working out the kinks in our system before the entire world.

Our major considerations in choosing to use *VIRGO* to catalog images were cost and availability. The NOTIS system was already available in the Fine Arts Library. *VIRGO* provided features that earlier stand-alone systems could not: powerful and sophisticated keyword searching, circulation control, and a MARC structure. Our only initial needs were an additional 486 PC workstation that could be connected to the LAN (local area network), and slide-size laser labels on which could be printed OCR (Optical Character Recognition) numbers for circulation control. In addition, the staff was already thoroughly familiar with the structure and coding for *VIRGO,* making the learning curve relatively slight and computer programmers completely unnecessary.

Having records on *VIRGO* for images not in the cataloged collection relieves staff of having to know where every image is housed. *VIRGO* allows for minimal-level records which may never be updated or expanded. Since so many of our titles are invented, it makes little difference that most of the images in our notebook collection are incompletely identified. We can simply concoct a title and then add as many subject terms as necessary—from a visual inspection of the image rather than from research—to describe the image, permit keyword searching, and locate the image in a particular notebook.

Another primary goal was to resolve the persistent problem of providing access to individual images within the context of collection-level cataloging. This is particularly difficult to resolve in the paper environment. For example, because the subject headings for the collection of historical views of New York are very general (Historic views—New York), it is difficult to lo-cate, among the eighty-three slides of historic views, that specific picture of a dead horse in the streets of New York in the 1930s. But, if we were to use a specific subject heading to identify "dead horse," it would not apply to every image in the collection of historical views—for which there is only a collection-level card set. NOTIS allows at least two means of dealing with this, neither perfect but both easier than typed card sets. Clemson chose to use collection-level records listing the detailed descriptions in a searchable note field. UVa opted to provide access to the details by creating a record for each item; the items are grouped together both physically and in the database by the basic call number for the group of images. There are advantages and disadvantages to each approach. Collection-level cataloging requires fewer records and fewer subject headings, but information about the details is lost. Item-level cataloging, on the other hand, allows a greater degree of subject analysis and thus greater access to a wealth of details, but it quickly fills up OPAC index screens.

VIRGO allows for easy copying of records (the *derive* function). A base record can be created that applies to the whole structure or set of images, and then additional records can be derived and altered to fit the specific image in hand, i.e., delete a general subject heading and/or add a more specific or relevant one. For example, we may catalog a plantation as a whole but own images of its plans, exteriors, gardens, furniture, and staircases. The base record records the name of the plantation, its place and date, etc., and the *Art and Architecture Thesaurus* (AAT) subject "Plantation houses" in a 654 field. The record for the staircase is derived from the base record but a heading for "newel staircases" is added in another 654 field to provide access to that particular image. The heading "newel staircases" does not apply to any other image in the set and does not appear in the record of any other image in the set. Thus while we still group the images together physically at the collection level using the classification scheme, we can now provide intellectual access to individual images within that collection. Nonetheless, this seems a cumbersome solution to the problem—shared with both art image and book cataloging—in that it can produce many index screens listing the same building title in the OPAC.

Lastly, being on *VIRGO* provides access to images for any patron with a modem, whether on Grounds or off. We have always had patrons from outside the School of Architecture, particularly from the language departments, Religious Studies, and the Graduate Business School; but it is often difficult for these patrons to find what they want without knowing the names of specific buildings or architects—which they rarely know. Given our staffing, it was impossible to provide the kind of detailed access they needed using a paper environment. *VIRGO* allows us to relatively quickly input the access points they need—without having to type or revise large card sets or file duplicate images in different drawers—and allows them to do the sophisticated searching necessary to combine these access points.

Process

One of the more exciting aspects of our project was its interconnection with the ongoing Digital Image Study Project. DISP is a group of professionals from several areas of the university that began meeting in the winter of 1991 to develop a digital imaging pilot project for art and architecture at the university. Initially included were the slide curator from the Art Department, a sys-

tems analyst from Information Technology and Communication (our computer gurus), and the three librarians from the Fine Arts Library. As we began to ponder how to provide intellectual access to the digitized images, we also drew in faculty who were Fellows in the Institute for Advanced Technology in the Humanities, the Systems Librarian for Information Services, and the Head of the library's Original Cataloging Unit.

We briefly considered trying to use Standard Generalized Markup Language (SGML, used by the publishing industry to mark texts for editing and printing) rather than MARC as a package for intellectual access. Although we eventually abandoned this, the exercise of devising field names for an SGML description of images—in the absence of the Getty's Art Information Task Force categories still under development at that time—gave us a long list of possible descriptors. This list was developed with the assistance of a professor in the English Department who was working on a project linking Rossetti's writings and paintings on an image and text database.[2] He was already using SGML to mark the texts. Our mission was to devise field tags to help him describe the images. During this process it became apparent that different project participants had not only different image information needs, but differing abilities to describe an image. To accommodate this we decided to describe images at three levels that build upon each other:

- The first level of descriptors is intended for use by general catalogers who may not necessarily know much about the artistic content of the image but who can garner basic information from a book caption or from data provided by a vendor. This information includes name of designer, title of work, date of work, and information essential for an OCLC record, such as image file size (if digitized) or whether the image is color or black and white (see figure 7-1).

- The second level includes descriptors from the first level but adds subject headings and other, more in-depth descriptors that might be provided by visual resources curators after researching the image (see figure 7-2).

- The third level is intended for the end user who could, in a networked environment, download records to his/her own files and add information relevant only to his/her project; e.g., who was the patron for a painting, who was the model Rossetti used for the angel, what is the symbolism of the cannon, which sketch or poem is the

MARC Field Tag Number	Description
046	BCE dates
100	Designer: Name of artist or architect with |d for life dates
110	Corporate name for architectural firms
111	Name of meeting/conference/exposition
245|a+	Title: Title statement
245|h	Media designator: <slide>
245|b+	Location of work: City, country or state
245|p	Type of view depicted in image: plan, exterior, interior, landscaping, artifacts, etc.
260|c	AD dates: Date, or range of dates, that work was conceived and/or constructed
851*	Location: |c street address, |d country
300*+	Physical description: size of digital file, slide
340*	Medium for art; special construction materials for architecture
510*	Source of image: Author/title or call number of book photographed
535*	Location of original art works, e.g., museum name
655*	Form/Genre heading

* = repeatable field
\+ = mandatory fields (must be included in record)

Figure 7-1 | First Level of Descriptors Used

MARC Field Tag Number	Description
099*	Local free text call number
240	Uniform title
242*	Translation of title
340|b*	Size: Dimensions of original work
440*	Artist's series: Series statement if series was artist's intent
505*	List of descriptions/Contents: Image descriptions for unanalyzed sets.
510*	Standard catalog no.: From standard catalogs on artist's works
520*	Description of view: e.g., detail of cornice; exterior: south facade; plan: first floor, etc.
545*	Restored/remodeled: Use biographical or historical note
600*	Subject: Personal name
610*	Subject: Corporate name
611*	Subject: Conference or meeting name
650*	Subject: Topical/LC
651*	Geographic subject
654*	Subject: AAT term
654*	Medium: AAT Materials Facet
654*	Form or genre: AAT Objects Facet: Image and Object Genres; Document Types
690*	Subject: Local heading/Iconclass
700*	Joint artist/architect; corporate name of larger complex: Additional artists or architects
710*	Additional architectural firm, or firm in which designer is a member
711*	Conference or exposition added entry
740*	Variant title: Title traced differently; Title of larger complex
755*	Physical characteristics: |y chrono and |z geo subdivisions
773*	Host item entry: Name of larger unit or complex

* = repeatable field
\+ = mandatory fields (must be included in record)

Figure 7-2 | Second Level of Descriptors Used

MARC Field Tag Number	Description
260|e	Where produced: Imprint—Place of manufacture
340*	Physical description of frame
500*	Documentary evidence: Note on documents relating to work
500*	Related studies: Preliminary sketches, photos, etc.
500*	Intended site: Site for which work was created
500*	Influence of the work on other works
500*	Kinds and dissemination of reproductions of the original
500*	Internal evidence: Signatures, dates, and other markings on work
534*	Original version note
561*	Provenance
581*	Related literature: Citation of writing about the work
583*	Conservation: Preservation strategies
585*	Exhibition record
600*	Patron: Subject (personal name)
600|e*	Name of sitter or model
700*	Added entry: Personal name

* = repeatable field
\+ = mandatory fields (must be included in record)

Figure 7-3 | Third Level of Descriptors Used

painting related to, etc. (see figure 7-3). Guidelines for using fields would be provided and, if followed consistently, the enhanced records could be copied back to the main database when the additional information might prove useful to others. This level is theoretical for the moment.

After much discussion, we decided to use SGML as a *package* for MARC fields—thus freeing us to concentrate on determining which MARC fields might most appropriately match our field names. We used OCLC's manual describing MARC fields for their version of the Visual Materials Format (although the format chosen will be immaterial once format integration is widespread); but we also compared our initial list to that of Clemson, Syracuse, the Cleveland Museum of Art, the AVIADOR Project, and to a prepublication copy of James Bower's article on the VRA MARC project—kindly provided by Helene Roberts.[3] The DISP group met nearly every week from January through April 1993 to review the MARC list and to try to actually use the fields to describe images brought in from the Rosetti project. In addition, we tried using the fields to describe the images digitized by a history professor working on a Civil War imaging project. He had scanned a few paintings by unknown artists into his database, but the images were mostly of old photographs and maps. By defining the MARC fields flexibly we were able to "catalog" these images as well.

As we developed the list, we simultaneously worked on an application manual (our local substitute for AACR2) which included the OCLC description of the field as well as decisions we had made on how the field was to be applied to images of art or architecture (figure 7-4).[4] Having with us a cataloger who was intimately familiar with the MARC record was vital to this enterprise as he kept us from going too far afield in our definitions and led us to alternate MARC fields that served our purposes when necessary. We were quite fortunate that he understood that cataloging images required using the MARC format and AACR2 rules flexibly. However, it was decided that our records would not be contributed to OCLC because they were too "non-standard" to meet OCLC input standards, even though they will actually provide more detailed intellectual access for images than a typical MARC/LCSH record does for a book. It is unfortunate that we will not be contributing to OCLC since without that capability we will be able to share cataloging records only over the Internet and not through a bibliographic utility.

The fields we chose to use are listed, with brief definitions, in figures 7-1 through 7-3. The title field (245) is probably the most packed with information. We use it not only for the name of the structure, but also to indicate its location as well as the type of view depicted (plan, rendering, exterior, interior, furniture, landscaping, etc.), correlated to decimals in the call number.

One of our most difficult decisions was how to indicate location. We could have used the 851 to record the street address. We originally considered using the 260 (place and publisher) but were quickly dissuaded by our cataloging consultant. We also could have used the 650 and 654 subject fields with geographic and chronological subdivisions, but this seemed unnecessary duplication of information available in the 245|b, which we settled on in order to be able to sort buildings with similar names on the OPAC index screen (see figure 7-5). We chose the 099 for our call number as we have no intention of reclassifying (and relabeling and refiling!) our entire collection. For image collections, a standard classification scheme seems unnecessary; there is no reason for each collection not to keep its own system—as long as the scheme is represented in the same field of the MARC record by all who use MARC records. The 099 is designed specifically for locally devised classification (i.e., filing) systems.

Our initial anxiety over training students to catalog, though not completely abated, was eased somewhat by the revelation that we could create a template record in *VIRGO* and then derive additional records from it. As long as the template is not mistakenly overwritten it is available as an online workform that both automatically lists and fills in the essential fields, and provides reminders of what goes into the other fields of the base record. (For the fixed fields we use macros that automatically fill in all required codes except for the date.) We chose for the template (figure 7-6) the fields from level one and two that we use most frequently for images that are not complicated. There was, of course, never any intent that all of the fields in each level be used for every record; but rather to provide for as many as we could think of, while actually using only those appropriate to the image in hand.

600: Contains: (1) names of persons who actually or probably lived, (2) names of families, (3) names of persons used with the phrase *in fiction, drama, poetry,* etc., and (4) personal author/title subject added entries. ****Image cataloging:** Use |a for names of sitters in portraits (i.e., who the work is about) with |x Portraits; or to name the model in a work that is not a portrait with |e Model. Also can contain name of the person or persons who commissioned the art or built work with |e Patron.

Figure 7-4 | Sample Field Description from Local Application Manual

St. Paul's Church <slide>:	Alexandria, Virginia; Exterior details
St. Paul's Church <slide>:	Baltimore, Maryland; Plans
St. Paul's Church <slide>:	Buffalo, New York; Exteriors
St. Paul's Church <slide>:	Brighton, England; Interiors
St. Paul's Church <slide>:	Edenton, North Carolina; Renderings
St. Paul's Church <slide>:	London, England; Furniture
St. Paul's Church <slide>:	Norfolk, Virginia; Exteriors
St. Paul's Church <slide>:	Philadelphia, Pennsylvania; Plans
St. Paul's Church <slide>:	Rome, Italy; Interiors

Figure 7-5 | Sample OPAC Index Screen

```
LTVR DONE                                              AKJ3594
                          NOTIS CATALOGING GUVK
    VR- AKJ3594 FMT F RT g BL m DT 06/15/93 R/DT 06/25/93 STAT nn
    E/L 7 DCF a D/S S SRC d PLACE xx LANG eng MOD   T/AUD   D/CODE s
    DT/1 ???? DT/2 ???? T/MAT s TECH n GOVT   A/MAT   R/TIME nnn
    ME/B 0

    040: :     |a VA@ |c VA@
    049: :     |a VA@
    099/1: :   |a (local call number)
    100:1 :    |a (Architect, last name first), |d (dates).
    245:10:    |a (Title) |h [slide] ; |b (city, state/country) : |p (image type).
    260: :     |c (date).
    300/1: :   |a 1 slide: |b (col./b&w)
    520/1: :   |a (slide description).
    510/2:3:   |a (source).
    654/1: :   |a (Subject tracing, repeat field as necessary). |2 aat
    851/1: :   |a (address).
```

```
LTVR DONE                                              AKJ3594
                        NOTIS COPY HOLDINGS GUVK

    VR VM
    (Architect, last name first), (dates).
     (Title) <slide> : (city, state/country) ; (image type). -- (date).
    STATUS a DT 06/15/93 AD none
    NOTES
    001 0A CN |a visr,cat |b (call number)          |d 06/15/93
        NOTES |a template record for slide cataloging
```

Figure 7-6 | *VIRGO* Template

For name authority work we must first rely on the records in *VIRGO*, regardless of whether our previous image collection records are more complete. These are either Library of Congress name authority records from OCLC or locally established headings. In the past if we did not find a name in UVa's local catalog we checked OCLC, which verified about 40 percent of the names we needed. Consultation with other visual resources curators has confirmed that RLIN with its Avery records is a better choice for architects' names. In addition, we rely on the *Macmillan Encyclopedia of Architects*, Thieme-Becker, Benezit, Colvin, Withey, *ProFile, Contemporary Architects*, and the Avery catalog and periodical indices, all of which are happily available outside our door in the reference area of the library.[5] We can also consult our manual authority file of architects and firms, compiled over the last eleven years, for names that do not appear in *VIRGO*.

For subject authority we use, nearly exclusively thus far, the *Art and Architecture Thesaurus*.[6] Having the electronic version is a considerable improvement over the hardcopy. The ability to search, display notes, and paste the chosen term into the record while still in *VIRGO* is a significant time-saver. After consulting with catalogers in the library's Special Collections Department, and remembering many discussions at AAT workshops and conference sessions, we chose to use single terms rather than to construct strings of terms. In light of our staffing situation, our planned use of student catalogers, and our decision not to contribute to OCLC, our overriding principle was to keep it simple. For that reason we also abandoned the idea of trying to use *Library of Congress Subject Headings* fairly early on.[7] The AAT is much more appropriate to our situation than is LCSH, and provides the detailed level of access that is required to effectively locate images.

Conclusion

A year into implementation we still consider our MARC project to be a work in progress. Over 4,100 records were input from mid-June 1993 to mid-June 1994, nearly all of it by one half-time library assistant. A student assistant who had cataloged on paper for us previously has recently been learning the new system and is pleased with the reduction in duplicate effort and paperwork; it is no longer necessary to write down all of the cataloging information on a piece of paper and then transfer it to card stock using a typewriter and photocopier. Steps have been eliminated and online authority records (both name and AAT) have enabled us to create records more quickly. Research remains the most time-consuming part of the process. At some point we will probably indulge in a retrospective conversion project, but that will require additional staff and workstations. In the meantime, our older records are still available in our card catalog; and new images added to the collection are added only to *VIRGO*.

There are problems and questions remaining, of course. One is the need for a linking mechanism for architecture (and complicated art) records to enable us to connect parts, pieces, wings, remodellings, interiors, exteriors, landscaping, plans, drawings, etc., to the whole; buildings to a complex; or illustrations/illuminations to a book. Collection-level records do not provide enough detail for most images. Item-level records are necessarily repetitious and create too many screens of OPAC indexes. It seems that it might be more appropriate to have a different type of record, one where there is basic information about the structure or complex (like the current MARC record) from which hang records or fields for each view. These records or fields would have additional information about the specific view and could be organized or grouped thematically and be searched online—yet would somehow eliminate the long indexes in the OPAC. This sort of arrangement could also work for parts of altarpieces, details of paintings, illuminated manuscripts, or even books within a series needing

analytics. The AVIADOR project at the Avery Library created a 789 field that goes a long way toward solving this problem, although it lacks an essential subject subfield(s); and the SPIRO project at the University of California–Berkeley could also be a prototype.[8]

Perhaps even more important is the need for MARC fields to be defined more flexibly, and for bibliographic utility input standards and AACR2 rules to be revised to accommodate our access needs and staffing levels. The seminal work done by the ARLIS/UK and Eire Joint Working Group to revise AACR2 to meet the needs of visual resources collections must be joined.[9] The utilities will continue to think of our records as substandard until we devise the standards; and we will not be able to easily share our cataloging work until we can contribute to the utilities. The very near future includes a picture of images embedded in online catalogs. It should be the job of visual resources curators to define how these images are described and how access to them is provided for patrons. There is, indeed, too much visual information available for us to be able to operate in vacuums anymore; and our patrons need more access points than we can keep in our heads.

NOTES

1. See in particular these publications of conference sessions or workshops: Brent Maddox, "Toward Automation—Implementing Standards in Visual Resource Collections," *Art Documentation* 4, no. 2 (summer 1985): 71–72; Cathy Whitehead and Amy Lucker, "Workshop: Non-Book Database Design," *Art Documentation* 6, no. 2 (summer 1987): 59; Rosann Auchstetter, "MARC-ing the Visual Document: Innovative Efforts in Visual Information Management," *Art Documentation* 6, no. 2 (summer 1987): 65–66; Christine Hennessey, "Creating a Database for Art Objects: The National Museum of American Art's Inventory of American Sculpture," *Art Documentation* 6, no. 4 (winter 1987): 147–149; Annette Melville, "One-Stop Shopping: Access to Visual and Archival Materials—Use of VIM and AMC Formats," *Art Documentation* 7, no. 2 (summer 1988): 47; Micheline Nilsen, "Visual Resources Collection Management: Cataloging Procedures and Other Issues for Automated Systems," *Art Documentation* 7, no. 2 (summer 1988): 51; Jeanne M. Keefe, "The Use of the Visual Materials Format for a Slide Library Integrated into an OPAC," in *Beyond the Book: Extending MARC for Subject Access*, edited by Toni Petersen and Pat Molholt (Boston: G. K. Hall, 1990, 25–41); Janet L. Stanley, "Symposium: Implementing the Art and Architecture Thesaurus—Controlled Vocabulary in the

Extended MARC Format," *Art Documentation* 8, no. 3 (fall 1989): 121–124; Maryly Snow, "Visual Depictions and the Use of MARC: A View from the Trenches of Slide Librarianship," *Art Documentation* 8, no. 4 (winter 1989): 186–190; James Bower, "Sharing the Wealth: Software for MARC-based Cataloging of Visual Materials," *VRA Bulletin* 17, no. 3 (fall 1990): 23–26; Phyllis Pivorun, "Summary of a Pilot Slide Automation Project Using the NOTIS On-line Library System," *VRA Bulletin* 17, no. 4 (winter 1990): 18–19; Phyllis Pivorun, "Why and How MARC Is Being Used for Automating the Architecture Slide Collection at Clemson University," *VRA Bulletin* 18, no. 2 (summer 1991): 18–21; and Susanne Warren, "Workshop—Using the AAT: Practical Applications," *Art Documentation* 11, no. 2 (summer 1992): 63.

2. Jerome McGann, "The Complete Writings and Pictures of Dante Gabriel Rossetti: A Hypermedia Research Archive," *Art Documentation* 12, no. 4 (winter 1993): 155–158.

3. Ann Abid, Eleanor Scheifele, Sara Jane Pearman, et al., "Planning for Automation of the Slide and Photograph Collections at the Cleveland Museum of Art: A Draft MARC/Visual Materials Record," *VRA Bulletin* 19, no. 2 (summer 1992): 17–21; James Bower, "The Visual Resources Association MARC Mapping Project," *Visual Resources* 9, no. 3 (1993): 291–327; *Online Systems Audiovisual Media Format,* 2nd ed. (Dublin, Ohio: Online Computer Library Center, 1992); Jeffrey J. Ross, *Cataloging Architectural Drawings: A Guide to the Fields of the RLIN Visual Materials (VIM) Format as Applied to the Cataloging Practices of the Avery Architectural and Fine Arts Library, Columbia University, Developed for Project AVIADOR,* Topical Papers, no. 1 (Tucson: Art Libraries Society of North America, 1992); Deirdre Stam and Ruth Palmquist, *SUART: A MARC-based Information Structure and Data Dictionary for the Syracuse University Art Collection* (Syracuse: Museum Computer Network, 1989).

4. Michael Gorman and Paul W. Winkler, eds., *Anglo-American Cataloguing Rules,* 2nd ed., 1988 revision (Chicago: American Library Association, 1988).

5. *Macmillan Encyclopedia of Architects,* ed. Adolf Placzek (New York: Free Press, 1982); Ulrich Thieme and Felix Becker, *Allgemeines lexikon der bildenden Kunstler von der antike bis zur gegenwart* (Leipzig: W. Engelmann, 1907–1950); Emmanuel Benezit, *Dictionnaire critique et documentaire des peintres, sculpteurs, dessinateurs . . .* (Paris: Librairie Grund, 1976); Howard Colvin, *A Biographical Dictionary of English Architects, 1660–1840* (Cambridge: Harvard University Press, 1954); Henry Withey, *Biographical Dictionary of American Ar-*

chitects (deceased) (Los Angeles: New Age Pub. Co., 1956); *ProFile: Professional File, Architectural Firms* (Philadelphia: Archimedia, 1978–1993); *Contemporary Architects,* ed. Ann Lee Morgan and Colin Naylor (Chicago: St. James, 1987); *Avery Obituary Index of Architects* (Boston: G. K. Hall, 1980); *Avery Index to Architectural Periodicals* (Boston: G. K. Hall, 1968); *Catalog of the Avery Memorial Architectural Library of Columbia University* (Boston: G. K. Hall, 1968 and supplements).

6. *Art and Architecture Thesaurus: The Authority Reference Tool,* Version 1.0 (New York: Oxford University Press, 1992). Second edition available spring 1994.

7. Library of Congress, Subject Cataloging Division, *Library of Congress Subject Headings,* 12th ed. (Washington, D.C.: Cataloging Distribution Service, Library of Congress, 1989), v. 1–3.

8. Ross, *Cataloging Architectural Drawings,* 52; and Maryly Snow, "SPIRO:FAQ; Frequently Asked Questions about SPIRO," *Visual Resources Association Bulletin* 21, no. 2 (summer 1994): 14.

9. Roy McKeown and Jane Savidge, "ARLIS/UK and EIRE Joint Working Group Revision of *AACR2* to Accommodate Cataloging of Art Reproductions: A Document for Discussion by LABL," *VRA Bulletin* 20, no. 4 (winter 1993): 19–27.

BIBLIOGRAPHY

Bales, Kathleen. "The USMARC Formats and Visual Materials." *Art Documentation* 8, no. 4 (winter 1989): 183–185.

Barnett, Patricia J. "Subject Analysis and AAT/MARC Implementation." *Art Documentation* 8, no. 4 (winter 1989): 171–172.

Hennessey, Christine. "The Inventory of American Sculpture: MARC-ing Realia." In *Beyond the Book: Extending MARC for Subject Access,* edited by Toni Petersen and Pat Molholt, 145–155. Boston: G. K. Hall, 1990.

Parker, Elisabeth Betz. *LC Thesaurus for Graphic Materials: Topical Terms for Subject Access.* Washington, D.C.: Library of Congress, 1987.

Pearman, Sara Jane. "An Opinion: Mumblings of a Slide Librarian." *Art Documentation* 7, no. 4 (winter 1988): 145–146.

Petersen, Toni, and Pat Molholt, eds. *Beyond the Book: Extending MARC for Subject Access.* Boston: G. K. Hall, 1990.

MARCing Architecture

David Austin

Background

Sir Martin Conway (Lord Conway of Allington), connoisseur, art critic, lecturer, explorer, and politician, began collecting pictures as a kind of *aide memoire* for his study of art. He later found, as do most art historians and critics, that materials of this sort are valuable research and teaching tools when helping others to understand and learn about art. At first he went about his efforts in a casual way during the last decades of the nineteenth century, but two events influenced his life early in the new century. The resulting change in his strategy made him a great benefactor of those whose careers are dedicated to providing visual information to students and scholars.

Sir Martin's long-standing interest in Flemish art led him to attend a special exhibit of paintings by the Van Eyck School, which was displayed in Bruges in 1902. He also attended a symposium associated with the exhibit where he came into contact with scholars of international renown. The experience showed him that art history could be a serious and worthwhile occupation and inspired him to become more inclusive and systematic in gathering materials for his lectures and studies.

The second influential event bearing on Sir Martin's collecting habits was a chance meeting with Robert Witt and his wife in Siena. Over dinner one evening Sir Martin learned that his newfound friend also collected photographs of works of art.

> Both of us then decided to make a serious business of photograph collecting, the only difference between us being that I collected photographs and prints of works of art of all kinds—architecture, sculpture, painting, the decorative arts of all kinds—and of all periods from prehistoric man down to modern times, while they confined themselves to reproductions of paintings and drawings.[1]

The decision to divide up their worlds of collecting enabled Sir Martin to focus his collecting energies within a narrower area while, at the same time, building a larger, more specialized library of pictures with more depth.

To make his collection comprehensive he sought out and purchased commercially available photographs, view cards, and postcards. He also bought stock-in-trade from the estates of dealers, bid at auctions for other collector's treasures, sought out sale and exhibition catalogs before others began to collect and preserve them, and accumulated the scholarly detritus of antiquarians. If a book or magazine contained some pictures of value to his collection, he cut it out, mounted it on heavy stock and added it to his collection. If the publication contained illustrations on both sides of the pages, he purchased two copies and usually discarded the text. Finally, he attempted to purchase every major publication issued before the Great War in his effort to make his collection as complete as possible.

In 1931 Lord Conway presented his drawings and photographs to the University of London, where it became part of the Courtauld Institute of Art. The collection is very much alive today and continues to grow through purchase, staff photographic expeditions, and donations from scholars and other collectors. It currently contains approximately one million images and is an important international research collection for the study of architecture and other aspects of art history. Its contents also hold value for others who rely upon visual information to supplement their studies and illustrate their research.

The Conway Library provided access to its photographs at its London location in Portman Square until 1989 when it, along with the other components of the Courtauld Institute, moved to newly remodeled quarters within Somerset House. The organization of the library's contents continued to follow the pattern established by its founder. Standard-size Library Bureau pamphlet boxes contain the mounted photographs, along with an occasional periodical article, brochure, or detailed guidebook, which will be interfiled among the photographs to which it is related. The boxed photographs are shelved by category: architecture, architectural drawings, sculpture, medieval arts, and manuscripts.[2]

A brief overview of the collection shows that subdivision by country and general period begins the sorting process for photographs of architecture and sculpture. Architecture associated with the British Isles breaks down by cathedrals, other sacred establishments (i.e., monasteries and abbeys), and then secular buildings, all of which are grouped alphabetically by site or city within their respective categories. For the rest of the world, alphabetical listing of sacred and secular buildings within city or site, from A to Z, determines the order of the photographs on the shelves. Photos of architectural drawings and sculpture subdi-

vide into anonymous works following those by named artists (again alphabetically organized). The pattern of organization for medieval arts begins with a generic typological division (i.e., sculpture, ironworks, etc.) and period. Once again, anonymous works follow works by known artists and craftspeople.

Until 1987 users had access to the photographs only at the Conway Library where professionals stood ready to orient them to the organization of the collection. The staff also helped researchers obtain photographic copies from negatives whose copyright the library held. Students and faculty of the Courtauld Institute constituted the largest number of users of the visual information, but visitors from the United Kingdom, and often from overseas, found visiting the collection worth the investment of time and money. Occasionally the Conway librarian and his or her staff attempted to compile indexes, either on three-inch-by-five-inch cards or sometimes on personal computers, to parts of the collection. However, the pressures of workload and time prohibited the construction of a comprehensive index to the whole collection.

Emmett Publishing's microfiche of the Conway Library changed all that.[3] Those seeking visual information about architecture and art objects will now find the collection more accessible in the published version, but finding specific items within it may be more difficult without the helpful staff standing at their side. As accessibility to the collection grows we may assume that more art and architectural historians and their students will use it, but will those from other disciplines also seek information here? Use by non-Courtauld Institute students and staff increased after the library's move to Somerset House, next to King's College of the University of London. General user studies available to us also suggest that scholars in a variety of fields other than art and architecture desire greater access to visual information.[4] We may speculate with some certainty that there will be many users who lack skills to ferret out hidden information in the Conway Library Microfiche. Moreover, users from other scholarly disciplines will probably apply knowledge from their own fields when they search for information in the collection. Unfortunately, one cannot predict with any certainty how scholars will use it or what kinds of information they will seek until large database indexes, such as that proposed for the Conway Library Microfiche, provide transaction logs for analysis.

Though the needs of many of the potential users of the Conway Library Microfiche cannot be fully anticipated, work has been undertaken to compile a database index to the photos. A fresh look at the contents of the photographs will help to build an index that will be comprehensive and flexible enough to attempt to answer as yet unasked questions from those seeking images. Let us look, for example, at pictures related to the *Cathedral of Notre Dame* in Paris. In the collection, major structures, such as Notre Dame, begin with ground plans. In this case there are three, one by R. N. Hadcock, an anonymous one, and one from Tome II of François Blondel's *Cours d'architecture enseigné dans l'Académie royal d'architecture* (Paris, 1675–1683). Because *Notre Dame* existed for several centuries before the invention of photography, earlier documentation of the building must include drawings, engravings, lithographs, and paintings. Some of these are from publications, such as Maurice Vloberg's *Notre-Dame de Paris et les vœu de Louis XIII: la vie de la cathédrale aux XVIIe et XVIIIe siècle racontée par l'image* (Paris, 1926), Claude Chastillon's *Typographie françoise, ou Representation de plusieurs villes, bourgs, chasteux, maisons de plaisance, ruines & vestiges d'antiquitez du royaume de France* (Paris, 1655), and Jean Marot's *L' Architecture françoise, ou Recueil des plans, élévations, coupes et profils des églises, palais, hôtels & maisons particulières de Paris* (Paris, c. 1680, also known as *La Grand Marot*). Other visual documents are from drawings and paintings in collections held by the Musée Carnavalet and the Bibliothèque National, Cabinet des Estampes.

When photographs of the cathedral make their appearance in the collection, several generations of visual documentation are represented. Some of them bear the byline of a professional photographer, such as James Austin, Achille Quinet, or Tim Benton. Others were purchased from the Alinari Archive or transferred from the Royal Institute of British Architects. Fragments from the cathedral are also represented by photographs from the Musée de Cluny or the Metropolitan Museum of Art in New York. Access to the image must be provided by the name of the structure and by the names of the various people, corporate bodies, and titles mentioned earlier if the work is worth the effort.

In general, series of images of buildings begin with general views, move on to individual exterior facades, then on to interiors if they warrant interest. For simple structures, such as rural pilgrims' chapels, only a few images may exist, but for large, intricate buildings, such as *Chartres Cathedral,* more than two thousand may be present.

Drawings of a particular structure, whether sketches or formal composite plans, particularly if they are by named architects, may be found in any of the first three parts. Many of these documents may be owned by an archive or a library. Credit must be given to their owners, as with Lemercier's drawings of the Musée du Louvre's *Pavillon de l'Horloge* held by Stockholm's Nationalmuseum. When the museum's inventory number appears on the frame, it, too, will be included to provide access for the users of the microfiche. Drawings can be part of museum or gallery exhibitions. This is the case with Robert de Cotte's drawings for the *Hôtel de Toulouse,* which are housed in the Berlin Kunstbibliothek, but were exhibited as part of *200 Französisches Meister Zeichnungen* at Carlsruhe, Bremen, and Berlin in 1972. Once again, access to the drawings must be provided in various ways, including the name and place of the institution that possesses the drawings, and the name of the exhibits in which they may have appeared.

Once inside a structure such as a cathedral or abbey church, a number of sculptures may be encountered. These, along with other freestanding, three-dimensional works placed in parks, squares, and libraries, and on fountains, will be found in parts one, two, and four of the microfiche. Access to them must be provided by name of a sculptor or sculptors, name(s) of subject(s), particularly if the work is intended to be a monument or portrait, or title of the piece, and its location. For example, the results of a search for Gioacchino Rossini's sepulchral monument will be enhanced by an answer that contains the name of its sculptor, Giuseppe Cassioli, and its location in the north aisle of Florence's *Santa Croce.* Similarly, someone seeking a picture of Jean Caffieri's bust of *Jean de Rotrou* will find value in an answer that points out that the work appears in both a plaster version in the Bibliothèque Sainte-Geneviève and in a marble version in the Théâtre française.

Other parts of an interior, which are not necessarily fixed to the fabric of a structure, such as church furniture, appear in part five of the microfiche. Many of these are not easy to find without a detailed index. For example, a more than cursory scan of the collection revealed Guillaume I Coustou's marble statue of *Louis XIII* in part four, and the reliefs on the choir screen begun by Jean Ravy and completed by Jean Bouteiller and an article about "Notre Dame's Vanished Glass" by Henry Krauss in two parts of the *Gazette des Beaux-Arts* (September 1955, 131–148 and February 1967, 65–78) in part five. For well-documented, older English churches, numerous pieces of church furniture, such as fonts, rood screens, and sword rests, will be scattered over several different microfiche. A researcher coming to the collection without considerable foreknowledge and experience will find them only by accident.

Planning the Index

An analysis of 2 percent of the images randomly selected from the microfiche revealed nine basic data fields necessary to provide access to the content of the images whose sources are so varied. Not all fields will be required all the time for all images and objects. Those identified in the sampling were: object name, personal name, object site, object date, form of representation, source of representation, a memo field, subject access to the object, and microfiche location of the image. Only information presented on the microfiche frame, such as words and phrases of import that appear on the photographs or are written on their mounts, will be considered in the indexing project as explicit information for access to the images. The visual content of the photograph will provide any implicit information for access.

Object Name (240, 243, 245, 246, 740)

The name of an object is often more important than the name of its creator, that is, the person or body that possesses primary intellectual responsibility for its creation. This is especially true of elements of the built environment that were constructed before the eighteenth century. Full names in the vernacular will be used whenever possible. The index will follow the practice related to the cataloging of music in which the caption information found on the frame will supply the title (245, 246).[5] Additionally, a title supplied from a standard reference source (240, 243), such as Nikolaus Pevsner's *Buildings of England* series, the volumes of the *Guida d'Italia* published by the Touring Club Italiano, the *Dictionnaire des Églises de France,* or George Dehio's *Handbuch der Deutschen Kunstdenkmäler,* will gather "together all catalogue entries for a work when various manifestations of it have appeared under various titles."[6] Confusion in alphabetical sorting will be avoided by spelling out all abbreviations.

The object name data field will also include subfields to contain such data as aspect (exterior or interior relationship to the viewer of the object) (|b),

subsidiary or subordinate section of the object (including chapels within a church), and part of the object that may make up an ornamental or structural component on the object (|p). Subdivision by aspect may reduce the amount of information the researcher will need to filter in a search for a particular view or set of views. For objects less elaborate than buildings, aspect, subsection, and even part may be superfluous.

Personal Name (100, 110, 600, 700, 710)

Names of people who possess primary responsibility for the creation of objects, whether individual (100) or corporate (110), may play a less prominent role in indexing than they do for bibliographical information. Often we may not know who created something, but we do know for whom it was created or whom the object depicts. The name of a patron (700 |r), rather than the architect or sculptor, may be more important to a researcher from another discipline. The data field for the name of the creator (100) will include biographical date(s) (|d), the term defining the relationship of the creator to the object (i.e., architect, sculptor, iron smith as supplied by the *Art and Architecture Thesaurus*) (|e), and any modifications that may reflect probable, but as yet unverified, names, such as "Delvaux, Laurent (?)" or "Torrigiano, Pietro, attr." or a group name such as "Canova, Antonio, Workshop of" (|g), even though they may be altered by future scholarship.

Information related to the identification of the person or persons who posed for or were the subject of a piece of sculpture will also be provided as an additional access point (600, |d, |e) for those seeking an image of a person rather than an individual work of art.

Object Site (752)

Location of an object often provides important modifications of the object's name, particularly when the object bears a frequently used, although important, name, such as *Notre Dame, Saint Mary's,* or *Santa Maria.* Many cities in France and Belgium contain a church bearing the name *Notre Dame* (Bodilis, Jugon, and Poissy, to name a few). The index must provide for a distinction between them. Even the distinction of the type of church (cathedral, parish church, abbey church, etc.) lacks enough specificity to differentiate between the *Notre Dame* Cathedrals of Paris and Amiens.

Additional access to locations of objects, particularly those smaller than buildings, to which objects may have migrated from their original locations will also be provided. Location will be presented in a repeatable secondary object site field (852) for those who look for such objects as marble busts, capitals from ruined buildings, or ivory diptychs, in either their original or later settings. The repetition of the field may also be of use to the researcher who may want to trace the provenance of an object from its original site, through various collectors' hands, to its current home, perhaps a museum far from its original site. Consider also the location of coins or medals. Few of them probably will remain in the city where they were originally minted, but such information may be of importance to a researcher who is seeking to establish the relative importance to a community of a person whose profile fills one side of the coin.

Object site (752 |a, |b, |c, |d, |e) will include fields for country, subordinate part of country (i.e., county, department, region, state, etc.), city, and landmark. Refinement by landmark part may occasionally be required to provide better access. Attention to site hierarchy not only makes a distinction between Cranbrook, in Kent, U.K., and Cranbrook, in Michigan, U.S.A., but also separates the Newport in Essex from the Newport on the Isle of Wight. Vernacular nomenclature of the country where the object is located will be preferred. For example: France—Calvados—Caen—Abbaye Saint-Étienne. The practice follows that established by the Getty Art History Information Program and its *Thesaurus of Geographic Names,* except that it goes beyond the city name and attempts to establish uniform names of landmarks or institutions. When an object is no longer located at its original site (as in the case of carved stonework from demolished buildings, ivory carvings, etc.), the field indicating object site will be repeated as often as necessary to place the object in its original city and at any subsequent site indicated on the image or in the photomount annotations.

Object Date (240 |f, 243 |f, 245 |f, |g)

The Conway Library seems to assume that many who use the collection bring experience and information with them in their search for images of architecture and sculpture. Therefore the library places minimal emphasis on incorporating dates of construction information on the photomounts. Dates associated with the objects in the photos generally appear as spans or years, century or centuries, and even questionable or probable forms.

The date field of the index recognizes that times associated with art objects are not always presented to us in nice tidy packages and may be fuzzy and liable to future modification, or even correction. Construction of cathedrals may span several centuries, dates of other objects may be deduced only through a knowledge of a craftsman's career, or we may only be able to attribute a general date or span of dates based on stylistic comparison. A date field for an index such as the one under discussion must tolerate a kind of vagueness and provide not only for a single date, but also for spans of years, multiple listings of centuries, and even questionable dates. As a reaction to the lack of emphasis on dates, the index will not include a separate field for dates of construction or manufacture (260), but will include any important temporal information in the object name (245 |f or |g) or uniform object name fields (240 |f, or 243 |f).

Form of Image (007 /01, /02)

Although images represented in the Conway Library are primarily represented by photographs, some of which may have originally appeared in other sources (such as periodical articles, exhibition catalogs, sales catalogs, and books), reference to such sources should be indicated. For purposes of the index, photographs that have not been published as part of a book, periodical, exhibition catalog, or auction catalog will be called photographs (007/02). Other types of photographs that have previously appeared in publications (books, sales catalogs, etc.) will be referred to as published photographs. Image types may also be from a variety of nonphotographic processes, including engravings, sketches, and paintings. Form of representation (007/01) presents three choices for the indexer: photograph, drawing, or painting.

Source of Image (503, 581)

In all cases the index will indicate the source of the illustration when it is identified in the microfiche frame (503, 581). The Conway Library owns copyright for many of the negatives and will print them for a nominal fee. They are marked by a six-digit figure stamped on the mount and will be listed as "Conway no. _____" in the source of representation field. Many others indicate a source such as "Tim Benton negative" or "Alinari Photo Archive." The source field (503 or 581) will list author and title (and page number if necessary) information from publications; title, institution, city, and date for exhibition catalogs; and auction house and date, or some other clear indication of marketing status, for images from sales catalogs.

Memo (500)

A memo field (500) may be included in the index. This field is conceived as a kind of catchall for such things as dimensions, medium, or provenance note, which may sometimes be provided by caption on the photomount. It should again be stressed that no information, except that on the photograph itself or added to the mounting stock, will be added here or anywhere else in the index record.

Subject Terms (654, 655)

Access will be provided to images in the collection by topical means (654), similar to the manner of subject access for printed material. Fortunately, nearly all the objects presented in the microfiche images may be described by terms selected from the hierarchies of the various facets of the *Art and Architecture Thesaurus* (AAT).[7] The AAT provides several advantages for subject retrieval of image content on the microfiche. First, it provides consistency for both index constructors and for index users because it is a controlled vocabulary. The hierarchical structure of the AAT reflects the arrangement, whole to part and general to specific, of the frames on the microfiche. Solid support in North America and growing recognition by major documentation centers in England and on the Continent indicate that those who apply the terminology see its advantages. Efforts to construct a multilingual version will expand its usefulness. Even the differences between American English and Anglo English terms and spellings are recognized by the *Thesaurus,* and appropriate alternatives are provided to satisfy the needs of those two user communities.

The Conway Library Microfiche Index will apply appropriate terms selected from the *Art and Architecture Thesaurus* in a hierarchical fashion (654) and to such extent as is appropriate to the degree of specificity of the image represented in the microfiche. For example, "City views" or "Assembly halls" will be sufficient for some images, but the string: "Cathedrals," "Crossings," "Columns," and "Capitals" will be necessary for others. Occasionally some images may also

warrant iconographic reference, such as "angel with rebec." Iconographic interpretation may be provided on the photomounts, but the form of its appearance in the subject field will be provided by ICONCLASS, an international standard vocabulary for such information (655).[8]

Fiche Location (099)

The index format provides a location key by part number, fiche number, frame number, and, for those frames that present more than one image, sector letter (099).

Construction of the Index

An extracted version of MARC appeared ideal to hold all the information necessary to provide full access to the photos in the Conway Library Microfiche. Unfortunately, large-scale data storage networks that use MARC as their foundation and currently provide shared cataloging and access are not yet capable of providing a fully relational search engine for users. Therefore a relational database manager was necessary to build an index powerful enough to provide access to the richness of the Conway Library Microfiche.

Among the database managers surveyed for the purpose, dBase IV proved to be the best among those commonly available. For those complex structures that contain images distributed over several parts of the microfiche, dBase IV has the ability to draw relational links between a master record and all those that relate to it. Various people who somehow were responsible for the creation of an object, whether they are architects, sculptors, benefactors, or subjects of a funeral monument, must be related to the object, and dBase IV can link them to the master record. A large number of records can be handled by the database manager, and it can contain both fixed and variable fields. Essential information can be entered in named fields of fixed lengths, which can be determined through a sampling of information supplied on the microfiche. Less essential information, which may not always need to be included, can be entered into a memo area of variable length. Mixing field sizes in this manner will conserve electronic storage space.

Authority files also will be constructed to ensure the accuracy and consistency of information recorded in the index. Some names required for access to the images on the microfiche may already exist in authority files of the United States Library of Congress and the Avery Library, and the resources of the Getty Art History Information Program's *Union List of Artist Names* (ULAN) will be consulted.[9] Other names will require standard reference tools to determine a preferred form and provide variations of the form.

In figure 8-1, Italy, Tuscany, and *Santa Maria della Pieve,* respectively, will be listed as alternate terms for Italia, Toscana, and Pieve de Santa Maria in the authority file of the Conway Library Microfiche Index Project.

Complete access to all the information in figure 8-2 requires that the name of the exhibition, the gallery where it was held, and the dates of the event (all listed in the Sources of Image field) must be found by users.

In figure 8-3, Mossehaus is the preferred object name, but *Verlagsbebäude Rudolf Mosse* appears as an alternate version in the authority file. If a person using the index asks for information related to "Neutra, Richard Joseph, 1892–1970, Architect," "Benton, Tim, Photographer," "Hajos, Elisabeth Maria, Author," or "Zahn, Leopold, 1890–, Author," relational links will provide access to the image. Likewise a user looking for all photographs from *Berliner Architektur der Nachkriegszeit* found in the Conway Library Microfiche will find them through links between the monograph title and images in the collection.

The Future of the Index

The index described here was designed to provide access to the large body of images available in the Conway Library Microfiche. The product is, at this writing, a commercial Web site, http://www.emmettpub. co.uk, accessible by password as provided by the pub-

---

Uniform Object Name [240]: **Santa Maria, Pieve (Arezzo).** *Aspect* [|b]: **Interior. To East** *Object Part* [|p]: **Nave.**
Object Name [245]: **Santa Maria della Pieve.**
Location [752]: *Country* [|a]: **Italia.** *Part* [|b]: **Toscana.** *City* [|c]: **Arezzo.**
Image Type [300]: *Extent* [|a]: **2 frames.** *Type* [|b]: **Interior photos.**
Source of Image [503]: **Conway Library; No. 040589**
Memo [500]: **Also known as Santa Maria della Pieve.**
Term [654]: **Parish churches ; Naves**
Fiche Location [099]: **1/0780:26**

Figure 8-1 | Screen Showing Alternate Terms

Agent: Name [100]: **Gabo, Naum.** *Date(s)* [|d]: **1890-1977.** *Role* [|e]: **Costume designer.**
Uniform Object Name [240]: **Chatte, La.** *Date* [|f]: **1926.** *Part* [|p]: **Costume design.**
Medium [|h]: **Pencil and graph paper.**
Object Name [245]: **Costume sketch for 'La Chatte'.**
Location [752]: *Country* [|a]: **United Kingdom.** *Part* [|c]: **Greater London.** *City* [|d]: **London.**
Image Type [300]: *Extent* [|a]: **1 frame.** *Type* [|b]: **Black-and-white Drawing.** *Medium* [|3]: **Pencil on graph paper.**
Source of Image [581]: **From: Naum Gabo. The Constructive Process. Tate Gallery, 1976-1977.**
Terms [654]: **Ballets. Costume designs.**
Terms [654]: **Art museums. Exhibition catalogs.**
Additional Site [852]: *Country* [|a]: **United Kingdom.** *Part* [|c]: **Greater London.** *City* [|d]: **London.** Site [|e]: **Tate Gallery.**
Fiche Location [099]: **4/1112:56**

Figure 8-2 | Screen Showing Image Source Data for Exhibitions

---

Agent [100]: Name: **Mendelsohn, Erich.** *Date(s)* [|d]: **1887-1953.** *Role* [|e]: **Architect.**
Uniform Object Name [240]: **Mossehaus.** *Date* [|f]: **1921-1923.** *Part* [|p]: **Exterior.**
Object Name [245]: **Mossehaus.**
Location [752]: *Country* [|a]: **Deutschland.** *Part* [|c]: **Berlin.** *City* [|d]: **Berlin.**
Image Type [300]: *Extent* [|a]: **1 frame.** *Type* [|b]: **Exterior photo.** *Medium* [|3]: **book illustration.**
Memo [500]: **Negative for photo by Tim Benton. Co-architect of Mossehaus was Richard Neutra. Building also known as Verlagsbebäude Rudolf Mosse.**
Source of Image [581]: *Berliner Architektur der Nachkriegszeit* (1923), by E. M. Hajos and L. Zahn.
Terms [654]: **Publishing offices.**
Added Agent [700]: **Neutra, Richard Joseph,** *Date(s)* [|d]: **1892-1970.** *Role* [|e]: **Architect.**
Added Agent [700]: **Hajos, Elisabeth Maria,** *Role* [|e]: **Author.**
Added Agent [700]: **Zahn, Leopold,** *Date(s)* [|d]: **1890- .** *Role* [|e]: **Author.**
Variant Object Name [740]: **Verlagsbebäude Rudolf Mosse.**
Fiche Location [099]: **2/1130:88**

Figure 8-3 | Screen Showing Use of the Memo Field

lisher of the microfiche. In addition to providing access to specific images, the index can also serve as an electronic reference tool for other managers of visual information collections, because it uses personal names, names of objects, and site names in a consistent fashion. Variants of these names and sites will also be available as alternative searching terms, but only one will be used as the preferred authority through the index.

The concept of shared access to information about objects and images currently receives a great deal of attention, especially in the museum community.[10] The format used in constructing the Conway Library Microfiche Index is a step toward a cooperative database for museum and academic facilities. Its simplicity allows flexibility in a way that traditional, full-level cataloging cannot. Institutions that include only pictures of an object, rather than the object itself, will probably be satisfied with a simplified, minimal-level record. Those institutions that own the object, however, will want to expand the minimal-level record to include information learned through firsthand inspection of the object. If they rely upon an in-house system for access to information about their holdings, they may enter confidential data, such as name of donor or the object's insurance valuation, in additional fields that can be protected by secure passwords. Finally, for those agencies committed to Machine-Readable Cataloging (MARC) for access to information, the format of the index may easily be mapped to either USMARC or UNIMARC information structures.

NOTES

1. Sir Martin Conway (of Allington), *Episodes in a Varied Life* (London: Country Life, 1932), 106.

2. Lord Conway's original collection did not include manuscript photographs. They were a later addition that although considerably strengthening the library's holdings, fall outside the scope of this study.

3. The 1987 publication followed the organization of the photographs as they exist at the library. It is available in six parts: I. Architecture of France and Italy; II. Architecture of the United Kingdom and the rest of the world; III. Architectural drawings; IV. Sculpture; V. Medieval arts; and VI. Manuscripts. The 1993 update deepens coverage of some structures and expands photographic documentation to many sites not represented before, particularly in Eastern Europe, and includes many manuscripts that the public sees only briefly when the items appear at auction.

4. Constance C. Gould, *Information Needs in the Humanities: An Assessment* (Stanford, Calif.: Research Libraries Group, 1988); Constance C. Gould and Mark Handler, *Information Needs in the Social Sciences: An Assessment* (Mountain View, Calif.: Research Libraries Group, 1989); Marilyn Schmitt, gen. ed., *Object. Image. Inquiry. The Art Historian at Work* (Santa Monica: The Getty Art History Information Program, 1988), particularly 16–22, 50–53; and Lawrence Dowler, "Conference on Research Trends and Library Resources," *Harvard Library Bulletin*, n.s., 1, no. 2 (summer 1990): 4–14.

5. Information enclosed in square brackets relates to numeric field codes of various MARC formats. Information explaining the codes may be found in: OCLC, Inc., *On-line Systems. Scores Format* (C80-2) and *Sound Recordings Format* (C80-3) (Dublin, Ohio: OCLC, 1980); Linda J. Evans and Maureen O'Brien Will, *MARC for Archival Visual Materials: A Compendium of Practice* (Chicago: Chicago Historical Society, 1988); Deirdre C. Stam and Ruth Palmquist, *SUART: A MARC-based Information Structure and Data Dictionary for the Syracuse University Art Collection* (Syracuse: Museum Computer Network, 1989); Patsy Gerstner and Jennifer Compton, *A Manual for Cataloging Historical Medical Artifacts Using OCLC and the MARC Format* (Cleveland: Cleveland Medical Library Association, 1990); and Canadian Centre for Architecture, *Canadian Centre for Architecture Collections Documentation Guide*, 1994.

6. Michael Gorman and Paul W. Winkler, *Anglo-American Cataloguing Rules*, 2nd ed. (Chicago, Ottawa: American Library Association, Canadian Library Association, 1978), 441.

7. *Art and Architecture Thesaurus*, 2nd ed., 5 vols. (New York: Oxford University Press, on behalf of the Getty Art History Information Program, 1994).

8. Henri van de Waal, *ICONCLASS: An Iconographic Classification System;* completed and edited by L. D. Couprie with R. H. Fuchs and E. Tholen (Amsterdam: North-Holland Publishing Company, 1973–1985).

9. *Union List of Artist Names* (New York: G. K. Hall, on behalf of the Getty Art History Information Program, 1994).

10. See in particular papers by Alan Seal, David Bearman, Rachel M. Allen, and Dr. Leonard D. Will, in the section "Bibliographic Database Development and Applications of Systems," in *Sharing the Information Resources of Museums*, Proceedings of the Third Conference of the Museum Documentation Association, York, England, 14–18 September, 1989 (Cambridge: The Association, 1992).

National Gallery of Art Slide Library, Washington, D.C.

9

Gregory P. J. Most

The slide library at the National Gallery of Art was instituted in 1941, the same year the building opened to the public. Originally, the slide library was part of the education division. The mission of the slide library initially was to provide access to images of works of art to the staff of the National Gallery as well as to professors at area colleges. Two separate slide collections were developed, one for staff and one for outside use. Anyone could use the lending collection whenever he or she liked. As the number of slide collections in the area grew and access to images became less difficult, the collections became more expensive to maintain. The cost of both commercially produced and in-house produced slides grew rapidly in the 1980s as did the price of slide mounts and other supplies. Replacement expenditures for lost or stolen slides steadily increased. Staff time devoted to serving outside patrons and maintaining a second collection became unreasonable. The focus of the department changed. In 1989, the department was transferred to the Gallery's library, which already included the photographic archives. In 1992, the lending collection was limited to slides of National Gallery of Art objects

and outside borrowing was achieved by using the interlibrary loan system.

The scope of the staff slide collection is encyclopedic but concentrates heavily on Western art from the late medieval period to the present. Collection strengths include Italian Renaissance and Baroque art, French art of the eighteenth and nineteenth centuries, American art, and the early modern movements. There are a number of special collections. Most important are a spectacular set of slides of illuminated European manuscripts, slides of exhibitions held at the National Gallery since 1971, and the Gowans Collection of Images of North American Living.

Excluding special collections, the holdings number 160,000 slides. The slide library serves the needs of the staff of the Gallery, principally curators, conservators, educators, fellows of the Center for Advanced Study in the Visual Arts, and docents, as well as visiting lecturers and curators. There are over 150 regular staff users. Public users range from students to college professors and museum curators. Around 30,000 slides are circulated per year. There are five professional staff: the chief slide librarian and two associate and two assistant slide librarians. Four volunteers work on average twenty-six hours per week cleaning and filing slides, organizing special collections, and cataloging slides.

The classification system dates to 1948 and is based on a model from the Art Institute of Chicago. It has been modified several times. The arrangement of the slides and retrieval of information was of great concern to the Gallery's first curators and educators. Memoranda dating to 1947 between the curator of education and the slide librarian discuss various manual ways to provide access to the collection. After the transfer of the department to the library in 1989, the importance of providing easy retrieval of slides and information became paramount. This also meant that automation of the collection became a primary concern.

The catalogs of all three library departments are mounted on one system. Each department has a separate account. To be consistent with the primary catalog, the reference library catalog, use of the MARC format was a given. The information is accessible through terminals of our online public access catalog. A reference terminal is located on the circulation desk of the slide library. Users can also gain access to the catalog from any one of sixty-four other terminals located throughout the museum by entering the command /lib and selecting "slide library" from the menu (see figure 9-1). Searching strategies are simple. Information is retrievable by entering a/ for artist names, owner or location of works of art or architecture, and exhibitions (by title). Boolean (b/), keyword (w/), call number (c/), and title (t/) searching is also available and easy to use. Subject (s/) headings include Library of Congress, *Art and Architecture Thesaurus* (AAT), and local subject headings (see figures 9-2 and 9-3).

Use the following commands to access the Slide Library Database:

Artist/Proper   Enter A/artist's name (last name first),
Name Search   city, building name, museum

     Example: A/Tintoretto, Jacopo or A/Venice

Title Search   Enter T/title of the art work or group
                     title

     Example: T/Last Supper or T/Maestà

Subject Search   Enter S/subject term(s)

     Example: S/Landscape France or S/John, the
     Baptist, Saint

Keyword Search   Enter W/keyword(s)

     Example: W/gouache or W/Rembrandt portraits

Boolean Search   Enter B/combine two keywords using
                     'and', 'or', or 'not'

     Example: B/Leonardo and painting B/Paris not
     architecture

It is NOT NECESSARY to CLEAR the screen before or after your search.
To use the Novice User Search System, enter ?

Figure 9-2 | Help Screen

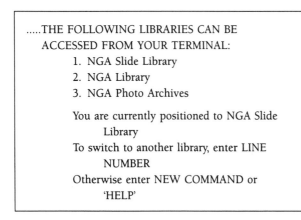

.....THE FOLLOWING LIBRARIES CAN BE
ACCESSED FROM YOUR TERMINAL:
     1. NGA Slide Library
     2. NGA Library
     3. NGA Photo Archives

You are currently positioned to NGA Slide
     Library
To switch to another library, enter LINE
     NUMBER
Otherwise enter NEW COMMAND or
     'HELP'

Figure 9-1 | Library Account Menu Screen

NGA Slide Library - - - - - - VTLS - - - - - - AUTHORS
YOU SEARCHED: a/metropolitan

1.		Metro, Israhel van, c.1445-1503.
2.	115	Metropolitan Museum of Art (New York, N.Y.)
3.	2	Metsu, Gabriel, 1629-1667.
4.	1	Metsu, Gabriel, follower, 1629-1667.
5.		Metsys, Quentin, 1465 or 66-1530.
6.		Meucci, Vincenzo, 1699-1766.
7.	1	Meyer, Alice, 20th century.
8.	160	Meyerhoff, Jane, 20th century.
9.	160	Meyerhoff, Robert E., 20th century.
10.		Meyerhoff, Robert E., Mrs.
11.	1	Meyrl, Johann, active 2nd half of 18th century.
12.		Meytens, Martin van, 1695-1770.
13.	1	Meytens, Martin van, School, 1695-1770.
14.	1	Miami, Florida.
15.		Michael Hasenclever (Gallery).

Enter the line number of the item you want to see, or
PS.......Previous screen   NS...........Next screen
?.....Menu-driven search   HELP..About this screen
.......Any command or /?

Figure 9-3 | A/ Screen

Preparation

Groundwork for the automation of the collection was laid in 1992. The program was implemented in October 1993. The chief slide librarian with the head of the library's cataloging section selected the MARC fields and subfields, and determined which fields would deviate from standard usage and what local fields would be used. Certain fields were used to correspond with the same information recorded in the photographic archives. At a future date the slide and photograph database will be merged, and this step will facilitate the transition. The chief slide librarian frequently consulted with the head of research services regarding access to different types of information in order to make the new catalog as easy to use and as flexible as possible.

As in many other visual collections utilizing the MARC format, the object described in the record is not the object at hand (the slide) but rather the work of art it represents. The information about the surrogate is not the primary interest of the user, but rather the work of art itself. This is the one aspect of the MARC format that most visual resources curators consider the most difficult to overcome. Changing the precepts of MARC's Visual Materials Format from surrogate to original challenges closely held ideas of what MARC is and how it is to be used. When one makes the leap and views MARC as a means to an end or as a tool, the concept becomes logical and the possibility of standardization of records a reality.

Online Computer Library Center's (OCLC) *Audiovisual Media Format* (2nd ed., rev.) and Research Libraries Group's *Visual Materials Format* (6th ed.) were the guidelines for determining what fields and subfields would describe the works of art. Whenever possible, fields and subfields were used as intended. When a deviation from standard use occurred, fields were chosen that most closely matched the original intention. Local needs were a primary factor in many of these decisions.

Record Description

The library had already selected VTLS (Virginia Tech Library Software) as its system software. The slide library adapted its needs to fit with the abilities of the software. An additional challenge to automation was to see if the software could meet the needs of a large visual collection. Initially several test records were input to investigate how the system would index and retrieve information.

Fixed Fields

The system supplies most of the preset, fixed fields we need but certain fields must be entered or changed to suit our requirements. The operator identification number and type of record fields are set at the beginning of each cataloging session. Any other modifications are made manually for each record.

Type of material is changed to "s" for slides. *US-MARC Code List for Countries* is used for the country field. We record any modifications in the office copy of the *Code List* for future reference (for example, Flanders = fl). Beginning and ending creation dates are recorded in the dates fixed field. No B.C.E. dates are used.

Variable Fields

Variable fields described in the following chart assume subfield "a" except where noted. Repeatable fields are indicated by an asterisk (*). Subject added entries are abbreviated as SAE, while AE is used for added entries. Deviations from the format are listed in bold type.

Field **Deviation**	No.	Format of field and subfield[s] **deviations in bold** Explanations and examples
System Control Number	035	System supplied number
Call Number	099	Codes for country, medium, cutter number, subject & title & number This field contains a local, free text call number. IT Ptg M623 RS FA 1

(Continued)

Field Deviation	No.	Format of field and subfield[s] **deviations in bold** Explanations and examples
Personal Name **Artist - Individual**	100 1	Surname, forename, |q qualification |b numeration |c **association,** |d dates. No deviation from standard practices. Association of a work of art to an artist is qualified by using one of three terms: attributed, after, or school. The use of *school* supersedes the use of similar terms, such as *workshop, circle, follower, style, manner,* or *studio,* despite the subtle differences in the terms. The 700 tag is used for former attributions with relator subfield |e **former attribution** following the date field. The 700 tag is also used for collaborating artists. The primary artist (for the 100 field) is chosen by contribution or by alphabetical location. The 700 tag is used for the secondary artist(s) with the addition of the relator subfield |e **collaborator** following the date field. 100 1 Oldenburg, Claes, |d 1929– . 700 Bruggen, Coosje van |d 1942– . |e collaborator.
Corporate Name **Artist - Corporate**	110 2	Name (direct order), |d date of activity. No deviation from standard format. Uses the same format as individual artist, specifying firm active dates when available. Used for firms and manufacturers. 110 2 New Mexico Artisans, Inc. |d firm active 1912–1934. 110 2 Hellmuth, Obata & Kassabaum, |d 1955– .
Title	245	Title |b other title information |p part. Title established by owning institution or conventional use. Following title, |b additional information deviates from standard use. Terms used for information, such as study, sketch, foreign language titles, secondary titles, etc., are listed in parentheses. Second indicator used for number of nonfiling characters.
Edition Statement **Edition, State**	250	Deviates from format. Used for editions of prints, sculpture, or any other object produced in a limited quantity, such as photography and some decorative arts. Different states or proofs of prints also use this tag.
Imprint **Date of Work**	260	|c **Creation date** |g **later date** |e place of manufacture. The creation date is the date or period of a work's completion. If an object is reworked at a later date or set aside for an extended period of time, use subfield |g for that information. When a place of creation or manufacture is relevant to the object's creation, use subfield |e. 260 |c 1959. 260 |c c. 1985.

Field Deviation	No.	Format of field and subfield[s] **deviations in bold** Explanations and examples
		260 |c mid-15th century. 260 |c 1884–5, |g 1918. 260 |c 1747, |e Dresden.
Physical Description **Medium/Dimensions**	300	**Medium & support, |c dimensions.** The medium and support deviates from the standard format because it describes the work of art. The description is listed as completely as possible and is not abbreviated. Dimensions are always listed in height, width, and diameter order (H × W × D), which is not specified unless only one dimension is given and clarity is desired. The use of centimeters is always preferable to inches, and the form of measurement is always listed. The abbreviation for centimeters is always used, but the words *feet* or *inches* are always spelled out. bronze, |c h. 8 feet 3½ inches. oil on canvas transferred from panel: oval, |c 34.5 × 42 cm. watercolor, pen and black ink, with scraping out on cream wove paper, |c 8 × 7 inches. tempera on oak panel, |c d. 45.8 cm. tin-glazed earthenware, |c 5 × 3¼ × 3¼ inches.
Series Statement, Title **Group Title**	440*	Group title or series. This tag is used to link related works, such as studies, models, and sketches for a work of art, series, sketchbooks, dispersed panels from polyptychs, or architectural decorations by a series of artists over a period of time (e.g., *Sistine Chapel*). This record is used in combination with tag 245. Maestà. Course of Empire. Brushstroke Series.
General Notes	*500*	General Notes This field is used for general information that is related to the work at hand. This might include a project description for a building, biographical or genealogical information about a sitter of a portrait, the identification and order of sitters in a group portrait, a description of the work at hand, or some other relevant facts. This field is unformatted and has no subfields.
Exhibitions Note **NGA Exhibition #**	585*	**Cat. # or cat. page #.** The location of a work of art in a National Gallery of Art exhibition catalog is listed in this field. The field is used in conjunction with an exhibition tag (711) listing the official exhibition title (which is often cross-referenced on the authority screen by a brief or more common exhibition title).

(Continued)

Field Deviation	No.	Format of field and subfield[s] **deviations in bold** Explanations and examples
Local Note **Citation Notes**	590*	Name, |c year, number, main work, chapter, verse, etc. Citations used include catalogue raisonné and numbers, Biblical or literary citations, etc., and they are keyword searchable. Benesch, |c 1973, 41. Luke, |c 2:12–15. Ovid, |c Metamorphoses 3:3. Dante, |c Divine Comedy: Inferno 5. Shakespeare, |c Hamlet: act I, scene 3.
Local Note **Inscriptions**	591*	Position, content, and description. Signatures, dates, and any other written information are recorded giving the location of the writing and its content. Signed and dated lower left: "C. Monet 1877" At bottom: *PARVVLE PATRISSA, PATLÆ VIRTVTIS ET HÆRES/ESTO, NIHIL MAIVS/..."*
SAE: Personal name **Person depicted**	600*	Surname, forename, |b numeral, |c associated terms, |d dates. Elizabeth |b I, |c Queen of England, |d 1533–1602. Leman, Mary Elizabeth |q (Betty), |d m. 1965– d. 1979. Treese, Gary George, |c Dr., |d 1947–1990. Luisa da Mantova, |d 13th century. Peter, |c Saint, Apostle. Catherine, |c of Siena, Saint, |d 1347–1380. Moses (Biblical leader). When well-known works of art are depicted in other works of art or for literature frequently used as subject matter in art, use this form. Manet, Edouard, |d 1832–1883. |t Olympia. Dante Alighieri, |d 1265–1321. |t Divine Comedy.
SAE: Corporate name **Place depicted**	610*	**City (Modifier: country or state). |b structure.** Used for the built environment and for views of cities or towns. The subfield for structure lists notable buildings, not a simple house. On rare occasions, a further subdivision may be needed. Use |x. London (England). Paris (France). |b Pont-Neuf. Houston (Texas). |b Penzoil Place. Washington (D.C.). |b National Gallery of Art |x West Building.
SAE: Topical term **General/local subject**	650*	**Subject** |x general subdivision |z geographic subdivision |y **century or period** subdivision

Field **Deviation**	No.	Format of field and subfield[s] **deviations in bold** Explanations and examples
		This tag is used for general subjects, which may be subdivided geographically or by period and which are not in the *Art and Architecture Thesaurus*.
		Portraits |z France |y 19th century. Flowers |x Roses. Mythology |z Greek |x Apollo.
SAE: Geographic name **Geographic place depicted**	651*	Site name (Modifier, e.g., country, state) Used for depictions of elements of the natural environment. Pecos Valley (New Mexico). Rhone River (France). Lago Maggiore (Italy).
SAE: Local **Medium - Region - Period**	690*	**Medium category |z Country |y century or period.** This tag creates additional searching ability. Painting |z United States |y 18th century. Architecture |z Italy |y Early Christian. Sculpture |z Greek |y Hellenistic Period.
SAE: Local **AAT Subject**	695*	Term (modifier, if any). *Art and Architecture Thesaurus* hierarchies are checked for potential subject headings when describing the content of an image. All AAT terms are tagged 695. The form of the heading is modified to conform to departmental standards. Sample terms: De Stijl. Palladian windows. Locks (hydraulic structures). Activists. Exedrae (site elements). Tapestries.
AE: Personal name **Individuals, private owners, collaborating artists**	700*	Surname, forename, |c association, |d dates, |e relator *Association = Attributed School** After* This field is used for collaborating artists, former attributions, and named private collectors. Use subfield |e plus the appropriate relator term for an artist's name. For individual collectors, use subfield |x and Art Collections. Husband-and-wife entries are always made individually and cross-referenced when possible. Family collections or corporate collections use the 710 tag. For NGA objects, see below. Giorgione, |d 1477–1511. |e collaborator. Boucher, François, |d 1703–1770. |e former attribution. Cross, Joseph D., |d 1958– . |x Art Collections. Cross, Joseph D., |c Mrs., |d 1960– . |x Art Collections.

(Continued)

Field **Deviation**	No.	Format of field and subfield[s] **deviations in bold** Explanations and examples
		NGA objects: Major donors to the National Gallery of Art's collections are also noted in the record. The donor's name and dates are listed and |e collector is used. Named funds are not indicated. The 710 field must also be modified (see below). Dale, Chester, |d 1883–1962. |e collector. NGA objects donated by an artist *of* the artist's own work are treated in a different manner. Add the term *collector* in parentheses to subfield |d before the period. Lichtenstein, Roy, |d 1922– (collector). Stieglitz, Alfred, |d 1864–1946 (collector).
AE: Corporate name **Location, owner**	710*2	**Museum** or corporate name, |b subordinate unit. Museums, anonymous private collections (modified by geographic location when known), auction houses, foundations, and corporate collections are specified using this tag. Metropolitan Museum of Art (New York, N.Y.). Museum of Fine Arts, Houston. National Gallery of Art (U.S.). National Gallery of Art (U.S.) |b Chester Dale Collection. Private Collection. Private Collection, France. Sotheby's |b New York. Hiram Butler Gallery. For auction houses and commercial galleries, indicate the date of sale or exhibition date in the general note field (500) in year, month, day order (e.g., yyyy/mm/dd or 1959/01/17).
AE: Corporate name **NGA Accession #**	710	|n NGA: accession number. NGA: 1993.3.1.a.
AE: Corporate name **Location: Architecture**	710*1	**City (Modifier, e.g., Country, State).** Use for city or building site for architecture or archaeological site. Lascaux (France). Houston (Texas).
AE: Meeting name **Exhibitions**	711*2	**Title of exhibition (Exhibition : city, country) |d (year/s).** Certain types of exhibitions are tracked in the database. All National Gallery of Art exhibitions, all Salon and Royal Academy annual exhibitions, and other landmark exhibitions, such as the Impressionist exhibitions, the Armory Show, etc., are recorded. Exhibition titles are cross-referenced as needed. Glory of Venice (Exhibition : National Gallery of Art) |d (1995). Impressionist Exhibition (Exhibition : Paris, France) |d (1874). Salon (Exhibition : Paris, France) |d (1903). Armory Show (Exhibition : New York, New York) |d (1913).

Authorities

Authorities include the *Art and Architecture Thesaurus*, the *Union List of Artist Names* (ULAN), *Library of Congress Subject Headings*, and Library of Congress Name Authority File. Most name authorities are copied into the slide library catalog directly from the reference library catalog to maintain proper authority control. Some name authorities are updated using ULAN. Local iconographic subject headings are also used. These headings are constructed to be consistent with AACR2. ICONCLASS is not used and there are no plans to implement it in the future.

Technical Specifications

The data for all library accounts are maintained on a Hewlett-Packard HP 3000 mainframe, model 957 with 3.5 gigabytes of memory. The system software used by all library departments is VTLS (Virginia Tech Library Software). At present, IBM 386 and 486 personal computers, a Compac Deskpro 5100, and a Power Macintosh 6100/60 computer are available to staff. The circulation desk terminal is an HP 2392A. Personal computers use Reflections software to communicate with the mainframe. VTLS is developing the ability to link text to images. At present [1994], the slide library is not planning to take advantage of this technology but hopes to in the near future as funds become available.

Item-level information is recorded online. Source citations, vendors and item numbers, copy numbers, location of the slide, availability, information regarding full views, details, models, and so on are recorded in the item screen. The circulation functions of the software will not be utilized until 40 percent of the collection has been automated.

There are some limitations to using VTLS for image collections. Item-level information needs better support and more descriptive space. Each account should be able to preset fixed fields in order to save time. At present, it does not seem possible for VTLS to write a viable and user-friendly program that will transfer information from selected fields to a word-processing program to suit the demands of this collection. The program sent to us by VTLS was cumbersome and required constant manipulation to get three lines of text in a font that was too large. Currently labels are created and printed using WordPerfect 5.1 through a Windows application. Information can be cut and pasted from VTLS to WordPerfect in quick, short steps. In some ways, greater flexibility and control are possible with this less-than-perfect method. Labels are printed on a Hewlett-Packard LaserJet 4M Plus printer (four lines of text at 8 pitch).

Four lines of information are placed on each label. Line one contains the call number and copy number of the slide. Line two lists the artist, while title information, often abbreviated, is placed on line three and part of four as space permits. Line four also contains the date field and location. On occasion the date field is eliminated to provide more title space. Because full electronic records exist and are readily accessible from any one of six computers, the need for extensive label information is reduced. A bar code is attached to each slide and backup card.

Conclusion

Staff received several weeks of training on the basics of using MARC and VTLS. A new, abbreviated manual was developed to serve as a reference tool during cataloging. The use of the MARC format at the National Gallery of Art slide library is an evolving process. The manual is a symbol of that evolution. It changed from a cataloging aid to a small, easily used booklet that has been updated several times and will be updated and expanded in the future as time permits.

Many people question whether the MARC format is necessary for cataloging image collections. It is important that directors of these collections learn, in these times of shrinking budgets, diminishing staff, and exploding technological advances, how to best utilize limited resources. The most radical yet logical way to handle the limits placed on our time and budgets is to share cataloging of works of art by loading these records in a national database utility, such as RLIN or OCLC. A single, albeit flawed, system with a proven history of shared use is better than trying to map information from multiple systems into one's local database. The development of standard fields and subfields for description will be key to a viable system for shared cataloging. Changing the MARC format to better suit the needs of its potential users and accepting the input of those users are more important than asking visual resources curators to abandon a tool that could prove revolutionary.

The following figures are examples of search results on public access screens (figures 9-4 through 9-6); MARC and public access screens, including item information, for the same painting (figures 9-7 through 9-10); and MARC and public access screens for a more complex record of a painting (figures 9-11 and 9-12).

NGA Slide Library - - - - - - - - - VTLS - - - - - - - - - - SUBJECT
YOU SEARCHED: s/lake wall

1.	1	Lake Schroon (New York).
2.	1	Lake Wallenstadt (Germany).
3.	1	Lake Winnepesaukee (New Hampshire).
4.	13	Lakes.
5.		Lambert, Isabel (Mrs. Constant), 1912-1992.
6.	1	Lamberti, Pietro di Niccolo, 1393-1435. Saint Mark.
7.	15	Lambs.
8.	3	Lamps.
9.	1	Lancaster (Massachusetts). First Church of Christ.
10.	7	Lances.
11.	7	Landscape.
12.	1	Landscape -- Argentina -- 19th century.
13.	1	Landscape -- Australia -- 20th century.
14.	8	Landscape -- Austria -- 20th century.
15.	3	Landscape -- Bahamas -- 19th century.

Enter the line number of the item you want to see, or
PS.......Previous screen   NS...........Next screen
?.....Menu-driven search   HELP...About this screen   ....Any command or /?

Figure 9-4 | S/ Screen

NGA Slide Library - - - - - - - - - - VTLS - - - - - - - - - - - TITLE
YOU SEARCHED: t/lute

1.	1	Luscher Color Test.
2.	4	Lute Player.
3.	1	Lynnewood Hall.
4.	1	Lyons Cafe.
5.	1	M. Bochet.
6.	1	M. Ruelle.
7.	1	Ma Jolie (Woman with a Zither or a Guitar).
8.	1	The Maas at Dordrecht.
9.	5	Mabou.
10.*	17	Mabou: 1975-1992.
11.	1	Mabou Mines.
12.	1	Mabou, Nova Scotia.
13.	2	Mabou Winter Footage.
14.	1	Macchiette.
15.	1	Madame Cave.

Enter the line number of the item you want to see, or
PS.......Previous screen   NS...........Next screen
?.....Menu-driven search   HELP...About this screen   ....Any command or /?

Figure 9-5 | T/ Screen

NGA Slide Library - - - - - - - - - VTLS - - - - - - - - - KEYWORDS SEARCHED

1.   picasso & dogs   7 ENTRIES

            BOOLEAN OPERATORS: AND (&); OR (+); NOT (–)

Enter the line number of the item you want to see, or
E #......Erase one entry   E #/#........Erase range   E ALL..........Erase all
?.....Menu-driven search   HELP...About this screen   ....Any command or /?

Figure 9-6 | Keyword Screen

NGA Slide Library - - - - - - - VTLS - - - - - MARC BIBLIOGRAPHIC RECORD   (5/9)
YOU CHOSE: rembrandt & mellon

Local lvl: 4   Analyzed: 0 Operator: 14   Edit:
CNTL: Rec stat: Entrd: 940516   Used: 951128
Type: g Bib lvl: m Govt pub: Lang: eng Source: Leng:
        Enc lvl: Type mat: s   Ctry: ne   Dat tp: MEBE: 0
Tech: Mod rec: Accomp mat:
Desc: Int lvl: Dates: 1635

   1.   035   0001-92660
   2.   099   DU Ptg R3851 PM MA 4
   3.   100 1   Rembrandt van Rijn, |c and School, |d 1606-1669.
   4.   245   Man in an Oriental Costume, |b (formerly "A Turk").
   5.   260 |c c. 1635.
   6.   300   oil on canvas, |c 98.4 x 74cm.
   7.   500   Govert Flinck is probably the other hand responsible for this painting.
   8.   585   Cat. # 1.
   9.   591   center left: [R]embrandt ft
  10.   650   Jewelry in art.
  11.   650   Portraits |x Male |z Netherlands |y 17th century.
  12.   690   Painting |z Netherlands |y 17th century.
  13.   700   Mellon, Andrew W., |d 1855-1937. |e collector
  14.   700   Flinck, Govert, |d 1615-1660. |e collaborator?
  15.   710 2   National Gallery of Art (U.S.) |b Andrew W. Mellon Collection.
  16.   710   n NGA: 1940.1.13.
  17.   711 2   Rembrandt in the National Gallery of Art (Exhibition : National Gallery of Art) |d (1969).

Enter
PS.......Previous screen   C......Copy availability   HR...........Hold a book
?.....Menu-driven search   HELP...About this screen   ....Any command or /?

Figure 9-7 | MARC Bibliographic Record

NGA Slide Library - - - - - - - - - - VTLS - - - - - - - - - - - - CATALOG CARD
YOU CHOSE: rembrandt & mellon   (5/9)

CALL NUMBER: DU Ptg R3851 PM MA 4
ARTIST: Rembrandt van Rijn, and School, 1606-1669.
TITLE: Man in an Oriental Costume, (formerly "A Turk").
DATE: c. 1635.
MEDIUM: oil on canvas, 98.4 x 74cm.
NOTE: Govert Flinck is probably the other hand responsible for this painting.
INSCRIPTION: center left: [R]embrandt ft
EXHIBITION: Rembrandt in the National Gallery of Art (Exhibition : National Gallery of Art) (1969).
NGA EXH.:   Cat. # 1.
SUBJECT: Jewelry in art.
SUBJECT: Portraits -- Male -- Netherlands -- 17th century.
SUBJECT: Painting -- Netherlands -- 17th century.
ADDED ENTRY: Mellon, Andrew W., 1855-1937. collector
ADDED ENTRY: Flinck, Govert, 1615-1660. collaborator?
LOCATION: National Gallery of Art (U.S.) Andrew W. Mellon Collection.
LOCATION: NGA: 1940.1.13.

Figure 9-8 | Catalog (OPAC) Screen

```
NGA Slide Library - - - - - - - - - - VTLS - - - - - MENU OF COPIES AND VOLUMES
YOU CHOSE: rembrandt & mellon                    (5/9)


    CALL NO:  VARIES FOR EACH ITEM *** SEE INDIVIDUAL ITEM RECORDS
    AUTHOR:   Rembrandt van Rijn, and School, 1606-1669.
MAIN TITLE:   Man in an Oriental Costume, (formerly "A Turk").
  PUBLISHER:  c. 1635.
    FORMAT:   slide


        LOCATION       STATUS      ITEM-ID      COPY UNITS
   1.   MAIN LIBRARY   Available   1000005153   1 FACE
   2.   MAIN LIBRARY   Available   1000005154   2 FACE
   3.   MAIN LIBRARY   Available   1000005147   1 FULL VIEW
   4.   MAIN LIBRARY   Available   1000005148   2 FULL VIEW
   5.   MAIN LIBRARY   Available   1000005149   3 FULL VIEW
   6.   MAIN LIBRARY   Available   1000005150   4 FULL VIEW
   7.   MAIN LIBRARY   Available   1000005145   1 HAND - LEFT
   8.   MAIN LIBRARY   Available   1000005146   2 HAND - LEFT
   9.   MAIN LIBRARY   Available   1000005162   1 HAND - RIGHT
  10.   MAIN LIBRARY   Available   1000005161   2 HAND - RIGHT
  11.   MAIN LIBRARY   Available   1000005151   1 HEAD
  12.   MAIN LIBRARY   Available   1000005152   2 HEAD
  13.   MAIN LIBRARY   Available   1000005160   1 MANTLE
  14.   MAIN LIBRARY   Available   1000005159   2 MANTLE
  15.   MAIN LIBRARY   Available   1000005157   1 TORSO
  16.   MAIN LIBRARY   Available   1000005158   2 TORSO
  17.   MAIN LIBRARY   Available   1000005167   1 TURBAN
  18.   MAIN LIBRARY   Available   1000005156   2 TURBAN
  19.   LENDING        Available   1000005166   1 FACE
  20.   LENDING        Available   1000005163   1 FULL VIEW
  21.   LENDING        Available   1000005164   2 FULL VIEW
  22.   LENDING        Available   1000005171   1 HAND - LEFT
  23.   LENDING        Available   1000005170   1 HAND - RIGHT
  24.   LENDING        Available   1000005165   1 HEAD
  25.   LENDING        Available   1000005169   1 MANTLE
  26.   LENDING        Available   1000005168   1 TORSO
  27.   LENDING        Available   1000005155   1 TURBAN


Enter the line number of the item you want to see, or
PS.......Previous screen     NS...........Next screen      CA....Longer description
?.....Menu-driven search     HELP...About this screen       .......Any command or /?
```

Figure 9-9 | Menu of Copies and Volumes

NGA Slide Library - - - - - - - - - - VTLS - - - - - - - - - - COPY DESCRIPTION
YOU CHOSE: rembrandt & mellon   (5/9)

   AUTHOR: Rembrandt van Rijn, and School, 1606-1669.
MAIN TITLE: Man in an Oriental Costume, (formerly "A Turk").

1.   ITEM CALL NO: DU Ptg R3851 PM MA 4.4
2.   ITEM NUMBER: 1000005158   8.   UNITS: TORSO
3.   COPY NUMBER: 2   9.   PRICE: $.00
4.   LOAN PERIOD: 30   10.   LOCATION: MAIN LIBRARY
5.   CIRC. COUNT: 0   11.   TEMP. AT:
6.   ENTRY DATE: 24May94   12.   LAST CHECKED IN: 24May94
7.   ITEM CLASS: 1   13.   CIRCULATION COUNT SINCE 24May94: 0
                                    14.   NGA 1/88

------> Available

Enter the line number of the field you want to change, or
PS.......Previous screen   HR........Hold this book   MA......Full MARC record
?.....Menu-driven search   HELP...About this screen   ....Any command or /?

Figure 9-10 | Copy Description

NGA Slide Library - - - - - - - - - - VTLS - - - - - MARC BIBLIOGRAPHIC RECORD
YOU CHOSE: Pantoja de la Cruz, Juan, 1551?-1608?

Local lvl: 4   Analyzed: 0 Operator: 11   Edit:
CNTL: Rec stat: Entrd: 940302   Used: 951206
Type: g Bib lvl: m Govt pub: Lang: eng Source: Leng:
       Enc lvl: Type mat: s Ctry: sp Dat tp: MEBE: 0
Tech: Mod rec: Accomp mat:
Desc: Int lvl: Dates: 1605
  1. 035   0001-22360
  2. 099   SP Ptg P198 PF MA 1
  3. 100 1 Pantoja de la Cruz, Juan, |d 1551?-1608?
  4. 245   Margaret of Austria, Queen of Spain.
  5. 260 |c 1605.
  6. 300   oil on canvas, |c 91 x 51 inches.
  7. 500   A similar full-length portrait of Margaret, dated 1606, is in the Prado. The pendant to the Houston
             painting, Philip III of Spain, is in the collection of the Banco de Espana, London. The pair was
             commissioned by the Queen for Don Antonio de Toledo, Count of Alba de Aliste.
  8. 500   Suspended above the double strand of pearls is a large pendant known as the "joyel rico" or "joyel
             de los Austrias", which is frequently seen in portraits of Margaret. The pendant, created for the
             royal family at the beginning of the seventeenth century, was made of a square diamond called
             the "Estanque" and a 58 ½ carat pearl known as the "Pellegrina". In 1972, a pearl believed to
             be the "Pellegrina" was in the collection of the actress Elizabeth Taylor. One of her dogs has
             apparently chewed on the pearl.
  9. 591   at lower left: Jues Pantoja de la +. Facieba[t] Vallesolito 16[0]5
 10. 600   Margaret |c of Austria, Queen of Spain, consort of Philip III, |d 1584-1611.
 11. 650   Portraits |x Female |z Spain |y 17th century.
 12. 650   Jewelry in art.
 13. 690   Painting |z Spain |y 17th century.
 14. 695   Pendant (companion piece).
 15. 695   Pendant (jewelry).
 16. 695   Ruffs.
 17. 700   Kress, Samuel Henry, |d 1863-1955. |e collector
 18. 710 2 Museum of Fine Arts, Houston.

Enter
PS.......Previous screen   NS..........Next screen   C......Copy availability
HR..........Hold a book
?.....Menu-driven search   HELP..About this screen   ....Any command or /?

Figure 9-11 | MARC Bibliographic Record

Slide Library - - - - - - - - - - VTLS - - - - - - - - - - - - CATALOG CARD
YOU CHOSE: Pantoja de la Cruz, Juan, 1551?-1608?

CALL NUMBER:	SP Ptg P198 PF MA 1
ARTIST:	Pantoja de la Cruz, Juan, 1551?-1608?
TITLE:	Margaret of Austria, Queen of Spain.
DATE:	1605.
MEDIUM:	oil on canvas, 91 x 51 inches.
NOTE:	A similar full-length portrait of Margaret, dated 1606, is in the Prado. The pendant to the Houston painting, Philip III of Spain, is in the collection of the Banco de Espana, London. The pair was commissioned by the Queen for Don Antonio de Toledo, Count of Alba de Aliste.
NOTE:	Suspended above the double strand of pearls is a large pendant known as the "joyel rico" or "joyel de los Austrias," which is frequently seen in portraits of Margaret. The pendant, created for the royal family at the beginning of the seventeenth century, was made of a square diamond called the "Estanque" and a 58 ½ carat pearl known as the "Pellegrina." In 1972, a pearl believed to be the "Pellegrina" was in the collection of the actress Elizabeth Taylor. One of her dogs has apparently chewed on the pearl.
INSCRIPTION:	at lower left: Jues Pantoja de la +. Faciеba[t] Vallesolito 16[0]5
SUBJECT:	Margaret of Austria, Queen of Spain, consort of Philip III, 1584-1611.
SUBJECT:	Portraits -- Female -- Spain -- 17th century.
SUBJECT:	Jewelry in art.
SUBJECT:	Painting -- Spain -- 17th century.
SUBJECT:	Pendant (companion piece).
SUBJECT:	Pendant (jewelry).
SUBJECT:	Ruffs.
ADDED ENTRY:	Kress, Samuel Henry, 1863-1955. collector
LOCATION:	Museum of Fine Arts, Houston.

Figure 9-12 | Catalog (OPAC) Screen

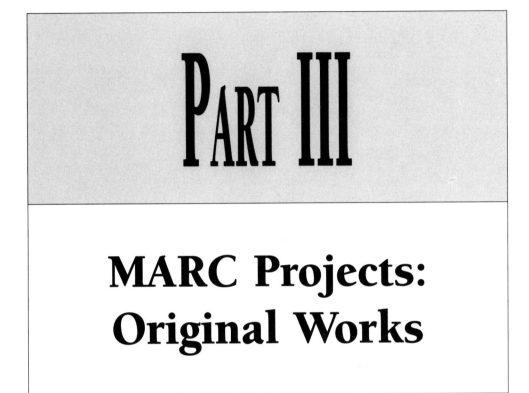

PART III

MARC Projects: Original Works

The Inventories of American Painting and Sculpture: Cataloging in MARC

Christine Hennessey

In 1985, the National Museum of American Art was one of the first museums in the country to utilize the MARC format in creating a database for art objects. With funding from the Henry Luce Foundation, the Inventory of American Sculpture was implemented using an adaptation of the Visual Materials Format.[1] Based on the success of that early implementation, the museum's other major national art inventory program, the Inventory of American Paintings Executed before 1914, was converted to the MARC format in 1991.[2]

Together, the Inventories of American Painting and Sculpture reference over 323,000 art works in public and private collections worldwide. The Paintings Inventory includes oils, watercolors, and pastels created by artists born or active in the United States before 1914. The Inventory of American Sculpture, which has no cutoff date, references works from colonial to contemporary times and includes traditional carved and cast pieces, modernist assemblages, and site-specific works. Of note, the Sculpture Inventory includes an estimated thirty thousand survey reports

from the Save Outdoor Sculpture! (SOS!) program, documenting the history and condition of America's publicly owned outdoor sculpture.[3]

Information for each of the Inventories is compiled from a variety of published and unpublished sources. Information is culled from museum collection and exhibition catalogs, theses, dissertations, and catalogues raisonnés, and reports supplied by historical societies, public art programs, private collectors, and special survey projects.

The Inventories reside on an online integrated networked system at the Smithsonian called SIRIS (Smithsonian Institution Research Information System). The SIRIS database, which utilizes NOTIS software, includes the holdings of Smithsonian libraries, archive and manuscript collections, and specialized research bibliographies. SIRIS is available on the Internet at http://www.siris.si.edu, or can be accessed by modem dial-in at (202) 357-4303.[4]

Each year, nearly three thousand researchers call, write, or visit the Inventories seeking information on

American painters and sculptors, and over nine thousand off-site searches of the database were logged in during the first six months of Internet availability. Among our users are curators, conservators, professors, students, collectors, and publishers. Their queries range from broad to specific:

> Can you give me a list of all Winslow Homer paintings?
>
> Did Homer do any watercolor paintings of Bermuda in the 1890s?
>
> Are there any outdoor monuments commemorating Martin Luther King Jr. and the Civil Rights movement in Birmingham, Alabama?

The Inventories have been structured to answer such questions as these. Essential information recorded for each art work includes: artist, title, dates, medium, version identification and markings information, current and past ownership or location information, subject matter, related bibliographic citations, historical remarks, and, for SOS!-surveyed outdoor sculpture, condition assessments and conservation treatment histories.[5] Each art work is cataloged at the item level, using an adaptation of the Visual Materials Format. Figure 10-1 has a complete listing and brief description of the MARC fields and subfields used by the Inventories. Figure 10-2 shows an example of an item included in the Sculpture Inventory and figures 10-3 and 10-4 are the OPAC and MARC screens created for this sculpture. OPAC and MARC screens for a painting can be seen in figures 10-5 and 10-6.

Wherever possible, we have tried to conform to national USMARC tagging practices. However, even with the 1987 expansion of the Visual Materials Format to include three-dimensional realia, and the more recent advent of format integration, we have had to adopt a flexible approach in defining fields and deciding on standards for recording data content.

As the sample records illustrate, we rely heavily on 5XX fields and had to define several local 59X fields to meet our needs for ownership, provenance, and condition information.

Particularly problematic for the Inventories is the detailed ownership and location data we record. Because the art works are not in our possession, we need to be able to record full owner name, street address, city, state, and ZIP code, in an easily readable and equally retrievable format. Our researchers, for example, might request a list of all pre-1914 American paintings owned by the Maryland Historical Society;

or want entries for all outdoor sculpture in Denver, Colorado. We also need to capture provenance histories, tracing the ownership and location of an art work over time (for example, all art works formerly in the collection of John D. Rockefeller); or generate a list of pre-1914 American paintings for sale at Sotheby's in the 1960s. Unfortunately, the existing 852 (location) field has only a single subfield |e for address information, and the 561 (provenance) field is structured primarily as a note field. Thus we opted to define several 59X fields, with specific subfields for each type of information, in order to facilitate retrieval and report capabilities.

Similarly, condition assessment information is an area where we've defined local fields to accommodate indexing needs. As part of the SOS! program, the first-ever national survey and condition assessment of America's outdoor sculpture, information was collected on the overall condition of each sculpture and any specific types of deterioration or damages. A follow-up questionnaire, now being designed, will track subsequent conservation treatments performed, and basic conservation information will be added to the SOS! records. Although the 583 (actions) field would be the logical choice for placement of this information, we found again that the current definitions and structuring of the subfields within that field did not meet our specific needs, and so adapted several local 59X fields to record both sculpture and base damage. Although SIRIS supports such local fields, these fields remain nonstandard for national utilities, including OCLC and RLIN.

Another problem for structuring in MARC are the multiple titles often associated with an art work. Titles of art works are key access points in the Inventory, and art works are often known by many titles. Paintings may have been exhibited under titles not originally assigned by the artist. Sculptures often acquire popular names—*The Statue of Liberty* versus *Liberty Enlightening the World*. Before format integration, we used the 740 field to record other "known-by" titles. With format integration, however, that field has been redefined to capture only analytic titles. If we opt to use the 247 (alternate indexing title) field, newly redefined indicator values can no longer be set to skip initial articles, thus hampering indexing of such titles as *The Statue of Liberty*.

Ease of retrieval and sharing of information are, of course, the Inventory's primary goals, and in our descriptive cataloging practices we have tried to follow existing standards and vocabulary. New names going

Field Tag Number	Field Type	Subfields
100	Artist	1 |aLast name, first name, |b Jr., |c Rev.,|d Life dates (b., d., ca., active),|e Role (e.g., painter/sculptor.)|g Qualifier (e.g., attributed to, copy after)
110	Corporate artist	2φ |a Firm name,|e Role.|g Qualifier (e.g., attributed to/copy after)
245	Title	1_ (second indicator value varies) |aTitle,|h (Painting/sculpture).
260	Execution date	|c Execution date display.
300	Dimensions	|a # of pieces|c Size phrase &/or measurements (weight).
340	Media	|a primary media:|c Secondary|e support|h Media display note.
510	Ref/source	3 |a Source or bibliographic citation (Author, "Title," Place of Publication: Publisher, Yr.)
520	Description	8φ |a Subject description.
530	Photo	|a Image on file.|c Photographer|d Juley #
530	Illus	|b Published reproductions.
562	Marks	|a Inscriptions|b Signed/unsigned|c Founder's mark appears.
585	Exhibits	|a Title, institution, city, year, notes (possibly shown at).
591	Owner/location	|9 Qualifying phrase|a Owner/location name,|b Division,|b Subdivision2,|c Street,|d Site,|e City,|f County,|g State,|h Country|I Zip|l Accession number
592	Location type	|a Type, e.g., post office, state capitol
593	Provenance	|9 Qualifying phrase|a Owner/Location name,|b Division,|b Subdivision2,|c Street, |d Site,|e City,|f County,|g State|h Country|I Zip|t Time|n Notes.
594	Remarks	|a Cast number and historical notes.
595	Related work	|a Linking note (Model for: record control #)
596	Conservation hist.	|a Treatment history.
597	SOS! survey	|a Surveyed|b 1992 June.|c Treatment needed.|n Conditions note.
598	Sculpture damage	|a Type, e.g., stained
599	Base damage	|a Type, e.g., cracks
650	Subjects	04 |a Primary term|x Secondary term|y Tertiary term
655	Object type	φ7 |a Type, e.g., mural, mobile|2 Source (e.g., aat, lctgm, local)
700	Addtl. artists	11 |a Last name, first name,|b Jr.,|c Rev.,|d Life dates,|e Role (e.g., painter/ sculptor.)|g Qualifier (e.g., attributed to/copy after)
710	Addtl. firms	21 |a Firm name,|e Role (e.g., founder, fabricator)|g Qualifier (e.g., attributed to/copy after)
740	Addtl. title	_1 (first indicator value varies) |a Title,|h (Painting/sculpture).
HOL	Record number	|a IAP/IAS|b ########

Figure 10-1 | MARC Field Summary Guide

into the database are checked against LCNAF (Library of Congress Name Authority File) and ULAN (Getty's Union List of Artist Names). If no match is found, new names are established following AACR2 (*Anglo-American Cataloguing Rules*, 2nd ed., 1988 revision).[6]

Terms used in the 340 (media) and 655 (object type) fields are checked against the AAT (*Art and Architecture Thesaurus*) and LCTGM (*Library of Congress Thesaurus for Graphic Materials*).

Figure 10-2 | "Sybil Ludington," by Anna Vaughn Hyatt Huntington, c. 1960. (By permission of City of Danbury/Danbury Public Library, Danbury, Conn.)

ARTIST:　　Huntington, Anna Vaughn Hyatt, 1876-1973, sculptor.
　　　　　　Roman Bronze Works, founder.
TITLE:　　Sybil Ludington, (sculpture).
DATE:　　1960. Dedicated Sept. 11, 1971.
MEDIUM:　　Sculpture: bronze. Base: stone.
DIMEN:　　Sculpture: approx. 6 x 3 x 5 ft.; Base: approx. 3 x 2 x 4 ft.
MARKS:　　(Back of base:) Anna H. Huntington/ROMAN BRONZE WORKS INC. N.Y. (Front of base:) SYBIL
　　　　　　LUDINGTON/ON APRIL 26, 1777, THIS BRAVE SIXTEEN-/YEAR OLD GIRL RODE THROUGH THE/
　　　　　　ENEMY-INFESTED COUNTRYSIDE FOR/THIRTY MILES IN PUTNAM COUNTY, NEW/YORK, TO
　　　　　　WARN THE LOCAL MILITIA THAT/BRITISH TROOPS WERE ATTACKING AND/PLUNDERING
　　　　　　DANBURY, CONNECTICUT. / DONATED BY ANNA HYATT HUNTINGTON. signed Founder's mark
　　　　　　appears.
SUBJECT:　　A young girl, Sybil Ludington, riding sidesaddle on the proper left side of a horse. Her proper right hand
　　　　　　is raised above her head and she clutches a branch as a makeshift whip. She holds the reins of the horse
　　　　　　in her proper left hand. Her mouth is open, as if yelling. She wears a dress and her hair is in a pony tail.
　　　　　　One foot is in the stirrup.
　　　　　　Portrait female - - Ludington, Sybil - - Full length
　　　　　　History - - United States - - Revolution
　　　　　　Equestrian Monument
OWNER (outdoor site:)
　　　　　　Administered by City of Danbury, Department of Public Works, 155 Deerhill Avenue, Danbury,
　　　　　　Connecticut 07810. Located Danbury Public Library, 170 Main Street, Danbury, Connecticut, 06810
PROVEN:　　Formerly in the collection of Huntington, Anna Vaughn Hyatt, Redding Ridge, Connecticut 06876
　　　　　　1960-1971.
REMARKS:　　IAS files contain copies of Danbury News Times (Danbury, CT) Sept. 13, 1971, which discusses the
　　　　　　dedication of the piece, its transportation and placement by Mafiano brothers; and Danbury News Times,
　　　　　　Nov. 27, 1984, pg. 12, which discusses a larger version of the work, located in Carmel, New York.
CONDIT:　　Surveyed 1993 April. Treatment urgent. Horse's tail is broken and the whip in the figure's hand is missing.
　　　　　　Visible cracks and staining on the sculpture. Water collects in recessed areas.
REF:　　Save Outdoor Sculpture, Connecticut survey, 1993.
ILLUS:　　Image on file.
REC NO:　　CT000014

Figure 10-3 | Inventory of American Sculpture: OPAC Record

PS-ABH2148 FMT F RT r BL m DT 04/06/94 R/DT 06/21/94 STAT mn E/L x DCF D/S D
SRC d PLACE xxu LANG und MOD T/AUD g D/CODE r DT/1 1960 DT/2 1971
T/MAT a TECH n GOVT   A/MAT   R/TIME nnn ME/B ?

100:1 :|aHuntington, Anna Vaughn Hyatt,|d1876-1973,|esculptor.
245:10:|aSybil Ludington,|h(sculpture).
260: :|c1960. Dedicated Sept. 11, 1971.
300: :|cSculpture: approx. 6 x 3 x 5 ft.; Base: approx. 3 x 2 x 4 ft.
340: :|ametal:|cbronze|hSculpture: bronze. Base: stone.
510:3 :|aSave Outdoor Sculpture, Connecticut survey, 1993.
520:8 :|aA young girl, Sybil Ludington, riding sidesaddle on the proper left side of a horse. Her proper right hand is raised above her head and she clutches a branch as a makeshift whip. She holds the reins of the horse in her proper left hand. Her mouth is open, as if yelling. She wears a dress and her hair is in a pony tail. One foot is in the stirrup.
530: :|aImage on file.
562: :|a(Back of base:) Anna H. Huntington/ROMAN BRONZE WORKS INC. N.Y. (Front of base:) SYBIL LUDINGTON/ ON APRIL 26, 1777, THIS BRAVE SIXTEEN-/YEAR OLD GIRL RODE THROUGH THE/ENEMY-INFESTED COUNTRYSIDE FOR/THIRTY MILES IN PUTNAM COUNTY, NEW/YORK, TO WARN THE LOCAL MILITIA THAT/ BRITISH TROOPS WERE ATTACKING AND/PLUNDERING DANBURY, CONNECTICUT./DONATED BY ANNA HYATT HUNTINGTON.|bsigned|cFounder's mark appears.
591:00:|9Administered by|aCity of Danbury,|bDepartment of Public Works,|c155 Deerhill Avenue,|eDanbury, |gConnecticut|i07810
591:00:|9Located|aDanbury Public Library,|c170 Main Street,|eDanbury,|gConnecticut,|i06810
592: :|alibrary
593:00:|9Formerly in the collection of|aHuntington, Anna Vaughn Hyatt,|eRedding Ridge,|gConnecticut|i06876 |t1960-1971.
594: :|aIAS files contain copies of Danbury News Times (Danbury, CT) Sept. 13, 1971, which discusses the dedication of the piece, its transportation and placement by Mafiano brothers; and Danbury News Times, Nov. 27, 1984, pg. 12, which discusses a larger version of the work, located in Carmel, New York.
597: :|aSurveyed|b1993 April.|cTreatment urgent.|nHorse's tail is broken and the whip in the figure's hand is missing. Visible cracks and staining on the sculpture. Water collects in recessed areas.
598: :|abroken parts|acracks|astained|awater collects in recessed areas
650:04:|aPortrait female|xLudington, Sybil|yFull length
650:04:|aHistory|xUnited States|yRevolution
650:04:|aEquestrian
655: 7:|aMonument|2aat
710:21:|aRoman Bronze Works,|efounder.
Holdings Record: |aIAS|bCT000014

Figure 10-4 | Inventory of American Sculpture: MARC View

ARTIST: Eakins, Thomas, 1844-1916, painter.
TITLE: The Artist and His Father Hunting Reed Birds on the Cohansey Marshes, (painting).
DATE: ca. 1874.
MEDIUM: Oil on canvas.
DIMEN: 27 x 17 7/8 in. (67.3 x 43.5 cm.).
MARKS: (Lower center, inscribed on bow of boat:) BENJAMIN EAKINS FILIUS PINXIT
SUBJECT: Two full-length male figures, Thomas Eakins and his father, seated in a rowboat hunting.
            Recreation - - Sport & Play - - Hunting
            Landscape - - Marsh
            Portrait male - - Eakins, Thomas - - Full length
            Portrait male - - Eakins, Benjamin - - Full length
OWNER: Virginia Museum of Fine Arts, 2800 Grove Avenue, Richmond, Virginia 23221
PROVEN: Gift of Mellon, Paul, Mr. & Mrs., Upperville, Virginia
REF: Rasmussen, William M. S., "American Art to 1900," Antiques, vol. 138 (August 1990), pg. 284.
ILLUS: Image on file.
REC NO: IAP 70620131

Figure 10-5 | Inventory of American Paintings Executed before 1914: OPAC View

PS-ABH2148 FMT F RT r BL m DT 04/06/94 R/DT   STAT mn E/L x DCF D/S D
SRC d PLACE xxu LANG und MOD T/AUD g D/CODE s DT/1 1874 DT/2
T/MAT a TECH n GOVT   A/MAT   R/TIME nnn   ME/B ?

100:1 :|aEakins, Thomas,|d1844-1916,|epainter.
245:14:|aThe Artist and His Father Hunting Reed Birds on the Cohansey Marshes,|h(painting).
260: :|cca. 1874.
300: :|c27 x 17 7/8 in. (67.3 x 43.5 cm.).
340: :|aoil:|ecanvas|hOil on canvas.
510:30:|aRasmussen, William M. S., "American Art to 1900," Antiques, vol. 138 (August 1990), pg. 284.
520:80:|aTwo full-length male figures, Thomas Eakins and his father, seated in a rowboat hunting.
530: :|aImage on file.
562: :|a(Lower center, inscribed on bow of boat:) BENJAMIN EAKINS FILIUS PINXIT
591:00:|aVirginia Museum of Fine Arts,|c2800 Grove Avenue,|eRichmond,|gVirginia|i23221
592: :|9Gift of|aMellon, Paul, Mr. & Mrs.,|eUpperville,|gVirginia
650:04:|aRecreation|xSport & Play|yHunting
650:04:|aLandscape|xMarsh
650:04:|aPortrait male|xEakins, Thomas|yFull length
650:04:|aPortrait male|xEakins, Benjamin|yFull length
Holdings Record: |aIAP|b70620131

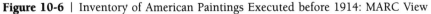

Figure 10-6 | Inventory of American Paintings Executed before 1914: MARC View

To meet the needs of our database users, some local in-house term lists have also been developed and are used either in lieu of or to supplement existing national authority lists. Among these is an in-house list of exhibition titles (used for field 585) and subject terms (used in field 650). Because of the inadequacy of broad LCSH (*Library of Congress Subject Headings*) terms for specialized collections, and to remain consistent with other art databases in the museum, we opted to use an in-house *Subject Term Guide,* initially designed in the 1970s for the museum's Slide and Photograph Archives. In keeping more with museum practice, we follow CHIN (Canadian Heritage Information Network) conventions for capitalization of titles and chose not to use ISBD punctuation.[7]

Despite the Inventories' deviations in tagging and descriptive practices, however, the USMARC format has proven to be a viable system for recording art data. For the future, in addition to fully implementing format integration, we are eager to implement an expanded artist authority file that would not only serve basic authority control needs, but also function as a biographical reference database that the public could search and understand. In creating such a file, we would like to record all the biographical information now collected on our manual worksheets, including preferred and variant names; place and dates of birth, death, and activity; minority status; primary occupations; and source citations. Unfortunately, however, the current MARC authority record structure is much more limited in scope, and the NOTIS system, like most MARC-based catalogs, does not support the display of authority records on the OPAC.

We also hope soon to begin an imaging project, eventually making the Inventories' sixty thousand plus images available online, along with the descriptive text of the record. As with any visual resources application, copyright concerns will dictate whether, once scanned, the images can become available online outside the Smithsonian.

Much has changed since our initial MARC experiment began. As this *Sourcebook* attests, the number of MARC-based visual resources catalogs is growing, and we remain hopeful that the MARC structure, accompanying cataloging standards, and bibliographic utilities all designed initially for book materials will become more accommodating for nonbook materials.

NOTES

1. In 1985, the Inventory of American Sculpture was implemented on the Smithsonian Institution Bibliographic Information System (SIBIS), a GEAC-based system. Articles about the Sculpture Inventory's early use of the MARC format appeared in *Art Documentation* 6, no. 4 (1987): 147–149; *Visual Resources* 4 (winter 1988): 373–388; and *Beyond the Book: Extending MARC for Subject Access,* edited by Toni Petersen and Pat Molholt (Boston: G. K. Hall, 1990).

2. The Inventory of American Paintings Executed before 1914 was begun in 1970 and resided on a Honeywell mainframe, using a generic Smithsonian programming format known as SELGEM.

3. The Save Outdoor Sculpture! (SOS!) program is jointly sponsored by the National Museum of American Art and the National Institute for the Conservation of Cultural Property. The goal of the project is to inventory and assess the condition of America's outdoor sculpture and to raise community awareness about the long-term preservation needs of outdoor sculpture.

4. Per NOTIS conventions, each of these catalogs has been defined as a separate institution group. Within the Art Inventories catalog, the painting and sculpture databases have been implemented as separate processing units, so researchers can search both inventories together or "set the catalog" to search just for paintings or just for sculpture. Before 1994, the SIRIS system resided on a GEAC mainframe. At the time of conversion to NOTIS, many of our fields were renumbered and restructured.

5. Until the 1991 conversion of the Paintings Inventory to the MARC format, only fifteen fields of information were defined. Historical remarks, provenance, and markings fields were among those not previously recorded for paintings.

6. Even when matches of terminology or names can be found, we sometimes differ in our choice of a heading. For example, for creator names entered in the 100 and 700 fields, preference is given to "exhibited under" names versus the fullest form of a name often cited in artists' dictionaries and picked up by LCNAF and ULAN. We also always add death dates when known.

7. Although tagged as 650 topical subjects, some of our subject strings may include a mix of personal and geographical terms, in addition to the topical term. These nonstandard headings had to be tagged as 650 subfields a, x, and y because of NOTIS OPAC subject indexing conventions.

The National Art Library, Victoria and Albert Museum, London

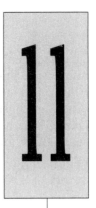

Jane Savidge

The Institution and Its Collections

The National Art Library (NAL) has a long history of collecting the documentation of art and design. With holdings currently estimated at more than one million items and annual acquisitions of approximately fifteen thousand titles, it is the largest collection of its kind in the United Kingdom and as such plays a major national and international role as a centre for art documentation.

The NAL originated as the Library of the Schools of Design, founded in 1837 following parliamentary concern about the nature of instruction in design. The schools and library moved to Marlborough House in 1852 where the small teaching collection of objects grew rapidly. Acquisitions from the Great Exhibition of 1851 supplemented the nascent museum collection and the library also continued to expand, moving with the museum to the new South Kensington site in 1857 and eventually into its present home in the Victoria and Albert Museum.[1]

In 1870, the publication of the *Universal Catalogue of Books on Art,* compiled in part from the holdings of the library, signaled a Victorian desire for comprehen-sive coverage of the subject area.[2] Today collection development is based upon a detailed collection profile. Subjects covered include those central to the work of the museum: prints, drawings and paintings, furniture and woodwork, textiles and dress, ceramics and glass, metalwork, sculpture, the art and design of the Far East, of India, and of Southeast Asia, and those relevant to the library's curatorial role covering the history of the art, craft, and design of the book. This core material is supplemented by literature concerned with a much broader subject field.

Major strengths are the holdings of eighteenth- and nineteenth-century sales catalogues and nineteenth-century exhibition catalogues, artists' books, comics and graphic novels, children's literature, trade literature (including a major collection of material issued by Liberty & Co.), and an outstanding collection of nineteenth-century periodicals.

The numerous special collections include two significant nineteenth-century libraries, that of the Rev. Alexander Dyce (1798–1869), a major collector of Shakespeare's works; and that of John Forster (1812–1876), which includes manuscripts and first editions of many of Charles Dickens's novels. There are many other important collections, among them the Mikhail Larionov Collection (material relating to the theatre and opera in Europe, especially in Russia and France, and work by Larionov and Nataliia Goncharova); the Clements Collection of armorial binding; the Osman Gidal Collection (magazines documenting the use of photo reportage in the 1920s and 1930s); and the Piot Collection (pageantry, fêtes, and ceremonies, sixteenth to nineteenth centuries).

In 1978, the foundation of the Archive of Art and Design (AAD) widened NAL collecting responsibilities to include archives. We currently hold more than two hundred relating to individuals, businesses, and societies involved in the production, marketing, promotion, and study of art and design, among them the sculptor Sir Eduardo Paolozzi's "Krazy Kat Arkive," an archive of twentieth-century popular culture. The library also administers the museum's own archive and registry.

The library collections include items in a wide range of formats, from manuscript material to videodisc. Although individual prints, drawings, and photographs are not currently collected (they are the responsibility of the museum's Department of Prints, Drawings, and Paintings), they are present in large numbers in certain of the library's special collections. The Linder Collections of the work of Beatrix Potter, for example, comprise a bequest of over 1,500 drawings, twenty sketchbooks and illustrated manuscripts, about two-hundred photographs (mainly from the period 1878–1912), and memorabilia, supplemented by a further collection of 278 drawings and thirty-eight books held on long loan. Many of the drawings and sketches relate directly to illustrations in the published works.[3]

Many of the archives held by the AAD also include wide-ranging materials in different formats. The "Krazy Kat Arkive" includes books and magazines, tear sheets and press cuttings, prints and posters, and many 3D objects, including a collection of toy robots.

Many other NAL collections require a cataloguing approach that emphasises the physical form and features of items (for example, the collections of bindings, illuminated and calligraphic manuscripts, fine printing, artists' books, and book art) and this has also informed our use of MARC fields, especially the implementation of fields 655 and 755. Book art in particular (defined as those artists' books produced from 1960 onward that experiment with the traditional structure, materials, and layout of the book) has been central to our reevaluation of the traditional forms of

access offered by libraries and our efforts to extend research-level access by genre and physical features to books as art objects.

NAL cataloguing policy reflects the library's dual function as a research and reference library and as a curatorial collection. The level of cataloguing applied, dependent upon the particular collection to be dealt with, ranges from enhanced level for rare book and special collections, through AACR2R Level 3 cataloguing for the bulk of the library's holdings, to minimal-level cataloguing for certain categories of ephemera.

In cataloguing visual materials, we consult Elisabeth W. Betz's *Graphic Materials: Rules for Describing Original Items and Historical Collections* (Washington, D.C.: Library of Congress, 1982), in conjunction with *Descriptive Cataloging of Rare Books,* 2nd ed. (Washington, D.C.: Library of Congress, 1991). For book art we have developed detailed cataloguing rules following guidelines established by the ARLIS/UK and Ireland Cataloguing and Classification Committee in 1989, which represent an expansion of AACR2R. For a full list of the authorities and standards we follow, see appendix 1 at the end of this chapter.

Automating the Collections and Our Use of USMARC

The NAL has been automating its collections since 1987. The Dynix Library System is used to provide an integrated online computer catalogue that now includes some 250,000 titles. We are a full member of OCLC, deriving catalogue records where available (approximately 60 percent). We are also working on a number of retrospective conversion projects to transfer entries from the manual catalogues into machine-readable form. A World Wide Web site for the National Art Library has recently been made available and the Computer Catalogue can be accessed directly using telnet.[4]

The decision to adopt USMARC arose naturally from our use of OCLC as a source of records. This proved advantageous as USMARC included a number of fields unavailable in UKMARC at that time, especially those defined for use in analysing the genre and physical features of items (655 and 755) and the definition of a field specifically for faceted subject strings (654).[5]

In our implementation of the format, we follow standard field definitions as embodied in the US-

MARC and OCLC manuals. In keeping with this, we minimise local variation in our use of fields. Where we have identified a need for modification of the field or its application, for example, in our use of 654, 655, and 755, we promote the changes required with those administering the format. For a breakdown of the main fields in use, see appendix 2 at the end of this chapter and the notes on specific fields later in the chapter. Additional notes on locally defined fields and NAL implementation are in appendix 3.

Developing an Integrated Catalogue

The great diversity of the National Art Library collections and the experience of using a multiplicity of separate manual catalogues reinforced our view that the complete holdings of the library should be accessible within a single database under unified authority control. This would enable all related material to be shown together, regardless of format. To illustrate this with an example from the Linder Collections, NAL holdings of publications by and about Beatrix Potter can be viewed alongside the original drawings and watercolours by her, revealing relationships between preliminary sketches and the books in which they appear.

To achieve this, we have also set up authority files that support all formats encountered. Names in the catalogue are present in a single name authority file. This covers individuals and institutions as authors and as subjects, and also includes names associated with the physical production and provenance of items.

This is not to say that all types of material within the library can be accessed effectively using identical searching methods. We recognise that certain collections require additional search options. For example, sale catalogues need to be searchable by date of sale; archives and manuscript collections by manuscript number; and bindings collections by type of binding and other physical characteristics, such as material, technique, and so on. To achieve this additional flexibility, we have set up numerous special indexes that operate on subsets of the total pool of catalogue records, accessed using submenus of the public catalogue. These submenus also assist the end user interested only in a specific type of material by narrowing the search and avoiding the distraction of entries relating to other formats. Catalogue records are mapped to these indexes using either codes in the record leader or in local field 049|l, for example, "s" to flag all sale catalogues; "a" to flag all artists' books, and so on. Prints, drawings, and photographs can also be separately identified in this way.

At present, we have submenus for sales and serials. Further indexes and submenus currently under development will cover NAL and AAD archives and manuscripts, the children's book collections, and the publications and research of the museum.

Archival Cataloguing and the Use of Analytic Records

The inclusion of archives in the integrated catalogue led us to develop a method of analytic cataloguing that enables parent/child relationships between parts of an archive to be revealed. Archival cataloguing is inseparable from the process of sorting and arranging a gathering of material to reveal the creative or administrative hierarchies that generated it. We wanted to make explicit original order and provenance using a hierarchically arranged group of linked MARC records.

The analytic software we use for this purpose was developed for us by Dynix UK and beta tested by the NAL. A version of it has since been incorporated into the standard Dynix software in a somewhat different form.[6]

To establish a structure of parent/child records, the cataloguer sets up a MARC record for the archival group, creating further independent MARC records to represent subgroups, classes, items, and/or piece as the archive is sorted and analysed. These are linked to form a complex tree structure of records representing up to five levels of analysis, allowing thousands of child records to be connected at different levels. Figures 11-1 through 11-3 show examples of an analytic record structure used to describe an archive.

This machine linkage is based on the standard USMARC field 773 (host item entry). The local Dynix record number of the parent or host item is added to subfield |w of each lower-level record attached directly to that parent. The reciprocal relationship (top level down) is achieved using an index to the record numbers of parent records linked from below in this way (invisible to the cataloguer or user).

08 OCT 96   The Victoria & Albert Museum - National Art Library   04:17pm
PUBLIC ACCESS CATALOGUE

This record describes part of a group or set of related items.
For more information about the related records, type SET

NAME(S)   Heal & Son Holdings Plc.
Heal, Ambrose, Sir, 1872-1959.
Heal, Anthony, 1907-1995.
Storehouse Plc.
Mansard Gallery, Heal & Son.
Worshipful Company of Furniture Makers (London, England).
Heal & Son.
Dunn's of Bromley.

TITLE   Heal & Son Holdings plc : records, 1810-1988.

COLLATION   ca.3500 items.

- - - - More on Next Screen - - - -

Press <Return> to see next screen :
Commands: SO = Start Over, B = Back, RW = Related Works, C = Copy status,
 <Return> = Next Screen, ? = Help

---

08 OCT 96   The Victoria & Albert Museum - National Art Library   04:18pm
PUBLIC ACCESS CATALOGUE

This record describes part of a group or set of related items.
For more information about the related records, type SET
Continued...

HISTORY   The family firm of Heal & Son was established in 1810 as a feather-dressing
business. In 1818, it moved to Tottenham Court Road and began to expand into bedding,
bedstead and furniture manufacture and retail. By the end of the century it ranked among
the best known London furniture houses and, in 1905, it converted from a partnership
into a limited company. Under the leadership of Sir Ambrose Heal (1872-1959), who
joined the firm in 1893, Heal's became renowned for promoting modern design in Britain
by encouraging and employing talented young designers. Sir Ambrose also expanded Heal's
own promotional activities and commissioned the best illustrators, graphic designers
and photographers to

- - - - More on Next Screen - - - -

Press <Return> to see next screen :
Commands: SO = Start Over, B = Back, RW = Related Works, C = Copy status,
 <Return> = Next Screen, F = First Screen, ? = Help

Figure 11-1 | Example of the Top Level of an Analytic Record for an Archive as Displayed on the Public Catalogue.
The record continues with several screens of history and provenance information and an abstract of the
contents.

```
08 OCT 96   The Victoria & Albert Museum - National Art Library      04:24pm
                     PUBLIC ACCESS CATALOGUE

             This record describes part of a group or set of related items.
               For more information about the related records, type SET

CONTAINED        Heal & Son Holdings Plc.
IN:              Heal & Son Holdings plc : records,

TITLE            Printed ephemera, [1926?]-1984.

COLLATION        30 items.

ARRANGEMENT      Class level description.




Press <Return> to see Copy status :
Commands:   SO = Start Over, B = Back, RW = Related Works, NT = Next Title,
            PT = Previous Title, ? = Help
```

Figure 11-2 | Example of a Lower-Level Analytic Record for an Archive

```
08 OCT 96   The Victoria & Albert Museum - National Art Library      04:21pm
                     PUBLIC ACCESS CATALOGUE
   Linked Set
  *---------------------- Higher Level --------------------------------------------*
  | 1. Heal & Son Holdings Plc.       AAD/1978/2 : AAD/1986/1 :            |
  |    Heal & Son Holdings plc : records,           1810-1988.            |
  |    *---------------------- Current Level ---------------------------------------*
  |    | 2.                                                               |
  |    |   Other records,                            [ca.1850]-1985.     |
  |    |   *------------------ Lower Level -----------------------------------------*
  |    |   | 2.1                                                         |
  |    |   |   Printed  ephemera,                     [1926?]-1984.      |
  |    |   | 2.2                                                         |
  |    |   |   Heal's wartime ephemera,               1939-1951.         |
  |    |   | 2.3                                                         |
  |    |   |   Personal papers : Sir Ambrose Heal,    [ca.1890]-1944.    |
  |    |   | 2.4                                                         |
  |    |   |   The Royal Warrant Holders Association : rec  1955-1981.   |
  *---*----*------------------------------------------------------ <more> ------*

Enter line number(s) to display title(s) :
Commands:   SO = Start Over, B = Back, DL# = Display Lower Level,
            <Return> = more titles, ? = Help
```

Figure 11-3 | Hierarchical Display Showing the First Three Levels in an Archive. Further levels are present below and can be displayed by entering the command DL.

Where further levels of analysis are required, each record attached to the parent can also have children attached. To continue the analogy, the top level is now the grandparent; the next level, the parent; and the third level, the child. As illustrated by figure 11-4, the links made at each level by the addition of local record numbers in 773 |w enable a complex structure of records to be built up.

Alongside their use for archives, this method of analysis can be used to show, for example, relationships between a group of drawings contained within a portfolio, or between studies that relate to a finished work. In the NAL they are used extensively to catalogue multiple items contained within a single physical volume (for example, to link the separate catalogue entries relating to a bound volume of sale catalogues).

For those searching the catalogues, the linked records can be accessed at the top (group level) and the hierarchical structure entered. From this point it is possible to move to a lower-level record and select it for display. Alternatively, a lower-level record may be identified directly and, upon discovering that it forms part of an archive, the end user may choose to enter the hierarchy and move up or down, viewing related records as required. All the connected MARC records are indexed and accessible using the full range of search options.

To help locate the record within the hierarchy, brief details from the parent record continue to display at the head of the screen when the end user moves from level to level. Up to three levels can be displayed at one time. We felt that any more than this would be confusing, given the constraints of a DOS environment and the limited space available on the screen.

Work with analytic record structures has involved reconsideration of certain aspects of cataloguing policy. The extent to which information needs to be repeated at different levels within a hierarchy is one aspect under review. The group record describing the archive of a stained glass manufacturer, for example, may have numerous subgroup records attached, each covering

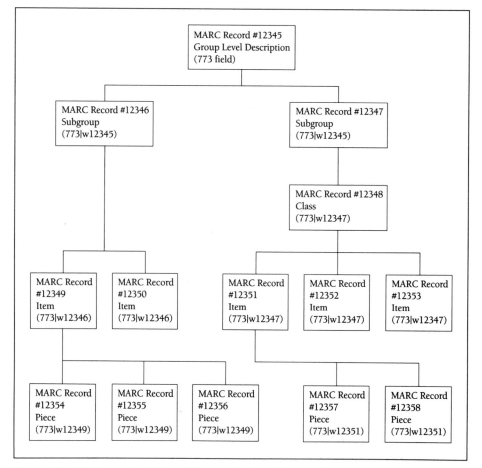

Figure 11-4 | Group Level Record for an Archive Showing the Attached Hierarchy of Linked Lower-Level Records

correspondence and designs relating to a particular project. Each subgroup may have item- or piece-level records describing the individual designs or letters attached below. To avoid extensive repetition of the same information at different levels, we try to consider the group of records as a whole when determining where to place an entry point within the hierarchy.

When a name or subject heading is required, this is placed at the highest level to which it relates. It is not repeated in each of the records attached, even though it may be entirely appropriate as a heading for these records (i.e., the subject string or name heading must apply to all the documents described by records attached). We would not make a name heading at group level for an individual responsible only for designs present in a subgroup. The heading would be given in the record for that subgroup with no further repetition of the name in the attached item records that describe the individual designs.

The main difficulty with analytic cataloguing concerns export of the record group. The links between records must be retained and the group of records viewed as a whole to make sense. We have been following with interest the discussion of whole/part relationships in USMARC as relevant to this problem. We have also begun to investigate the potential of using SGML and EAD in combination with the hierarchical MARC record structure as an alternative means to manipulate and make available the quantities of information contained in archival finding aids.

A further immediate problem affects search results when analytic records are retrieved using Boolean logic. If, in a Boolean AND search, one of the selected subject words is attached high up in a hierarchy because it applies to a large group of records and the second selected word is present only at a lower level, the Boolean AND search will not retrieve the record despite its relevance to the search. This occurs because the current version of the software takes no account of the links between records when searching the indexes.

MARC Issues Associated with Implementation of the *Art and Architecture Thesaurus*

Another area in which we are developing and adjusting our use of MARC fields relates to our implementation of the *Art and Architecture Thesaurus* (AAT) as the means to support both subject analysis and object

description of the collections. Our intention is to use this thesaurus both to support cataloguing activity and to extend the search options offered to the end user of the public catalogue.

Since the early 1990s, we have been using the AAT as the main source of new terminology required for NAL subject headings although the headings continue to be structured following in-house rules using fields 690 and 691. We have also implemented the AAT as the source of terms added to USMARC fields 655 (form/genre) and 755 (physical characteristics), with the intention of linking all these headings to the relevant hierarchies of the thesaurus.

We are now in the process of translating more than twenty-six thousand subject headings present on Dynix into the standard faceted structure and vocabulary of the AAT using MARC tag 654. To achieve this, we are working with the Getty Information Institute on an automated conversion of our local subject strings to the AAT, generating in the process large numbers of candidate terms for consideration and possible addition to the thesaurus (including many alternative U.K. English forms).[7]

In the 654 field, we make use of precoordinated subject strings to achieve indexing precision, combined with Boolean search operators to provide exhaustivity and flexibility where required.

We have now carried out two trial matching exercises against the AAT, enabling identification of patterns of NAL headings that cause false matches and correcting the programming to take account of these. We have also been able to sort out some of the inconsistencies in our source data and to identify types of headings to be edited in their AAT form before proceeding to load them onto the catalogue.

A typical and fairly straightforward heading, such as 690|aFashion photography, will be automatically generated as 654|cKT#135798|aFashion photography |2aat, while in other cases considerable editing of the headings will be required.[8]

This has also shown up certain problems with the structure of MARC field 654, which we have been attempting to resolve. In converting the file of NAL headings we identified a need for a second focus term in 654, for example, an item about the conservation of nineteenth-century French panel stamp bindings requires the heading Panel stamp bindings—France —19th century—Conservation, with "conservation" as the second focus term.

We subsequently worked with the AAT on a proposal to make the 654 |a subfield repeatable (approved by MARBI), which now permits the 654 coding: 654

|cp|aPanel stamp bindings|zFrance|y19th century|ck |aConservation.

Another area of difficulty affecting both 654 and 655 relates to the use of other sources of terms when the required descriptor is not present in the AAT.

The AAT is a subject-defined thesaurus and cannot attempt to be universal in its coverage. Inevitably in analysing subject content, intellectual genre, or form of material, other term lists and thesauri have to be used. When NAL cataloguers locate relevant subject terms elsewhere, they submit these as candidate terms for consideration and inclusion in the AAT. However, this still leaves some subjects completely outside scope.

When an entire string heading is derived from an alternative thesaurus, the source of the heading can be given in |2 using an appropriate identifying code, for example, identifying a heading from one of the RBMS thesauri. Problems arise, however, when most elements of the string derive from the AAT with perhaps a single term from another source.

In deciding how to deal with this type of heading, options open to us were to code these as local in |2 or to drop such terms completely out of the string, entering them in a separate MARC tag in order to retain the AAT coding.

Neither of these options is particularly satisfactory. If the first is adopted, the authority of the string is undermined. It is, in every other respect, a perfectly valid, correctly constructed AAT heading that may be of use to other institutions. It appears unhelpful to disguise the source of most of the terms within it by replacing AAT with local as the |2 code.

The second option removes a key element from the string, reducing the effectiveness of precoordination. Although the term is still present in the record, its relationship to the (possibly multiple) subject headings assigned to the item may be far from clear.

Our preferred solution is to pursue the definition of a new subfield for use in fields 654 and 655. This would be used to flag the presence of a descriptor taken from a source other than the primary thesaurus. The |2 could be repeated to give the code of the subsidiary source and/or |5 added as a variant of "institution to which the field applies," giving the library's holdings code to indicate the library responsible for the local term.

A further modification to MARC fields 654 and 655 will be needed if the underlying structure of the thesaurus is to be made available to the end user. Alongside straightforward Boolean searching of precoordinated subject headings or object descriptors, we want to make the broader and narrower structure of the AAT transparent, allowing the end user to select specific term(s) from the precoordinated string and display these in thesaurus view. Once in the thesaurus, the structure of the hierarchies will be used to broaden or narrow the search as required.

To achieve this, each term used in a heading must be linked to its correct location within the thesaurus. Our intention is to use the control number held in the MARC authority record for each AAT term, to use this to locate the term in the hierarchies when thesaurus view is selected.

In existing headings covered by the NAL/AAT matching exercise, however, it has been necessary to include this information within the 654 string itself, expanding the 654|c field to include the relevant control numbers: 654|cKT#53592|aBookbinding|cxKM #74760|bcompetitions, where the numbers present in the string are the AAT record numbers used to find the right place in the hierarchy when the end user wants to see a specific term in context.

MARC Fields Used in Developing Access by Form, Genre, and Physical Characteristics

In our use of MARC fields for the description of form, genre, and physical characteristics, we continue to distinguish form and genre in field 655 from physical characteristics in field 755, based upon the view that 655 describes what the item is (in a textual and a physical sense), while 755 gives access to its physical attributes.

The indexes based upon 655/755 enable end users to search for object type alone or in combination, making a distinction, for example, between a book jacket still present on the book to which it relates and a book jacket detached from the item (in an archive with its associated designs, for example), or between a watercolour sketch in a sketchbook and a single-leaf watercolour drawing. The MARC fields are used to achieve this. They also enable object type/genre to be separated from the long list of associated physical features when records are displayed.

To date, the precoordinated headings used in NAL records have been held in separate authority files. However, they are now stored using a single MARC authority record tag 155 regardless of the source tag 655 or 755. Following the deletion of 755, we are actively seeking a way to separate out object type and genre from physical attributes but have not yet arrived

```
LEADER  00842nam  2200217a45eO
008      920612s1984      txua        000 0 eng d
100  1  Grant, Susan kae
245  10 Giving fear a proper name : |bDetroit /|cSusan kae Grant.
260     Dallas, Texas :|bBlack Rose Press,|cc1984.
300     1 v. (unpaginated) :|bill. ;|cc1984.
500     Artist's book which explores the nature of phobia, based upon Grant's experiences as a resident of inner-city
        Detroit.
500     "In the Summer of 1979, I moved to Detroit, Michigan. The following images are interpretations of dreams,
        recollections, fears, nightmares and day to day experiences that were recorded in a journal from 1979-1981"
        -- Introduction.
500     Each double page opening comprises a text relating to the named phobia and a collage which consists of a
        black and white photograph of the artist, overlaid and stitched through with pins, hair, nylon thread and wire.
        Miniature cap gun attached with thread acts as a book mark.
500     "The photographs are contact prints from segments of the body that have been collaged, sewn, painted and
        probed. They also contain hair, teeth, a miniature telephone, barbed wire and various other three dimensional
        objects" -- Artist's statement.
500     "The text is Palatino Roman printed on paper made by Blake Alexander. The boxes were constructed by Brad
        Metcalf. In a limited edition of fifteen" -- Colophon.
500     The book is bound in pink cadillac car vinyl between boards in a hollow back binding and tied with black
        ribbon.
500     "Housed in a simulated bullet proof case" -- Artist's statement.
500     Portraits reprinted from Portrait of the artist and her mother. Madison, Wis. : Black Rose Press, c1979.
590     Library's copy is no. 11, signed by the artist.
600  10 Grant, Susan kae.
655  7  Artists' books|zU.S.A.|y1984.|2aat
655  7  Book art|zU.S.A.|y1984.|2local
690     Phobias|xDepictions.
690     Dreams|xDepictions.
700  11 Alexander, Blake,|epapermaker.
700  11 Metcalf, Brad,|ebox maker.
755     Collages|zU.S.A.|y1984.|2aat
755     Contact prints|zU.S.A.|y1984.|2aat
755     Handmade papers|zU.S.A.|y1984.|2rbpap
755     Deckle edges|zU.S.A.|y1984.|2aat
755     Typefaces|xPalatino Roman|zU.S.A.|y1984.|2aat
755     Found objects|zU.S.A.|y1984.|2aat
755     Miniature objects|zU.S.A.|y1984.|2local
755     Human hair|zU.S.A.|y1984.|2local
755     Teeth|zU.S.A.|y1984.|2aat
755     Barbed wire|zU.S.A.|y1984.|2aat
755     Toy guns|zU.S.A.|y1984.|2aat
755     Vinyl bindings|zU.S.A.|y1984.|2aat
755     Perspex boxes (containers)|zU.S.A.|y1984.|2aat
755     Limited numbered editions|zU.S.A.|y1984.|2local
```

Figure 11-5 | Edited Catalogue Record Illustrating the Use of Object Type and Physical Characteristics

at a means to achieve this without the addition of a further MARC field to the format.

Perhaps our treatment of the item to reveal its physical object characteristics is best revealed by an example from the artists' books collection.

The catalogue record in figure 11-5 shows our use of genre and physical characteristics fields in combination. The record also illustrates the use of multiple thesauri. All the 655 and 755 headings coded local in |2 or associated with codes other than AAT have been developed as candidate terms and supplied to the AAT for inclusion in the thesaurus. Descriptive notes support, explain, and provide a context to the controlled headings assigned.

Conclusion

In our implementation of USMARC, we have found the format to be eminently flexible, even when dealing with unique artists' books, such as Colin Hall's decomposing *Book in a Jar* or the unopenable *Book of Nails*.[9] We have been able to use the format to bring out the unusual physical format and copy-specific features of these works. For an integrated collection such as the NAL, the use of the MARC format provides a common structure underpinning a standardised approach to all the different types of material we encounter, facilitating comparison and critical analysis of related holdings.

We await with interest the outcome of discussions about the integration of USMARC and UKMARC, which we hope will widen the lively discussion of its strengths and weaknesses as a format and the continuing exploration of its flexibility in a wide range of cataloguing contexts.

NOTES

1. A detailed history of the development of the museum and library on the South Kensington site is given in John Physick, *The Victoria and Albert Museum: The History of Its Building* (London: Victoria and Albert Museum, 1982). For a description of the developing museum collection, see Anna Somers Cocks, *The Victoria and Albert Museum: The Making of the Collection* (Leicester: Windward, 1980).

2. *The First Proofs of the Universal Catalogue of Books on Art: Compiled for the Use of the National Art Library and the Schools of Art in the United Kingdom,* 2 vols. (London: Chapman and Hall, 1870).

3. A number of published catalogues give details of these collections: Anne Stevenson Hobbs and Joyce Irene Whalley, *Beatrix Potter: The V&A Collection. The Leslie*

Linder Bequest of Beatrix Potter Material (London: Victoria and Albert Museum; Frederick Warne, 1985); *The Linder Collection of the Works and Drawings of Beatrix Potter* (London: National Book League; Trustees of the Linder Collection, 1971); and, in preparation, *Catalogue of Drawings in the Linder Collection,* to be published by Frederick Warne and the Trustees of the Linder Collection.

4. For the World Wide Web, use <http://www.nal.vam.ac.uk>; for catalogue access, use <telnet nal.vam.ac.uk>.

5. As the result of an initiative by the Library Association Rare Books Group, these fields have subsequently been made available in UKMARC.

6. At time of writing, the NAL has just completed the process of upgrading the Dynix System to Release 142. This has involved some change to the functionality of the analytics.

7. This project has been described in detail in the following articles: Jane Savidge, "Developing Online Access to a Subject Thesaurus: Implementing the *Art and Architecture Thesaurus* in the National Art Library OPAC," *Computers and the History of Art* 3, no. 2 (1993): 27–37; Douglas Dodds, "The National Art Library and the *Art and Architecture Thesaurus,* Part 1," *AAT Bulletin,* no. 22 (1994): 1–5; Toni Petersen, "The National Art Library and the *Art and Architecture Thesaurus,* Part 2," *AAT Bulletin,* no. 22 (1994): 6–8; and Joseph A. Busch, "The National Art Library and the *Art and Architecture Thesaurus,* Part 3: Automated Mapping of Subject Headings into Faceted Index Strings," *AAT Bulletin,* no. 22 (1994): 9–12.

8. To give just one example, the NAL heading Birds—Depictions has been automatically generated as Shuttlecocks—Depictions. There is no animals hierarchy in the thesaurus and "Birds" is present as a UF term leading to shuttlecocks.

9. Both these examples present a particular challenge to the cataloguer: Colin Hall's *Book in a Jar* (S.l: The Artist, 1984) is a kilner jar containing fragments of a decomposing sketchbook or diary sealed in with sour milk and rice. *The Book of Nails* (Madison, Wisc.: Xexoxial Endarchy, 1992) was made by Floating Concrete Octopus, an intermedia/performance group that changes its name every year. The item comprises a book on Vincent van Gogh, glued shut, and then sealed with nuts and bolts.

APPENDIX 1
Main Standards, Authorities, and Term Lists
Used by the NAL Cataloguing Section

Descriptive Entry

Anglo-American Cataloguing Rules. 2nd ed., 1988 revision. Ottawa: Canadian Library Association; London: Library Association; Chicago: American Library Association, 1988. (AACR2R)

Betz, Elisabeth W. *Graphic Materials: Rules for Describing Original Items and Historical Collections.* Washington, D.C.: Library of Congress, 1982.

Cook, Michael, and Margaret Procter. *A Manual of Archival Description.* 2nd ed. Aldershot, Eng.: Gower, 1989.

Descriptive Cataloging of Rare Books. 2nd ed. Washington, D.C.: Library of Congress, 1991.

Hensen, Steven L. *Archives, Personal Papers, and Manuscripts: A Cataloging Manual for Archival Repositories, Historical Societies and Manuscript Libraries.* 2nd ed. Chicago: Society of American Archivists, 1989.

Personal and Corporate Name Headings

Anglo-American Cataloguing Rules. 2nd ed., 1988 revision. Ottawa: Canadian Library Association; London: Library Association; Chicago: American Library Association, 1988. (AACR2R)

OCLC Name Authority File. Contains records from the Library of Congress and records submitted by NACO (Name Authority Cooperative Project) participants.

Names as Subject

Personal and corporate names as subject, established according to the preceding sources, are subdivided by addition of a Library of Congress subject subdivision from Library of Congress *Subject Cataloging Manual: Subject Headings.*

H 1105: *Free-floating Subdivisions Used under Names of Corporate Bodies.*

H 1110: *Free-floating Subdivisions Used under Names of Persons.*

Subject Headings

Art and Architecture Thesaurus. 2nd ed. New York; Oxford: Oxford University Press on behalf of the Getty Art History Information Program, 1994.

Library of Congress Subject Headings (LCSH) via OCLC.

Physical Characteristics and Provenance

Art and Architecture Thesaurus. 2nd ed. New York; Oxford: Oxford University Press on behalf of the Getty Art History Information Program, 1994.

Binding Terms: A Thesaurus for Use in Rare Book and Special Collections Cataloguing. Prepared by the Bibliographic Standards Committee of the Rare Books and Manuscripts Section (ACRL/ALA). Chicago: Association of College and Research Libraries, 1988.

Paper Terms: A Thesaurus for Use in Rare Book and Special Collections Cataloguing. Prepared by the Bibliographic Standards Committee of the Rare Books and Manuscripts Section (ACRL/ALA). Chicago: Association of College and Research Libraries, 1990.

Printing and Publishing Evidence: A Thesaurus for Use in Rare Book and Special Collections Cataloguing. Prepared by the Bibliographic Standards Committee of the Rare Books and Manuscripts Section (ACRL/ALA). Chicago: Association of College and Research Libraries, 1986.

Provenance Evidence: A Thesaurus for Use in Rare Book and Special Collections Cataloguing. Prepared by the Bibliographic Standards Committee of the Rare Books and Manuscripts Section (ACRL/ALA). Chicago: Association of College and Research Libraries, 1988.

Type Evidence: A Thesaurus for Use in Rare Book and Special Collections Cataloguing. Prepared by the Bibliographic Standards Committee of the Rare Books and Manuscripts Section (ACRL/ALA). Chicago: Association of College and Research Libraries, 1990.

Genre Terms

Art and Architecture Thesaurus. 2nd ed. New York; Oxford: Oxford University Press on behalf of the Getty Art History Information Program, 1994.

Descriptive Terms for Graphic Materials: Genre and Physical Characteristic Headings. Compiled and edited by Helena Zinkham and Elisabeth Betz Parker for the Library of Congress, Prints and Photographs Division. Washington, D.C.: Cataloging Distribution Service, 1986.

Genre Terms: A Thesaurus. Prepared by the RBMS Standards Committee. 2nd ed. Chicago: Association of College and Research Libraries, 1991.

APPENDIX 2
Record Description

Main USMARC Fields Used in NAL Catalogue Records

The standard NAL catalogue record for original cataloguing may include some or all of the following fields as appropriate to the particular title to be catalogued. Other fields may be entered as required or defined in USMARC/OCLC manuals. For full details of mandatory/ optional status and content of each field, see these manuals.

This list reflects the USMARC format before format integration. We are currently remapping our use of fields to bring them into line with recent changes to the format.

Record Leader
  Status
  Type of record
  Bibliographic level
  Encoding level
  Descriptive cataloguing form

007	Physical description fixed field		
08	Fixed field	Int lvl	Main entry
	Updated	Repr	Fiction
	Date type	Contents	Biography
	Date 1	Govt Publication	Language
	Date 2	Conf Publication	Modified record
	Country	Festschrft	Cataloguing source
	Illus	Index	

010	LC control number (if no ISBN)
020	ISBN
041	Language code
049	|l Local code
100	Personal name
110	Corporate name
111	Conference name
130	Uniform title (main entry)
240	Uniform title (not main entry)
243	Collective title
245	Title and statement of responsibility
250	Edition
260	Imprint
300	Physical description
440	Series
490	Series
500	Notes
502	Thesis note
504	Bibliography note
505	Formal contents note
510	Citations/References note
520	Summary/abstract
583	Action note
590	Local notes
600	Name as subject

610   Corporate name as subject

611   Conference name as subject

630   Uniform title as subject

654   Faceted subject string.

655   Genre/Document type (controlled terms)

690   NAL local subject heading—topical

691   NAL local subject heading—geographical

700   Added personal name

710   Added corporate name

711   Added conference name

730   Added uniform title

740   Added title entry

755   Physical characteristics (controlled terms) [now deleted by USMARC]

773   Host item entry

APPENDIX 3
Supplement

Presented here are further notes on locally defined fields and NAL implementation.

049|l

This is a local field containing a single-letter code used to manipulate subsets of the total body of catalogue records to produce listings, provide reports, develop submenus within the library OPAC, and so forth.

Examples of codes used include:

    a   artists' books

    b   broadsheets

    c   children's books (examples)

    e   exhibition catalogues

    f   noteworthy bindings

    m   manuscripts

    p   private press books

    s   sale catalogues

    t   trade literature

    v   V&A publications

    x   prints

    y   drawings

    z   photographs

100, 110, 111; 600, 610, 611; 700, 710, 711
Name Fields

In explaining the role of or relationship between a named individual or institution and the specific item described, we use relator terms entered in the |e subfields of 1XX and 7XX fields, for example, |edonor, |eprinter, |epapermaker, and so on. This supplements the descriptive text contained in any statement of responsibility in 245|c and within the note fields.

5XX   Note Fields

We make extensive use of descriptive notes using the 500 (general note) field and the full range of specific notes, which, until MARC format integration, were frequently format defined and which are now becoming generally available. These include summary or abstract of the coverage of the item in 520, citation notes in 510, and detailed notes on provenance in 561. Where necessary, descriptive notes are used to justify and explain controlled headings assigned in other fields.

583   Action Note

This tag is used specifically to record details of local actions to reproduce NAL originals described in catalogue entries (e.g., the existence of microform masters, slides, etc.). It is also used to record full collation details of special collection items (supplementing the information given in field 300 [physical extent] and elsewhere in the notes), including information about physical damage to NAL items. (In addition, the holdings record associated with the MARC record contains coded data identifying the conservation status of the item.)

690, 691, 654   Subject Fields

Field tags 690 and 691 are locally defined subject fields that contain NAL in-house subject headings (corresponding to the division between topical and geographical headings found in 650 and 651). We are currently working toward the replacement of these local fields (and their contents) with field 654.

In making subject entries we are not generally dealing with detailed iconographic subject analysis as the bulk of the collections do not require this. Where such analysis is required we make use of the standard subdivision *depictions* to indicate the difference in the approach to the subject. We supplement this by detailed analysis of genre using field 655 (see the following section).

655   Intellectual Genre/Object Type Field

All special collection items are assigned controlled terms that describe the intellectual genre or physical form of the whole item. Thus this field defines the genre or object type—what the item is as opposed to what physical features it exhibits (755) or what it is about (654).

Terminology in this field is derived from the *Art and Architecture Thesaurus*, supplemented by other relevant thesauri. Terms found in sources other than the AAT are submitted to the AAT as candidate terms.

755   Physical Characteristics

Terms have been supplied for all special collection items using controlled terminology. This repeatable field has been used to describe the physical features and makeup of the object identified in field 655, for example, paper, printing methods, binding features, and so on. Terminology is derived from the AAT and other sources, as described above. The 755 field has now been deleted from USMARC.

The 655 and 755 fields are searchable through separate indexes or by a combined search. Thus the terms corresponding to physical process and the attributes of an object (in 755) can be separated from the named object (the form term in 655) or searched in combination, for example, all Bibles with marbled endpapers. This enables us to distinguish a book jacket that forms part of an item from a book jacket alone, or a watercolour sketch in a sketchbook from a single leaf.

773   Analytic Linking Field

The use of this field was developed for the NAL by Dynix to provide for the requirements of cataloguing whole/part relationships (in archives, bound volumes, etc.). A hierarchy of linked records can be created to express the structure and intellectual relationships between different parts of an archive. Independent MARC records are set up for each group, subgroup, class, item, or piece. These are then linked into a hierarchical structure to display relationships. Field 773 (host item) is a standard MARC field that contains an additional subfield |g (unique identifying number of subordinate item). (The numbers are system supplied when a command is entered to link the records.) These fields can be used to show, for example, relationships between groups of drawings contained within a portfolio or between studies and sketches that relate to a finished work. We currently use them to show physical connections between separate catalogue entries, for example, where bound together, or to reveal the administrative and creative structures that generated the archives of an individual or corporate body. [At time of writing, USMARC is discussing the use of 7XX fields to describe whole/part relationships.]

Additional Notes on Fields as Applied to the Linder Collection

007   **Fixed field (physical description)**

     GMD   k

     SMD   [most often relevant are:]

     d   drawings

             watercolours treated as drawings, not paintings (e); 655 and 755 to be kept consistent

     h   photo prints

     j   prints

Fixed field positions:

003   colour: usually c, a, or b

004   primary support

005   secondary support

049   **Local holdings**

A local field to enable manipulation of records sorting and searching by submenu as required.

Codes relevant to the Linder Collection are:

|l   x   prints

           y   drawings

           z   photographs

100   **Main entry—Personal name**

Artist's name entered even if unsigned work if attribution is secure.

245   **Title statement**

The date is sometimes included as part of the title.

Cataloguers' omissions are rare; punctuation follows Betz 1.A3.

|h   [art original]

|b   See Betz 1.F2

|c   Artist/creator rarely entered here as many of the items are unsigned.

Rules adapted as follows:

250   **Edition statement**

Not used for drawings and photographs (only for prints in a numbered edition)

260   **Publication date**

|c   Date is the only subfield used for original drawings and photographs.

A detailed date is given where possible (optional according to AACR2, but desirable: (see Betz 2.H1), e.g., 1880 Sept. 27.

300   **Physical extent**

|a   1 art original :

|b   The most striking medium/predominant technique is normally given first, following practice as outlined in Betz and normal practice of the V&A Print Room.

In this subfield there is some freedom of description using uncontrolled vocabulary (supplemented by the use of controlled terms in 655/755). The type of support need only be included here (as well as in **340**) if very unusual; if recto and verso drawings are present, these are described separately.

|c   Measured in mm not cm following Betz 3.D2.2. This is essential and is approved practice for the description of drawings and paintings; both dimensions are always given.

Any inscription or other text included in picture area should be included in the measurement (3.D3).

If both recto and verso drawings are present, these are described separately.

We would usually indicate if paper is an irregular shape ("irreg. sheet"), but give further details (torn off, cut down, corner cut out, etc.) in 500 notes; important to include dimensions of secondary support (Betz 3.D3.6: "optional addition") here: it may be original, and especially may include part of the image or a border image (*type* of support, both primary and secondary, described under 340); the U.K. term "window mount" is used instead of "mat."

340   Physical medium

|a   Type of support described here.

|c   Give a brief description only if there is much detail in 300 |b.

|e   Type of support described here.

500   Notes

Including:

Source of title, e.g., "supplied by cataloguer."

Other title matter, e.g., variations in title; continuation of title.

Description of subject depicted including any lines of text if, e.g., there is an illustration for a rhyme. We would generally give detailed descriptions here, keeping any supplied title in 245 fairly succinct.

Captions along with signatures and other inscriptions frequently noted together as they are often physically linked (although captions are fairly rare in the Linder Collection).

List of all inscriptions in the notes area: signatures first, then inscriptions according to importance and/or prominence, followed by the various markings. Inscriptions would generally include medium and indicate line endings, giving exact punctuation, including, for example, lack of full stop at end, quotation marks, underlinings, superscript characters, decorative lettering, and so on. The clearest method is to describe each inscription in a new 500 field (unless closely related).

Markings of all kinds are described, including their **medium.** Watermarks would normally be described in a separate note.

Expansion of the physical description would include: pinholes, patches, tears, etc.; also more detail on technique and palette.

506, 530   Restricted access notes

Details of access are given in a general entry referring to the Linder Collection as a whole, not in each individual catalogue entry.

555   Finding aids note

561 **Provenance note**

For example, "Originally collected by Leslie Linder" is entered for each item; for the general entry referring to the Linder Collection as a whole, supplemented by |b "presented . . . and housed at . . . ; on loan . . ."

585 **Exhibitions note**

655 **Index term—Genre/form**

Many headings are used for this kind of material. Where terms are not available in the AAT, other thesauri are consulted.

730 **Added entry—Uniform title** (for titles of published works to which drawings, etc., relate)

755 Many headings are used for this type of material to indicate technique and materials used. [Now deleted by USMARC.]

12 Washingtoniana II: Cataloging Architectural, Design, and Engineering Collections in the Prints and Photographs Division of the Library of Congress

Karen Chittenden

Prints and Photographs Division Collections and Readers

Over 13.5 million pictorial materials, including documentary and master photographs; popular and fine prints; posters; and architectural, engineering, and design drawings, are in the custody of the Prints and Photographs Division (P&P), a unit of the Library of Congress established in 1897.[1] Due to a variety of factors, including decades of understaffing, "only" about three million items had been processed and were available for service to researchers. Since 1990, however, a major Library of Congress initiative, with increased resources, has been to process and catalog huge backlogs in P&P and other divisions. The Arrearage Reduction Program has so far made more than three million additional items in P&P available to the public.

Every year more than 25,500 researchers consult the collections in the Prints and Photographs Division, either in person, or by telephone, or by mail. These scholars, publishers, media representatives, and members of the general public have very diverse backgrounds and a wide array of research needs.

The Washingtoniana II Project

Between 1989 and 1996, the Prints and Photographs Division conducted a project to preserve, organize, and provide access to approximately forty thousand of its unprocessed architectural, design, and engineering drawings. The project is called Washingtoniana II because it includes mainly architectural drawings that relate to the Washington, D.C., metropolitan area. (An earlier project, Washingtoniana I, dealt with photographs relating to Washington, D.C.[2]) Washingtoniana II was funded in large part by the Morris and Gwendolyn Cafritz Foundation.

Scope

The bulk of the materials in the project are architectural drawings, ranging from eighteenth-century developmental drawings for the *U.S. Capitol,* to nineteenth-century designs for the *Library of Congress* and twentieth-century working drawings by local architects for Washington row houses and stores. A Frank Lloyd Wright drawing for the unbuilt *Sugar Loaf Mountain Automobile Objective and Planetarium,* recent designs for an elegant Maryland residence by Cesar Pelli, and U.S. Federal Housing Administration drawings for public housing further indicate the breadth of topics. More than five hundred designers are represented—some by only a single drawing, most by several projects, and a few by archives of thousands of drawings and office records, such as those of Waggaman & Ray and Arthur B. Heaton. A variety of media and processes were used to produce the drawings, including ink, watercolor, graphite, blueprint, diazo print, and photographs. The materials were acquired over many years as copyright deposits, purchases, and gifts.

Goals

The original goals of the Washingtoniana II project were:

1. to provide access to the architectural, design, and engineering drawings and related materials through project-level catalog records, an item-level finding aid, and a microfilm;

2. to preserve the drawings by cleaning, repairing, and limiting handling of these usually fragile items; and

3. to publish an illustrated guide with essays and descriptive entries.

Phases

It took almost eight years to plan the project and to proceed through stages to preserve the drawings; physically process, house, and store them; record data to be used in the preparation of the catalog records; produce MARC format catalog records; and produce the finding aid.

PLANNING PHASE

The planning phase of the project involved setting up a team in which a cataloger, two library technicians, and two conservators worked with the division's curators and a reference staff representative. We talked to staff at other institutions who have cataloged architectural drawings, such as the Avery Library at Columbia

University and the Prints and Drawings Department of the American Institute of Architects Foundation. With our conservators, we developed strategies for preserving, housing, and storing the drawings. We talked to other curators and reference librarians as well as some scholars and researchers about their data retrieval and service needs. We surveyed the materials to get a general idea of what we had, where it was stored, and what condition it was in. We devised a system of assigning nonclassified call numbers in which each building project was given a sequential unit number. We elected to use a nonclassified filing system because we needed to store drawings as compactly as possible, and we wanted to avoid having to shift collections frequently to interfile newly acquired materials in a subject classified scheme.

PRESERVATION PHASE

The majority of architectural drawings in the Washingtoniana II project were never intended to be used as primary sources for research. Their purpose was to aid in the construction of buildings; once they had served their purpose they were rolled or folded and stored in usually less-than-ideal conditions for extended periods. Because of this, many of the drawings in the project needed some degree of conservation attention. It took about five years to complete the preservation phase of the project. A system was devised by a library conservator to humidify and flatten large quantities of drawings, which enabled two library technicians to treat over eighteen thousand drawings in less than two years. Two project conservators, as well as other conservators who were hired as consultants, surveyed the materials to assess treatment needs, performed treatments, and supervised the system for flattening the drawings.[3]

PHYSICAL PROCESSING PHASE

Once the materials were surveyed and preserved, physical processing could begin. Staff sorted the drawings into groups by building project and then subarranged them either by following the numbering system present on the drawings or, when no numbering system was present, by drawing stage (e.g., preliminary drawings, working drawings) and then by method of representation (e.g., plans, elevations, sections, details). See figure 12-1.

This intellectual arrangement is preserved within each project through an item number assigned to each

```
        Preliminary drawings
            Plans
            Elevations
            Sections
            Details
        Working drawings
            Plans
            Elevations
            Sections
            Details
```

Figure 12-1 | Arrangement of Unnumbered Drawings

drawing regardless of its size. The complete call number contains a prefix for the P&P collection area, or filing series (ADE for Architectural, Design, and Engineering drawings); a UNIT number representing the building project; an item number for the drawing; and a storage designation based on the size of the drawing's housing, which determines whether it will be stored in a print box, a map case drawer, or a tube. See the example below.

```
        ADE - UNIT 248,   no. 1   (E size)

collection area    project       item    storage designation
```

As a library technician hand-marked each drawing with its call number, she dictated information about it to another technician who recorded the information in a computer database (dBase IV software). This information became the basis for cataloging work-sheets, finding aid entries, shelf lists, and other reports. The drawings were then housed in polyester or paper folders and stored. Folders were labeled with call numbers printed from the dBase database.

CATALOGING PHASE

A three-tiered approach provides access to the materials. Collection-level MARC format catalog records are created for the archives of architects or architectural firms. The collection-level catalog records summarize information pertinent to the entire body of drawings, such as overall span dates and predominant subjects or building types, and provide context, such as acquisition source or architectural firm history. The second tier of this system is MARC format catalog records at the group, or unit, level, which provide access to the drawings pertaining to a single building or design project. The third tier is an item-level finding aid, which provides more specific information about each drawing and permits a single drawing to be located, thus reducing physical wear and tear on the whole unit when it is pulled or refiled.

FINDING AID PHASE

The finding aid provides specific information about each drawing, such as notable subjects, media, support, and any reproduction numbers. Additional information is provided for drawings of high research value, such as signatures, inscriptions, and precise measurements.

The finding aid (figures 12-2 and 12-3), currently contained in three-ring binders, is produced by formatting and printing electronic data captured in the

Title:	Architectural drawings for a <u>hotel ("Capitol Park Hotel")</u>, North Capitol Street and E Street, N.W. (lots 160-162, square 268), Washington, D.C.
Call Number:	**ADE - UNIT 13**
Summary:	Includes preliminary and working drawings showing site, hotel, offices, and bars as site plans, plans, elevations, sections, details, perspective projections, and schedules; renderings; electrical systems, structural systems, and mechanical systems drawings; engineering drawings; plats.
Medium:	41 items : ink, colored ink, graphite, and blueprint ; in folder(s) 117 x 192 cm. or smaller.
Date:	1914.
Creator:	A.B. Mullett & Co., architect.
Note(s):	UNIT title devised.
	Commission no. 450.
	Some drawings signed by client (illegible).
	Forms part of A.B. Mullett & Co. Archive.
Source:	Gift; Suzanne Mullett Smith; 1987; (DLC/PP-1989:104).
	Gift; Suzanne Mullett Smith; 1986; (DLC/PP-1986:R006).

Figure 12-2 | Sample Entry in Finding Aid

Call number:	ADE - UNIT 13, no. 1 (C size)
Notable subject(s):	Perspective
Media/support:	Ink on illus. board
Note(s):	
Reproduction number(s):	
Call number:	ADE - UNIT 13, no. 2 (F size)
Notable subject(s):	Sub-basement plan
Media/support:	Ink on linen
Note(s):	Signed by client
Reproduction number(s):	
Call number:	ADE - UNIT 13, no. 3 (F size)
Notable subject(s):	Basement plan
Media/support:	Ink/graphite on linen
Note(s):	Signed by client
Reproduction number(s):	
Call number:	ADE - UNIT 13, no. 4 (F size)
Notable subject(s):	1st floor plan
Media/support:	Ink/graphite on linen
Note(s):	
Reproduction number(s):	
Call number:	ADE - UNIT 13, no. 5 (F size)
Notable subject(s):	Mezzanine floor plan
Media/support:	Ink/graphite on linen
Note(s):	Signed by client
Reproduction number(s):	
Call number:	ADE - UNIT 13, no. 6 (F size)
Notable subject(s):	2nd floor plan
Media/support:	Ink/graphite on linen
Note(s):	Signed by client
Reproduction number(s):	
Call number:	ADE - UNIT 13, no. 7 (E size)
Notable subject(s):	3rd floor plan
Media/support:	Ink/graphite on linen
Note(s):	Signed by client
Reproduction number(s):	
Call number:	ADE - UNIT 13, no. 8 (F size)
Notable subject(s):	3rd floor plan
Media/support:	Ink/graphite on linen
Note(s):	Signed by client
Reproduction number(s):	
Call number:	ADE - UNIT 13, no. 9 (F size)
Notable subject(s):	North Capitol Street elevation
Media/support:	Ink/colored ink on linen
Note(s):	Signed by client
Reproduction number(s):	

Figure 12-3 | Sample Entry in Finding Aid

physical processing phase of the project in an item-level listing, interfiled with group-level information derived from the catalog record.

We are planning to encode the finding aid in the new SGML (Standard Generalized Markup Language) Document Type Definition (DTD) called Encoded Archival Description (EAD) so that information about each drawing can be accessed online in relation to its building project. The item-level information will link to the project-level information, which in turn will link to any collection-level information.[4]

PUBLISHED GUIDE PHASE

Simultaneous to the processing and cataloging phases of the project, Prints and Photographs Division curatorial staff was coordinating the production of a published guide to the project. The guide contains essays written by scholars, biographical entries on the architects in the project, and reproductions of selected materials.

Description of Catalog Records

Catalog records for the architectural drawings are created in the MARC Visual Materials Format, with one group record for each of the almost three thousand units and some collection-level records for summarizing the large archives that contain many units. See figure 12-4 for a list of MARC tags used. By using the MARC format, we can integrate the records into the Library of Congress central computer catalog, to be available with records for other Prints and Photographs Division materials, such as photographs or posters, as well as books, manuscripts, and maps in other areas of the library. Researchers are thus able to search for a single subject across a wide spectrum of materials. The records will also be available on RLIN, OCLC, and the Internet, enabling the public to search the catalog without having to travel to Washington, D.C., to visit our Reading Room.

Standards

In constructing our catalog records, we follow the rules of entry in AACR2 (*Anglo-American Cataloguing Rules*, 2nd ed., 1988 revision) and the supplementary descriptive rules for pictorial materials (*Graphic Materials: Rules for Describing Original Items and Historical Collections*, 1982). We draw topical subject

```
Fixed fields:
    Leader Bytes
    Minaret and MUMS displays
    001   Control Number
    005   Date and Time of Latest Transaction
    007   Physical Description Fixed Field-General
          Information
    008   Fixed-length Data Elements
Variable-length fields:
    010   LC Control Number
    017   Copyright Registration Number
    035   System Control Number
    040   Cataloging Source
    050   LC Call Number
    100   Main Entry-Personal Name
    110   Main Entry-Corporate Name
    245   Title Statement
    260   Publication, Distribution, etc. (Imprint)
    300   Physical Description
    500   General Note
    505   Formatted Contents Note
    506   Restrictions on Access Note
    520   Summary, Abstract, Annotation, Scope, etc.
          Note
    530   Additional Physical Form Available Note
    540   Terms Governing Use
    541   Immediate Source of Acquisition Note
    555   Cumulative Index/Finding Aids Note
    580   Linking Entry Complexity Note
    600   Subject Added Entry-Personal Name
    610   Subject Added Entry-Corporate Name
    650   Subject Added Entry-Topical Term
    651   Subject Added Entry-Geographic Name
    655   Index Term-Genre/Form
    700   Added Entry-Personal Name
    710   Added Entry-Corporate Name
    773   Host Item Entry
    852   Location
    908   Local Fixed Field
    985   Local Record History
```

Figure 12-4 | List of Fields Used in ADE - UNIT and LOT Catalog Records

headings and terms for indexing form of material from TGM (*Thesaurus for Graphic Materials*), adding new terms as required. The AAT (*Art and Architecture Thesaurus*) is the main source we consult when proposing new terms relating to architecture for TGM.[5]

Architect names, some client names, and significant building names are also included in the catalog records as access points. The names are taken from LCNAF (Library of Congress Name Authority File) and LCSH *(Library of Congress Subject Headings)*. When the names are not found in these files, we establish them following AACR2 and the LCSH *Subject Cataloging Manual*.[6] A data dictionary documents field content and tagging in detail (see appendix B).

Approach

After the planning, preservation, and physical processing phases of the project were completed, the MARC format catalog records were ready to be written. The cataloger began by analyzing the data captured during physical processing, which had been formatted into cataloging worksheets, and making decisions on what information to incorporate in the records and how to incorporate it.

In most cases, main entry is given to the architect in a 1XX field. If more than one architect's name is on the drawings, the first architect named is assigned as the main entry and additional names are included as added entries (7XX fields). The architect is defined as the person or corporate body responsible for the design of the structure or the documentation of the design of the structure.

Using the architectural drawing for the hotel in figure 12-5 as an example, the title (245 field) is devised

Figure 12-5 | A.B. Mullett & Co., Architects, "Capitol Park Hotel," Washington, D.C., 1914. Library of Congress, Architecture, Design and Engineering Collections ADE - UNIT 13, no. 1 (C size), LC-USZ62-114046. Used with permission.

to include the primary drawing purpose (e.g., architectural drawings), the building type (e.g., hotel), what the building was called on the drawing (e.g., Capitol Park Hotel), the client's name (illegible in the case of this example), and the address (e.g., North Capitol Street and E Street, N.W. [lots 160–162, square 268], Washington, D.C.).

For the physical description (300 field), the total number of drawings in the unit is entered followed by the specific material designation of "items" (see figure 12-6). We use the term *items* because the units often contain a variety of materials, including original drawings, reproduction processes (e.g., blueprints and diazo prints), photographs, and photomechanical processes. The specific media and dimensions of the largest housing used in the unit are also entered in the physical description.

Commission numbers and notes useful for documenting the material or relating it to other materials are included in general notes (500 field). A summary note (520 field) is used to summarize the drawing types, subjects represented, methods of representation, secondary drawing purposes, and other document types included in the unit.

When a building client's name can be verified in a reference source, it is given as an added entry (700, 710 fields) with a relator term of "client." If the structure depicted is for the use of the client, and his or her name has been verified, a subject added entry (600, 610 fields) is also used, with a subdivision elucidating the relationship of the client to the structure (e.g., "Homes and haunts" for personal names and "Buildings" for corporate bodies). Specific topical terms are also included as subject added entries (650 field). Genre terms (655 field) are mainly limited to drawing purpose. Physical form terms are not indexed, as this information is available in the 300 and 520 fields and in the finding aid. Figure 12-7 shows the preceding information as it appears on-screen for a user.

Challenges

Working with architectural drawings has provided us with some challenging issues. For example, the drawings themselves are very difficult to handle, house, and store. In addition, the way in which architects work generated some cataloging questions. The MARC format had fields for all the information we wanted to record, but implementation systems that take advantage of the codes and links are still needed.

Because the drawings are often quite large, sizable work space and storage space are required. The drawings can also be fragile, having been executed on tracing paper or reproduced as blueprints and diazo prints, which require extreme care in handling. The mixture of original drawings and reproductions places limitations on housings, since these types of materials should not be interfiled for preservation reasons. It also can be time-consuming to decipher written information given the handling constraints.

Because architectural drawings are created in a variety of media and processes, the choice of main entry is sometimes difficult. When cataloging original drawings, clearly the architect is assigned as the main entry, following AACR2 Rule 21.1A1, as the person "responsible for the creation of the intellectual or artistic content of a work," whether or not he or she delineated the work. In the case of reproductive processes, such as blueprints or photographs of drawings, AACR2 Rule 21.16B seems appropriate:

> Enter a reproduction of an art work (e.g., a photograph, a photomechanical reproduction, or a reproduction of sculpture) under the heading for the original work. Make an added entry under the heading for the person or body responsible for the reproduction, unless the person or body is merely responsible for manufacture or publication.

Most of the time the work-in-hand supports these choices of main entry because of the way the names are expressed on the drawings.

Occasionally the choice becomes less clear when, for example, the work-in-hand is an engraving of an architectural drawing. Is the engraving a reproduction of an art work, requiring that the architect be given main entry, or is it an adaptation of an art work, which necessitates following AACR2 Rule 21.16A:

> Enter an adaptation from one medium of the graphic arts to another under the heading for the person responsible for the adaptation. . . .

Strict adherence to the rules would probably lead to the conclusion that the engraving is an adaptation of an art work rather than a reproduction. However, in many cases, the prints were made to be used in the design or documentation of the design of a structure. We concluded that the purpose of the prints cataloged in the context of the Washingtoniana II project was reproductive, and assigned the architect as main entry.

The biggest disadvantage of the MARC format was related to implementation rather than to the format

```
OCLC:     95858272        Rec stat: n   Entrd: 950721        Used: 19960912
Type: k   Bib lvl: d   Govt pub:     Lang: eng      Source:      Leng: nnn
          Enc lvl:      Type mat: l   Ctry: xxu      Dat tp: s
Tech: n   Mod rec:     Accomp mat:
Desc: a   Int lvl:     Dates: 1914,
COM:k     FMD:l    OR:|    CL:u   PRS:u         SSN:u
```

050 00	|aADE - UNIT 13 |u<P&P>
010	|a 95858272 /PP
040	|aDLC |cDLC |egihc
110 2	|aA.B. Mullett & Co., |earchitect.
245 10	|aArchitectural drawings for a hotel ("Capitol Park Hotel"), North Capitol Street and E Street, N.W. (lots 160-162, square 268), Washington, D.C. |h[graphic].
260	|c1914.
300	|a41 items : |bink, colored ink, graphite, and blueprint ; |cin folder(s) 117 x 192 cm. or smaller.
500	|aUNIT title devised.
500	|aCommission no. 450.
500	|aSome drawings signed by client (illegible).
520 0	|aIncludes preliminary and working drawings showing site, hotel, offices, and bars as site plans, plans, elevations, sections, details, perspective projections, and schedules; renderings; electrical systems, mechanical systems, and structural drawings; engineering drawings; plats.
541	|cGift; |aSuzanne Mullett Smith; |d1987; |e(DLC/PP-1989:104).
541	|cGift; |aSuzanne Mullett Smith; |d1986; |e(DLC/PP-1986:R006).
580	|aForms part of A.B. Mullett & Co. Archive.
540	|aMay be restricted: Information on reproduction rights available in LC P&P Restrictions Notebook.
506	|aOriginal materials served by appointment only.
555 8	|aFinding aid (unpublished): Filed by UNIT number, available in Prints and Photographs Reading Room.
650 7	|aHotels |zWashington (D.C.) |y1910-1920. |2lctgm
650 7	|aOffices |zWashington (D.C.) |y1910-1920. |2lctgm
650 7	|aBars |zWashington (D.C.) |y1910-1920. |2lctgm
655 7	|aArchitectural drawings |y1910-1920. |2gmgpc
655 7	|aRenderings |y1910-1920. |2gmgpc
655 7	|aElectrical systems drawings |y1910-1920. |2gmgpc
655 7	|aStructural drawings |y1910-1920. |2gmgpc
655 7	|aMechanical systems drawings |y1910-1920. |2gmgpc
655 7	|aEngineering drawings |y1910-1920. |2gmgpc
655 7	|aPlats |y1910-1920. |2gmgpc
773 0	|tA.B. Mullett & Co. Archive (Library of Congress) |w(DLC) 95858231
852	|aLibrary of Congress |bPrints and Photographs Division |eWashington, D.C. 20540 USA |ndcu
908	|a q e
985	|app/wii

Figure 12-6 | MARC Bibliographic Record

itself: the inability to link collection-level information to project-level information to item-level information in parent-child relationships. However, as the project progressed, technology was taking major steps forward. The development of an SGML DTD for archival finding aids will solve part of the problem. Information relating to individual drawings that we intended to provide in a hard-copy finding aid will be encoded in SGML and linked to the project-level MARC records through the 856 field. Both levels of information will be accessible electronically. The development of linking fields, especially the 773 (host item entry) field, has also given us the ability to make a link between the project-level catalog record and the collection-level catalog record. We considered using the 789 (component item entry) field, the approach developed by the Avery Library, but held off because of MARC record size limits and confusing local system displays.

Records 11 through 11 of 90 returned.

Author:	A.B. Mullett & Co., architect.
Title:	Architectural drawings for a hotel ("Capitol Park Hotel"), North Capitol Street and E Street, N.W. (lots 160-162, square 268), Washington, D.C. [graphic].
Published:	1914.
Description:	41 items : ink, colored ink, graphite, and blueprint ; in folder(s) 117 x 192 cm. or smaller.
LC Call No.:	ADE - UNIT 13
Notes:	UNIT title devised.
	Commission no. 450.
	Some drawings signed by client (illegible).
	Includes preliminary and working drawings showing site, hotel, offices, and bars as site plans, plans, elevations, sections, details, perspective projections, and schedules; renderings; electrical systems, mechanical systems, and structural drawings; engineering drawings; plats.
	Gift; Suzanne Mullett Smith; 1987; (DLC/PP-1989:104).
	Gift; Suzanne Mullett Smith; 1986; (DLC/PP-1986:R006).
	Forms part of A.B. Mullett & Co. Archive.
	May be restricted: Information on reproduction rights available in LC P&P Restrictions Notebook.
	Original materials served by appointment only.
	Finding aid (unpublished) : Filed by UNIT number, available in Prints and Photographs Reading Room.
Subjects:	Hotels -- Washington (D.C.) -- 1910-1920. lctgm
	Offices -- Washington (D.C.) -- 1910-1920. lctgm
	Bars -- Washington (D.C.) -- 1910-1920. lctgm
	Architectural drawings -- 1910-1920. gmgpc
	Renderings -- 1910-1920. gmgpc
	Electrical systems drawings -- 1910-1920. gmgpc
	Structural drawings -- 1910-1920. gmgpc
	Mechanical systems drawings -- 1910-1920. gmgpc
	Engineering drawings -- 1910-1920. gmgpc
	Plats -- 1910-1920. gmgpc
Location:	Library of Congress Prints and Photographs Division Washington, D.C. 20540 USA dcu
Control No.:	95858272 /PP

This display was generated by the CNIDR Web-Z39.50 gateway, version 1.08, with Library of Congress Modifications.

Figure 12-7 | Catalog Screen

Status of the Project

The preservation, physical processing, housing and storage, and preliminary cataloging phases of the Washingtoniana II project were finished in 1994. The final cataloging and finding aid phases of the project were completed in December 1996. The proposed publication date for the book is 1998.

The original plan of producing a microfilm as a surrogate for the drawings was abandoned midway through the project because of dissatisfaction with microfilm as a surrogate as well as budgetary reasons. Copy photographs of a selection of more than five-hundred drawings will provide the means for creating a partial visual surrogate through digitizing the copy negatives and transparencies.

Conclusion

Now that the processing and cataloging phases of the Washingtoniana II project are coming to a close, we will continue to use the access system that we developed for this project to process and catalog other architectural materials that did not fall within the scope of Washingtoniana II. The MARC format has proven to be flexible enough to accommodate architectural materials, especially because it soon will be possible to make links between levels of records. Finally, the ability to communicate information on national networks, which the MARC format provides, gives researchers the best possible access to our collections.

NOTES

1. For additional information, see: Library of Congress, *Library of Congress Prints and Photographs: An Illustrated Guide* (Washington, D.C.: Library of Congress, 1995); and C. Ford Peatross, "Architectural Collections of the Library of Congress," *The Quarterly Journal of the Library of Congress* 34, no. 3 (1977): 249–284. The division's World Wide Web homepage is at http://lcweb.loc.gov/rr/print, with access to the text portion of catalog records. Selected collections are available with digital images at the American Memory Web site: http://lcweb2.loc.gov/ammem.

2. Kathleen Collins, *Washingtoniana Photographs: Collections in the Prints and Photographs Division of the Library of Congress* (Washington, D.C.: Library of Congress, 1989).

3. Michele E. Hamill, "Washingtoniana II: Conservation of Architectural Drawings at the Library of Congress," *The Book and Paper Group Annual* (The American Institute for Conservation of Historic and Artistic Works) 12 (1993): 24–31.

4. Library of Congress EAD Web site address: <http://www.loc.gov/rr/ead/eadhome.html>.

5. *Anglo-American Cataloguing Rules,* 2nd ed., 1988 revision (Chicago: American Library Association, 1988); Elisabeth Betz, comp., *Graphic Materials: Rules for Describing Original Items and Historical Collections* (Washington, D.C.: Library of Congress, 1982); Library of Congress, Prints and Photographs Division, *Thesaurus for Graphic Materials,* 2nd ed. (Washington, D.C.: Library of Congress Cataloging Distribution Service, 1995); and *Art and Architecture Thesaurus,* 2nd ed. (New York: Oxford University Press, on behalf of the Getty Art History Information Program, 1994).

6. Library of Congress, *Subject Cataloging Manual: Subject Headings,* 4th ed. (Washington, D.C.: Library of Congress Cataloging Distribution Service, 1991–).

13 MARC Format for the Photograph Collection at the Milwaukee Public Museum

Susan Otto

Background

The Milwaukee Public Museum is a large natural history museum that has, over the past one hundred years, systematically assembled and maintained collections that number over 4.5 million specimens. Its significant collections and research fields include: North American Indian ethnology, New World archaeology, ethnobotany, Milwaukee and Wisconsin flora and fauna, Paleozoic brachiopods, and European firearms and decorative arts. The photograph collection of the museum serves as an institutional archive. As such, most of the approximately 250,000 photographs in the collection were taken by museum staff and reflect the work of the museum: its fieldwork, specimens, exhibits, and activities.

The photograph collection is part of the museum reference library. The 125,000-volume library, along with the museum, serves a broad community from the general public to serious professionals. However, most of the users of the photograph collection are from the academic community who use the images for research and publication.

Most of the 250,000 images in the photograph collection are black-and-white photographs. Because the photographs were taken by museum staff, the collection holds both the negatives and prints. Because of the increasing demand for color photographs, there has been a shift away from black-and-white negative/print images toward the use of color slides. Most of the color slides are taken by the museum curators and are kept in the curatorial departments as part of the curators' ongoing research. Slides of general, less academic interest are held in the photograph collection. The photograph collection now holds approximately 25,000 35mm color slides. The slides are stored in 20-slide archival sheets and filed by broad subject area. There is an inventory list for the slides in the collection.

The black-and-white photographs are arranged in two different systems:

1. Photographs taken before 1960 are stored in archival boxes and arranged in broad subject categories. Each image has a negative number (essentially an accession number) and a corresponding catalog

card that contains the information about the image. Because the catalog cards are arranged by negative number, it is impossible to search the card catalog by subject. However, there is a loose-leaf inventory/index finding aid to assist the user in determining which boxes contain the desired image.

2. Photographs taken since 1960 are arranged by museum department, and the information about the images is written on the negative envelope. These photographs are mounted into loose-leaf binders and are arranged by negative number. Although there is a semblance of subject grouping for some of these images, most of the photographs were simply assigned the next negative (accession) number and added to the back of the last book.

Until recently, access to the images has been through various inventory lists and staff memory. At present, the only electronic access to the images that have been cataloged is through the computer in the photograph collection. However, the museum has recently established a Web site and will be using the site to make the catalog of photographs (as well as catalogs of other museum collections) available to the public.

Preparation

In 1991, the photograph collection acquired a computer, and the library staff decided to make those photographs for which there is a high demand more accessible by cataloging them into a computer database. We chose the Minaret database (developed by Cactus Software) because it is a MARC format database that is used by several other archival institutions. While the decision to use a MARC format database reflects the librarian bias of the staff, we felt that because the MARC format has an established track record and is generally accepted as standard in libraries and archives throughout the country, we would eventually be able to transfer our records to other, national databases. The MARC format also provides us with the flexibility to catalog different collections of photographs within the larger collection at different levels of completeness and detail depending on the importance and use of each smaller collection. We decided to catalog three different collections at three different levels of cataloging: photographs of the North American Indians, photographs by Sumner W. Matteson, and photographs of the artifacts in the anthropology department.

North American Indian Photographs

Fieldwork among North American Indians by the museum staff between 1910 and 1970 resulted in some twelve thousand images of Indians in the Southwest, Great Basin, Northwest Coast, and Wisconsin. The North American images were chosen to be cataloged first because of their heavy use.

Work on the American Indian photograph catalog began in 1991. About 95 percent of the photographs were in the pre-1960 arrangement system. These photographs were taken over a period of some sixty years, over many geographic regions, by several different photographers. This meant that, although the photographs had catalog cards, they had never been brought together in one meaningful arrangement. The first task was to locate all the North American Indian photographs and sort them, first into general geographical areas/cultural groups (e.g., Plains Indians, Woodland Indians, Northwest Coast Indians, etc.), then by tribe. The images were further sorted by photographer, location (reservation), date, and subject.

Beginning with the Woodland Indians, the Wisconsin Indian group was cataloged first, followed by the other groups and tribes within the other geographical areas. Although it is important to have access to the images on an item level, we did not want to produce a record for each photograph. We thus decided to treat the photographs as if they were part of a series. Images were arranged into meaningful groups by the preceding criteria and given a descriptive group title, a group being anything from a single photograph to more than one hundred photographs. However, each image in the group was given its own separate field containing the negative number and a brief description. Because the Photograph Collection has only one staff member, it took just over three years to complete the catalog for the American Indian photographs. The catalog was completed in spring of 1995.

The standard used to do the cataloging was Elisabeth W. Betz's *Graphic Materials: Rules for Describing Original Items and Historical Collections,* and the MARC conventions used were those of OCLC. Records were entered in the Minaret OCLC database, Visual Materials (VM) Format. Full level I cataloging of these records uses the variable fields shown in figure 13-1. The variable fields for a record look like those in figure 13-2.

MARC Tag Number	Local Use
100:	Photographer.
245:	Descriptive title of the collection.
260:	Place, publisher, date.
300:	Physical description of the collection.
440:	Series title: generally a statement of place and date that the photographs were taken.
520:	Description of individual photographs: Negative number: description proper {type of negative [g=glass, n=nitrate, s=safety, x=no negative] ; whether or not a print is on file [+=yes, –=no]}.
650:	Library of Congress subject heading.
690:	Local subject heading (i.e., subject headings not permitted by LCSH).

Figure 13-1 | Variable MARC Fields Used for Photograph Collection

100	1	‖a Barrett, S.A. ‖q (Samuel Alfred) ‖d 1879-1965.
245	10	‖a Chippewa Dream Dance Drums / ‖c photographed by S.A. Barrett.
260		‖a Milwaukee : ‖b Milwaukee Public Museum, ‖c 1910.
300		‖a 4 photographs: negative and/or print.
440	0	‖a Lac Court Oreilles, WI fieldwork, 1910.
520	8	‖a #2710:Dream Dance at Whitefish showing the two ceremonial drums {n/g ; +p}
520	8	‖a #2715:Close-up of one of the Dream Dance Drums showing symbolic decoration in beadwork {n/g ; +p}
520	8	‖a #2717:Close-up view of one of the circles of the drummers {n/g ; +p}
520	8	‖a #20213:Dream Dance at Whitefish showing the two ceremonial drums {n/n ; +p}
650	0	‖a Ojibwa Indians ‖Music
690		‖a Chippewa Indians ‖Music

Figure 13-2 | MARC Bibliographic Record

The Sumner W. Matteson Photograph Collection

The second collection that is being put into electronic format comprises the photographs of the turn-of-the-century photojournalist Sumner W. Matteson. Matteson, a contemporary of Edward Curtis, traveled throughout the United States, Mexico, and Cuba photographing the changing frontier. His images are important for their artistic quality as well as their anthropological/historic value. Although many of Matteson's images are in collections across the country, the Milwaukee Public Museum has the largest number—some five thousand of his original negatives (see figure 13-3 for an example).

The Matteson Collection had been purchased from the Matteson estate in 1922 and accessioned into the pre-1960 system. Because all the images were accessioned at the same time, all the catalog cards were together. In 1983, the museum published a book about the work of Matteson, and an inventory of the photographs was done at that time. Because of the importance of this collection, the heavy use it receives, and its relatively small size, we decided to catalog this collection at an item level. It took almost two years to enter all the Matteson photographs at this minimal-level cataloging. Although this level of cataloging is not totally satisfactory, it gives good access to the images. Later we would go back and upgrade the cataloging to I level using the variable fields shown in figure 13-4 entered in the Minaret visual materials database. The variable fields for a record look like those in figure 13-5.

Figure 13-3 | "Horse Boy outside of medicine lodge. Ft. Belknap Reservation, Mont., 1905." Photo by Sumner W. Matteson. (By permission of the Milwaukee Public Museum©.)

```
MARC
Tag
Number    Local Use

033:      Date.
035:      Negative number.
050:      Copy negative number.
080:      Lantern slide number.
100:      Photographer.
245:      Descriptive title.
300:      Physical description.
440:      Series/portfolio title.
650:      Library of Congress subject heading.
```

Figure 13-4 | Variable MARC Fields Used in Database

```
033        |a 1908
035        |a 41179
050        |a SWM-1-G-235.
080        |a 674.02:60
100  1     |a Matteson, Sumner W.
245  10    |a Two large logs on the Columbia River.
300        |a 1 |b Nitrate.
440        |a Oregon.
650   0    |a Lumbering |y Oregon.
```

Figure 13-5 | MARC Bibliographic Record

```
MARC
Tag
Number    Local Use

033:      Date of photograph.
035:      Negative number.
100:      Photographer.
245:      Descriptive title for photograph.
260:      Place, publisher, date.
300:      Physical description.
752:      Hierarchical place name access.
518:      Place and date of photograph.
530:      Lantern slide catalog number.
533:      Duplicate or copy negative.
650:      Library of Congress subject headings.
690:      Local subject heading (i.e., subject headings
            not permitted by LCSH).
```

Figure 13-6 | Variable MARC Fields Used in Database

```
033 0      |a 1907
035        |a 106659
100  1     |a Matteson, Sumner W., |d 1867-1920.
245  5     |a [The new post office in Mexico City,
             second to none in the world] / |c
             photographed by Sumner W. Matteson.
260        |a Milwaukee : |b Milwaukee Public
             Museum, |c 1922.
300        |a 1 : |b Glass ; |e Contact print.
752        |a Mexico |b Federal District |d Mexico City.
518        |a Mexico City, 1907.
530        |a Lantern slide: 917.265:13.
533        |a Copy negative: SWM-1-D-653.
650 10     |a Post offices |y Mexico.
```

Figure 13-7 | MARC Bibliographic Record

Recently we have begun to upgrade the Matteson catalog using I-level input standards. As with the photographs of the North American Indians, the standard used to do the cataloging is Betz, *Graphic Materials*, and the MARC conventions used were those of OCLC.

Full level I cataloging of these records uses the variable fields shown in figure 13-6. The variable fields for a record look like those in figure 13-7.

Cataloging for both the North American Indian and the upgraded Sumner W. Matteson photographs follows the rules and conventions set down in Betz and OCLC. There is no deviation from standard practices.

Photographs of Artifacts in the Anthropology Department

An experiment was begun to make the photographs of the artifacts in the anthropology collection more accessible. All these photographs are arranged in loose-leaf binders by negative number. Any available information about these images (often very little) is written on the negative envelope.

Beginning with the first photograph in the first book and using the information on the negative envelope, we made a very brief, quick-and-dirty database record using the Minaret Museum Collections database. See figure 13-8. The record looks like the one shown in figure 13-9.

It took a little less than two years to get the two thousand plus images into this database. As hoped, the effort has made the photographs more searchable.

MARC Tag Number	Local Use
035:	Negative number.
245:	Descriptive title of artifact.
500:	Expanded description of the artifact, if necessary.
	Use for geographic location identification.
503:	Name of anthropology collection (if any).
518:	Anthropology's accession/cataloging number for the artifact.
535:	Where/how collected.

Figure 13-8 | Variable MARC Fields Used in Database

```
035    |a A-504-F.
245    |a Bowl and forks.
500    |a Fiji.
503    |a Stanley Collection.
518    |a Cat. #59370/26347 -- large fork.
518    |a Cat. #58638/19424 -- small fork.
518    |a Cat. #59366/20347 -- bowl.
650    |a Material culture |y Fiji.
```

Figure 13-9 | MARC Bibliographic Record

The librarian can call up the records for all material culture for Fiji and, by scrolling through the records, the curator can usually tell what photograph he or she wants without having to page randomly through the binders containing the photographs.

Conclusion

Recent cutbacks in the museum budget have made it necessary to reduce museum staff. The photograph collection staff was cut from one full-time librarian to one quarter-time librarian. Therefore, although work on upgrading the remaining Sumner W. Matteson photographs into the catalog is progressing, it is doing so at a greatly reduced rate. The establishment of a Web site for the museum opens up the possibility of putting the catalog, and eventually the photographs themselves, online. Plans are being made in the hope that funding can be found.

BIBLIOGRAPHY

Betz, Elisabeth W. *Graphic Materials: Rules for Describing Original Items and Historical Collections.* Washington, D.C.: Library of Congress, 1982.

Online Systems Audiovisual Media Format. 2nd ed. Dublin, Ohio: Online Computer Library Center, 1986.

Cataloging Images in MARC at the California Historical Society

Patricia Keats

Until the summer of 1995, the California Historical Society (CHS) in San Francisco was housed in a late-nineteenth-century Pacific Heights mansion built for John D. Spreckles, a turn-of-the-century entrepreneur who established the sugar beet industry in California, and founded railroads, utilities, and a street railway. The society's new address is 678 Mission Street, San Francisco, California 94105. The society, a private nonprofit institution, is designated by the state legislature as the official historical society of California, dedicated to collecting, preserving, and interpreting information about California and the West. The library of the society, the North Baker Library, is housed in the Spreckles mansion at 2099 Pacific Avenue; its holdings include historical texts, manuscripts, maps, and several special collections found nowhere else in the country. In addition to housing the most complete history of printing and lithography in the western

United States, the library includes an estimated 500,000 photographs. These materials are divided into four main collections: reference and research, manuscripts, the Kemble collection of western printing and publishing, and the photographic collection.

The reference and research collection includes thirty thousand published books and pamphlets, hundreds of thousands of ephemera, 3,700 maps, posters, and broadsides, and 2,500 serials, including periodicals, newspapers, and microfilm. The books in the collection are titles relating to the history of California from 1535 to the present, emphasizing local history, early exploration and growth of the state's fifty-eight counties; and twentieth-century materials focusing on the history of women, ethnic and other minority groups, transportation, and business and labor history. Pamphlets include documents, reports, and shorter works, such as governmental publications,

Reprinted with permission of the *Visual Resources Association Bulletin* and Patricia Keats from "Cataloging Images in MARC at the California Historical Society," *VRA Bulletin* 22, no. 4 (winter 1995): 19–35.

local histories, brochures, and corporate and individual publications. Among the periodicals housed at the society are rare Gold Rush newspapers and original issues and microfilm editions of the *Alta California* and the *San Francisco Call*. The collection of ephemera contains biographical, business, and theater materials, including personal recollections by families of their pioneer ancestors. Also included in this part of the collection is a small amount of sheet music. The library's three thousand maps and seven hundred posters and broadsides include original maps of the Fremont expedition, early boundary maps, the earliest city and county maps, and Gold Rush material.

The society's manuscripts encompass over 3,500 collections, including diaries and letters of Gold Rush miners, early settlers, and ranchers, as well as material from nineteenth-century businesses and political organizations, and leaders such as Adolph Sutro, Gertrude Atherton, Mary Austin, Dan DeQuill, and Bret Harte. The Kemble collection on western printing and publishing is named for the pioneer California printer and publisher, Edward Cleveland Kemble. This collection consists of more than four thousand volumes, extensive pamphlet and ephemeral materials, the third largest collection of type specimen books in the United States, photographs from the archive of the Western Printer and Lithographer, more than three hundred periodicals, archives of several printing firms, including Taylor & Taylor, and significant manuscript holdings all pertaining to the history of printing and publishing, especially in California and the West.

The photographic collection is divided into the general collection and the special or restricted collection. The general collection includes 450,000 prints, 4,000 oversize prints, 38,500 film negatives, and 4,100 glass plate negatives, providing an extraordinary breadth and depth of historical documentation. The special collection includes 115 daguerreotypes, 240 other-cased photographs, ninety-five mammoth plate prints, 150 glass stereo views, 241 photographic albums, thirty-five photographic rare books, and 2,400 photographs arranged by photographer. Some of the photographers represented include Carleton Watkins, Eadweard Muybridge, Arnold Genthe, and Minor White. Subjects include San Francisco's Chinatown and the 1906 earthquake, stereoscopic views of California by Watkins, the Panama-Pacific International Exposition of 1915, and the Golden Gate International Exposition.

The society also has a fine arts collection which includes paintings, drawings, watercolors, furniture, and decorative arts objects. This part of the collection includes historical artifacts such as campaign buttons, firemen's badges, wooden pipes, miniatures, souvenirs, and miners' money belts. Much of this part of the collection is in storage but is currently being more fully cataloged and entered into a database.

Most of the printed collections at the society are cataloged, but there remains an enormous amount of unprocessed material. The photographic collection is by far the most organized, but was also in the process of having its shelf list revised as the visual imaging project was begun. The library collection is organized, but according to a wide variety of schemes. Over the years, different classification systems have been used —the Dewey system, the Library of Congress Classification System, and several local systems such as biographies classed alphabetically, and some items classed by accession number. To begin to standardize and automate the collection, a few years ago the library went through an online retrospective conversion project, and eighteen thousand records were put into RLIN by adapting already existing records. There still remain many unclassified items, items needing original cataloging, as well as totally unprocessed items.

The visual imaging project at the society began as a desire to create a catalog of its entire library and museum collections which would be accessible to the public by computer either through the Internet or the statewide California system, MELVYL, which includes libraries in the University of California and the California State University systems, and the state library. Since so much of the collection is unique, getting our records online could make our library available to a wider audience than those who are able to visit our Pacific Heights location. After we converted a large portion of our book records to a MARC format on RLIN, we began to work on other parts of our collection not so readily transferable to the MARC format—namely images and objects.

The images, which have been scanned and cataloged, are only available on our local terminals, but we hope to be able to mount both our catalog and our images on Internet Web pages in the future.

Getting Started

The visual imaging project began in 1993 as part of a project to automate the society's collections. As with many collections, the cataloging was not consistent over the years. Many items were unprocessed and ir-retrievable. CHS tried to anticipate standards that would be available five or ten years into the future, and, in doing so, assembled a powerful, user-friendly network of client-server workstations. Searching for the right computers was the first step. The criteria used in making the selection included the computer's ability to handle digital images, strong database management, file security, institution-wide networking, ability to integrate a wide array of software tools, and a friendly graphical interface. CHS chose the UNIX-based NeXT computers as the basis for the automation effort because of their ability to handle all of our requirements. NeXT computers were purchased and networked for the society through funding obtained from the William G. Irwin Charity Foundation. Document and image scanners were also purchased, and we began to decide which items to use in our initial project. These decisions were based on the popularity of the image as well as the object's rarity and fragility. As of 1995, spread throughout the library building, seven TCP/IP Ethernet-connected workstations were in use by the staff, with an attached array of three flat-bed image scanners, one high-speed document scanner, a printer on each of the three floors of the building, with floppy, optical, CD, and DAT (digital audiotape) drives providing any type of file loading or backup capability.

The decisions on equipment were made by the curatorial director of photography, Robert MacKimmie, and the library director, Jeffrey Barr, both of whom had experience using either DOS or UNIX-based computers. After the equipment was purchased, further funding was sought to hire people to scan, catalog, and enter the images and their records. The Durfee Foundation in Los Angeles provided these funds in 1994, and the society's desire to create a catalog consisting of both images and text data from the library, photograph collection, and fine arts collections began to be realized.

Due to the variety of images at CHS, choosing the first ones to be scanned proved to be complex and challenging. Historical importance, state of preservation, as well as the beauty and appeal of the image figured in the decision-making process. Since the first year was to serve as a pilot project, the variety of types of images scanned and cataloged was important. At first a theme of the Gold Rush was considered, but this was eventually expanded to include images covering all of California history. The format of the image was also a consideration. Since the society has many different images in different formats, we decided to pull images from many parts of the collection; therefore, we scanned and cataloged images on sheet music, fruit labels, wood engravings from nineteenth-century illustrated periodicals, watercolors, pencil sketches, oil paintings, artifacts such as miners' money belts, souvenir fans from Sonoma County, as well as the more conventional photographs and book illustrations.

Before the catalogers, Barry Lee Johnson and I, arrived in March 1994, some preliminary selection had been done, but most of the process was completed after we began working with the materials every day. Many photographic images had been scanned, but as with some of the other items in the collection, some preliminary information had to be provided before cataloging could occur. The photography curator, library director, or fine arts curator assisted by identifying the type of photograph, or whether the book illustration was a wood or steel engraving, or what media had been used in producing a sketch by a nineteenth-century artist.

Scanning was performed at the highest resolution allowed by our equipment and then taken offline and stored on optical disk. Images are recorded as 1-bit line art, 8-bit gray scale, or 24-bit color as dictated by the material. When sufficient optical disks are filled, the digital information is transferred to DAT as a short-to-intermediate-term archiving method until more permanent archival storage becomes cost effective. This method allows fast retrieval and display of images, with the assurance of high-quality versions in the vault if high-resolution files are required, or if the screen version needs upgrading.

Once we solved the scanning problems and discovered what scanned well and what did not, we began to tackle the cataloging problems. While the museum and library staff now fully appreciates the fact that the MARC format can define any type of collection material, this was not always the case. At first, neither the photography curator nor the fine arts curator believed that the information from their items would fit into a MARC record because MARC records were only for books—or so they thought.

Before beginning to catalog, we studied Elisabeth W. Betz's *Graphic Materials: Rules for Describing Original Items and Historical Collections* (Washington, D.C.: Library of Congress, 1982) and the American Library Association's *Anglo-American Cataloguing Rules*, 2nd ed. (Chicago: ALA, 1978). Since both catalogers had extensive backgrounds in cataloging a wide variety of formats—slides, books, rare books, sheet music, music, broadsides, newspapers, and realia—we felt comfortable deciding how to handle the different formats we encountered. Barry Johnson had just come from the RLG (Research Libraries Group) project at Northwestern University where he had been cataloging a collection of French historical photographs, so he was familiar with the Visual Materials (VIM) format in RLIN. Both of us were used to using LCSH for our subject headings, and I had become familiar with *Art and Architecture Thesaurus* (AAT), having learned about it over the last few years from articles and conferences.

The library director, Jeffrey Barr, had a copy of the manual by Deirdre Stam and Ruth Palmquist, *SUART: A MARC-based Information Structure and Data Dictionary for the Syracuse University Art Collection* (Syracuse, N.Y.: Museum Computer Network, 1989) which discusses cataloging collections with MARC tags. I had also read *Beyond the Book: Extending MARC for Subject Access*, edited by Toni Petersen and Pat Molholt (Boston: G. K. Hall, 1990) which deals with using the MARC format for a variety of cataloging projects. *The Guide to Indexing and Cataloging with the Art and Architecture Thesaurus*, edited by Toni Petersen and Patricia J. Barnett (New York: Oxford University Press, 1994, on behalf of the Getty Art History Information Program), was also a great help. The chapters that were particularly relevant to our collections were "Archives and Special Collections," by Victoria Walch, "Books and Other Bibliographic Materials," by Arlene Taylor, "Objects," by David McFadden and Gregory Tschann, and "Visual Resources," by Alfred Willis.

Many of our decisions on how to apply the MARC format to a particular image were made after reviewing what other institutions had done in RLIN, by asking other institutions on the listserves, and by discussing among ourselves what would be the most logical and straightforward way to proceed. Enormously helpful was the input of two catalogers (with twenty-five years of experience between them), one library director who has been involved with rare books for years, a photography curator who has also been in the field for years, and a fine arts curator with years of museum experience. We tried to incorporate everyone's ideas, and for the most part agreed on the final solution.

For cataloging, standard thesauri are being used —*Library of Congress Thesaurus for Graphic Materials* (LCTGM), *Art and Architecture Thesaurus* (AAT) as well as *Library of Congress Subject Headings* (LCSH).

Our goal is to offer the society's members a database in which their search will provide them with a wide array of research material—not only books on a topic, but photographs, images from books, sheet music, ephemera, and fine arts objects. We hope this will make a researcher's work more fruitful and productive and will also utilize the society's collections to the fullest. The image database will also aid the curators in planning exhibitions, doing research, and providing information for the public.

The Project

Carrying out the project became a bit more complicated than anyone had anticipated because of limited funds. We originally were to be cataloging on the VTLS system, which is an automated library system that can handle cataloging, online public access catalogs, and, in this case, an image database. Unfortunately, funding was not obtained for the full VTLS system and we were limited to using the demonstration software. While waiting for funding to buy the full system, we decided to purchase a temporary system to use for our online catalog. Jeffrey Barr decided upon the Columbia Library System (CLS) software for its low cost and ability to store full USMARC records. Although intended for public and school libraries, we found it versatile, adaptable, and accepting of nearly all the MARC fields we wanted to use.

Our procedure was to catalog the items into the RLIN database, a national online utility that is used by research institutions internationally, and then pass the records to floppy disks and load them into our local online catalog, CLS. The first few weeks of the project were spent setting up the CLS system and working with customer service people at both CLS and RLIN to resolve how to transfer records from RLIN into CLS, how to get the fields we wanted to appear in the record, and how to customize the public catalog screens.

The next step was to select images, and then to customize the fixed and variable fields we would be using in the MARC record. The photographs cataloged were chosen by Robert MacKimmie to show the breadth of the society's collections—chronologically, geographically, topically, and by photographic process. The book images were selected with the guidance of Jeffrey Barr. To verify the engravers and book illustrators, we used *California on Stone* by Harry T. Peters (New York: Doubleday, Doran & Company,

1935) and a preliminary list of important early book illustrations in California history obtained from Gary Kurutz, special collections librarian at the State Library of California in Sacramento. Later in the project, we turned to cataloging items in the fine arts collections selected with the guidance of Katherine Holland, the fine arts curator. She was able to suggest artifacts, paintings, drawings, lithographs, etc., that were historically notable as well as visually memorable. As the project progressed, connections were made among the three major areas of the collection (library, photography, and fine arts) and we eventually found, for example, that a subject heading such as "fire houses" would retrieve materials from all parts of the collection.

At first our intention was to catalog a broad sampling of images from throughout the collection, but as we developed methods for cataloging different formats our intentions changed. We began to focus on small, contained collections within the society, such as a series of Carlton Watkins photographs, the Jones Pantoscope (a series of about twenty-five pencil drawings from the 1870s), or a collection of pages detached from nineteenth-century periodicals featuring wood engravings of California-related topics.

Although we began using item-level cataloging, this focus on special collections led us to do some collection-level cataloging as well. Collection level was particularly good for items that showed a progression of events, such as harvesting a crop of fruit, building a department store in downtown San Francisco after the earthquake, or a group of images depicting the same view over the years. Our image records are interfiled with our book, pamphlet, and library records, which was one of the major aims of the project. Because of the limited size of our collection, in comparison to a large university collection, we feel we can continue to interfile our records and not create an unsearchable database. Even though many of the subject headings are similar, e.g., "California—Gold discoveries" or "Hats," we utilized an option in LCTGM that allows the cataloger to attach a date at the end of the subject heading. This breaks down some of our larger subjects by date. For example, under "Hats," we have the date of the image as a subdivision in our online catalog, i.e., "Hats—1856" or "Hats—1860–1880."

While some users may wish to search a general topic such as a picture of a gold miner, others may have specific needs, such as a picture of Montgomery Street in San Francisco before the earthquake of 1906, showing what people were wearing at that time.

Therefore we needed to be able to put specific subject headings on our image records. This was also our reason for doing more item-level cataloging, and less collection-level cataloging. There are advantages and disadvantages to both methods. Collection-level cataloging requires fewer records and fewer subject headings, but information about details is often lost. Also, within a given span of time, many more images can be cataloged by using the collection-level method. Item-level cataloging, on the other hand, allows a greater degree of subject analysis, and therefore much greater access to details in each image. But this type of cataloging takes an enormous amount of time and often entails research and consultation with the curators. Fortunately, since this was a pilot project and we were not tied to producing huge numbers of records, we were able to do in-depth item-level cataloging.

After a few months our cataloging procedure evolved into the following steps: (1) catalog on a worksheet, (2) type into RLIN, putting the record into a SAVE file so changes could still be made, (3) revise (sometimes working with the curator or librarian), (4) proofread for errors, (5) go back into the RLIN record, correct any errors, make changes, and then PRODUCE, which finalizes the record and produces a set of catalog cards for our institution, and (6) pass the record from RLIN onto a floppy disk and load into our local OPAC (CLS).

One of the first issues we had to resolve in using a MARC record for an imaging project was where to put an image ID number that would link the image to the text record. The photography curator devised a Visual Imaging Project (VIP) number which is assigned to each image we catalog. This acts as the link between the record and the image in our VTLS system. Since this number is a locally assigned number, we chose to put it in a 590 field, the MARC field for local notes.

Another concern was what to do with call numbers or local shelf list numbers that were too long to fit into the eight-digit OPAC field. For the many items that did not have typical "call numbers" these had to be created. For book illustrations we chose to use the call number of the book from which it was taken as the call number for the image. Other items in the collection proved more challenging. The photographs, for example, have separate file numbers and their own system of shelflisting (e.g., SF-Russian Hill-Ante 1906). Because a call number is really a finding aid (a flag to users and staff identifying the location of the item), we decided to put the word "Photo" in the call number field. Thus when patrons are searching through our online catalog, the word "Photo" in the upper left corner of the record (where a regular call number would appear) will tell them that they are looking at a record for a photograph. We would have preferred to place the photographs' shelflisting in the call number field, but for most of the photographs this information exceeds our local OPAC's eight characters line limit; the shelf list number is stored in the 555 MARC field instead. This is the cumulative index/finding aids note field, which is basically what the shelf list is for the staff. Fortunately, the photographs were the only items for which we could not fit in a call number that would tell staff where to find the item.

Our broadside images all have simple identifying numbers—Vault B-12, for example—so these were used as the call number. Sheet music is arranged by year in twelve boxes, so we decided to give the location, item description, and year in the call number. A similar approach was used for the fruit labels which are part of the Kemble collection. The location, description of item, and an identifying number on the containers housing the items are given. The fine arts collection has a wide array of items, but nearly all of them have unique accession numbers. We decided to use this accession number in the call number field and to precede it with the abbreviation FA for all of these collections, for example, FA 78-6-2. No location was specified with these objects since they were to be stored in various areas, as yet undetermined, in the new building. The fine arts curator maintains a detailed listing of the whereabouts of these pieces.

The Process

Figure 14-1, a cover from a piece of sheet music from 1906, is an example of one of the many types of formats with which we worked. Because each format required different solutions, as we progressed we decided to create a manual. We began by developing a basic cataloging worksheet that was used for all of our materials. When other fields were needed, we simply added them. There is space on the worksheet to write in long titles, long notes, and many subject headings. Our basic worksheet contains the MARC fields shown in figure 14-2.

RLIN has different files for different formats. VIM is the RLIN visual materials format, and we used that for the photographs and the book illustrations. Images on sheet music covers are recorded in the SCO format (scores format in RLIN), and broadsides are

recorded in the BKS format (books format in RLIN). The decision to use formats in addition to the VIM format was based on precedent. Other institutions had already put cataloging of similar images into these other formats. In addition, these formats had the specific fields that were needed for our cataloging purposes. Now, with the coming of format integration, some of this may change.

All the worksheet fields are variable fields in RLIN. Some of these fields, such as title and physical description, must be input for each record; but there are also optional fields such as the 590 (local notes) and the 755 (descriptive terms) fields. While we were working with a particular format, we made a list of the fixed field values that were needed and used them throughout the group of images we were cataloging. The only things that changed in the fixed fields were the dates and whether item-level or collection-level cataloging was used. These values are given in the manuals for USMARC, as well as for RLIN and OCLC, and can easily be looked up for each format.

In general, the author field (100/110) was used for the artist or producer of the image—e.g., a photographer, a painter, an engraver. If a photographic firm was responsible for a photograph, its name was entered in this field. The title (245) was sometimes taken from the item (often printed on the image or handwritten somewhere on the item), in which case we noted in a 500 note field where the title was taken from on the item. When there was no visible title, which was often the case, we supplied one. When a title was supplied, it was put in brackets to indicate that it was devised by the cataloger. The imprint area (260) was fairly straightforward. Often there was no place or date on an item, but we recorded what was on the item using Betz's book as a guide and AACR2 as a backup when needed. If the date is not known but can be estimated, a question mark after the date indicates that it was supplied by the cataloger. The physical description area (300) included the extent of the item (what it is; i.e., a drawing, an engraving) and other physical details such as the materials used (graphite on paper, albumen, metal and leather) and the dimensions of the item. All dimensions were rounded up to the next centimeter, except for photographs, which were given to the nearest centimeter.

All of these decisions were made by using the Betz book in conjunction with AACR2. In a few cases we bent the rules to please curators and ourselves when we felt we needed more information or more flexibility. This was done rarely, and usually only in cases that

Figure 14-1 | "The Stricken City," by Ella Wheeler Wilcox. Vault Sheet Music, 1906, for Piano and Voice. (By permission of the Photographic Archives, California Historical Society Library, San Francisco, Calif. FN 30348 VIP 04005.)

MARC Tag Number	Local Use
040	Cataloging source (contains a code for CHS, and the abbreviation "egihc" for the Betz book, *Graphic Materials*)
043	Geographic area code; for most of our items which were about California we used "n-us-ca" (North America-U.S.-California)
100/110	Author
245	Title
260	Imprint
300	Physical description
440	Series
590	Local notes (We put the VIP number here so it appears as the first note in our online catalog display.)
500	Notes
505	Contents
555	Finding aids
590	Local notes (Any other local notes appear in this position.)
600/610	Personal/Corporate names - subject headings
650	Subject headings
651	Geographical subject headings
653	Local subject headings
654	Faceted topical subject headings (AAT)
655	Descriptive terms
691	Local geographic terms (We have used this field for indicating blocks on streets.)
700/710	Personal/Corporate names - added entries
755	Descriptive terms

Figure 14-2 | MARC Fields Used on Worksheet

would not create any conflicts in the RLIN database. The notes used in the 500 field varied from format to format. They usually explained the image or gave information physically found on the item, such as a handwritten note on the back of a photograph.

The subject heading fields were a bit more complex since we were using both LCTGM and AAT as thesauri and sometimes LCSH. We also had to use local subject headings from time to time. This resulted in a wide variety of subject heading fields, but all the fields were legal MARC fields. For personal and corporate names (600/610), we utilized the Library of Congress Name Authority, which we have access to on CD-ROM. (The CDs are available from the Library of Congress Cataloging Distribution Service, Washington, D.C. 20541, and come with manuals on how to use them.) Having the Library of Congress name authority files on CD has been an enormous help, and because we were

entering our records into a national utility (RLIN), it has also been necessary to follow Library of Congress in this regard. Often our names were not in the name authority files and then we used a variety of standard sources to ascertain the correct form of the person's name, and birth and death dates, if possible. Corporate names, such as photographic firms, were also found in the Library of Congress Name Authority File. In addition, we have been using the *Index to American Photographic Collections,* edited by Andrew H. Eskind and Greg Drake (Boston: G. K. Hall, 1990). There is now a third enlarged edition, published in 1995, which updates many entries. Our photography curator scanned this into our NeXT terminals, along with an index to San Francisco photographers, thus providing easy access to both of these sources. For names of geographic locations (651), we used the Library of Congress Subject Authority which we also have on CD-ROM.

The regular subject headings were located in the 650 field. To specify which thesaurus we used, MARC requires a different indicator. A "7" indicates the source specified in subfield "2." The abbreviation for the source was given after the subject heading. For example, 650 7 Hats|2lctgm indicates we used the subject heading "Hats" from the LCTGM thesaurus.

With each thesaurus the subject could be divided by a date and, if indicated, by a geographic place as well. Place subdivisions were usually formed by state and then by city, by country and then by city, or by nationality—650 7 Beaches|zCalifornia|zSan Francisco. |2lctgm. If a specific date was important, it was added at the end of the string of subjects—650 7 Beaches |zCalifornia|zSan Francisco|y1885.|2lctgm. Ranges of dates could also be indicated, such as 1860–1885. This date corresponded to the date in the imprint field, 260.

When using subdivisions in the AAT, we followed the AAT rules for subdividing. Because AAT utilizes a faceted heading, the terms had to go into the 654 MARC field, which is for faceted topical terms. We have used many AAT terms, but fewer faceted terms, because of the confusing way the headings look when they appear in RLIN and in our OPAC; but, if there was no other way to indicate a subject heading, we did use the AAT faceted term. Our rule of thumb has been to use LCTGM first if our subject heading could be found there. If not, we moved on to the AAT, then to LCSH. We did not include the same term from each thesaurus, and were well aware of the problems this would eventually cause in our OPAC and in RLIN. Our local OPAC does have a system for authority control, but we have used it minimally. For the small number of records we have for images, it has not been a problem. We have found that when the image records are interfiled with the book records in our online catalog, there have not been any authority conflicts—so far.

We were surprised to find that certain subjects could not be found in any thesaurus. Such terms as *stampedes, tree stumps, wooden sidewalks,* and *opium dens* were not to be found. We have been regularly submitting these terms to both LCTGM and AAT and most of them have been accepted. If we needed to include a subject before it was accepted by a thesaurus, we included it in the MARC field 690, the field for local subject headings. We also used the 653 field, which is the field for uncontrolled index terms. Our most common use of a 690 field was the 691 field, which is for local geographic terms. We wanted to indicate a specific street block, if known, on photographs and images. We noted that other institutions had created a subject string in the 691 field, such as 691 Montgomery St. (San Francisco, Calif.)|c200 Block. When we have a large number of records, all with the same street as a subject heading, this subdivision helps our researchers narrow their search.

Cataloging Examples

The following examples include a photograph, a book illustration (lithograph and an engraving), a lithograph on the cover of a piece of sheet music, a color lithography fruit crate label, and a leather money belt. Each item utilized the basic MARC fields, but the items also required flexibility in the use of other MARC fields.

The photographs were originally intended to be cataloged at the item level, and the examples represent item- or monographic-level cataloging. We hope to eventually do more collection-level cataloging with the photographs, but for our current purposes the item level seems to be more useful, although very time-consuming. Figure 14-3 is a photograph we titled ourselves because it lacked any title on the item. Since the name and address of the photographic firm appeared on the mount, it was given in the 110 field. Because Brown is such a common name, we felt it necessary to indicate that it was a firm, and then to give a location as well. This was constructed according to AACR2 rules.

Figure 14-4, a copy of the RLIN record, shows how we fit the pertinent information into the MARC format. The title was given in brackets because it was created by the cataloger since no title appeared on the item. Subfield h indicated the medium of the item. In this case, the general material designation (GMD) or medium was "graphic," which is taken from Betz's *Graphic Materials.* The 300 field was straightforward for cataloging photographs. The term "photoprint" is from Betz, and if the photograph was mounted it was indicated here, for example: "1 paris card." These mounts/cards are standard, and the terminology is from *Descriptive Terms for Graphic Materials,* compiled and edited by Helena Zinkham and Elisabeth Betz Parker (Washington, D.C.: Library of Congress/Cataloging Distribution Service, 1986). The process was noted by our photography curator, and the terminology used was also taken from the above book. The dimensions given were not rounded up to the nearest centimeter because our photography curator did not want them rounded up. In the end, we compromised when we felt

Figure 14-3 | "Three Women Painters," Photo by Brown, c. 1880s. (By permission of the Photographic Archive, California Historical Society Library, San Francisco, Calif. FN-04198 PT-Kirk Jessie.)

```
040      CHi|cCHi|eegihc
043      n-us-ca
110 2    Brown (Firm : San Francisco, Calif.)
245 10   [Three women painters posing in the studio with their field kits]|h[graphic]
260      San Francisco :|bBrown,|c[ca. 1855]
300      1 paris card :|balbumen ;|cimage 24 x 17 cm., mount 25 x 18 cm.
590      VIP00106.
500      On back: Jessie Kirk, Clara McChesney, K. Hooker-Katherine Putnam Hooker.
         Probably taken in the 80s [1880s]
500      On mount: Brown, 606 Kearney Street, San Francisco.
555 0    PT-(Kia-Kiz)|cShelf List (Location)
590      FN-04198
590      Gift of Marian O. Hooker, February, 1952.
600 10   Kirk, Jessie.
600 10   McChesney, Clara,|d1860 or 1928.
600 10   Hooker, Kate Putnam.
610 20   Brown (Firm : San Francisco, Calif.)
650 7    Artists' models.|21ctgm
650 0    Umbrellas and parasols.
650 0    Photography, Artistic.
650 7    Artists' materials.|21ctgm
650 7    Hats|y1855.|21ctgm
650 0    Women painters.
655      Portrait photographs.|2lctgm
653      Plein-air painting.
755      Albumen photoprints.|2gmgpc
755      Card photographs.|2gmgpc
796 11   Hooker, Marian O.,|edonor.
```

Figure 14-4 | MARC Bibliographic Record for Photograph

it would not create a problem either in RLIN or in our local OPAC. If the photo was mounted on a card, the size of the mount was also given.

Notes for photographs varied widely but the main notes included a comment about where the title was found (photo, mount, back of photograph), a note either quoting or paraphrasing what was on the back of the photograph, and any other information we needed to put in the record. We used the note area, the 500 field in MARC, to include information that was important enough to be searchable in our OPAC, since it does search the note field. The 505 MARC field was used when we did a collection record, since this field is for formatted contents notes. We listed the photos in this field when there were a small number of photos in the

collection record, perhaps ten or so. The 585 MARC field (exhibitions note) was used when a photograph had appeared in an exhibition. We knew this would be helpful from the curatorial point of view.

The 590 (local note) field was used not only for our VIP number, but also for File Negative numbers (FN), and any other locally assigned number associated with the photograph. Any note referring only to our copy of a photograph—for instance, the condition of our copy, the stamp of a collection to which the photograph belongs, or the noting of the item as a gift to the society—was put in a 590 field. If the item was a gift, we traced the donor in a 796 or 797 MARC field, which are the fields for local added entries (personal and corporate names). We made sure that there was a differentiation between a "donor" and a "former owner," since often it was not clear whether the person or institution had donated the item or whether it was from a collection that had been disbanded or sold. These fields are used similarly in book records, and we felt comfortable in applying the same rules to images.

Book illustrations were handled a little differently in that we had to record from what book the image was taken. Figure 14-5 shows a wood engraving entitled "High and Dry" from Frank Marryat's book *Mountains and Molehills* (New York: Harper, 1855). In our record, figure 14-6, we used field 773 in MARC, which is for the host item entry. This field contains information concerning the host item for the component part described in the record. Since the wood engravings and, in other books, lithographs, were part of a larger whole, we decided this MARC field suited our purposes. Not only could we get the author and title of the work in this field, but it also accommodated publication information which was important since there are so many different editions of books.

Figure 14-6 shows the RLIN record for this wood engraving, and because there was both an artist and an engraver, we listed the artist, Frank Marryat, in the 100 field, and then put the engraver, J. W. Orr, in the 245 subfield c, which is the statement of responsibility area. Mr. Orr's name appears on the engraving along the bottom left, just under the end barrel and package, "J. W. Orr, N.Y." The title page of the book states, "With illustrations by the author." We then traced J. W. Orr in an added entry field, 700, gave his dates, and noted he was the engraver. This form of his name, John William Orr, 1815–1887, was taken from the Library of Congress Name Authority File. In the 260 field, we described the place, publication, and date of the wood engraving, not of the book, always

remembering we were cataloging the image and not the book. In this case, we enclosed the entire field in brackets since the actual image is not dated, but can be assumed from the publication date of the book. Only a place and date were given, because the printer of the engraving is not known.

In the physical description field, 300, the dimensions given were of the engraved area only, not of the size of the entire page in the book. The 500 field shows a good example of a note which included information visible in the image that was important enough to be included in a note, but not necessarily in a subject heading. The 590 note indicated that the library owned a second copy of this book, which also indicated a second copy of the image.

This record also has an example of our use of LCSH, in that we used the terms "Chinese" and "Mexicans" and then subdivided them geographically. The 755 field (added entry—physical characteristics) appears on every image record we created. Here we used the terminology from *Descriptive Terms for Graphic Materials,* whose abbreviation you can see at the end of the field, "gmgpc." We actually cataloged two other examples of this same image, one from another edition (London: Longman, 1855) of the same book, which reproduces the image in a color lithograph, and another which is a photograph of J. W. Orr's engraving. Now when a patron searches under Marryat, Frank, or Orr, J. W., or even "High and Dry," all three records will be found. Thus one valuable outcome of this project is the way it brings together different parts of the collection.

Another small collection was of sheet music, and since other institutions were cataloging images from sheet music, we decided that a portion of our collection should also be cataloged. Because other institutions

Figure 14-5 | "High and Dry," Graphic from Frank Marryat, *Mountains and Molehills* (New York: Harper, 1855). Vault 917.94.M3491855b. (By permission of the Photographic Archive, California Historical Society Library, San Francisco, Calif. FN-30349 VIP 07410.)

```
040      CHi|cCHi
043      n-us-ca
110 1    Marryat, Frank,|d1826-1855.
245 10   High and dry|h [graphic] /|c [engraved by] J.W. Orr.
260      [New York :|bs.n.,|c1855]
300      1 print:|bwood engraving;|c13 x 19 cm.
590      VIP07410.
500      Illustration by Frank Marryat.
500      Bubb Grubb & Co., Col. Tibbs, dentist, and Boggs not verified.
590      Library owns 2 copies.
610 20   Niantic Hotel (San Francisco, Calif.)
610 20   Niantic (Ship)
610 20   Eagle Saloon (San Francisco, Calif.)
610 20   Eastin & Co. (San Francisco, Calif.)
650 7    Business enterprises|zCalifornia|zSan Francisco.|21ctgm
650 7    Printing industry|zCalifornia|zSan Francisco.|21ctgm
650 0    Chinese|zCalifornia|zSan Francisco.
650 0    Mexicans|zCalifornia|zSan Francisco.
650 7    Carts & wagons.|21ctgm
700 1    Orr, John William, |d1815-1887, |eengraver
755      Wood engravings.|2gmgpc
773 0    |7p1am|aMarryat, Frank.|t Mountains and molehills.|dNew York : Harper,
         1855.
```

Figure 14-6 | MARC Bibliographic Record for Wood Engraving

were using the SCO or score format, we decided to use that as well as it offered the fields we needed. Figure 14-7 shows a cover of "The Hank Monk Schottische" composed by J. P. Meder in 1878. Figure 14-8 shows the RLIN record for this image. The 048 field was included because it contains, in coded form, information which "specifies the medium of performance for a musical composition and also the number and types of instrumental and vocal parts" (AACR2). Although it is not a required field, the other sheet music images we found did include this field. Two other institutions whose records we studied, Johns Hopkins and Brown University, were also cataloging sheet music. Brown was using the note area to describe their images, and we tried to follow their form since they have been doing this for quite some time. We were worried that we would be offending music catalogers by some of our use of MARC fields, but cataloging images on sheet music was already being discussed by music catalogers. We were told not to treat the music and the image in separate records, so we used LCTGM and AAT for subject access to the images, and LCSH for subject access to the music. Therefore, in the first 650 fields we used LCSH headings for the type of music—Piano music

and Schottisches. The rest of the subject headings dealt with the image on the cover of the music.

The author, title, imprint, and physical description fields were all fairly straightforward, since this was dictated by regular music cataloging rules (see chapter 5, "Music," in AACR2). Only the height of the music is indicated. Music cataloging has a definite order in which the notes must be listed, and after we had ascertained that order, the cataloging went fairly quickly. This particular image was more complex than most because it is a lithograph, and it also included some fairly well known figures in the early West. There was a printed dedication at the head of the title, as well as a caption under the illustration. The note fields in figure 14-8 related this additional information. The second 500 note indicated where the title is taken from, the third indicated other important information printed on the title page. The next 500 field was a description of the image, and gave any names associated with producing the image. These names cannot be given in the 100 field which, when cataloging music, is for the composer of the music. The fifth 500 field noted where the lithography was done, "Lith. Phila.," which was important since this is the

Figure 14-7 | "The Hank Monk Schottische." Composed by J. P. Meder, for Piano, 1878. (By permission of the Photographic Archive, California Historical Society Library, San Francisco, Calif. FN-30354 VIP 03908.)

```
040        CHi|cCHi
148        ka01
100  1     Meder, J.P.
245  14    The Hank Monk Schottische.|ccomposed by J.P. Meder.
260        Carson City, Nev. :|bJohn G. Fox,|cc1878.
300        5 p. of music :|bill.,|c36 cm.
590        VIP03908.
500        For piano.
500        Cover title.
500        "Dedicated to Miss Lillie Swift."--cover, at head of title. "Keep your Seat Horace,
           I'll get you thar on time."--cover, caption under illustration.
500        Cover illustration: Stagecoach being driven over a small creek by four galloping
           horses. There are passengers on top, one Chinese, and inside the coach.
           Mountains appear in background./J.P. Marshall. Thos. Hunter
500        Lith. Phila. "Pioneer Stage Co. Coach-U.S. Mail," appears on stagecoach
           depicted on cover.
500        Hank Monk, the dean of the "whips," famous for the speed and skill with
           which he covered the mountain roads. He drove Horace Greeley and Mark
           Twain, their trip described in Roughing It (1872). Cf. A Companion to
           California.
590        Imperfect copy: Library's copy lacks all music but p.5.
600  10    Monk, Hank.
600  10    Greeley, Horace,|d1811-1872.
650  0     Piano music.
650  0     Schottisches.
650  7     Stagecoaches|y1878.|21ctgm
650  7     Horses.|21ctgm
650  7     Postal service|y1878.|21ctgm
650  7     Clothing & dress|y1878.|21ctgm
650  7     Passengers|y1878.|21ctgm
650  7     Chinese|zWest (U.S.)|y1878.|21ctgm
700  10    Marshall, J.P.,|eillustrator.
700  10    Hunter, Thos.,|q (Thomas),|elithographer.
710  20    Pioneer Stage Co.
755        Lithographs.|2gmgpc
```

Figure 14-8 | RLIN Record for Sheet Music

only place this information was recorded. The final 500 field gave background information on the image when we felt that additional information was needed. We usually took this information from *A Companion to California* by James D. Hart (Berkeley: University of California Press, 1987) and either quoted or paraphrased and noted "Cf. A Companion to California" at the end of the note. This is a standard practice in book cataloging and suited our purposes. The illustrator, J. P. Marshall, and the lithographer, Thos. Hunter, both received added entries in the 700 fields, as did the Pioneer Stage Co., which is painted on the stagecoach in the image. The subject headings used were derived the same way as for any other image, by actually looking at the image. Dates were added since the date of the sheet music could serve as a date for the image.

Some of the ephemera which we cataloged included fruit crate labels. Figure 14-9 shows one of the more beautiful labels, "Diving Girl Brand California Apples." These labels were part of a group in the Kemble Collection. We decided to catalog these in the VIM format, and treated them the same way that ephemera would be cataloged in a special collections

Figure 14-9 | "Diving Girl Apples." Lithograph, Kemble-Labels-Schmidt1-001. (By permission of the Photographic Archive, California Historical Society Library, San Francisco, Calif. FN-30347 VIP 07903.)

situation. Figure 14-10 shows the RLIN record for this image. Since all of the labels were done by the Schmidt Lithography Company, that became the corporate author. We did encounter labels printed in the Los Angeles and Seattle offices of the company, and the entry would reflect that location. The dates were ascertained by the printing company records noting that the labels were printed mainly between 1920 and 1950. When no date appeared on the label, we put this range in the date field. Some of the labels had a date in the margin of the label, and in these cases we were able to use a specific date.

The title of the label was always taken from the label itself. The process was always color lithography. We measured the labels as any other piece of ephemera, and rounded up to the nearest centimeter. The note field contained any other text that appeared on the label that we felt was important, such as specific organizations or wording that gave some information about the product or its production. The final note was usually a description of the image itself, which we tried to keep fairly simple. In this case, we also had a 510 field which contains the name of a publication in which the work has been cited, indexed, or abstracted. There happens to be a book solely on fruit crate labels, and if we found our label cited there, we noted it in field 510. This is also a standard MARC field, and was useful in cataloging other items, such as lithographs or engravings which were cited in bibliographies on California publishing and artists.

The fine arts collection proved interesting to catalog since there were not only graphic materials (paintings, drawings, and watercolors), but actual objects such as badges, pins, gold miners' pans, souvenir items, and a traveler's money belt. Figure 14-11 shows the record for the money belt in RLIN. Usually there was

040	CHi|cCHi|eegihc
110 2	Schmidt Lithography Company (San Francisco, Calif.)
245 10	Diving girl brand California apples |h [graphic]
260	|c[ca. 1920]
300	1 label : |bcol. lithograph ; |c24 x 27 cm.
590	VIP07903.
500	"Newtown Pippins. Produce of U.S.A., Watsonville, Cal. Packed and shipped by Watsonville Apple Selling Organization."
500	Image of a woman wearing a red bathing suit diving into the water and two apples.
510 4	McClelland, Gordon T. Fruit box labels,|cp76.
650 7	Apples.|21ctgm
650 7	Bathing suits.|y1920.|21ctgm
650 7	Diving.|21ctgm
655 7	Fruit crate labels.|2gmgpc
655 7	Labels.|2gmgpc
710 2	Watsonville Apple Selling Organization.
755	Chromolithographs.|2gmgpc

Figure 14-10 | RLIN Record for Fruit Crate Label

040	CHi|cCHi
245 10	[Leather money belt of Isaac Perkins, Salem, Massachusetts.]|h[Realia]
260	|c[1850?]
300 1	money belt :|bleather, cloth and metal;|c80cm. long.
500	Title supplied by cataloger.
590	VIP6206
520	Leather and cloth money belt with buckles still attached. Leather dyed red in parts. Back of larger of two pouches inscribed, "Isaac Perkins-Salem. Panama May 20, 1850. Sacramento, 1850." Front and back sections of belt connected by cloth band. Other smaller pouch has no inscription.
600 1	Perkins, Isaac|xClothing.
650 7	Money belts.|2aat
650 0	Overland journeys to the Pacific.
650 0	California|xHistory|y1846-1850.

Figure 14-11 | RLIN Record for Object in Fine Arts Collection

no author involved for these objects or artifacts, and no title either. We tried to create a title that described the item clearly. Rather than being a "graphic," these items were given a GMD of "realia," which is also taken from AACR2. The dates of these items were often estimated, and therefore indicated in brackets, often with a question mark. The 300 field gave what the item was (money belt), the medium or what the item was made of (leather, cloth and metal), and finally a measurement (80 cm. long). The guidelines for realia can be found in chapter 10 of AACR2, "Three-Dimensional Artifacts and Realia." Measurements can be given of one dimension, or two or three, as long as the dimension given is noted.

The first 500 field noted that the "Title is supplied by cataloger" and the next was our local note for our VIP number. The 520 MARC field (summary note) contains an unformatted note that describes the scope and general contents of the materials. Here the item was described fully, including any writing which appeared on it, in this case an inscription which dated and identified its owner. Here we also used LCSH for subject access, since the item was used in an overland journey to the Pacific, and also was a part of California's history from 1846 to 1850, the Gold Rush period.

Not many artifacts have been cataloged, mainly because we are limited to those that can be laid flat on a scanner. Eventually we hope to have more three-dimensional objects to catalog, as well as large paintings and pieces of furniture and sculpture. So far, we have cataloged a group of pencil sketches of the West done in the 1870s, a set of watercolors of the missions throughout California, and wood engravings from nineteenth-century periodicals such as *Harper's Weekly* and *The Pacific Rural Press*.

Conclusion

After a year's work, we felt we had accomplished some basic groundwork for the cataloging of all major types of items found in our collections. Having dealt with photographs, books, book illustrations, ephemera, sheet music, broadsides, artifacts, and fine arts graphics (paintings, drawings, etc.), we felt that we had manipulated the MARC format enough that we could probably make it fit anything—or make anything fit into it. We have an extensive background in cataloging not only books, but other items as well, from Icelandic texts in a special collections department to stuffed animal patterns in a public library and slides in an art museum. Our prior knowledge of AACR2, the MARC format, and Library of Congress rules and subject headings has served us well in adapting the MARC format to the cataloging of images.

The one-year grant period was spent not only on cataloging; we also developed a way in which to choose which items to catalog, established a method by which different classification and record-keeping procedures could be integrated into a MARC record, and discovered relationships and connections between parts of our collections that had not previously been linked.

The cataloging process was refined as we went along, but still involves much consultation between the catalogers and the curators of each collection. The curators know what they want to get out of each record and the catalogers know how to fit that information into the MARC record. Even with online authorities, the task of researching subjects, and checking authorities and reference works (e.g., city directories, standard reference works, and local histories) is still time-consuming but necessary. Fortunately, we were able to take the time needed to iron out problems, because we did not have to produce a large number of records during the first year. Now our task will be to choose which images and which collections would benefit the most from being cataloged online, whether it be from a research or a preservation point of view. Much of our material is very fragile, and the mere act of a researcher looking at a manuscript, book, or photograph may damage the item. Having its digitized image online not only saves the fragile item from much nonessential handling, but also provides the researcher a better look, since the image can be enlarged and zoomed in on for detailed examination.

Since our OPAC searches on virtually all fields and can perform Boolean searches, good subject access results are achieved. We are also quite pleasantly surprised at how well the image records intersperse with the book records. The first day we loaded image records into the OPAC happened to be a public day for the library; within an hour we received a sheet music request based on one of the image records that had been loaded that morning. The system works! Our existing system can handle five thousand records and images, but in an abbreviated version of the MARC record. For our next steps toward a system which can display the full MARC record and image together, we will need additional equipment. We expect to be able to acquire the needed equipment within the next few years; until then we will keep producing records for our images.

The variety of formats we worked with has given us an unusual chance to deal with both traditional and nontraditional cataloging. Yet, we feel we have followed standard MARC format, AACR2 rules, and graphic materials guidelines, and have used standard thesauri in the proper manner. The combining of library, photograph, and museum items into one database has been an exciting endeavor, and one which we hope will be more the norm than the exception in the future. By utilizing an already existing structure, MARC, we feel we have made available items which before had been inaccessible to researchers using standard national utilities such as RLIN, OCLC, and even local systems such as MELVYL. Managers of image and object collections need to cooperate to make their records and images available to the public. The MARC format seems to have worked well for us. We hope other such diverse collections will make some of the same decisions we have made.

From Cuneiform to MARC:
A Database for Ancient Near
Eastern Cylinder Seals Owned
by the Pierpont Morgan Library

Elizabeth O'Keefe

The Institution

The Pierpont Morgan Library is a major repository of artistic, literary, and historical materials dating from the fifth millennium B.C.E. to the modern era. The core of its holdings is composed of the collection of books, manuscripts, drawings, and ancient Near Eastern seals acquired by J. Pierpont Morgan, the American financier. When Morgan died in 1913, his library and the palazzo-like structure designed by Charles McKim to house it passed to his only son. J. P. Morgan Jr. shared his father's ambition to bring the best of European culture to the United States, and to make it "available in every way possible for the advancement of knowledge and for the use of learned men of all countries."[1] In 1924, he transferred the library and an endowment to provide for its maintenance to a board of trustees; soon afterward, it was incorporated as a public institution.

The library's holdings are divided among eight curatorial departments: the Archives, Autograph Manuscripts, Drawings and Prints, the Gilbert and Sullivan Collection, Medieval and Renaissance Manuscripts, Music Manuscripts and Books, Printed Books and Bindings,

and Seals and Tablets. The Morgan maintains a reference collection of approximately fifty-five thousand titles, including monographs, periodicals, pamphlets, photographs, and microforms, which is intended to support research on the rare material. Qualified scholars have access to both rare and reference material in the library's Reading Room; prints and drawings may be examined in the Print Room. The library mounts three major exhibitions a year; sponsors numerous lectures, seminars, workshops, concerts, and readings; and issues exhibition and collection catalogs and facsimiles.

Although visual material is a component of all the collections, only two departments, the Department of Drawings and Prints and the Department of Seals and Tablets, are concerned exclusively with nontextual material. This article focuses on a project to create a MARC database for the library's ancient Near Eastern seals. Few readers are likely to encounter a collection of this kind; nevertheless, a description of the project will, I hope, demonstrate how one can successfully apply MARC to the most unlikely objects, while laying the groundwork for integrated access to the objects themselves and to related research material.

The Seals Collection

The library's holdings consist of 2,011 seals, spanning a period of almost five thousand years (5000–400 B.C.E.) and ranging in place of origin from Iran to Cyprus. The overwhelming majority are cylinder seals, although the collection also contains several hundred stamp seals. The first seals were in the form of stamps; they predate the use of cylinder seals by about two thousand years. Cylinder seals first appeared about 3500 B.C.E. at Uruk in southern Mesopotamia and at Susa in modern-day Iran, just before the development of writing. As their name indicates, they are stone cylinders engraved in reverse with designs that leave an impression when the seal is rolled over a plastic material, such as clay or mud. The cylinders were perforated lengthwise and worn on a cord or string. See figures 15-1 and 15-2.

Seals served both a practical purpose—marking ownership, securing goods against theft, and identifying the senders of written communications—and an amuletic function, depicting figures or events meant to protect or benefit the owner of the seal. As the only surviving objects from the ancient Near East for which we can construct a historical sequence of over three millennia, they are an invaluable source of knowledge for the art and culture of the region, as well as beautiful objects in their own right.

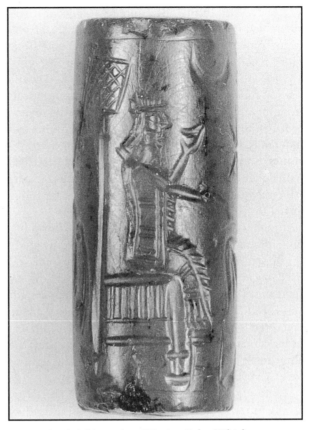

Figure 15-1 | "Attendant Waving Palm Whisk over Table before Seated King," cylinder seal, Neo-Assyrian (c. 900–700 B.C.E.), Chalcedony, 27 × 12 mm. (By permission of the Pierpont Morgan Library, New York. Corpus #776.)

Figure 15-2 | Modern Impression of Seal 776 Showing Ritual Scene with Two Attendants and a Seated King. (By permission of the Pierpont Morgan Library, New York. Corpus #776.)

About two-thirds of the library's collection was assembled for Pierpont Morgan by the American collector William Hayes Ward between 1885 and 1908. More recently, the library received two major gifts: 144 seals from the collection of Robert F. Kelley and a study collection of 453 cylinder and 230 stamp seals from Jonathan P. Rosen. The library also owns several bronze foundation figures, a large clay foundation cylinder of Nebukadnezer II inscribed with text, two eye-stones, and a small number of clay tablets inscribed with cuneiform texts (most of the three thousand clay tablets acquired by Pierpont Morgan were later transferred to the Babylonian Collection at Yale).

Each seal is housed with a modern polyform impression made from the seal. Scholars normally study the impression made from the seal rather than the seal itself, because the designs are cut in reverse into a very small area (the average seal measures 2.5 cm in height and 1.5 cm in diameter), making it difficult to read the seal directly.[2] Photographs of the seals and of the seal impressions are another important research tool; the latter must be taken using controlled, raking light in order to bring out the details of the design.

Although the Morgan seals are studied chiefly by art historians, archaeologists, and historians, they have also been the object of research by scholars in the fields of cosmology, religion, optics, gemology, and the history of technology. For many years, the curator of the collection, Dr. Edith Porada, who was also professor emerita of art history and archaeology at Columbia University, offered seminars to graduate students, and images of the library's seals are often reproduced in scholarly publications.

Documentation of the Collection

All the seals acquired by the library before 1948 were published by Edith Porada in the *Corpus of Ancient Near Eastern Seals in North American Collections. The Collection of the Pierpont Morgan Library* (cited throughout this chapter as the *Corpus*.)[3] Later acquisitions are documented in printed catalogs or lists.[4] But the *Corpus* and the other sources were issued only in limited quantities and are now out of print; moreover, they offer none of the features that make electronic finding aids so useful: keyword searching, multiple indexes, ability to locate subsets of records based on Boolean queries,

and the ability to produce hard copy in a number of different formats (printed lists, container labels, exhibition labels, etc.).

Dr. Porada, who served as honorary curator of seals and tablets from 1956 to 1994, was fully alive to the benefits of computerized access to collection information. She was one of the first Morgan staff members to acquire a home computer, and as early as 1984 she was investigating the possibility of developing a system that would allow users to retrieve and display multiple images of seals on a television screen. But she was advised that the technology was still too new and too costly, and that it would be better to wait until it was more fully developed.

In 1992, the library formed a computer cataloging committee to explore the question of how to provide access to its collections through the use of computer technology. Information on the library's holdings is presently kept in a variety of formats, ranging from handwritten accession books to card files to list-processing files to RLIN records (for reference books and some rare books). It is seldom possible to determine our holdings in a given area by looking in only one source, and significant portions of the collections are uncataloged or documented only by sketchy or outdated records. There are no institution-wide cataloging standards and policies, and departmental cataloging practices are by and large homegrown and eclectic, or a continuation of library and archival practices predating the computer.

As the first step in the planning process, the computer cataloging committee visited each curatorial department to gather information on current cataloging and record-keeping procedures, and to inquire into the various information needs of the curators and of the constituencies served by each department. Dr. Porada expressed great interest in the committee's aim. With her help, committee members compiled a list of data elements that would be useful in the description of seals. This list formed the basis for the data dictionary used in the project, though some additional fields were added later. Dr. Porada's chief reservation had to do with the absence of a common vocabulary within the field. There are no established vocabulary lists, and indeed no consensus on accepted terms for styles, iconographic terms, materials, shapes of seals, or period names (for some periods, the range of years covered by the period names is still in dispute). She was not aware of any move to develop a standardized format for cataloging seals, although various repositories probably had their own local databases. Nonetheless, Dr. Porada welcomed the prospect of improved access to the material in her collection, and would undoubtedly have played an active role in planning had it not been for her death in March 1994.

Dr. Porada bequeathed to the Morgan her reference library, her papers, and her extensive collections of modern seal impressions, photographs, and drawings. The library, which contains some 1,705 monographs, thirty periodicals, and several thousand offprints, constitutes a definitive assemblage of printed material relating specifically to seals, as well as works dealing with the art and archaeology of ancient cultures from the Mediterranean to the Indus Valley. Dr. Porada's modern seal impressions include not only seals from the major museums, but also from many private collections; the impressions from museums and collections in Baghdad and Teheran are particularly valuable because the seals from which they were taken are now inaccessible to most Western scholars.

The task of processing and cataloging the material fell to the cataloging department, of which I am head. Normally the first thing one has to do in connection with a large gift is to obtain funding to cover the additional staff and material required to process it. I was spared this headache, because, with characteristic foresight and thoughtfulness, Dr. Porada had arranged for the Joseph Rosen Foundation to underwrite the costs associated with making her bequest accessible to scholars. As a result, we were able to get down at once to listing the books and serials in RLIN.

When all is said and done, though, the cataloging problems presented by the offprints are still within the ambit (admittedly, an ever-widening one) of traditional library cataloging. Cataloging the seals themselves posed a much greater challenge. When I learned in June 1994 that the Morgan's newly appointed curator, Sidney Babcock, had been assigned the task of compiling a computerized list of the seals, I offered to work with him on the project, because it seemed to me that everything in the library relating to seals, whether rare or reference, formed an entity, and would benefit from an integrated approach. I brought to this endeavor an abysmal ignorance of seals and of the ancient Near East, but about fifteen years' experience with book cataloging and some recent experience with mapping the MARC format to the fields used by our curators of illuminated manuscripts. Sidney Babcock, a former student of Dr. Porada and presently curator of the Rosen collection of ancient Near Eastern art, knew a great deal about seals and the ancient Near East and almost nothing about cataloging

in an electronic environment. We hoped that working together, we could come up with a record structure for the seals that could also be used for the seal impressions and photographs, and that the records we created could later be transferred to whatever system the library chose without having to do extensive reprogramming or data conversion. Collaboration would also, we hoped, make it possible to develop a shared list of indexing terms that could be used for everything in the library related to seals, from the objects themselves to images of seals to printed works and archival material.

We agreed to defer the question of imaging until the library was ready to tackle it on an institution-wide basis. Neither of us had the technical expertise to evaluate different imaging systems, and the library does not yet have the hardware or software required to make image capture, storage, and retrieval viable. If we could manage to have records ready to be linked with images when the time came, that would certainly be to our advantage.

Planning

We began the planning process with a discussion of which part of the seals collection ought to be listed first. Although there was a certain appeal to beginning with the less well documented seals, we agreed that the need to do original cataloging before we could choose and test a format would complicate the task too much. Instead, we decided to begin with the 1,157 seals documented in the *Corpus*. Insofar as standards of any kind may be said to exist within the field, Dr. Porada's work set the standard for seals cataloging by virtue of its meticulous classification, its clear presentation, and its precise descriptions of pictorial content. By using the *Corpus* terms for figures and objects, we could build up an internally consistent vocabulary familiar to scholars in the field, even if they chose to use variant terms in their own publications.

The next step was to identify appropriate data elements and to choose a format. We began with the list supplied to the computer cataloging committee by Dr. Porada, and added fields drawn from the MARC format, such as a field indicating the availability of reproductions and a field describing restrictions on access (see figure 15-3). Some of the information pertaining to the new fields, such as the control numbers for photographic negatives, will have to be collected and added to records after the initial records are created. Other

MARC Tag Number	Description
035|a	Local data field (used for accession number, e.g. Morgan Seal 1, Morgan Seal KC 72) +
040|a	NUC code for library creating record +
040|c	NUC code for library transcribing record +
046|a	B.C.E. Datetype (normally a q, for questionable) +
046|b	1st date (B.C.E.) +
046|d	2nd date (B.C.E.)
046|e	2nd date (A.D.)
245|a	Brief description of the scene +
245|h	Graphic material designation +
260|c	Date phrase +
300|a	Extent of item +
|b	Material +
|c	Dimensions +
500|a	Notes (general; include notes on reuse, recutting; horizontal vertical inscriptions; intaglio vs. reverse; in future, may include information on string holes and on weight of the seal)
506|a	Terms governing access
506|a	Arrangements for access
510|a	Citations to the seal (in catalogs) &
510|c	Locations within source &
520	Full description of the scene +!
|A	Main pictorial elements +!
|B	Subsidiary pictorial elements +&!
|C	Decorative elements +&!
524|a	Preferred citation +
530|a	Photo/Surrogate image available (e.g. negative/slide/b & w photograph/seal impression) &
|b	Photo/Image source (e.g. Photographic Records Dept.)
|d	Photo/Image order no. (e.g. Neg. no. XXX) &
535|a	Location of original (will be used for records for study collection of seal impressions, negatives, photographs, etc.)
540|a	Terms governing reproduction
541|a	Immediate source of acquisition (used for gifts)
|e	Accession number
544|a	Comparanda (use for cf.able seals or objects) &!
546|a	Language of inscription (e.g. Sumerian, Akkadian) &
546|b	Alphabet used in inscription &
561|a	Provenance (history of ownership)
562|a	Inscription transliterated &!
562|b	Translation of inscription &!
581|a	References to discussions of the seal &
585|a	Exhibitions (including venue, date, etc.) &
590|a	Condition (e.g. damaged, chipped, etc.)
653|a	Iconographic term +&#
	The first indicator is used to distinguish among figures that appear in a primary scene (Indicator = 1), secondary scene (Indicator = 2), or as decorative motif (Indicator = 3) +!

Figure 15-3 | MARC Fields Used to Catalog Seals

MARC Tag Number	*Description*
654	Description of the physical/stylistic characteristics of the object #
654|O	Object type (e.g. cylinder seal, stamp seal, tablet) +#
654|P	Period +#
654|Y	Style (e.g. linear, modeled, drilled, cut) #
654|L	Color + [repeatable for multi-colored objects] #
654|M	Material +#
654|S	Shape (for stamp seals only; e.g. pyramidal, conical, gabled) #
654|Z	Place made (if known) #
655|a	Genre scene (e.g. combat scene, contest frieze, presentation scene) #
797|a	Added entry under the repository designation for the seal #
852|a	Library name +
852|e	Library address +

Guide to symbols:
+ = mandatory
& = repeatable
! = deviation from MARC standard
= fields requiring authority control

Figure 15-3 | MARC Fields Used to Catalog Seals (Continued)

fields, especially those that consist of "boilerplate," such as the library's name and address, were typed once, and then duplicated from one record to another.

At the same time, we were investigating other databases of ancient Near Eastern objects. The main focus of our inquiry was the data fields used, rather than the specific system or software. Existing databases were likely to be highly customized applications; even if the institution that used the software was able or willing to give us a copy, there was no in-house support for adapting it to our own needs. Like many museums, the Morgan is collection-rich and technology-poor, and one part-time staff member is expected to cope with all the institution's computing needs. (The library recognizes that more computer staff will be required to implement an online public catalog, but that goal is several years down the road.)

In August 1994, Sidney Babcock and I visited the Babylonian Collection at Yale. Under the supervision of Ulla Kasten, the department has built up an impressive database of twenty-nine thousand records for its collection of clay tablets. It was instructive to see their field types, although the fields needed to describe tablets, which are primarily textual rather than pictorial, are rather different from those needed for seals. For example, there is a field for the number of lines occupied by the text, but no field for style or for iconographic terms. The Yale staff were very happy with the software

they were using—SPIRES, which was developed at Stanford; it offers unlimited record-size, flexible-length fields, Boolean search capabilities, the ability to index and sort on any field, and various report formats. But SPIRES works only on a mainframe (not an option for us); moreover, the vendors had announced not long before our visit that they were no longer going to support the package, so the Babylonian Collection was soon going to be in the market for new software.

We also obtained some sample screens from the Metropolitan Museum's objects database. Again, it was interesting to see which fields another institution had identified as important; but the focus of the Metropolitan Museum's system is collection management, and it contains many fields for information we were not concerned to track, such as photographic records data and conservation history, while making no provision for essential categories such as color, genre, and iconography.[5]

The final decision—in one sense, unorthodox, in another, extremely conservative—was to use the MARC format for the seals database. The following considerations played a part:

- I was familiar enough with MARC to be able to map our fields to MARC relatively quickly; the learning curve for adopting some other data structure would be much longer.

- Others have used MARC for visual material and art objects. By now there is a substantial body of literature on the topic, and the MARC documentation itself is extremely copious and detailed.

- Using MARC would allow us to use the same format for the seals and for the reference material relating to seals. Records for both could eventually reside in the same database, and share the same authority files.

- Given the nature of the Morgan's collections, which are composed preponderantly of material traditionally found in library collections (books, manuscripts, ephemera), the system eventually chosen by the library will most likely be MARC-based.

- Using MARC would allow us to disseminate the records through RLIN to a much wider audience long before we had a system of our own that could offer remote access.

- MARC is a widely known and accepted standard. If either of us were to leave the library, the work we had begun could be continued by our successors without too much difficulty.

- MARC-compatible software for PCs is now available that can be used to create MARC records for subsequent loading into bibliographic utilities and into our own in-house system. We wanted to be free to work in various locations, in and out of the library, and to experiment and make mistakes before going public on RLIN.

Mapping the fields we had chosen to MARC proved relatively simple, though it required fine-tuning for a couple of fields, and we ended up taking a few liberties with the format (see below for details). The biggest problem was not how to shoehorn the data into a limited number of fields, but how to resist the temptation to go wild and use every imaginable field. When we asked Donald P. Hansen, who is professor of art history and archaeology at the New York University Institute of Fine Arts, to review an experimental record we had entered in the VIM file in RLIN (RLIN id number NYPRF-1), he pointed out that the record was much too long, and that we were giving away curatorial research (the record was about three pages long and contained copious comparanda and citations to discussions of the seals). It was a useful reminder that bibliographic records in national databases should function as finding aids, not as curatorial files, pointing scholars to where the object is located

but not making them privy to every piece of information the museum has ever gathered about the object.

Software

The software we chose, Minaret (available from Cactus Software), had already been used for a number of years by several other collections in the New York metropolitan area.[6] It was demonstrated at a meeting of the Graphic Collections Catalogers and Curators Group in 1992; users noted that the package supported full MARC records, and that RLG could load Minaret records stored on diskettes into RLIN.

Peter Simmons, manager of collections access at the Museum of the City of New York, was kind enough to give me a two-hour demonstration of Minaret in August 1994. He was using Minaret to catalog the Byron Collection, a large photograph collection, and found it worked very well. System features included data entry and report screens that he had customized for the museum's needs, Boolean searching (clunky but usable), and pop-up authority files. The authority files function as a data validation tool, but they are not linked with the bibliographic records in such a way that a change to the authority record changes all occurrences of a heading on the bibliographic records. Nor is global change possible within the system. What one can do is print out the terms in the authority files, decide which need to be changed, and then use Minaret's ASCII export feature to send the bibliographic records containing these terms to a word-processing file. After running a global change, the records can be reimported into the MARC format. It is a cumbersome method, but it works; and this was very desirable for a database likely to contain so many terms in flux.

Peter Simmons' main difficulty with Minaret was that he was unfamiliar with MARC at the start of the project. It is possible to use Minaret without ever learning anything about MARC, because the package comes with a number of forms that use natural-language field names, but users who want to create their own work screens or do more sophisticated Boolean searches need to know enough MARC to make the translations between the MARC field tags and their meaning in natural language (e.g., 260|a means the place of publication). Minaret provides separate "layouts" for music, visual materials, and archival and manuscript collections; with the advent of format integration, these separate formats are a bit out of date, but because any and all of the existing layouts

776. Brownish chalcedony. Cylinder. 27 x 12. Attendant waving palm whisk over table decked with cloth and cup before seated king(?) raising cup. Behind king, second attendant with fan and towel. In sky, wedge, winged sun disk, star, crescent. [Ward, Seal cylinders 741].

Figure 15-4 | Sample Entry from the *Corpus*

may be altered by the user, one could in effect implement format integration in Minaret even before it was available in the bibliographic utilities.

Peter had no experience with the system's method of handling diacritics, because all his records were English-language records. This was a concern to us, because some of the seals bear inscriptions, chiefly in Sumerian and Akkadian, which require the use of such characters as the hacek and the upadhmaniya. Minaret provides an extended character set, Minaret Slavic (Latin II), that permits the use of these and many other exotic characters and diacritics; how that translates when records are loaded into another system is a different, still unresolved issue.

With this encouragement, we bought a copy of the software and began to lay out the format for the records. After some trial and error, we ended up using the MARC fields shown in figure 15-3. Figure 15-4 represents a sample entry from the *Corpus*.[7] Figure 15-5 represents the MARC record in Minaret. Figures 15-6 through 15-8 represent the user-friendly version of the record we set up for data entry and for viewing.

Our use of most of the fields was relatively straightforward. In general, the deviations have occurred where standards remain problematical, or where we wanted to have a separate field for a type of information that MARC relegates to the general note field.

Comments on MARC Fields

Fixed Fields

The Minaret template we customized for the seals database contained the fixed fields associated with the Books format. We did not bother to change it, since we were not using any of the fixed fields associated with the Visual Materials Format. Before the records are sent to RLIN, we will add the appropriate VIM fixed fields to the records, and add the value "a" (for "art original") to the fixed field for type of material (USMARC 008 33).

Most of the information in the fixed fields does not vary from record to record; the only value that occasionally changed was the country code (USMARC 008 15–17). Normally it is "iq" (the USMARC code for Iraq, the modern name for southern Mesopotamia). The database does include a few records for Syrian, Cypriote, and Iranian seals, all of which are given the proper USMARC country code.

Variable Fields

245 TITLE

It will come as no surprise to catalogers of visual materials and art objects that the decision on what to put in the 245 (title) field turned out to be the most difficult part of the whole exercise. Like so many other art objects, seals are untitled, and our source, the *Corpus*, does not supply titles, although it does provide the raw material for someone attempting to construct them on the basis of subject content or material type.

One solution is to construct a title based on the subject content of the seal: for example, "Archer Attacking Winged Bull" (Morgan 620). We opted for this solution because it is commonly used when cataloging other visual material for which no title exists, such as photographs and drawings. But many of the seals present such complex scenes, or combinations of scenes, that it was difficult to reduce the lengthy descriptions to a succinct, meaningful phrase. For example, Seal 935 is described thus in the *Corpus*:

Undulating striped band dividing design into four themes: in first, three human heads, one animal head, two hands, all reversed; in second, hero with plumed helmet, holding weapon; in third, lion above gazelle, both reversed; fourth, hare over monkey beside column of inverted crescents above guilloche.[8]

In any case, constructing a title based on subject content is not a very satisfactory solution, because it does not reflect usage in the field. Although scholars often use descriptive phrases of this sort as captions for labels and for reproductions of seals, they normally refer to seals by their repository designation (e.g., Morgan 1) or their catalog number, when a catalog has been published (e.g., Nuzi 6).[9] AACR2 Rule 25.13B1c prescribes a similar procedure when formulating uniform titles for unnamed illuminated manuscripts, and this method seems applicable to many types of untitled art objects. We will probably end up redoing the 245 fields so that they consist of the phrase "Morgan Seal [accession number]," and relegating meaningful brief titles to field 246 (alternative titles).

```
ID:AM-776        RTYP:c  ST:s       MS:  EL:        AD:950816
CC:9664  BLT:rm        DCF:?  CSC:d  MOD:              UD:12/18/95
CP:xx    L:xx    INT:  GPC:  BIO:  FIC:0  CON:
PC:b     PD:  /      REP:    CPI:0  FSI:0  ILC:      II:0
 MMD:     OR:   POL:   DM:   RR:      COL:     EML:  GEN:    BSE:
```

035	|a(NNPM)Morgan Seal 776
040	|aNNPM|cNNPM
046	|aq|b721|d675
245 00	|aAttendant waving palm whisk over table before seated king|h[cylinder seal]
260	|c[between 721 B.C.E. and 675 B.C.E.?]
300	|a1 cylinder seal :|bbrownish chalcedony ;|c27 x 12 mm.
506	|aImpression of seal available for study to qualified researchers|caccess by appointment only.
510	|aWard, Seal cylinders,|bno. 741.
520	|AAttendant waving palm whisk over table decked with cloth and cup before seated king(?) raising cup -- |BBehind king, second attendant with fan and towel --|Cin sky, wedge, winged sun disk, star, crescent.
524	|aMorgan seal 776.
530	|ab & w photographs of seal impression available from|cPhotographic Record Dept.|dNeg. no. ?.
561	|aAcquired by Pierpont Morgan sometime between 1885 and 1908.
581	|a"Seals 770-777 may with certainty be classified as Neo-Assyrian cylinders of the latter part of the eighth and of the seventh century ... The robe of the worshiper in 775 suggests Babylonian influence in that it has folds at the back as in garments seen on Neo-Babylonian seals ... and in that the fringe appears only at the bottom of the robe instead of being drawn over the hip as in earlier Assyrian representations like 644. The attendants in 776 are similarly clothed, suggesting that both 775 and 776 were made in or after the time of Sargon, when marked Babylonian influence modified even the type of dress worn at court."|zPorada, CANES, p. 93-94
653 1	|aAttendants with palm whisks.
653 1	|aTablecloths.
653 1	|aCups.
653 1	|aSeated kings.
653 2	|aAttendants with fans.
653 2	|aAttendants with towels.
653 2	|aWinged sun disks.
653 2	|aWedges.
653 2	|aStars.
653 2	|aCrescents.
654	|PNeo-Assyrian|Ylate modeled-style|Lbrownish|Mchalcedony|Ocylinder seals|ZSouthern Mesopotamia|2aat
655 7	|aBanquet scenes.
797 2	|aPierpont Morgan Library.|kSeal.|nMorgan seal 776.
852	|aPierpont Morgan Library|e29 E. 36th Street, New York NY 10016

Figure 15-5 | MARC Record for Seal 776

300|c DIMENSIONS

The dimensions recorded are the height and diameter of the end of the seal, given in millimeters, with no rounding up to the next millimeter. For seals with convex or concave sides, where the diameter of the middle varies from the diameter of the end, the former is added in parentheses, for example, 25.5 x 25 (23) mm. For fragmentary seals where only the height or the diameter is ascertainable, only that measurement is given.

520 SUMMARY NOTES

Detailed descriptions of the subject content of the seals are transcribed in the 520. We took the liberty of breaking this field down into three subfields (usually it contains only subfield |a) that reflect the relative

RECORD#: AM-776
ACCESSION#: Morgan seal 776

Description of pictorial elements:
  <BRIEF DESC>: Attendant waving palm whisk over table before seated king
  <MAIN PIC ELEMENTS>: Attendant waving palm whisk over table decked with cloth and cup before seated king(?)
         raising cup --
  <SUBSID. ELEMENTS>: Behind king, second attendant with fan and towel --
  <SUBSID. ELEMENTS>: In sky, wedge, winged sun disk, star, crescent.
  <DECORATIVE ELEMENTS>:

Description of physical/stylistic characteristics:
  <OBJECT TYPE>: cylinder seals
  <PERIOD>: Neo-Assyrian
  <STYLE>: late modeled-style
  <COLOR>: brownish
  <OTHER ATTRIBUTES>:
  <MATERIAL>: chalcedony
  <SHAPE>:
  <PLACE EXECUTED>: Southern Mesopotamia
  <EXTENT>: 1 cylinder seal :
  <DIMENSIONS>: 27 x 12 mm.
  <CONDITION>:

Date (or dates) of object:
  NOTE: DATETYPE is always q; dates may consist of a range (e.g., 3200/3000)

  <DATETYPE>: q
  <B.C.DATE1>: 721
  <B.C.DATE2>: 675
  <A.D.DATE2>:
  <DATEINWORDS>: [between 721 B.C.E. and 675 B.C.E.?]

NOTES

Interpretations, comments:
  <NOTE>: "Seals 770-777 may with certainty be classified as Neo-Assyrian cylinders of the latter part of the eighth
         and of the seventh century ... The robe of the worshiper in 775 suggests Babylonian influence in that it
         has folds at the back as in garments seen on Neo-Babylonian seals ... and in that the fringe appears only
         at the bottom of the robe instead of being drawn over the hip as in earlier Assyrian representations like
         644. The attendants in 776 are similarly clothed, suggesting that both 775 and 776 were made in or after
         the time of Sargon, when marked Babylonian influence modified even the type of dress worn at court."
  <SOURCE OF NOTE>: Porada, CANES, p. 93-94

Figure 15-6 | User Screen for Seal 776

importance of the scenes: 520|A Primary scene; 520|B Secondary scene; 520|C Decorative elements.

The capital letters are another deviation from normal MARC practice (MARC subfields are always either lowercase or numerical). Capitals will make the subfields easier to recognize and to fix with a global change before we submit the records to RLIN.

544 COMPARANDA

Our use of the 544 is nonstandard, or stretches the standard. MARC uses the 544 to cite material once part of a collection or record group, but which is now in other hands. We wanted a separate field for comparanda (notes citing seals or objects with which comparisons may be drawn).

Published in:
    <BIB. CITATION>: Ward, Seal cylinders, no. 741

Comparanda:
    <OBJECT CITED>:
    <OWNER>:

<PREFERRED CITATION>: Morgan seal 776

Provenance:
    <PROVENANCE>: Acquired by Pierpont Morgan sometime between 1885 and 1908.

Exhibition data:
    <EXHIB>:

ACCESS INFORMATION

Photo/surrogate image data:
    <FORMAT>: B & w photographs of seal impression available from
    <ORDERINFO>: Photographic Record Dept.
    <ORDER#>: Neg. no. ?

Restrictions on access:
    <RESTRICTIONS>: Impression of seal available for study to qualified researchers
    <ACCESS HOW>: access by appointment only

Figure 15-7 | User Screen for Seal 776

562 INSCRIPTIONS

About two hundred of the seals described in the *Corpus* contain inscriptions; these inscriptions will be transcribed in the 562|a, and translations will be provided in the 562|b. MARC makes no provision for a field specifically designated for inscriptions; we decided to use the 562|a, which is used for identifying marks (not quite the same, but similar).

653 ICONOGRAPHIC TERMS

We used the 653 field, defined in MARC as the field used for uncontrolled subject added entries, to index the subject content of the seals. Our use of the first indicator is a little unorthodox. Normally it is used to distinguish primary and secondary descriptors, but we used it to indicate whether the term appears in a primary scene (indicator value is 1), a secondary scene (indicator value is 2), or as a decorative element (indicator value is 3). The terms themselves came directly from the *Corpus* descriptions (the question of vocabulary control is discussed in more detail in the section on Authorities).

654 DESCRIPTIONS OF THE PHYSICAL/STYLISTIC CHARACTERISTICS OF THE OBJECT

This field is normally used for subject terms broken down by facet. We used it for indexing terms related to the physical characteristics of the object—a category that used to be assigned to the 755 field and is now assigned to the 655 field (formerly for genre terms only, now for genre and form terms). We did this because using the same field for two different types of information created problems in Minaret; the software does not allow you to place on a form two different field labels for the same field tag. We wanted the customized work screen to have separate fields for form and for genre, so we decided to use the 654 for form and retain the 655 for genre.

The peculiar subfield designators were another response to the field label problem. We wanted to use AAT facets or subfacets: color, material, style, period, and shape. But we discovered that several of these facets are coded with the same letter:

|cf is used for period and for style; |cd is used for color and for shape.

INDEXING TERMS

Iconographic terms:
  <PRIMARY (1)/SECONDARY (2)/DECORATIVE (3)>: 1
  <ICONTERM>: Attendants with palm whisks.

Iconographic terms:
  <PRIMARY (1)/SECONDARY (2)/DECORATIVE (3)>: 1
  <ICONTERM>: Tablecloths.

Iconographic terms:
  <PRIMARY (1)/SECONDARY (2)/DECORATIVE (3)>: 1
  <ICONTERM>: Cups.

Iconographic terms:
  <PRIMARY (1)/SECONDARY (2)/DECORATIVE (3)>: 1
  <ICONTERM>: Seated kings.

Iconographic terms:
  <PRIMARY (1)/SECONDARY (2)/DECORATIVE (3)>: 2
  <ICONTERM>: Attendants with fans.

Iconographic terms:
  <PRIMARY (1)/SECONDARY (2)/DECORATIVE (3)>: 2
  <ICONTERM>: Attendants with towels.

Iconographic terms:
  <PRIMARY (1)/SECONDARY (2)/DECORATIVE (3)>: 2
  <ICONTERM>: Winged sun disks.

Iconographic terms:
  <PRIMARY (1)/SECONDARY (2)/DECORATIVE (3)>: 2
  <ICONTERM>: Wedges.

Iconographic terms:
  <PRIMARY (1)/SECONDARY (2)/DECORATIVE (3)>: 2
  <ICONTERM>: Stars.

Iconographic terms:
  <PRIMARY (1)/SECONDARY (2)/DECORATIVE (3)>: 2
  <ICONTERM>: Crescents.

Genre scene terms:
  <GENRETERM>: Banquet scenes.

Figure 15-8 | User Screen for Seal 776

This would have meant trouble with the customized work screens; so we decided to substitute capital letters for the AAT facets:

|P for period, |Y for style, |L for color, |S for shape.

A global change will correct these unorthodox subfield codes before the records are submitted to RLIN.

Authorities

The choice of indexing terms proved to be every bit as confusing as Dr. Porada had warned. No subject-specific word lists exist, so we used terms we found in the *Corpus,* which is at least internally consistent. Terms describing the physical characteristics of the objects are the most amenable to standardization; many of these terms can be matched to descriptors in word lists devised for more general purposes, such as the AAT or even LCSH. Terminology that reflects art historical judgments on content (e.g., iconographic and genre terms) is far more difficult to standardize, and needs to be worked out in the context of a cooperative effort within the field.

Physical and Stylistic Characteristics

The physical characteristics of the seal are probably the easiest to fit into existing thesauri. We used AAT facets for color, material, style and period, shape, and object type, and plugged in terms that were used in the *Corpus*. The overlap between the *Corpus* terms and the terms used in the AAT varies from category to category. Almost all the material terms used in the *Corpus* are to be found in the AAT; terms not found there will need to be checked to establish whether they are variants of existing terms or whether they need to be submitted to the AAT as candidate terms. Color terms are another matter altogether. The terms used in the *Corpus* represent what the author meant by "dark-green" or "bluish," while the AAT terms are based on the Universal Color Language (UCL). At some point, we will need to redo the color descriptions using the UCL.

Stamp seals are always characterized by shape: conical, pyramidal, octagonal, and so on. Dr. Porada had been working with other scholars to standardize the terminology, but no formal list as yet exists. For now, we are using the terms that appear in the published descriptions. AAT terms for shape were adequate for the *Corpus* records because Morgan's collection contained only a few stamp seals, but they were not sufficient for the Kelley seals, which come in a bewildering variety of shapes (hemispheroid, tabloid, lentil-shaped, gable-shaped, hammer-shaped).

AAT terms for period and style are far more specific than LCSH terms, and may be used with much greater flexibility. Catalogers are permitted to construct AAT strings using whichever AAT terms they deem appropriate, while catalogers using LCSH are limited to the combinations of terms enumerated in the list or sanctioned in the *Subject Cataloging Manual*. For example, the LCSH heading "Cylinder seals" may not be modified by an adjectival qualifier for style or period, or subdivided by a time period;

only geographic subdivisions (|z), such as the name of a region or a modern country or an ancient site, are permitted. By contrast, AAT allows us to specify "Akkadian" or "Kassite" or "Neo-Babylonian" cylinder seals. Moreover, AAT breaks periods down into much finer subdivisions; in place of LCSH's single, broad "Assyro-Babylonian," AAT offers five Babylonian periods and three Assyrian periods; this specificity is crucial for indexing objects, to say nothing of specialized reference materials.

Genre

Genre is one of the organizing principles within the *Corpus*. Seals are grouped by region, subdivided by period; within periods, the descriptions are organized by style (e.g., linear, cut, drilled, and modeled), by motif (the winged gate, the god with a crook, suppliant goddesses), and by genre (contest friezes, banquet scenes, offering scenes). These terms, or terms analogous to them, are widely used in other printed catalogs of seals. The logical next step will be to share our list with others in the field, and draw up an authoritative list of genres.

Names

Rather to my surprise, two types of names turned out to be far less troublesome than I had expected: place names and personal names. None of Morgan's acquisitions came from controlled excavations. During the period when he was acquiring his seals, there was no sense that a seal was less valuable because its source was unknown. Dealers and collectors alike viewed them not as cultural artifacts or archaeological data but as art objects comparable to the engraved gemstones that have been in demand by connoisseurs since the Renaissance.

Even seals excavated during a modern scientific dig cannot always be localized with certainty. Seals were eminently portable, and so durable that they were passed down through many generations: One Morgan seal made during the First Dynastic Period (c. 2900–2800 B.C.E.) bears an incantatory inscription in Neo-Babylonian characters, indicating that it was still in use about two thousand years later. For excavated and nonexcavated seals alike, localization is generally done using stylistic criteria that permit the scholar to assign the seal to a region rather than to a site, and the regions can be rather large. We ended up using "Southern Mesopotamia" as the place of origin (654|z) for more than half the seals in the *Corpus*.

Personal names of human beings play only a minor role in the study of seals. Seals' makers are unknown; so are their original owners, unless mentioned in inscriptions on the seal. Only about 20 percent of the seals listed in the *Corpus* contain inscriptions; only about half of these inscriptions mention human (as opposed to divine) names. Provenance, too, is blessedly uncomplicated: Because seals have been actively collected only for about a century, one is spared the intricate ownership histories that are characteristic of other types of art objects. For the most part, the seals in our collection made a fairly direct journey from the silent earth into the hands of a dealer, and thence to Mr. Morgan.

Divine names do figure largely in the study of seals. The question is: Which name form to use? Many of the gods depicted on seals can be recognized by their symbols and attributes: The sun god has rays, ascends a mountain, and carries a saw with which he measures out justice. But the sun god bears different names in different cultures: The Sumerian name is Utu, the Akkadian name is Shamash (also transliterated as Šamaš). Seals represent so many different periods and civilizations, almost all of which were influenced by each other, that it is very difficult to pinpoint the origin of individual seals. The *Corpus* tends to use descriptive rather than proper names, referring to "the sun god" rather than "Utu" or "Shamash," "the weather god" rather than "Ishkur" (Sumerian) or "Adad" (Akkadian). The trend in more recent scholarship is to assign the proper name whenever the seal can be confidently assigned to a particular culture, but there is still no agreement on which name forms to use even within a given language (Šamaš or Shamash?).

Nondivine Figures and Objects

In addition to gods, the seals also depict heroic, demonic, or monstrous figures (nude bearded heros, griffin-demons, lion-headed eagles) and human figures defined by role (worshipers, banqueters, combatants) or by costume or physical attribute (figures in long robes, figures with horned headgear, pigtailed women). For the most part, these figures are types rather than individuals; it is rare to find a character

who can be given a name out of legend or mythology, such as Etana, the mythical Akkadian shepherd king, who appears in Seal 236.

Natural and man-made objects (animals, plants, buildings, furniture, weapons, utensils) appear frequently, either in the possession of the figures or as independent items in the design. During the initial data entry, we used the *Corpus* terminology, but plan to match the terms later with LCSH terms and bring our vocabulary in line with LCSH as much as possible. There is substantial overlap, although a certain number of the terms will be unique (e.g., "Winged sun disks," "Griffin-demons," "Large-eared gods," "Fleece-kilted heros"). A list of these terms would form a useful starting point for a subject-specific thesaurus.

As we began the indexing, two questions quickly arose: To what extent did we want to precoordinate terms, and to what extent did we want to specify relationships (spatial, role, actor/acted upon) between figures? Many of the figures on the seals are identifiable only by the use of a string of terms: "pigtailed women" and "nude bearded heros" are distinct types, and it would be misleading to describe them simply as "women" or as "heros." But where does one draw the line between qualifiers that express what a figure is and those that express what the figure is doing (e.g., "kneeling pigtailed women," "nude bearded heros wrestling with lions")?

The ideal solution would be some sort of faceting scheme. One such scheme has been developed for seals by Françoise Digard.[10] Digard proposed a method for describing the relation of the elements to one another, and for breaking down the different aspects of the figures into various facets, each with its own subfacets. For example, the Beings category is divided into animate versus inanimate beings and, within that, further subdivided into human, divine, and hybrid beings; each type can be characterized by such attributes as costume, gesture, posture, role, and so on. The scheme is worked out in careful detail, and copiously illustrated with drawings so that the indexer can consistently index a given posture using a given term. Unfortunately, the scheme has never really gained acceptance, because the drawings are not always accurate, the interpretations of the drawings are often faulty, and the author did not distinguish between genuine and forged seals.[11] We settled for entering the terms mostly as they appear in the *Corpus*, and hoping that at some later date we might be able to develop a faceting scheme of our own or adapt one developed by someone else.

Status of the Project

As of November 1996 Minaret MARC records exist for all the seals listed in the *Corpus* and for the Kelley seals. The Rosen seals, which are documented only at the group level, await fuller description by the curator. Data entry was relatively speedy, once the fields had been mapped to MARC and the forms created; the average amount of time required to input a record (including the description and the assignment of indexing terms) was about fifteen minutes per seal. Once the curator has reviewed all the records, they will be sent to RLIN; in the meantime, the curator has access to the database and can retrieve records searching any field or combination of fields. We are also planning to export the descriptions to an ASCII file, and then import them into the Microsoft Access database maintained by the library's Department of Photographic Records. Staff in this department often receive requests for images of specific objects (a porcupine, a leaping stag); access to full records will make it much easier for them to process requests.

We added 820 subject headings related to the ancient Near East to our in-house authority file, which is kept in a Procite database. Most headings are from LCSH or AAT, although we have had to establish a few terms of our own: "Seal impressions," "Stamp seals," and "Strigils," as well as names for sites, for ancient peoples, and for various deities. We plan to submit some of the object terms to AAT, as we understand that its editors are very hospitable to new terms.

We have added about 475 names to our in-house name authority file. Many had already been established by the Library of Congress; others had not, and we contributed about forty new name authority records to the Library of Congress Name Authority File (the Pierpont Morgan Library is a participant in NACO, the Name Authorities Cooperative Project). Our records have mainly been for authors of articles, but also include the names of collectors, museums, and a couple of ancient Near Eastern rulers. We look forward to the day when the Library of Congress will allow NACO libraries to contribute the names of ancient sites to their authority file. Many of the names that appear in our offprints refer to specific sites, and not all are included in LCSH, or even in the recently published *Concordance of Ancient Site Names.*[12]

Once the records for all the seals are entered, we plan to print out lists of the indexing terms used, merge these terms with the headings that have been used thus far for indexing the books and offprints, and work on building up a coherent, controlled vocabulary list that can be applied to the printed material, seal impressions, photographs, and other study material in Dr. Porada's bequest. The list will be dynamic, growing as new terms are needed; it will include cross-references and scope notes. We will make it available to others in the field, and hope that it could form the basis for a vocabulary of terms related to ancient Near Eastern objects.

Conclusion

Many of the problems and issues that arose in the course of the project to catalog the Morgan seals are peculiar to the material being cataloged. Few readers will ever have to worry about the spelling of the Sumerian (or is he the Akkadian?) sun god's name, or the difference between a bull-man, a bull-demon, and a human-headed bull. But our experience suggests some general conclusions that may be useful to others documenting nonbook material or special collections.

One realization was that MARC can be used for just about anything. We were able to get all the data we wanted into the MARC format; sometimes we had to squeeze or cheat a little, but all the deviations were reversible (and, we hope, excusable, given the uncharted nature of the waters). Motivation was the key factor. The curator was convinced that the whole collection ought to be more accessible to researchers, and that researchers would want to have reference material in the same searching universe as the objects. MARC was the answer to both needs, at least for this institution.

This is not to say that MARC is perfect. But the defects that others have noted in the course of trying to use MARC for visual materials did not affect our project. The part-whole relationships that bedevil catalogers of architectural material were not an issue for us.[13] We did not have to agonize over the merits of item- versus collection-level records, because we were working with a relatively small number of objects, almost all of which had existing item-level descriptions. We do not plan to use the database as a collection management tool, so the fact that MARC is not designed to track museum (or for that matter, library) transactions did not put us off.

The issues that gave us the most trouble were issues that would present difficulties no matter which format was used. Problems with inadequate descriptive cataloging standards and terminology are the same whether you are inputting the data into MARC records, into a collection management system based on some commercially developed database management system, or onto clay tablets in a cuneiform script. Working with art objects gave me more insight into what makes visual materials catalogers so testy about trying to apply cataloging rules derived from what is normal for books (and books printed after 1800, at that!). I will be following with interest the fate of the draft rule interpretation on uniform titles for works of visual art that was submitted to the Library of Congress by the Cataloging Advisory Committee of ARLIS/NA. I also welcomed the opportunity to get better acquainted with the AAT; I hope that eventually scholars in the field of Near Eastern studies can work together with librarians to create tools as well designed and carefully maintained.

Working with the seals introduced me to a period and art form of which I knew next to nothing. The ability of carvers, working in reverse, to compress a drama into a few millimeters, or to impart a delicate modeling to tiny figures, struck me as little short of miraculous, and I found it very moving to hold objects that reflected the concerns of an owner dead and gone several millennia ago. I hope that our work on the Morgan seals database will introduce these objects to a much wider audience, and make it easier for researchers to study them.

NOTES

1. J. P. Morgan Jr., in a letter to the board of trustees of the library, Feb. 15, 1924. Quoted in: *The Pierpont Morgan Library: A Review of the Growth, Development and Activities of the Library during the Period between . . . February 1924 and the Close of the Year 1929* (New York: Pierpont Morgan Library, 1930), 2.

2. Michael Roaf, *Cultural Atlas of Mesopotamia and the Ancient Near East* (New York: Facts on File, 1990), 72.

3. *Corpus of Ancient Near Eastern Seals in North American Collections. The Collection of the Pierpont Morgan Library* (Washington, D.C.: Pantheon Books, 1948). Two catalogs were compiled much earlier by W. H. Ward: *Cylinders and Other Ancient Oriental Seals in the Collection of J. Pierpont Morgan* (New York: Privately published, 1909) (catalog of about 300 cylinder seals owned by Morgan); and *Seal Cylinders of Western Asia* (Washington, D.C.: Carnegie Institution of Washington, 1910) (contains descriptions and drawings of 219 seals Morgan purchased from the Metropolitan Museum).

4. *Eighteenth Report to the Fellows of the Pierpont Morgan Library 1975–1977* (New York: Pierpont Morgan Library, 1978), 373–387 (unillustrated checklist of the Kelley gift); *Twenty-first Report to the Fellows of the Pierpont Morgan Library 1984–1986* (New York: Pierpont Morgan Library, 1989), 440–449 (summary list of Rosen seals with three illustrations).

5. We learned of the existence of the Iconostasis database for Aegean glyptics only after the completion of our own project. The database is described by its creators, Janice Crowley and Anthony Adams, in "Iconaegean and Iconostasis: An Iconographic Classification and a Comprehensive Database for Aegean Glyptik," an article published in *Sceaux minoens et mycéniens* (Berlin: Gebr. Mann Verlag, 1995): 39–58. The database, which includes brief descriptions, images, and an iconographic classification, uses Microsoft FileMaker Pro; the authors plan to make the database and the classification system available on disc eventually.

6. We purchased version 1.70, which runs on a 286 or higher; a newer version with imaging is now available. Readers interested in learning about the new version should contact Cactus Software, Inc., 10 West 15th Street, Suite 720, New York, NY 10011; (212) 647-1470.

7. *Corpus,* p. 94.

8. *Corpus,* p. 123.

9. Nuzi refers to the catalog compiled by Edith Porada, *Seal Impressions of Nuzi* (New Haven, Conn.: American Schools of Oriental Research, 1947).

10. Françoise Digard, *Répertoire analytique des cylinders orientaux* (Paris: Editions du Centre national de la recherche scientifique, 1975).

11. Edith Porada, "Problems of Method in the Archaeology and Art History of the Ancient Near East," *Journal of the American Oriental Society* 102 (1982): 501–506.

12. Eileen Fry and Maryly Snow, eds., *Concordance of Ancient Site Names* (Raleigh, N.C.: Art Libraries Society of North America, 1995).

13. Lynda S. White, "Image Cataloging in MARC at the University of Virginia," *VRA Bulletin* 21, no. 3 (fall 1994): 26.

16

The Performing Arts Index at the Metropolitan Museum of Art

Judith Jaroker and Constance Old

Educators, researchers, performers, and others interested in the arts may seek performing arts–related images from artworks. Such images are found in drawings and paintings and in other media, such as ceramics and tapestry. Museum records customarily describe physical characteristics of artworks in detail, with somewhat less attention afforded to the objects' iconography. By focusing on the iconography of music, dance, and theater, the Performing Arts Index (PAI) at the Metropolitan Museum of Art fills a niche for those seeking such images for study or illustration. This chapter gives an overview of the Performing Arts Index in its present state as a collection of images of dance, theater, and music found on artworks in the Metropolitan Museum collection, and suggests how the PAI could be automated into an image database which would make it even easier to locate specific performing arts–related images.

Constance Old began work on the project in the 1980s by collecting examples of dance-related images on Metropolitan Museum artworks. The project was known as the Metropolitan Museum of Art Dance Index (MMADI) and was undertaken under the auspices of the Metropolitan Museum of Art's Musical Instruments Department. In the early 1990s the MMADI was expanded to include images relating to music and theater. The MMADI became the Performing Arts Index (PAI) to reflect this expanded focus. At this time an association was formed with the Research Center for Music Iconography (RCMI).

The Research Center for Music Iconography, directed by Zdravko Blažeković, is the American center of the *Répertoire International d'Iconographie Musicale* (RIdIM) and is located in the Graduate School of the City University of New York. It was founded in 1971 by City University Professor Barry Brook to develop

Updated from first appearance in *Dance and Technology III; Transcending Boundaries. Proceedings of the Third Annual Conference,* May 18–21, 1995, ed. A. William Smith, York University, Toronto.

methods for cataloging and classifying images relevant to music iconography. RIdIM is sponsored by the International Musicological Society, the International Association of Music Libraries, and the International Council of Museums. The biannual *RIdIM/RCMI Newsletter* charts the progress of the organization and provides further information for students of musicology and music iconography. National music iconography centers associated with RIdIM are active in thirteen countries: Croatia, the Czech Republic, Denmark, France, Germany, Hungary, Italy, Japan, the Netherlands, Poland, Sweden, Switzerland, and the United States. The task of these centers has been to assemble, catalog, and publish examples of music iconography in major museums and private collections. During the 1980s, a two-year grant from the National Endowment for the Humanities (NEH) funded the publication of music iconography inventories with images and image descriptions. To date, five volumes have been published covering the collections at the Cleveland Museum of Art; the National Gallery of Art, Washington, D.C.; the Frick Collection, New York; the Morgan Library (Medieval and Renaissance manuscripts only), New York; and the Art Institute of Chicago. Seven hundred images were assembled for a Metropolitan volume. This was not published and the images are now in the PAI.

The Performing Arts Index has provided source material for museum and university conferences, seminars, lectures, and tours. Articles and information have appeared in *Dance Magazine, RIdIM/RCMI Newsletter,* Mary Bopp's *Research in Dance: A Guide to Resources* (New York: G. K. Hall, 1994), newspapers, and other publications. For example, images from the project were used in the MMA publication, *Dance: A Very Social History* (Carol McD. Wallace, Don McDonagh, Jean L. Druesedow, et al., New York: Metropolitan Museum of Art/Rizzoli, 1986); in *Drumming at the Edge of Magic, a Journey into the Spirit of Percussion* (Mickey Hart, with Jay Stevens and Frederic Lieberman, San Francisco: Harper, 1990); in the Channel Thirteen/WNET eight-part series *Dancing* (1993); and as models for the cover designs of compact discs by Julia Prospero of Lyrichord Discs (1995). In addition, images have been selected for the forthcoming *International Dance Encyclopedia* to be published by Oxford University Press.

The PAI project has been supported by the MMA's Accessions and Catalog Department, Musical Instruments Department, Photograph and Slide Library, Photograph Studio, Systems and Computer Services, and the Watson Library.

From the beginning, the Index has offered black-and-white photographs of relevant images and cataloging information about objects in the museum collections. The information includes: museum accession number, curatorial department, negative number, artist/maker/school/workshop, artist's date of birth/death, title/object name, brief description, material/medium/technique, dimensions, credit, curatorial classification, period, and style. This data comes from the MMA Accessions and Catalog Department; it does not include information about iconography. Currently the PAI contains approximately three thousand dance, music, and theater images. They are filed in binders and arranged according to museum curatorial department.

The objectives of the PAI are to identify and catalog dance-, theater-, and music-related images, devise ways to index their iconography, and create an automated image database that would allow retrieval of images according to subject, similar to Germany's Bildarchiv Foto Marburg's *Marburg Information, Documentation and Administration System* (MIDAS). The PAI is being designed for maximum compatibility with current museum practices to insure that it will integrate smoothly into the Metropolitan Museum's system. The creation of the MMA collections management program, *The Museum System* (TMS), is a long-term project which is in an early stage of development.

Cataloging

The PAI contains images of relevant museum objects and text in the form of an organized object description or catalog record. In planning to automate these images and records, a cataloging system must provide for the way in which the information is organized into fields, what syntax is used to fill those fields, and what terms should be used within the syntax. The first two considerations and the use of a MARC-based system are discussed in this section; the third consideration is discussed in the following section on indexing.

A primary factor in PAI design was choosing catalog practices that are widespread. In describing the creation of a documentation system for the Deutsches Theatermuseum in Munich, Deputy Director Heinrich Huesmann put it aptly in his assertions that "[i]t would have had a devastating effect on the development of theatre documentation if each country had developed among its separate institutions diverse and independent documentation systems. This condition would have resulted in a Babylonian confusion of system languages. The problem of information exchange rests not solely on the deficient or successful compatibility of hard- and software systems, but foremost on terminology definitions, the foundation and systematic conceptual synthesis of . . . theatre."[1] The aim of compatibility underlies the PAI consideration of a MARC system, but consideration of RIdIM rules and Metropolitan host practices are also relevant.

The PAI is considering the RIdIM cataloging scheme. The RIdIM cataloging rules were developed by music iconographers. They are based upon, but are somewhat more detailed than, relevant sections of the standard library cataloging manual, *The Anglo-American Cataloguing Rules,* second edition, revised. Carla Tessari's *Catalogo italiano di iconografia musicale: Strutturazione dei dati delle schede* was developed in 1992 at the University of Pavia and the cataloging rules continue to be revised. Also of major concern, as has been stated above, is that PAI practices must be compatible with those of the Metropolitan Museum of Art. MMA cataloging practices are unique to the Museum and, moreover, there are differences amongst the different curatorial departments. In-house practices could be improved by adopting the terminology from the *Categories for the Description of Works of Art* developed for the museum world by the Art Information Task Force (AITF), a committee organized in 1990 by the Getty Art History Information Program.

Although MARC comes in different versions, such as USMARC (United States), CANMARC (Canada), and UKMARC (United Kingdom), basic MARC is an international standard. Nevertheless, there is some discrepancy in how MARC fields are interpreted when they are used to catalog art objects and images as revealed in a 1992 study of eleven MARC-based projects.[2] Despite such inconsistencies, MARC is a viable option. In her article in the *RIdIM/RCMI Newsletter,* Selima Mohammed suggested that RIdIM use for its cataloging well-developed international standards such as are provided by the Library of Congress and MARC.[3] MARC could satisfy PAI cataloging needs, but would it satisfy user needs? Precedents suggest that an analysis of user queries can be helpful in selecting a retrieval system. For example, data extracted from sample user queries were used to structure the automated image retrieval system of the National Library of Medicine.[4] User search patterns from the PAI and RCMI show that many performing arts researchers define searches according to time period and geographic location/

culture, performer, musical instrument, costume, props, or event. Because these elements of information can be accounted for in MARC fields, it is likely that MARC cataloging would satisfy the needs of PAI users.

In the MARC system, records contain information within coded and textual fields. The fixed-length coded fields which begin a record are filled with numbers or abbreviations; they may duplicate information in the textual variable-length fields. Many variable fields are preceded by coding in the form of field indicators and may be subdivided as well. The scheme proposed for the PAI is a MARC stripped of indicators to use only those coded fields which do not duplicate information in textual fields. Figure 16-1 gives a schematic view of a MARC record to demonstrate the order and use of some numbered fields that could be used to catalog performing arts images.

A catalog record for the PAI would describe the museum object and include essential elements of a field linking the image to its catalog record (field 856), an image of the object, a reference to the MMA image of the object (negative number field), and the subject (6XX fields). The MARC visual materials fields above, with the exception of fields for subject and for electronic location, correspond to fields which are already used in MMA cataloging.[5] For an application manual for syntax of field entry, the PAI could adopt the USMARC Bibliographic Format manual which includes fields for visual materials, and the format integration manual which is essential to supplement the USMARC manual. Complexities arise when these fields are used to describe an object's iconography, the purpose of the PAI. Minor adaptations of MARC for the PAI are suggested below.

What might a PAI record look like? Take, for example, a sample PAI record for Thomas Eakins' "Negro Boy Dancing" (see figure 16-2). The record (see figure 16-3) shows only fields which are relevant to the object being cataloged. The MARC numbers would not be visible on the user's screen display. Notice that there may be more than one entry for a single field, that is, fields may repeat. Also, notice indications of the origins of the indexing terms, whether *Library of Congress Subject Headings* (LCSH), the *Dance Collection Subject Headings* of the New York Public Library (NYPL), or RCMI's *List of Western Instruments Annotated from an Iconographical Point of View.*[6] The distinction in indexing term lists is discussed further in the following section.

The question of how to classify an image according to its subject is by no means straightforward

MARC Tag Number	Description
007	Object type
033	Date/time and place of object creation
035	System control number
040	Cataloging source
041	Language (language associated with an item)
043	Geographical area
044	Country of publishing/producing
045	Time period of content
048	Number of musical instruments or voice
090	[Locally defined]
1XX	Main entry—personal name, corporate name, etc.
240	Uniform title
245	Title
260	Imprint (publication, distribution, etc.)
300	Physical description
340	Physical medium
351	Organization and arrangement of materials
4XX	Series statement
500	General note
502	Dissertation note
506	Restrictions on access note
510	Citation/references note
511	Participant or performer note
518	Date/time and place of an event
530	Additional physical form (may use for negative number)
540	Terms governing use and reproduction note
545	Biographical or historical note
561	Provenance note
581	Publications about described materials note
585	Exhibition note
586	Awards note
600	Subject added (SA) entry: Personal name
610	SA: Corporate name (use for firm/factory/workshop)
611	SA: Meeting name (meeting or conference/exhibition)
630	SA: Uniform title
650	SA: Topical term
651	SA: Geographical name
655	SA: Genre/form
656	SA: Occupation
657	SA: Function (activity or function that generated the described material according to MARC manual)
69X	Local subject access fields
700–75X	Added entries
850	Holding institution
852	Location
856	Electronic location and access

Figure 16-1 | MARC Record

Figure 16-2 | Thomas Eakins, "Negro Boy Dancing," Watercolor on off-white wove paper, 1878. (The Metropolitan Museum of Art, Fletcher Fund, 1925 [25.97.1].)

007	Object	Watercolor
033	Date/time/place creation	1878
035	System control number (Acc.no.)	25.97.1
040	Cataloging source	Metropolitan
044	Country of publishing/producing	United States
045	Time period of content	postbellum South
048	Number of musical inst/voice	banjo (RCMI)
100	Artist	Eakins, Thomas (1844-1916)
245	Title	Negro Boy Dancing
300	Physical description	Watercolor on off-white wove paper 46 x 57.4 cm.
500	Notes	Eakins' interest in African Americans is also demonstrated in his "Pushing for Rail."
500	Notes	There is a preserved pencil sketch, some oil studies and a perspective drawing of this watercolor.
500	Notes	Originally called "The Negroes"
510	Citations/references	Weinberg, H. Barbara, "Thomas Eakins and the Metropolitan Museum of Art," *The Metropolitan Museum of Art Bulletin*, vol. LII, no. 3 (winter 1994-5): 22–23.
510	Citations/references	Gardner, A.T. *History of water color painting in America*. New York, 1966, p.79, pl.64
518	Date/time and place	Signed "EAKINS 78"
545	Biographical/historical note	Eakins entitled this "The Dancing Lesson" when he sent it to the 1889 *Exposition Universelle* in Paris.
561	Provenance note	Fletcher Fund, 1925.
585	Exhibition note	Washington, D.C. -- U.S. National Gallery of Art, Smithsonian Institution; Chicago -- The Art Institute of Chicago; Philadelphia Museum of Art [traveling exhibition, October 8, 1961-March 18, 1962].
586	Awards note	Silver medal at the Massachusetts Charitable Mechanics' Association Exhibition in Boston, 1878.
650	SA: Topical term	Children as dancers (NYPL) -- 19th century
655	Form/genre	Afro-American dance (LCSH)
850	Holding institution	Metropolitan Museum of Art
852	Local classification	American -- Drawings and Watercolors
8XX	Locally defined: Negative number	59862 H B
856	Electronic location of an image	(Example: C:\image\eakins\25971)

Figure 16-3 | Sample PAI Record

because one image may be said to have many subjects, depending upon the cataloger's perspective. The PAI might cope with this problem of image retrieval by subject, by providing both a list of subject terms in an index and by allowing users to look through many retrieved images. The following section describes how an indexing system could use text and images for maximum efficiency in image retrieval.

Indexing

Deciding upon the subject content of images is complex because, given the proverbial thousand words a picture is worth, it seems futile to assign one or two. Information professionals note the difficulties of indexing images.[7] Despite these difficulties, subject indexing within the performing arts is essential to the PAI.

The subject of an image, according to art historian Erwin Panofsky, can be defined on three levels: the basic level of what is seen in the image; the middle level of what the seen components signify; and the highest level of what the seen components mean within the culture that created the image.[8] It may seem that the form/genre and function 6XXs within MARC and Panofsky's middle and highest level of interpretation correspond, but actually these MARC fields are defined in terms of the form and function of the artwork itself and not of the form and function of the artwork's iconography. Take, for example, a Greek wine vessel on which is painted some youths playing wind instruments and dancing: The subject or function of the vessel is "wine holder" whereas the subject of the vessel's decoration would be "playing wind instruments." The PAI requires that the subject of the visual materials be indexed as well as the visual materials themselves. It would be useful for the PAI to keep these levels of indexing distinct.

When a cataloger determines that many images share a common iconographical subject, a single catalog record could be created for the group of images. Such generalized cataloging saves space and time, but would be too general for an index of the nature of the PAI. Even so, it would be useful to retain the general categories of dance, theater, and music. If an image can be classified as both dance and drama, there may be two entries in the 650 field. MARC cataloging allows for additional information to be added in a string after the main subject entry. For instance, the 650 field allows for a topical term, geographical term, general subdivision, chronological subdivision, and geographic subdivision. It would simplify matters for the PAI if, rather than enter information in standard MARC subfield strings, information was divided into different fields so that they might become locally assigned 650 subfields.

Subject indexing requires a controlled vocabulary, that is, a vocabulary with terms predetermined, so that more than one image may be retrieved by a single indexing term. In *Standard Cataloging,* Intner and Weihs explain that a sound indexing vocabulary contains terms that are not synonymous or otherwise ambiguous, that are precise for the particular topic, and that can be separated into hierarchies.[9] For specialized collections, precision of terms is key. Some performing arts collections have created their own indexing lists, such as the *Billy Rose Theatre Collection Subject Heading List* of the New York Public Library for the Performing Arts, and RCMI's *List of Western Instruments.* However, keeping in mind the Intner and

Weihs guidelines, it is clear that creating an indexing vocabulary—the technical term is thesaurus—is a formidable project, and that it is practical to use extant thesauri whenever possible. Two thesauri commonly used to index the subject content of images are the *Art and Architecture Thesaurus* (AAT) and ICONCLASS. ICONCLASS is not sufficiently precise for PAI requirements. The AAT includes terms for Musical Instruments and Sound Devices, Costume, and Built Environments. It might be a possibility for the PAI. The Harvard Theater Collection uses the *Library of Congress Thesaurus for Graphic Materials,* while the Dance Collection of the New York Library of the Performing Arts uses the *Library of Congress Subject Headings* (LCSH) and adds indexing terms as needed. No single thesaurus contains terms precise enough to accommodate dance, music, and theater indexing, but several thesauri could be combined for a richer supply of terms appropriate to the PAI, provided that indexers were aware of possible list overlap. Because the subject headings from the Library of Congress are in widespread use and are fairly broad in scope, they could serve as a backbone for PAI indexing although they would need to be supplemented. Other resources could include the NYPL's *Dance Collection Supplementary Headings* and the RCMI's *List of Western Instruments.*

The LCSH, enriched with terms from other thesauri, seems serviceable for the purpose of indexing PAI images, but the best test of an indexing system is in its application. As examples, two PAI images (shown in figures 16-4 and 16-6) are assigned the subject terms seen in figures 16-5 and 16-7. Even though the MARC system specifies thesauri in the second indicator of the code preceding a subject field, in these examples a proposed thesaurus is indicated in parentheses following the term.

For figure 16-4, musicologists could be asked to identify the instruments as precisely as possible, and theater scholars to identify by masks and dress the *commedia dell'arte* characters depicted.

Defining dance types as is suggested for figure 16-4 is difficult because it is rare to be able to identify a dance type from the single choreographic step captured in an image. An image of dance can be described objectively by noting apparent body positions, such as a raised leg, but such a description would be of little use to researchers. Who would enter "raised leg" as a key phrase? For this type of query, visual browsing of many small images, or "thumbnails," may be preferable.

Another way to locate images allows queries based on visual characteristics of images, such as

Figure 16-4 | Giovanni Domenico Tiepolo, "A Dance in the Country," Oil on canvas, c. 1750. (The Metropolitan Museum of Art, Gift of Mr. and Mrs. Charles Wrightsman, 1980 [1980.67].)

650	Men dancers (LCSH)
650	Women dancers (LCSH)
650	Actors (LCSH)
650	Musicians (LCSH)
650	Costume—Theatrical (LCSH)
655	Commedia dell'arte (LCSH)
655	Couple dance (NYPL)
656	Open air performances (NYPL added term)

Figure 16-5 | Subject Terms for *A Dance in the Country* Showing Proposed Thesauri

shape, color, or texture. As of 1996, the main body of research on retrieval of images according to visual properties has been for images which are not art-related, and so the software developed for retrieval by visual properties may have limited applicability in the domain of art. A few databases which use visual characteristics for image retrieval programs for art images are worth noting as possible models for the PAI. For example, the Art and Art History project at the University of California at Davis uses QBIC (Query by Image Content) software, as does Imagebase at the Fine Arts Museum of San Francisco and the image collections of the French Ministry of Culture. An image matching and retrieval program, Morelli, was developed with art uses in mind by art historian William Vaughan at Birbeck College in London. Morelli can locate images based on outline and motif. Its suitability to art images rests in its speed, ability to compare black-and-white with color images, and use of subject text searches.[10] Search properties of color and texture may not be too practical for the needs of PAI users, but searching by image outline might be helpful. The problem is with the technology—it takes much effort to choose which objects within each image should be outlined and it takes much time to do the outlining. Within the limits of the technology at present, this method is not recommended over an image retrieval system in which words retrieve thumbnail images that the user can browse.

The caveat for a system that uses text to retrieve images is that text terms must be applied to objects consistently and accurately. PAI users could learn which terms were incorporated into the indexing vocabulary by sifting quickly through a list of indexing terms entered into the database. Achieving accuracy in cataloging can be time-consuming and therefore costly.

A model for how detailed PAI cataloging might be accomplished might be the cataloging process described by Lynda White for a project of image cataloging using MARC at the University of Virginia. For this project, cataloging is divided into three steps: base cataloging which requires no special knowledge of the object; cataloging using additional fields such as the subject fields completed by specialists; and a theoretical system whereby data for a field such as related literature may be entered by the researcher using a particular image.[11] The first step and part of the second reflect what would be PAI procedure, because the PAI might use existing museum cataloging for objects. Subject cataloging must be done by those knowledgeable about art, dance, theater, or music history.

Hardware/Software

Advantages of automating the PAI are many. Computer searching of a database would allow images to be retrieved fast. A computer database could be updated easily and could produce hard-copy inventories in publishable form. A more complete PAI might be transferred to compact discs so that institutions or individuals would have access to the index tool.

A computer system to support automation of the PAI would require a server with ample storage space, a computer with a high-resolution monitor, a printer, and software to index text and images. Presumably the Museum's Unix server could be harnessed for the project. The MMA uses an IBM platform and the PAI would do the same in the interests of compatibility. A high-resolution color monitor would display color images to best advantage and a color laser printer would generate high-quality printouts. A high-resolution scanner would not need to be purchased: A service bureau could make digital reproductions of relevant slides. Choices in all categories are limited by Metropolitan Museum of Art guidelines as well as by available funds.

It would be ideal to have search software written expressly for the PAI, and comparable database projects have had software developed. For example, the *Marburg Information, Documentation and Administration System* (MIDAS) had the program Hierarchical Document Administrator (HIDA) written in the programming language C. HIDA allows searches by particular fields, in fields combined by Boolean operators AND, OR, and NOT, and by free text search for items retrieved in the aforementioned two search types.

Figure 16-6 | "Fan," French, 19th century. (The Metropolitan Museum of Art, Gift of Mrs. William Randolph Hearst, 1963 [63.90.131].)

650	Men dancers (LCSH)
650	Women dancers (LCSH)
655	Circle dances (NYPL)
655	Dance music (LCSH)
656	Social dancing (NYPL)

Figure 16-7 | Subject Terms for the Fan in Figure 16-6

In the absence of specially developed software, a Cuadra product called STAR coupled with Luna imaging software could be customized to PAI needs and could be an economical alternative. If the PAI did choose STAR and Luna, it would be in good company. Museums, including the Frick Collection in New York, have chosen the STAR text-retrieval system. Among the present clients of Luna are the Preservation Department of Columbia University, the Getty Conservation Institute, and the New York Theater Collection. STAR includes a flat-file database management system with text retrieval capabilities and an interface for MARC. It requires a Unix server to run, has an optional application program for the Images software, and an option for a World Wide Web browser interface. Luna Imaging, Inc., has developed Luna Image Server (LIS) and Insight software to manage and provide access to large digital image collections. Technically, the PAI would need three software programs to create its image database: STAR to operate through Windows; Luna Image Server (LIS) to link images to text (a software of which users would not be aware); and Insight to provide an interface for the images. The image software allows browsing of thumbnail images and the storing of images of one or two other resolutions on Photo CDs.

A typical search on the envisioned PAI system might go as follows. A user enters the keywords "stage" and "Harlequin" through the STAR interface. The Luna software locates and retrieves all images in which both words appear in the catalog record, retrieving, for example, eighteen relevant thumbnails. When the user clicks on the tiny image of greatest interest, the full catalog record is retrieved by STAR. The whole PAI system could reside on CD-ROMs. The three search systems could include catalog records with several thousand thumbnails, and other low-resolution images on a single CD, and high-quality reproductions of the images on additional CDs. STAR has an interface which allows it to be mounted on the World Wide Web so that, in the future, member mu-

seums might be able to enter data to an Internet-mounted PAI. Museums and educational institutions might use the PAI for a fee, which could be reduced for PAI museum members who contribute images and catalog records from their collections.

Conclusion

This chapter suggests preliminary stages in Performing Arts Index development and database design. The PAI would remain under the auspices of the Musical Instruments Department at the Metropolitan Museum of Art and would use mainly MMA cataloging fields within the rubric for USMARC visual materials format. It could use indexing terms from the *Library of Congress Subject Headings,* the *Art and Architecture Thesaurus,* the NYPL's *Dance Collection Supplementary Headings,* and the RCMI's *List of Western Instruments.* It would contribute new indexing terms for more precise performing arts indexing. To improve information retrieval the PAI would be designed to index visually as well as verbally. Catalog record input could begin as soon as funds were available, a system assembled, and software installed. Visitors would be allowed to use the automated database during its development and could keep their search result printouts. An inventory with accompanying illustrations could be published at intervals to reflect database contents and, when several thousand records and images for relevant dance-, theater-, and music-related images from Museum objects had been entered into the PAI, the database could be transferred to CD-ROM.

In the long term, other institutions might be invited to contribute records to expand the Performing Arts Index. Institutions could send reproductions of relevant images to the Metropolitan Museum of Art so that cataloging could be done by PAI catalogers, or else catalog guidelines could be distributed to encourage institutions to catalog their own images for the PAI. They would send completed records to the PAI for inclusion in the database. Ultimately, it could be made accessible via the Internet so that it would be available through an online terminal anywhere in the world.

NOTES

1. Heinrich Huesmann, "New Theatre Documentation Technology at the Munich *Deutsches Theatermuseum,*" *Theatre History Studies* 7 (1987): 119.

2. James M. Bower, "The Visual Resources Association MARC Mapping Project," *Visual Resources* 9, no. 3 (1993): 291–327.

3. Selima Mohammed, "RIdIM Documentation: A Proposal for Change," *RIdIM/RCMI Newsletter* 19, no. 1 (spring 1994): 32.

4. Raya Fidel, Trudi B. Hahn, Edie M. Rasmussen, et al., *Challenges in Indexing Electronic Text and Images,* ASIS Monograph Series (Medford, N.J.: Learned Information, 1994), 7–22.

5. Marica Vilcek, *Metropolitan Museum of Art Cataloging Manual* (New York: Metropolitan Museum of Art Cataloging Department, 1972, typescript).

6. *Library of Congress Subject Headings,* 19th ed., 4 vols. (Washington, D.C.: Library of Congress, 1996); Dorothy Lourdou, *Dance Collection Subject Headings* (New York: Dance Collection, New York Public Library for the Performing Arts, 1994, typescript); Terence Ford, compiler, *List of Western Instruments Annotated from an Iconographical Point of View* (New York: Research Center for Musical Iconography, 1987).

7. Sara Shatford Layne, "Some Issues in the Indexing of Images," *Journal of the American Society for Information Science* 45, no. 8 (1994): 583–588; Elaine Svenonius, "Access to Nonbook Materials: The Limits of Subject Indexing for Visual and Aural Languages," *Journal of the American Society for Information Science* 45, no. 8 (1994): 600–606; James M. Turner, "Subject Access to Pictures: Considerations in the Surrogation and Indexing of Visual Documents for Storage and Retrieval," *Visual Resources* 9, no. 3 (1993): 241–271.

8. Erwin Panofsky, "Iconography and Iconology: An Introduction to the Study of Renaissance Art," in *Meaning in the Visual Arts* (Garden City, N.Y.: Doubleday, 1955), 26–54.

9. Sheila Intner and Jean Weihs, *Standard Cataloging for School and Public Libraries* (Englewood, Colo.: Libraries Unlimited, 1990), 79–80.

10. Catherine Grout, "From 'Virtual Curator' to 'Virtual Librarian': What Is the Potential for the Emergent Image Recognition Technologies in the Art-Historical Domain?" in *Proceedings of the 1996 Electronic Imaging and the Visual Arts Conference, EVA '96,* ed. J. Hemsley (London: National Gallery of Art, 1996), 6, 10, 11.

11. Lynda S. White, "Image Cataloging in MARC at the University of Virginia," *VRA Bulletin* 21, no. 3 (fall 1994): 23–33.

ACKNOWLEDGMENTS

The authors thank Mathilda Rostoker and Anne Steel, *Performing Arts Index;* Dr. Selma Jeanne Cohen, editor, *International Encyclopedia of Dance;* Kevin Donovan, Luna director of Special Projects; Dr. Mark Franko, University of Santa Cruz; Catherine Johnson, managing director of the Dance Heritage Coalition; Dorothy Lourdou and Patricia Rader, New York Public Library Dance Collection; David Smith, Cuadra; Dr. Julia Sutton, New England Conservatory of Music; and Antonio Baldassarre, *Répertoire International d'Iconographie Musicale,* Switzerland.

BIBLIOGRAPHY

Besser, Howard. "Visual Access to Visual Images: The UC Berkeley Image Database Project." *Library Trends* 38, no. 4 (spring 1990): 787–798.

Bildarchiv Foto Marburg: From Printed to Digital Tradition of Art and History. A Study Project of the German Documentation Center for Art History (Deutsches Dokumentationszentrum für Kunstgeschichte (DDK)). Brochure demonstrating a range of IBM products, written by members of the Faculty of the University of Marburg, 1995(?).

Billy Rose Theatre Collection Subject Headings List. Updated by the Theatre Collection staff. New York: Billy Rose Theatre Collection, New York Public Library for the Performing Arts, n.d.

Bopp, Mary S. *Research in Dance: A Guide to Resources.* New York: G. K. Hall, 1994.

Bower, James M. "The Visual Resources Association MARC Mapping Project." *Visual Resources* 9, no. 3 (1993): 291–327.

Brook, Barry S. "RIdIM Inaugural Report." *Fontes Artis Musicae* 19, no. 3 (1972): 196–206.

Education and Cultural Heritage: Solid Partners for the NII: A Profile of Current and Emerging Projects and Approaches. Prepared by the Getty Art History Information Program, Eleanor Fink, director, following panel discussion in Washington, D.C., January 14, 1995.

Enser, P. G. B. "Progress in Documentation Pictorial Information Retrieval." *Journal of Documentation* 51, no. 2 (June 1995): 130–170.

Fidel, Raya, Trudi B. Hahn, Edie M. Rasmussen, et al. *Challenges in Indexing Electronic Text and Images.* ASIS Monograph Series. Medford, N.J.: Learned Information, 1994.

Ford, Terence, compiler. *List of Western Instruments Annotated from an Iconographical Point of View.* New York: Research Center for Musical Iconography, 1987.

Grout, Catherine. "From 'Virtual Curator' to 'Virtual Librarian': What Is the Potential for the Emergent Image Recognition Technologies in the Art-Historical Domain?" In *Proceedings of the 1996 Electronic Imaging and the Visual Arts Conference, EVA '96,* edited by J. Hemsley. London: National Gallery of Art, 1996.

Holl, Monika. "Die Katalogisierung von musiki-konographischen Inhalten in der bildende Kunst nach dem EDV-Programm MIDAS des Deutschen Dokumentationszentrums für Kunstgeschichte an der Universität Marburg." *RIdIM/RCMI Newsletter* 16, no. 2 (fall 1991): 18–28.

Huesmann, Heinrich. "New Theatre Documentation Technology at the Munich *Deutsches Theatermuseum.*" *Theatre History Studies* 7 (1987): 117–134.

Intner, Sheila, and Jean Weihs. *Standard Cataloging for School and Public Libraries.* Englewood, Colo.: Libraries Unlimited, 1990.

Keens, William, Leslie Kopp, and Mindy N. Levine, preparers. *Images of American Dance: Documenting and Preserving a Cultural Heritage.* Washington, D.C.: Dance program, National Endowment for the Arts, 1991.

Layne, Sara Shatford. "Some Issues in the Indexing of Images." *Journal of the American Society for Information Science* 45, no. 8 (1994): 583–588.

Library of Congress Subject Headings. 19th ed. 4 vols. Washington, D.C.: Library of Congress, 1996.

Lourdou, Dorothy. *Dance Collection Subject Headings.* New York: Dance Collection, New York Public Library for the Performing Arts, 1994. Typescript.

Markey, Karen. "Computer-Assisted Constructions of a Thematic Catalog of Primary and Secondary Subject Matter." *Visual Resources* 3, no. 1 (1983): 16–49.

Mohammed, Selima. "RIdIM Documentation: A Proposal for Change." *RIdIM/RCMI Newsletter* 19, no. 1 (spring 1994): 32–36.

Panofsky, Erwin. "Iconography and Iconology: An Introduction to the Study of Renaissance Art." In *Meaning in the Visual Arts.* Garden City, N.Y.: Doubleday, 1955, 26–54.

Smith, A. William. "EDDI-R, Electronic Database of Dance Images; Renaissance." In *Proceedings: The Fourth Biennial Arts and Technology Symposium, March 4-7, 1993, Connecticut College, New London, Connecticut,* compiled by David Smalley, Noel Zahler, and Pam Galvani. New London, Conn.: Center for Arts and Technology at Connecticut College, 1993.

Soergel, Dagobert. "Indexing and Retrieval Performance: The Logical Evidence." *Journal of the American Society for Information Science* 45, no. 8 (1994): 589–599.

Stam, Deirdre C. "Pondering Pixeled Pictures: Research Directions in the Digital Imaging of Art Objects." *Visual Resources* 10, no. 1 (1994): 25–39.

Svenonius, Elaine. "Access to Nonbook Materials: The Limits of Subject Indexing for Visual and Aural Languages." *Journal of the American Society for Information Science* 45, no. 8 (1994): 600–606.

Tessari, Carla. *Strutturazione dei dati delle schede.* Terza edizione riveduta e aggiornata. Pavia: Università degli studi di Pavia, 1992.

Turner, James M. "Subject Access to Pictures: Considerations in the Surrogation and Indexing of Visual Documents for Storage and Retrieval." *Visual Resources* 9, no. 3 (1993): 241–271.

USMARC Format for Bibliographic Data. 2 vols. Washington, D.C.: Library of Congress, 1994.

Vilcek, Marica. *Metropolitan Museum of Art Cataloging Manual.* New York: Metropolitan Museum of Art Cataloging Department, 1972. Typescript.

Weinstein, William. "Designing an Image Database: A Holistic Approach." *Visual Resources* 10, no. 1 (1994): 49–55.

White, Lynda S. "Image Cataloging in MARC at the University of Virginia." *VRA Bulletin* 21, no. 3 (fall 1994): 23–33.

APPENDIX A

Core Categories for Visual Resources, Version 2.0

Visual Resources Association
Data Standards Committee

General Guidelines

The *Core Categories for Visual Resources* are intended as a guideline for developing local databases and cataloging records. While they are not specific instructions for system-building or record structures, they may be used as a template for the foundation of such applications. For example, in a flat file database both work and visual document information might reside in a single record, while in a relational database environment, work information may be entered in a separate table and linked to visual document records.

The *Core Categories for Visual Resources* element set contains two groupings of elements, the *Work Description Categories* (nineteen elements), and the *Visual Document Description Categories* (nine elements). Because they are guidelines, it is not required that all of the categories be used to create a record for any one work or visual document. Users may also find the need to supplement the *Core* with additional elements for a fuller description of the work or visual document. In addition, the same data values may appear in more than one category within a record. In order to facilitate interoperability with other cultural heritage information resources, the *Core*, version 2.0 is mapped to the CDWA, MARC, and the REACH project data element set.

How the *Core* serves as a guide for cataloging practice:

- *Defining a "work"*: The *Core* includes both work and visual document information. However, what constitutes an art "object" is often difficult to determine. As the DSC discussed how different types of objects could be accommodated by the categories, it quickly became apparent how difficult it was to determine what constituted the relevant object for description. The DSC concluded that the *Core* should be flexible enough to accommodate a variety of local practice. For example, when the visual document is a work (a plan for *St. Peter's* by Michelangelo) that also functions as a document for another work (the building, *St. Peter's*), it may be approached in several different ways.

- *Choosing terminology:* The *Core* recommends a select group of controlled vocabularies and suggests the use of authority files for relevant categories. Although specificity of terminology (e.g., prints vs. etchings vs. soft-ground etchings) is outside of the scope of the *Core*, the Visual Resources Sharing Information Online Network (VISION) project records will demonstrate a variety of practices that could be used as models for local applications.

▪ *Data Content:* You will find specific examples of data values that could be used in each category (e.g., the term *refectory table* can be used in the Work Type category). These examples are used to better illustrate the scope of each category and are not meant to prescribe rules for data content. Category repeatability is noted, however, because many of these categories will require, at the level of specific content, more than one value (e.g., more than one subject term for a particular work of art). A set of data content rules is being developed for the VISION project.

Outline

I. WORK DESCRIPTION CATEGORIES

W 1. WORK TYPE
W 2. TITLE
W 3. MEASUREMENTS
W 4. MATERIAL
W 5. TECHNIQUE
W 6. CREATOR
W 7. ROLE
W 8. DATE
W 9. REPOSITORY NAME
W 10. REPOSITORY PLACE
W 11. REPOSITORY NUMBER
W 12. CURRENT SITE
W 13. ORIGINAL SITE
W 14. STYLE/PERIOD/GROUP/MOVEMENT
W 15. NATIONALITY/CULTURE
W 16. SUBJECT
W 17. RELATED WORK
W 18. RELATIONSHIP TYPE
W 19. NOTES

II. VISUAL DOCUMENT DESCRIPTION CATEGORIES

V 1. VISUAL DOCUMENT TYPE
V 2. VISUAL DOCUMENT FORMAT
V 3. VISUAL DOCUMENT MEASUREMENTS
V 4. VISUAL DOCUMENT DATE
V 5. VISUAL DOCUMENT OWNER
V 6. VISUAL DOCUMENT OWNER NUMBER
V 7. VISUAL DOCUMENT VIEW DESCRIPTION
V 8. VISUAL DOCUMENT SUBJECT
V 9. VISUAL DOCUMENT SOURCE

I. WORK DESCRIPTION CATEGORIES

A Work is an object, i.e., any physical entity that exists or has existed at some time in the past or an ephemeral event (happening, performance art) that may be captured in physical form as a visual document of the original work. Examples include works of art, architecture, and artifacts or structures from material, popular, and folk culture. The Work Description Categories are intended for description of the original object, work, or event that is depicted in the visual document (e.g., photograph, slide, digital image) of that object, work, or event. The term *work* is used throughout to refer to the object or event described.

W 1. WORK TYPE

Answers the Question: What is the work's generic name?

Type: Repeatable

Definition: The specific kind of work described (e.g., refectory table, altarpiece, portfolio, drawing, drinking vessel, temple, garden, palace, cathedral, burial mound, performance).

Guidelines: This category records a term or terms specifying the particular kind of work or group of works being described. The degree of specificity is a local decision, dependent upon what is most useful to the cataloging institution. For example, a cassone may be labeled by the term *furniture* in one institution, but such a general term would be insufficient in another where decorative arts are emphasized in the curriculum or collection.

A Work Type can change over time. The physical form or function of a work can change, such as when a sculptural group was originally used as a support for a table or when a train station has been converted into a museum. It may be necessary to record the Work Type of the work as it was created, as well as all subsequent functions and forms.

A work can be a single physical object, a fragment or part of a broken or dispersed work, an entity composed of many parts, or an event, such as a happening or other time-based, temporary manifestation. The names of parts of a work or the name of a work group should be identified in *Category W17— Related Work*. The nature of the relationship between the works should be recorded in *Category W18— Relationship Type*.

Terminology: The use of a controlled vocabulary is recommended, such as the *Art and Architecture Thesaurus* (especially the Objects facet), *Library of Congress Thesaurus for Graphic Materials,* or *Revised Nomenclature for Museum Cataloging.*

> *Mapping:*
> *REACH Element Set:* Type of Object
> *CDWA:* Object/Work-Type
> *MARC:* 655

W 2. TITLE

Answers the Question: What is or has the work been called or named?

Type: Repeatable

Definition: The title or identifying phrases given to a work (e.g., *Venus and Cupid, Noli me tangere, Portrait of Thomas Jefferson, Ceramic Fruit Bowl, Untitled, Getty Kouros, Serpent Mound, Great Stupa, White House, Chateau de Versailles, Petit Trianon, Winchester Cathedral, Expulsion*).

Guidelines: A work may have been given many different titles throughout its history. Sources for the title may include the creator, a prior owner, or a scholar's publication. It is also possible, especially in contemporary art, for a work to be called *Untitled.* The specific form of a title assigned by the creator may have a particular meaning; therefore, the creator's choice of wording, language, punctuation, and idiom should be given priority when known (e.g., Duchamp's *The Bride Stripped Bare by Her Bachelors, Even*).

Many works are known by a generic name rather than by a title (e.g., *Chandelier, Atlatl, Sarong, Barn with Rooster Weathervane,* or *Rolltop Desk*). Such names are sometimes based on classification terms or work types. They may also be modified by phrases that serve to identify and briefly describe the work itself. These names or terms therefore perform the same distinguishing function as a title. Some works, such as manuscripts, may be known by a particular numbering system, such as *Harley 609.*

If the work is part of a series that is identified by title, the series title should also be recorded in *Cat-*

egory W17—*Related Work* (e.g., *Le Cheval Rayé* from series *Les Anciennes Indes*). The nature of the relationship should be recorded in *Category W18— Relationship Type.*

Terminology: Use of an authority file is recommended. When possible, the title preferred by the repository should be recorded, even if it is not as the primary title.

> *Mapping:*
> *REACH Element Set:* Object Name/Title
> *CDWA:* Titles or Names-Text
> *MARC:* 24X

W 3. MEASUREMENTS

Answers the Question: What are the proportions or size of the work?

Type: Repeatable

Definition: Information about the size, shape, and scale of a work, particularly its dimensions (e.g., 39.5 × 67.4 cm, 45 cm [diameter], 14¾ × 20⅛ in [plate mark]).

Guidelines: Traditionally, dimensions are expressed height by width by depth (thus orientation is implied in the description of the dimensions). For example, dimensions of a painting of vertical orientation could be 52 × 42 in; however, more explanatory text may be required to express the dimensions of a Greek vase (e.g., 48.3 cm × 28.1 cm [diameter of mouth], 27.2 cm [diameter of body]).

The dimensions or numerical measurements of a work may be determined in different ways. For example, when measuring a coin or a piece of sculpture, weight is an important factor. For a painting, however, height and width are often sufficient. For a video or film, running time or length is the important measurement. Dimensions may or may not be particularly relevant for architectural works, depending on the collection's focus.

It is important to note the overall dimensions. However, a work may have several relevant dimensions. When measuring a manuscript, for example, the dimensions of the volume, the page, and the text block could be indicated, and the number of lines on the page could be recorded.

> *Mapping:*
> *REACH Element Set:* Dimensions
> *CDWA:* Measurements-Dimensions
> *MARC:* 340b

W 4. MATERIAL

Answers the Question: What is the work made of?

Type: Repeatable

Definition: The substances of which a work is composed (e.g., oil paint, ink, graphite, chalk, laid paper, wood, canvas, burlap sacking, ink, marble, gut, fur, quarter sawed lumber, cast iron, brick, clapboard).

Guidelines: The degree of detail with which a material is described (e.g., poplar vs. wood) is defined by local policy.

Terminology: The use of a controlled vocabulary is recommended, such as the *Art and Architecture Thesaurus* (especially the Materials hierarchy) and *Revised Nomenclature for Museum Cataloging.*

> *Mapping:*
> *REACH Element Set:* Medium/Materials
> *CDWA:* Materials and Techniques-Materials-Name
> *MARC:* 340ace

W 5. TECHNIQUE

Answers the Question: How was the work made or altered?

Type: Repeatable

Definition: The production or manufacturing processes, techniques, or methods used in the creation or alteration of a work (e.g., drawing, sculpting, painting, impasto, gilding, burnishing, overpainting, frame construction, cantilever construction, production techniques, restoration).

Guidelines: This category records all significant processes, techniques, and methods incorporated in the fabrication or alteration of a work. Materials can be fashioned, formed, or applied to a work in many different ways, with greatly varying results.

Terminology: The use of a controlled vocabulary is recommended, such as the *Art and Architecture Thesaurus* (especially the Processes and Techniques hierarchy).

> *Mapping:*
> *REACH Element Set:* Techniques/Process
> *CDWA:* Materials and Techniques-Processes or Techniques-Name
> *MARC:* 340d

W 6. CREATOR

Answers the Question: Who designed and/or created the work?

Type: Repeatable

Definition: The names, appellations, or other identifiers assigned to an individual, group of people, corporate body, or other entity that have contributed to the design, creation, production, manufacture, or alteration of the work.

Guidelines

Form of Name: The form of name chosen to identify the creator should, wherever feasible, be established by the use of an appropriate authority, where variant names should also be recorded. The name should be context sensitive to the work at hand. For example, corporate bodies should be identified by the name in use at the time the work was created, even if this has been superseded or abandoned (e.g., the work of Morris, Marshall, Faulkner and Company should be distinguished from the work of the later incarnation of the firm, Morris & Co.).

Multiple Creators: A work of art may be the result of a series of activities, sometimes accomplished over an extended period of time, for which a number of separate individuals or groups are responsible (e.g., both Michelangelo and Bernini contributed to *St. Peter's Basilica;* Leonardo contributed the angels to Verrocchio's *Baptism of Christ*).

Anonymous Creators: The Creator category is intended for established identities, including anonymous creators associated with an established identity, such as school of, workshop of, style of, etc. It also includes assigned identities (e.g., Hand G, Achilles Painter, Borden Limner, Master of the Munich Adoration, Master of the Housebook). When there is no information about a creator's identity, *Category W14—Style/Period/Group/Movement,* and *Category W15—Nationality/Culture* may be used to qualify or identify the work.

Terminology: The use of an authority file for personal and corporate names is recommended, e.g., *Library of Congress Name Authority File* and the *Union List of Artist Names.*

> *Mapping:*
> *REACH Element Set:* Creator/Maker
> *CDWA:* Creation-Creator-Identity-Names
> *MARC:* 1XX, 7XX

W 7. ROLE

Answers the Question: What part does the entity named in Creator play in the creation or design of the work?

Type: Repeatable

Definition: The role performed by a creator or maker in the conception, design, or production of the work (e.g., artist, painter, designer, draftsman, engraver, muralist, potter, modeller, sculptor, goldsmith, publisher, architect, patron, builder).

Guidelines: This category records the relationship between the Creator category and the described work. Distinguishing the specific role played by the creator is critical, particularly when multiple individuals or groups participated in the creation of the work. Whereas it may be sufficient to note the role generically as artist for the creator of a watercolor sketch, a print may have been created by multiple individuals, including a designer, engraver, and publisher. A structure may have an engineer, architect, stonemason, landscape architect, interior designer, etc.

Role distinguishes the contribution made by the creator to the work. It allows the researcher to locate all instances when an artist acted in one capacity as compared to another. For example, a researcher may want to locate all works for which Rembrandt acted as etcher as distinct from all instances when he was a painter.

Terminology: The use of a controlled vocabulary is recommended, e.g., the Agents facet of the *Art and Architecture Thesaurus.*

> *Mapping:*
> *REACH Element Set:*
> *CDWA:* Creation-Creator-Role
> *MARC:* 1XXe, 7XXe

W 8. DATE

Answers the Question: When was the work made or altered?

Type: Repeatable

Definition: Any date or range of dates associated with the creation, design, production, presentation, performance, construction, or alteration of the work or its components (e.g., 1667, ca. 1210, 17th century, before 952 BCE, 1821-1835).

Guidelines: A work may have been created over a span of time or may have multiple dates associated with the varying stages of its design, manufacture, production, performance, construction, or alteration. An example is Lorenzo Ghiberti's bronze doors for the *Baptistery* in Florence, which were completed twenty-three years after he designed the winning entry in the competition in 1401. A manuscript may have been illuminated in one century and bound in another century, while architectural structures may be created over a period of centuries. The dates of a photographic negative and the prints made from it can differ widely. Some types of works, such as ephemeral street art, may have a finite range of dates associated with their existence. Performance art, happenings, or installations may have taken place at specific dates and/or times.

Expressions such as "first half sixteenth cent.," or "fifth-fourth cent. BCE" can be used to describe ranges of approximate dates. Dates can be qualified with terms like *circa, about, before,* or *after* (e.g., after 1611 or ca. 830 BCE). Dates expressed as named eras should be recorded in *Category W14—Style/Period/Group/Movement* (e.g., Baroque, Flavian, Naqada II); their numerical equivalents should be recorded in Dates.

If dates are expressed according to systems other than the Gregorian calendar (such as Julian, Napoleonic, or Islamic calendars), this fact should be clearly designated, for example, "1088 AH [1677 CE]" notes the year in the Islamic calendar with the year in the Gregorian calendar in brackets.

The precise nature of the creative activities surrounding dates may be explained in *Category W19—Notes.* Examples include an Ansel Adams photograph, printed in 1983 from a negative dating ca. 1960; an album of drawings dated ca. 1550-1777, compiled 1789-1796, and rebound with additions in 1891; a sculpture from 1372, and reworked 1377-1379.

Terminology: The use of date guidelines is recommended, such as those outlined in the *Guide to Indexing and Cataloging* with the *Art and Architecture Thesaurus.*

> *Mapping:*
> *REACH Element Set:* Date of Creation/Date Range
> *CDWA:* Creation-Date
> *MARC:* 260c

W 9. REPOSITORY NAME

Answers the Question: What is the name of the administrative unit where work is located?

Type: Non-Repeatable

Definition: The name of the repository that currently houses the work, excluding temporary loans. If the work is lost, stolen, or destroyed, this category identifies the last known repository and states that the work has been lost, stolen, or destroyed, or that the repository is unknown (e.g., Graphische Sammlung Albertina; location unknown, formerly Dan Fellows Platt Collection).

Guidelines: The repository name can be a corporate name or a personal name, as in the case of a private collection. In some cases, the administrative unit that houses the work should be recorded as well as the parent institution to which that administrative unit belongs. For example, a mask might be housed in the Heye Foundation, which is part of the National Museum of the American Indian, which is part of the Smithsonian Institution. Or, the repository for a sarcophagus could be the Department of Egyptian Antiquities in the British Museum.

Terminology: The use of an authority file for personal names and corporate bodies is recommended; e.g., the *Library of Congress Name Authority File.*

> *Mapping:*
> *REACH Element Set:* Current Repository Name
> *CDWA:* Current Location-Repository Name
> *MARC:* 535a

W 10. REPOSITORY PLACE

Answers the Question: Where is the repository geographically located?

Type: Non-Repeatable

Definition: The geographic place where the repository is currently located. If the work is lost, stolen, or destroyed, this category identifies its last known geographic location (e.g., Vienna, Austria; formerly New York, NY, USA).

Guidelines: The location should be recorded at least to the level of city or town. Street addresses may also be recorded. For large repositories that have facilities in diverse locations, record the geographic location of the administrative unit that holds the work when this differs from the location of the main repository buildings. For example, the National Archives of the United States in Washington, DC, has an administrative unit that holds works in Arlington, VA; and the Smithsonian Institution in Washington, DC, has a unit, the National Museum of the American Indian, in New York, NY.

Special Note: For site-specific works, use *Category W12—Current Site* and *Category W13—Original Site,* instead of the repository categories. For example, the obelisk in Piazza Caprettari in Rome is not located in a "repository" but at a "site." Another example is an artifact that is now lost, and was last known to exist at an archaeological site; its location should be recorded in *Category W13—Original Site.*

Terminology: The use of a controlled vocabulary for geographic names is recommended, such as the *Thesaurus of Geographic Names, Library of Congress Name Authority File,* and *Library of Congress Subject Headings.*

> *Mapping:*
> *REACH Element Set:* Current Repository Place
> *CDWA:* Current Location-Geographic Location
> *MARC:* 535bc

W 11. REPOSITORY NUMBER

Answers the Question: What is the unique identifier used by the repository for the work described?

Type: Non-Repeatable

Definition: The unique identifier assigned to a work by the current or last known repository (e.g., H1/503/1913, 1967.776).

Guidelines: This category records any numeric or alphanumeric code (such as an accession number, shelf number, etc.) or phrase that uniquely identifies the work as belonging to the repository. The identifier usually contains coded information, such as the date of accession, donor, or physical location of the work within the repository. For works that are part of volumes or groups, the identifier may be a concatenation of unique identifiers for the work at hand and its larger contexts.

> *Mapping:*
> *REACH Element Set:* Current Object ID Number
> *CDWA:* Current Location-Repository Numbers
> *MARC:* 035

W 12. CURRENT SITE

Answers the Question: If the work is site-specific, where is it currently located?

Type: Non-Repeatable

Definition: The geographic place where a building, structure, sculpture, mural, or other site-specific work is currently located (e.g., Mesa Verde National Park, CO, USA; Salisbury Plain, Wiltshire, England; Rifle

Gap, CO, USA; Lake Havasu City, AZ, USA; Acropolis, Athens, Greece). For ephemeral works (e.g., performance works, environmental works) this category identifies the specific place where the work was performed or where it existed as depicted in the Visual Document.

Guidelines: Current Site is intended to accommodate architecture and other site-specific works such as performances, structures, sculptures, murals, mosaics, or monuments that do not reside in a repository. For example, Bernini's *Fountain of the Four Rivers* in Rome is not located in a repository but at a site—Piazza Navona, Rome, Italy. Location for works of architecture, such as Frank Lloyd Wright's *Fallingwater,* should be recorded in this category (Bear Run, PA), as should Christo's ephemeral *Surrounded Islands* (Biscayne Bay, FL, USA), or Richard Haas' *Homage to the Chicago School* (Chicago, IL, USA).

Terminology: The use of a controlled vocabulary for geographic names is recommended, such as the *Thesaurus of Geographic Names, Library of Congress Name Authority File,* and *Library of Congress Subject Headings.*

> *Mapping:*
> *REACH Element Set:*
> *CDWA:*
> *MARC:* 651, 752

W 13. ORIGINAL SITE

Answers the Question: If the work is site-specific, where was it originally located or discovered?

Type: Non-Repeatable

Definition: The geographic place where a work was originally located, excavated, or discovered (e.g., Tarquinia, Italy; Athens, Greece; Antwerp, Belgium). Use also for structures or other works that have been moved or that have not survived.

Guidelines: This category should be used to record the original location for architectural works that have been moved (e.g., *London Bridge,* originally in London, England, now in Lake Havasu City, AZ, USA), lost, or destroyed (e.g., *Sophienkirche,* Dresden, Germany); and to record the original site of archaeological finds or other works now residing in repositories elsewhere (e.g., the *Elgin Marbles,* original site is Athens, Greece, current repository is the British Museum, London, England). When using this category, be sure to record the current site in *Category W12—Current*

Site or the current repository in *Category W9— Repository Name* and *W10—Repository Place.*

The place where a work was found does not necessarily indicate where it was made, although it is an important clue to its past history and use. Knowing where an object was excavated contributes to analyses of trade patterns and cultural behavior. It may also be important for the dating and authentication of a work.

Terminology: The use of a controlled vocabulary for geographic names is recommended, such as the *Thesaurus of Geographic Names, Library of Congress Name Authority File,* and *Library of Congress Subject Headings.*

> *Mapping:*
> *REACH Element Set:* Place of Origin/Discovery
> *CDWA:* Context-Archaeological Excavation-Place, Context-Architectural-Building/Site Place
> *MARC:* 651, 752

W 14. STYLE/PERIOD/GROUP/MOVEMENT

Answers the Question: What stylistic characteristics does the work have, or with what group, period, or movement is the work commonly affiliated?

Type: Repeatable

Definition: Terms identifying a work that associates it with a defined style, historical period, group, school, or movement whose characteristics are represented in the work (e.g., Op Art, Fauve, Medieval, Neo Romanticist, Pre Raphaelite, Hellenistic, Feminist, Old Kingdom, Ming, Renaissance, Surrealist, Louis XVI, Mannerist, Ch'ien lung, Postmodern, Nayarit, Huari, Kano School, Pointillism).

Guidelines: Stylistic terms may be geographically derived (Etruscan, Limoges) or they may be based upon chronological periods or historical eras (Neolithic, Renaissance). Stylistic terms may be used to describe works produced under the aegis or reign of a specific individual or ruling group (Elizabethan, Victorian) or they may be used to describe works associated with a specific movement or school (De Stijl, Die Blaue Reiter). Terms used for this category may refer to works exhibiting similar decorative forms or characteristics (black-figure, Perpendicular Style) or to works which employ similar philosophies or concepts (Feminist Art, Erotic Art, Minimalism).

Style terms often have a hierarchical relationship (Byzantine can be broken into such styles as Comnenian or Palaeologan), and depending on local practice, the cataloger may choose to record both broader and narrower terms (e.g., Medieval Architecture and Perpendicular Style can be used to describe the same work).

Terminology: The use of controlled vocabularies is recommended, such as the *Art and Architecture Thesaurus* (especially Styles and Periods hierarchy) or the *Library of Congress Subject Headings.*

> *Mapping:*
> *REACH Element Set:* Style/Period/Group/
>   Movement/School
> *CDWA:* Styles/Periods/Groups/Movements-
>   Indexing Terms
> *MARC:* 655y

W 15. NATIONALITY/CULTURE

Answers the Question: With what nationality or cultural entity is the work associated?

Type: Repeatable

Definition: The name of the culture from which a work originates or the name of the nationality with which the work has been associated (e.g., English, Japanese, Sienese, Phrygian, Aztec, Berber).

Guidelines: Nationality can include the geopolitical area where the work was created or found. Places include current political nations and historical entities (e.g., kingdoms, city states) that no longer exist or no longer have the same boundaries (e.g., Flemish). To describe a work in terms of a distinctive style, rather than a regional affiliation, use *Category W14—Style/Period/ Group/Movement.* Use of the adjectival form, rather than the geographic place name is recommended.

Terminology: The use of controlled vocabularies is recommended, such as the *Art and Architecture Thesaurus* and *Library of Congress Subject Headings.*

> *Mapping:*
> *REACH Element Set:* Nationality/Culture of
>   Creator/Maker
> *CDWA:* Creation-Creator-Identity-
>   Nationality/Culture/Race-Citizenship;
>   Creation-Creator-Identity-Nationality/
>   Culture/Race-Culture
> *MARC:* 655x

W 16. SUBJECT

Answers the Question: What is the work of or about?

Type: Repeatable

Definition: Terms or phrases that characterize what the work depicts, what is depicted in it, or what concepts are expressed by the work. These include generic terms (e.g., woman, enclosed garden, sarcophagus lid, ceiling plaster, newel staircase), proper nouns and iconographic terms (e.g., Three Graces; George Washington; Asa-yama Mountain, Honshu, Japan), and concepts (e.g., truth, sacrifice). This category also accommodates the use of codes (e.g., ICONCLASS notations).

Guidelines: Subject matter can be drawn from standard motifs based on religion, literature, tradition, and other works, or it can be highly individual and the result of the creator's personal imagination. The subject of a painting may be a narrative scene such as Christ led before Pilate or the rape of Europa. The subject of a work may be an individual figure taken out of narrative context, such as Bathsheba, or it may be a portrait of a Dutch official. The subject of a work of architecture may be its order or type of brickwork; the subject of a vase can be its geometric decoration.

Three levels of subjects can be recorded in this category. The first is an objective description of what is depicted (e.g., a man in uniform). The second is an identification of the subject (portrait of George Washington). The third identifies deeper meaning as interpretation (Washington stands in a classical pose and leans upon a bundle of rods that signify the authority of Roman magistrates thus associating Washington with great and powerful Roman magistrates of antiquity).

Objective descriptions of the subject of a work may be made on the basis of direct observation. Traditional, conventional, and accepted names of subjects are gleaned from standard source books on subject matter and iconography. Books, articles, and catalogs provide current and historical interpretations of context and meaning. The creator may also have made a statement about the subject matter of a work.

Terminology: The use of a controlled vocabulary is recommended, such as the *Art and Architecture Thesaurus* or *Library of Congress Subject Headings.* For iconographic themes, controlled vocabularies include ICONCLASS and *Library of Congress Thesaurus for Graphic Materials.* For identified persons or groups, an authority file is recommended; vocabulary resources include *Library of Congress Name Authority File* and the *Union List of Artist Names.* For geographic places, an authority file is recommended; vocabulary resources include *Thesaurus of Geographic Names, Library of Congress Name Authority File,* and *Library of Congress Subject Headings.*

Mapping:
REACH Element Set: Subject Matter
CDWA: Subject Matter-Description-Indexing
   Terms, Subject Matter-Identification-Indexing
   Terms, Subject Matter-Interpretation-Indexing
   Terms
MARC: 6XX; for coded information, use 084

17. RELATED WORK

Answers the Question: To which work is the described work related?

Type: Repeatable

Definition: Works related to the work being described. The relationship can be temporal (chronological, historical), spatial, causal, associative, reproductive, or part/whole.

Guidelines: It is recommended that a link be made with works that have a direct relationship to the described work, particularly when the relationship may not be otherwise apparent. Information about relationships between works is used to analyze the creative process and to trace the influences between works. The amount of information recorded in this category will be determined by local practice, but basic identifiers, such as creator, title, and date are recommended. The purpose of this category is to direct the user to another work and should be done as economically as possible.

Works can be related to each other in the following ways:

- Temporal, as when one work is preparatory for another (e.g., Perugino's compositional study for the *Adoration of the Magi*, a model for a clock, a mold used to cast a bronze sculpture, a plan for a structure).

- Spatial, such as when two works were created to hang together as pendants (e.g., Gilbert Stuart's portraits of George and Martha Washington).

- Causal, as when one work provides stylistic inspiration for another (e.g., the works of Rembrandt or Delacroix reworked by Van Gogh).

- Associative, as when one work is depicted in the other (e.g., the "visual quotation" of the *Mona Lisa* by Marcel Duchamp).

- Reproductive, including copies after other works (e.g., Rubens' copy of Titian's *Bacchanal*

and George Baxter's nineteenth-century print of Raphael's *Descent from the Cross*).

- Hierarchical (part/whole or whole/part), including works such as altarpieces, drawings, or prints that are part of a volume or series, pages that are part of a manuscript, wings added to structures, buildings that are part of a larger complex, and physical groups that are made up of various objects or works. Historical part/whole relationships should also be recorded, such as a disassembled sketchbook and its former folios, dispersed panels that once were part of the same altarpiece, or architectural spolia that were once part of another structure. Record here the name of the larger entity to which the described work belongs, or the multiple parts of the larger work being described.

- Lost or destroyed work, such as an original Greek sculpture known only through Roman copies, or a model book that provided the source for an image found in many versions.

Terminology: The use of an authority file is recommended; vocabulary sources for architectural structures include *Library of Congress Name Authority File*. For titles of works of art, the name preferred by the repository should be used if possible.

Mapping:
REACH Element Set: Related Objects
CDWA: Related Work-Identification
MARC: 787

W 18. RELATIONSHIP TYPE

Answers the Question: What is the relationship between the Related Work and the described work?

Type: Repeatable

Definition: The kind of relationship between the described work and the Related Work (e.g., part of, larger context for, preparatory sketch, cartoon for, model for, study, plan for, printing of, copy after, derived from, probably a prototype for, possibly a copy after, wing of, adaptive reuse of, etc.).

Guidelines: This category includes terms or phrases to describe the type of relationship between the described work and the Related Work. The relationship should be reciprocal and terms used to describe the works should reflect this (e.g., prototype for, and based upon). Parallel relationships link one work to another work, implying a one to one, equal relationship (e.g., preparatory sketch, cartoon, model, study, plan, copy, appropriation). Hierarchical relationships link the whole work to its constituent parts, implying either a one to many relationship or a relationship which may include several levels from larger to smaller or smaller to larger. Hierarchical relationships may also require the notation of the placement within the sequence (e.g., folios in a manuscript, panels from an altarpiece, buildings within an architectural complex). Recording the type of relationship between two works allows the collocation of works sharing a common relationship to a given work, making it possible to establish sequences and chronologies among related works. Relationship Type allows the researcher to find, for example, all etchings printed from the same plate, sculptures that are copies of a lost work, or all works that are part of a particular album.

Terminology: The use of a controlled vocabulary is recommended, such as the *Art and Architecture Thesaurus* (especially the Information Forms and Visual Works hierarchies), *Library of Congress Descriptive Terms for Graphic Materials*, or *Revised Nomenclature for Museum Cataloging.*

> *Mapping:*
> *REACH Element Set:*
> CDWA: Related Work-Relationship Type
> MARC: 787g

W 19. NOTES

Answers the Question: What other relevant information is there about the work?

Type: Repeatable

Definition: This category provides a place for narrative text, including comments, interpretation, summarization, history of the work, explanation of the content of other categories, (e.g., justification of an attribution to a particular artist recorded in *Category W6— Creator*). The Notes category can also record differing opinions, evidence, additions, and explanations of adaptations, etc.

Guidelines: The Notes category accommodates free text narratives on the work or on the content of other categories which serve to enhance the record for the user.

> *Mapping:*
> *REACH Element Set:* Notes
> CDWA: Remarks
> MARC: 5XX

II. VISUAL DOCUMENT DESCRIPTION CATEGORIES

A visual document is any image that depicts a work. Visual documents can exist in different formats including photomechanical, photographic, and digital formats. Multiple visual documents may be associated with one work. This section of categories deals with describing the content of the visual document as well as the physical or electronic carrier of that image (e.g., the photograph of the sculpture, the slide of the cathedral, the digitized image of the painting).

V 1. VISUAL DOCUMENT TYPE

Answers the Question: What kind of visual document depicts the work?

Type: Non-Repeatable

Definition: The generic identification of the medium of the visual document (e.g., photograph, slide, digital image, video, moving image, CD-ROM).

Guidelines: Identification of the visual document type helps users to evaluate how the resource may be used. The visual document type also indicates what, if any, equipment (e.g., slide projectors) may be required to facilitate its use. The visual document type also indicates the amount of information it contains. For example, a slide of a performance piece shows one moment of the performance, while a videotape documents the entire performance. One might also want to know that a particular visual document is a duplicate, e.g., a duplicate slide is of lesser quality than the one made directly from the work.

Terminology: The use of a controlled vocabulary is recommended, such as the *Art and Architecture Thesaurus, Library of Congress Descriptive Terms for Graphic Materials*, or *Revised Nomenclature for Museum Cataloging.*

> *Mapping:*
> *REACH Element Set:*
> CDWA: Related Visual Documentation-Image
>   Type
> MARC: 533a

V 2. VISUAL DOCUMENT FORMAT

Answers the Question: How is the visual document stored?

Type: Repeatable

Definition: The format of the visual document (e.g., gelatin silver print, lantern slide, Beta, VHF, JFIF with

JPEG compression, TIFF, cibachrome print, Macintosh, Windows, DOS).

Guidelines: Recording image format makes it possible for users to identify visual document formats that are useful to their work and/or usable on available equipment. The format of the visual document also suggests the amount of detail that might be found in the visual document. A researcher may wish to convert a 35mm image to a JEPG image.

Terminology: The use of a controlled vocabulary is recommended, such as the *Art and Architecture Thesaurus* (especially the Visual Works and Information Forms hierarchies).

> *Mapping:*
> *REACH Element Set:*
> *CDWA:* Related Visual Documentation-Image
>   Measurements
> *MARC:* 533e

V 3. VISUAL DOCUMENT MEASUREMENTS

Answers the Question: What size is the visual document?

Type: Repeatable

Definition: The measurements of the visual document (e.g., 8 × 10 inches, 656K bytes, 1024 × 768 pixels, 35mm, 60 min.).

Guidelines: Recording image measurements makes it possible for users to identify visual documents of a size that is useful to their work. For example, a researcher will not be able to view a high resolution digital image because he or she does not have the appropriate monitor. The dimensions of the visual document also suggest to the researcher the amount of detail included in the image. It is important to know that a particular visual document is an 8 by 10 inch negative and not a 35mm negative, since the larger negative shows more detail.

> *Mapping:*
> *REACH Element Set:*
> *CDWA:* Related Visual Documentation-Image
>   Measurements
> *MARC:* 533e

V 4. VISUAL DOCUMENT DATE

Answers the Question: When was the visual document made?

Type: Non-Repeatable

Definition: Any date or range of dates associated with the creation or production of the visual document (e.g., 1983).

Guidelines: This category records the date that the visual document was created. It can be recorded either as numbers or text (e.g., first half twentieth cent. or late 19th cent.). Dates can be qualified with terms such as *circa, about, before,* or *after* (e.g., after 1911 or ca. 1830).

> *Mapping:*
> *REACH Element Set:*
> *CDWA:*
> *MARC:* 533d

V 5. VISUAL DOCUMENT OWNER

Answers the Question: Who owns the visual document and where is it located?

Type: Non-Repeatable

Definition: The identification of the repository, agency, or individual that owns the visual document, including the name and location of the owner (e.g., Frick Art Reference Library, New York, NY, USA; Museum of Fine Arts, Boston, MA, USA; Bunting Memorial Slide Library, University of New Mexico, Albuquerque, NM, USA).

Guidelines: The identification of the owner of the visual document assists researchers who may want to examine an image whose reproduction rights are held by one entity (e.g., Alinari), but which is owned by and located at another source (e.g., a photo study collection or university slide collection). The owners recorded in this category include educational institutions, commercial image libraries, museums or galleries, as well as cultural heritage or government agencies. The identification of the owner may be used by researchers who wish to see a copy of the image or obtain permission to reproduce it.

Use of this category is essential in a data sharing environment, because it identifies the entity that created a particular record and/or provided the digital visual document that is linked to that record.

Terminology: The use of consistent forms of personal and corporate names is recommended (e.g., *Library of Congress Name Authority File*). An authority of geographic places is recommended for the location of the owner; vocabulary resources include *Thesaurus of Geographic Names* and *Library of Congress Name Authority File.*

Mapping:
REACH Element Set:
CDWA: Related Visual Documentation-Image
    Ownership-Owner's Name
MARC: 533c

V 6. VISUAL DOCUMENT OWNER NUMBER

Answers the Question: What is the unique identifier used by the visual document owner?

Type: Non-Repeatable

Definition: The unique identifiers assigned to a visual document by the owner (e.g., A4S36.2).

Guidelines: This category records any numeric or alphanumeric code or phrase that uniquely identifies the visual document as belonging to the owner. It can take the form of numbers, codes, or other identification assigned to the visual document by the owner, including accession number (e.g., 009876) or bar code, or electronic ID number (GR/20.tif).

> *Mapping:*
> *REACH Element Set:*
> CDWA: Related Visual Documentation-Image
>   Ownership-Owner's Number
> *MARC:* 533n

V 7. VISUAL DOCUMENT VIEW DESCRIPTION

Answers the Question: What is depicted in the visual document of the work?

Type: Repeatable

Definition: Terms, phrases, or narrative text that describe the view of the work, as seen in the visual document (e.g., view from below; detail of hand; interior: ballroom; general view from East; bird's eye view; axonometric; plan; garden facade). Dates can also be included here to further clarify the view (e.g., pre-1978 cleaning, after 1952 landscaping, 1963 remodeling photograph).

Guidelines: A description of the view provided by the visual document makes it possible to evaluate the nature of the information it contains. For example, a view of the *Nike of Samothrace* from below may aid in determining how the work was originally intended to be seen. An aerial view of the Acropolis places the remains of the various monuments in their relative context.

This category can also help to differentiate among the various visual documents of a particular work. The information provides additional descriptive details to help precisely identify the work in the visual document in case of loss or damage. A view of the *Basilica of San Francesco* in Assisi before 1997 will document its state before the earthquake.

To avoid ambiguity, care should be taken in providing directional descriptions for built and anthropomorphic works. View East should be either View from the East or View toward the East; Left profile should be Profile from the left or Left proper profile.

Terminology: The use of a controlled vocabulary is recommended, such as the *Art and Architecture Thesaurus* (especially the Visual Works, Processes and Techniques, Attributes and Properties, and Components hierarchies).

> *Mapping:*
> *REACH Element Set:*
> CDWA: Related Visual Documentation-View
>   and Related Visual Documentation-View-
>   Indexing Terms
> *MARC:* 245p; 505; 520

V 8. VISUAL DOCUMENT SUBJECT

Answers the Question: What is the visual depiction of or about?

Type: Repeatable

Definition: Terms or phrases that characterize what the visual document depicts, what is depicted in it, or what concepts are expressed by it. These include generic terms (e.g., woman, enclosed garden, sarcophagus lid, ceiling plaster work, newel staircase), proper nouns and traditional iconographic terms (e.g., Three Graces; George Washington; Asa-yama Mountain, Honshu, Japan), and concepts (e.g., truth, sacrifice). This category also accommodates the use of codes (e.g., ICONCLASS notations).

Guidelines: Subject matter can be drawn from standard motifs based on religion, literature, tradition, and other works, or it can be highly individual and the result of the creator's personal imagination. The subject of a painting may be a narrative scene such as Christ led before Pilate or the rape of Europa. The subject of a work may be an individual figure taken out of narrative context, such as Bathsheba, or it may be a portrait of a Dutch official. The subject of a work of architecture may be its order or type of brickwork; the subject of a vase can be its geometric decoration.

Three levels of subjects can be recorded in this category. The first is an objective description of what is depicted (e.g., a man in uniform). The second is an identification of the subject (portrait of George Washington). The third identifies deeper meaning as interpretation (Washington stands in a classical pose and leans upon a bundle of rods that signify the authority of Roman magistrates thus associating Washington with great and powerful Roman magistrates of antiquity).

Objective descriptions of the subject of a work may be made on the basis of direct observation. Traditional, conventional, and accepted names of subjects are gleaned from standard source books on subject matter and iconography. Books, articles, and catalogs provide current and historical interpretations of context and meaning. The creator may also have made a statement about the subject matter of a work.

Special Note: This category refers to unique subjects found in the Visual Document that have not already been recorded in *Category W16—Subject.*

Terminology: The use of a controlled vocabulary is recommended, such as the *Art and Architecture Thesaurus* or *Library of Congress Subject Headings.* For iconographic themes, controlled vocabularies include ICONCLASS and *Library of Congress Thesaurus for Graphic Materials.* For identified persons or groups, an authority file is recommended; vocabulary resources include *Library of Congress Name Authority File,* and *Union List of Artist Names.* For geographic places, an authority file is recommended; vocabulary resources include *Thesaurus of Geographic Names, Library of Congress Name Authority File,* and *Library of Congress Subject Headings.*

> *Mapping:*
> *REACH Element Set:*
> *CDWA:* Related Visual Documentation-View-Indexing Terms
> *MARC:* 6XX; for coded information, use 084

V 9. VISUAL DOCUMENT SOURCE

Answers the Question: What is the source of the visual document?

Type: Repeatable

Definition: Information about the agency, individual, or repository from which the visual document was obtained, including name, location, owner number, or a bibliographic citation in the case of copy photography (e.g., Whitaker Studios, Richmond, VA, USA; Scala, Florence, Italy; Saskia Ltd. Cultural Documentation, Portland, OR, USA; Bildarchiv Foto Marburg, Mar-

burg, Germany; Service Photographique Réunion des Musées Nationaux, Paris, France; Maria Gimbutas, *The Language of the Goddess* [San Francisco: Harper and Row, 1989]).

Guidelines: The identification of the source of a visual document is important for researchers who wish to locate a copy for study or publication. Visual Resources collections systematically record the source of a visual document, whether it is a commercial vendor, a museum's photograph service, the name of the professor or student who photographed the work on site, or a reference to a publication where an image is reproduced.

> *Mapping:*
> *REACH Element Set:*
> *CDWA:* Related Visual Documentation-Image-Source-Name and Related Visual Documentation-Image-Source
> *MARC:* 541

Additional Categories Mapped in the Sourcebook

These are definitions of categories of information that institutions in Table 1 used in addition to the VRA Core Categories listed above.

WORK CATEGORIES

Variant Title: Titles other than the established title by which the work may also be known.

Translated Title: The title of a work translated into a language other than the original language.

Creator's Series Title: The name of a collective work intended by its creator to be in series (e.g., Goya's *Los Caprichos,* Monet's *Haystacks*).

Location Produced: The location where the creation, design, or production of the work of art or its components took place.

Provenance: The provenance or history of the owners of a work of art from its creation to the present. This includes the means by which a work passed from one owner to the next, an identification of any public sales involving the work or the names of any agents who aided the transfer of ownership, and the names of any dealers who handled the work or included it in their inventories. If a work has been lost, stolen, or destroyed, or has otherwise vanished from public view, this fact should also be indicated here.

Physical Description: A description of the appearance of the work expressed in generic terms, without reference to the subject depicted. This includes the names of any recognizable patterns, motifs, or textures used in the decoration of the work.

Critical Documentation: Citations to sources of textual information related to the work of art being described, including archival documents, unpublished manuscripts, and published bibliographic materials, and references to verbal opinions expressed by scholars or subject experts.

Exhibitions: A historical record of the public display of a work of art, including its installation in a gallery, inclusion in a special exhibition, and any loan during which the work was on public view, even if not part of a formal exhibition. Use the title or name of the exhibition as formulated by the organizing institution (e.g., *Michelangelo Draftsman,* Internationale Bauausstellung, Berlin, 1987).

Inscriptions: A description of distinguishing or identifying physical markings, lettering, annotations, texts, signatures, or labels that are a part of a work of art or are affixed, applied, stamped, written, inscribed, or attached to the work, excluding any mark or text inherent in materials.

Source of Acquisition: The means by which a work of art entered the collection of a particular individual or corporate body.

Conservation: An assessment of the overall physical condition, characteristics, and completeness of a work of art at a particular time.

VISUAL DOCUMENT CATEGORIES

Visual Document Classification: Placement of a visual document within a formal classification scheme based upon similar characteristics of the works depicted in the visual documents.

Visual Document Color: The characterization of the chromatic qualities of the image (e.g., black-and-white, color, sepia, monochrome).

Number of Images: For collection-level records, the number of images included in the collection.

Visual Document Series/Set: The group name of a purchased series or set of images.

VRA DATA STANDARDS COMMITTEE MEMBERS

Sherman Clarke (Liaison, MARC
Advisory Group)
Eileen Fry
Sheila Hannah
Carol Jackman-Schuler
Benjamin Kessler
Elisa Lanzi (Chair)
Linda McRae
Maryly Snow (Liaison, ARLIS/NA)
Margaret Webster
Dustin Wees
Lynda White

APPENDIX B

Washingtoniana II Data Dictionary

Anne Mitchell and Karen Chittenden

Fixed Fields and Leader

Fixed-field and leader data are displayed one way in Minaret and another way in MUMS. The Minaret display uses the OCLC format. This data dictionary will list these fields in the order they appear in the Minaret display. A key to corresponding MUMS boxes or fields is included.

CHARACTER POSITION	LEADER NAME
00-04	Logical record length 00000 (Minaret—nothing in this field)
05	Record status **n** = new
06	Type of record **k** = graphic
07	Bibliographic level **d** = subunit
08-09	Undefined character positions \\
10	Indicator count **2** *
11	Subfield code count **2** *
12-16	Base address of data **00000** *
17	Encoding level \ = full
18	Descriptive cataloging form **a** = AACR2
19	Linked record requirement \ *
20-23	*Entry map*
20	Length of the length-of-field portion **4** *
21	Length of the starting-character-position portion **5** *
22	Length of the implementation-defined portion **0** *
23	Undefined entry map character position **0** *

* Minaret assigns no value.

DEFAULT VALUE(S):   **MUMS boxes**

      LDR05 - **Rec stat: n**   Box _____

      LDR06 - **Type: k**   Box 41

      LDR07 - **Bib lvl: d**   Box 27

      LDR17 - **Enc lvl: ♭ (Min.) or - (MUMS)**   Box 1

      LDR18 - **Desc: a**   Box 36

DATA CONVENTIONS/COMMENTS: Most of these values are defaulted into every record in the WII database. Leader 05 indicates the status of the record; **n** is the code for new record. Leader 06 indicates the type of record; **k** is the code for two-dimensional non-projected graphic. Leader 07 indicates the bibliographic level; **d** means that it is a subunit record. Leader 17 is for the encoding level; **♭** or - for blank means that the catalog record is full level. Leader 18 contains the code for the descriptive cataloging rules used; **a** stands for AACR2.

These fields are reflected near the top of each record and appear with OCLC style tags. The other defaults at the top of the record are generated by Minaret, not used, or described elsewhere in this dictionary (008). None of the leader is repeatable. Do not make any changes in any of these fields. In the OCLC style format used for Minaret, these leader bytes appear as separate fields near the top of each record. The order in which they appear is altered to facilitate data entry.

PUNCTUATION: none

MINARET/OCLC DISPLAY:

OCLC: **001**   Rec stat: **leader/05**   Entrd: **008/00**   Used: **005**

Type: **leader/06**   Bib lvl: **leader/07**   Govt pub: **008/28** Lang: **008/35**   Source: **008/39**

Leng: **008/18**   Enc lvl: **leader/17**   Type mat: **008/33** Ctry: **008/15**   Dat tp: **008/06**

Tech: **008/34**   Mod rec: **008/38**   Accomp mat: **008/23**

Desc: **leader/18**   Int lvl: **008/22**   Dates: **008/07 008/11**

COM: **007/00** FMD: **007/01**   OR: **007/02**   CL: **007/03**   PRS: **007/04**   SSN: **007/05**

Example: Data for ADE - UNIT 3 in MINARET/OCLC Display:

OCLC: **95849455**   Rec stat: **n** Entrd: **950721**   Used: **19950818**

Type: **k** Bib lvl: **d**   Govt pub: **♭**   Lang: **eng**   Source: **♭**   Leng:**nnn**

Enc lvl: **♭**   Type mat: **l**   Ctry: **xxu** Dat tp: **i**

Tech: **n**   Mod rec: **♭**   Accomp mat: **♭♭♭♭♭**

Desc: **a**   Int lvl: **♭**   Dates: **1909,1910**

COM: **k**   FMD: **l**   OR: **|**   CL: **u**   PRS: **u**   SSN: **u**

MUMS BOXES:

01. Leader 17	02. 008/18-20	03. 008/33	04. 008/34	05. 008/32	06. 008/23-37	07.
08.	09.	10. 008/22	11.	12.	13.	14.
15. 008/35-37	16.	17.	18.	19.	20. 008/06	21. 008/07-10
22. 008/11-14	23. 008/15-17	24.	25.	26.	27. Leader 07	28. 008/38
29. 008/39	30. I.B. 32	31. I.B. 38	32. I.B. 39	33. Non-perm.dist.	34. 008/28	35. I.B. 10
36. Leader 18	37.	38. I.B. 16	39. Rec.dest.	40.	41. Leader 06	

(I.B.=Internal byte)

Example: Data from ADE - UNIT 3 in MUMS display:

01. -	02. nnn	03. l	04. n	05. -	06. ——	07.
08.	09.	10. -	11.	12.	13.	14.
15. eng	16.	17.	18.	19.	20. i	21. 1909
22. 1910	23. xxu	24.	25.	26.	27. d	28. -
29. -	30. y	31. -	32. -	33. 7	34. -	35. 7
36. a	37.	38. f	39. f	40.	41. k	

MARC TAG   MARC FIELD NAME

001   **Control Number (NR)**

No indicator or subfield codes.

DEFAULT VALUE(S): none

DATA CONVENTIONS/COMMENTS: This field contains a unique control number (in Minaret, a system-generated number which resembles an LCCN, which will eventually be changed to a pre-assigned LCCN before the record is loaded to MUMS).[1] This is the current control number of the catalog record. Records are created in Minaret and are loaded into MUMS, therefore, these numbers will correspond between systems. Each number has the same format. Data in this field correspond with data in the 010 except for the presence of |c <PP> in the 010. The Minaret to MUMS load program converts the Minaret 001 to 035. When the records are loaded into MUMS as verified records the program deletes the 035.

PUNCTUATION: none

EXAMPLE(S):

001   ƀƀƀ958494551ƀ

MARC TAG   MARC FIELD NAME

005   **Date and Time of Latest Transaction (NR)**

005/|a   Date and Time of Latest Transaction (NR)

DEFAULT VALUE(S): none

DATA CONVENTIONS/COMMENTS:

|a   This field contains a 16-digit number (MUMS) or an 8-digit number (Minaret) that indicates the date and time of the latest transaction. This information is system-generated in both MUMS and Minaret. A new date/time appears in this field each time that a record is altered in any way. A numeric string provides information as to the year, month, day, hour, minute, and second that this modification occurs.

PUNCTUATION: none

EXAMPLE(S):

MUMS:

005 |a19951017123442.0

(This means this record was modified on Oct. 17, 1995, 12:34:42 p.m.)

Minaret:

Used: 19951017

(Only year, month, and day are displayed in Minaret.)

MARC TAG	MARC FIELD NAME
007	**Physical Description Fixed Field**
007/00	Category of material
007/01	Specific material designation
007/02	Original versus reproduction aspect
007/03	Color
007/04	Primary support material
007/05	Secondary support material

DEFAULT VALUE(S): kl|uuu

DATA CONVENTIONS/COMMENTS:

|a   All information is contained in a single |a. The six-character string is coded information about the physical elements of the collection. Information derived from the 300 field and/or 5XX fields of the item(s) described in the catalog record is used to assign an alphabetic code which indicates the category of material to which they belong. Most materials cataloged as ADE - UNITs are non-projected graphics. For non-projected graphics, the 007 is a 6-character code.

007/00   k   Category of material is **non-projected graphic**. Some of the ADE - UNITs contain slides, and even though these materials are technically projected graphics, they will not be used as such, and this code reflects the way these materials are used.

007/01   l   A specific material designation for the non-projected graphic. WII records use an l (lowercase L) to indicate the specific material designation for the non-projected graphic is **technical drawings**.

007/02 | This code indicates whether the item is an original publication/production or a reproduction or facsimile. Because the usefulness of this character position is currently being questioned, institutions are advised to record a fill character (|) instead of one of the four codes available. WII records use |.

The last three positions are coded **u** for **unknown**. It is difficult to assign these codes to groups of architectural drawings because they may cover many of the available coding categories. In addition, limited physical description information is included in the ADE - UNIT catalog records. It would be difficult (and time-consuming) to, although in many cases, some of this information is accessible on an item level in the finding aid.

007/03   **u**   This code indicates that color characteristics of the materials are unknown. The 300 field includes the word "colored" (e.g., colored pencil, colored ink) if there are one or more occurrences of the use of color in the materials represented by the catalog record. One needs to consult the finding aid to access this detailed information about individual drawings in each UNIT.

007/04   **u**   This code indicates that the primary support material is unknown. Most of the drawings in ADE - UNITs are on paper, many are on linen, some are on plastic, and many contain more than one type of support materials. The primary support material for the UNIT is therefore difficult to determine in many cases. Because this information is accessible at the item level via the finding aid, it was not essential to determine an appropriate group-level code in the catalog record.

007/05   **u**   This code indicates that the secondary support material is unknown. In most cases, drawings in UNITs have no secondary support, and in cases where there are secondary supports, this information was not always recorded. Since it was not considered critical to compile this information, it is not available for coding in the catalog record.

Indicators: none

PUNCTUATION: none

MARC TAG   **MARC FIELD NAME**

   008   **Fixed-length Data Elements (NR)**

008/00-05 Date Entered on File

A six-digit date, generated by Minaret. The first two digits record the year, the next two the month, and the last two the day that a record is added to the database.
Example: Date added: **950917** (yymmdd)
(Record was entered into system on September 17, 1995)

008/06 Type of Date/Publication Status   (MUMS box 20)

This field contains a one-character alphabetic code to indicate the type of date(s) contained in the 008/07-10 (Date 1) and 008/11-14 (Date 2). ADE - UNIT records use either **s** (single date) or **i** (inclusive dates). A constant of **i** is defaulted into the records in Minaret. If there is only a single date, this code is changed to **s** during record editing.

008/07-10 Date 1/Beginning date of publication   (MUMS box 21)

In ADE - UNIT records, this field contains the year that the item(s) in the UNIT were produced. The date matches the year in 260/|c. In Minaret the date is entered in the field labelled **Dates:** <u>before</u> the comma (the spaces following the comma are for date 2). If there is more than one year in the 260/|c field, the earliest year is entered here. Washingtoniana II did not use unknown dates, therefore no **u** code (e.g., 185u) is used.

008/11-14 Date 2/Ending date of publication (MUMS box 22)

If there is an end date to a date span in the 260/|c, place that date here, otherwise, leave blank. In Minaret, this date is entered in the field labelled **Dates:** <u>after</u> the first date and comma. When there is no date 2, the Minaret layout defaults this to ƀƀƀƀ.

008/15 Country (MUMS box 23)

This field contains a code which indicates the place of production or execution. The field contains a default code for full level cataloging, that means unpublished items produced in the United States. The source of the code for this field is *USMARC Code List for Countries* maintained by the Library of Congress. Codes are input in lowercase.
Default: **xxu**

008/18 Length/Running time for motion pictures and videorecordings (MUMS box 2)

Default: **nnn** (for not applicable)

008/22 Category of material (MUMS box 10)

Default: **k** (for nonprojected graphics)

008/23 Accompanying material (MUMS box 6)

Default: ƀƀƀƀƀ (five blanks for not applicable)

008/28 Government publication (MUMS box 34)

Default: ƀ (blank indicates this is not a government publication) (This code is changed to **f** in a few instances where the work is created by a U.S. government agency.)

008/33 Type of visual material (MUMS box 3)

Default: **l** (lowercase L for "technical drawings")

008/34 Technique (MUMS box 4)

Default: **n** (not applicable)

008/35 Language (MUMS box 15)

This code indicates the language of the captions, accompanying text, and information in the title block, or the language associated in the materials.
Default: **eng** (English)

008/38 Modified record (MUMS box 28)

A one-character alphabetic code which indicates whether any data on a bibliographic record are a modification of information that appeared on the item(s) being cataloged. A blank in this field means this record is not modified.
Default: ƀ (blank)

008/39 Cataloging Source (MUMS box 29)

A blank indicates that the Library of Congress is the creator of the original cataloging data.
Default: ƀ (blank)

MARC TAG	MARC FIELD NAME
010	**Library of Congress Control Number (NR)**
010/|a	Library of Congress Control Number (NR)
010/_1	Undefined
010/_2	Undefined

DEFAULT VALUE(S): none

DATA CONVENTIONS/COMMENTS: This field contains a unique control number (in MUMS, an LCCN; in Minaret, a system-generated number which resembles an LCCN).

|a   All data are contained in a single |a. This field contains the control number (LCCN). This number consists of a two-digit year followed by a six-digit number, followed by a space, slash PP. The Minaret to MUMS load program converts the Minaret 010 to the 001 (LCCN) in MUMS.

Indicators: Both are undefined and blank.

PUNCTUATION: Three blanks precede the digits. A blank follows the digits and a slash precedes the PP.

EXAMPLE(S):

010 |aƀƀƀ95849469ƀ/PP

MARC TAG	MARC FIELD NAME
017	**Copyright Registration Number (R)**
017/|a	Copyright registration number (NR)
017/|b	Source (agency assigning number) (NR)
017/_1	Undefined
017/_2	Undefined

DEFAULT VALUE(S): none

DATA CONVENTIONS/COMMENTS:

|a   Contains the copyright registration number composed of one or more alphabetic characters indicating the class under which the registration is made, followed by a sequentially assigned number. The date range of WII copyright deposits is 1902–1968. The materials are registered in the following classes:

    G - (chromos & lithographs/works of art)

    H - (photographs/reproductions)

    I - (original works of art/drawings or plastic work of scientific or technical nature)

Most ADE - UNITs containing copyright deposits have only one copyright registration number recorded in a single |a. For UNITs with up to five copyright registration numbers, this subfield is repeated for each number. For UNITs with more than five copyright numbers, the first number is given, followed by a note indicating that this number is the first in a sequence of numbers.

|b   All WII catalog records contain a default: U.S. Copyright Office.

Indicators: Both are undefined and blank.

This field is input after field 300 and before the first note.

PUNCTUATION: Field does not end with a mark of punctuation unless field ends with an abbreviation, an initialism, or other data that end with a mark of punctuation. In all cases WII catalog records contain "U.S. Copyright Office" in |b and therefore do not end with a mark of punctuation.

EXAMPLE(S):

017 |aI10684|bU.S. Copyright Office

017 |aI15696|aI15695|bU.S. Copyright Office

017 |aI5806 (first of 29 sequential copyright numbers)|bU.S. Copyright Office

---

MARC TAG	MARC FIELD NAME
035	System Control Number (R)
035/‡a	System control number (NR)
035/_1	Undefined
035/_2	Undefined

DEFAULT VALUE(S): none

DATA CONVENTIONS/COMMENTS: This field contains a system control number and the NUC symbol for the system for a record belonging to a system other than the one whose number is contained in field 001 or 010. Source of code is *Symbols of American Libraries*. The 035 is generated by the Minaret to MUMS loading program. The program converts the Minaret 001 to 035. The program then deletes the 035 upon the actual load into MUMS. In MUMS, this number is an LCCN.

Indicators: Both are undefined and blank.

PUNCTUATION: The NUC symbol of the system/institution, enclosed in parentheses, immediately precedes the system control number.

EXAMPLE(S):

035 |a|(DLC)95-849455

MARC TAG	MARC FIELD NAME
040	Cataloging Source (NR)
040/|a	Original cataloging agency (NR)

040/	c	Transcribing agency (NR)
040/	e	Description conventions (NR)
040/_1	Undefined
040/_2	Undefined

DEFAULT VALUE(S): DLC in |a and |c; **gihc** in |e.

DATA CONVENTIONS/COMMENTS:

|a   The Library of Congress code **DLC** appears in the a and c subfields as the original and transcribing agency.

|e   Descriptive cataloging follows cataloging rules in *Graphic Materials*. The code for *GM*, **gihc**, is included in |e.

Indicators: Both are undefined and blank.

PUNCTUATION/SPACING: none

EXAMPLE(S):

040 |aDLC|cDLC|egihc

MARC TAG	MARC FIELD NAME
050	**Library of Congress Call Number (R)**
050/|a	Classification number (R)
050/|u	Local subfield containing custodial location information (NR)
050/_1	Existence in Library of Congress collection
050/_2	Source of call number

DEFAULT VALUE(S): <P&P> in |u.

DATA CONVENTIONS/COMMENTS: The bulk of the drawings are assigned local P&P ADE - UNIT call numbers. The UNIT filing series is used for items that are best described as a group, but must be served and/or tracked individually. A typical UNIT describes a single design project, alteration, or renovation. UNITs are accompanied by an item-level (or occasionally container-level) finding aid. ADE - UNIT numbers were assigned sequentially in the order that materials were processed and do not reflect the commission number of the architectural drawings. An architect's work may be dispersed among non-sequential UNITs.

Materials that need to be described, served, and/or tracked as groups are assigned LOT numbers. Many of these materials are bound.

|a   The entire call number goes into |a. This includes filing series designation in uppercase letters (ADE - UNIT or LOT) followed by the assigned number within the series. The call number refers to the entire UNIT, even if the UNIT contains only one item. The format of the call number is:

ADE - UNIT [#]

LOT [#]

|u   The default is the abbreviation for the custodial division Prints and
          Photographs: <P&P>. Storage locations are included only for LOTs
          because there are often multiple locations for each UNIT. (The find-
          ing aid notes UNIT locations.) In cases where there is a surrogate or
          microfilm which represents the drawings in the UNIT, the phrase USE
          MICROFILM or USE SURROGATE is placed after the <P&P>.

Indicators: First and second indicators are both 0. The first indicates the item
is in the Library of Congress collections, the second that the call number was
assigned by the Library of Congress.

PUNCTUATION/SPACING: In |a ADE is separated from UNIT with a space, hy-
phen, space. There is a space after UNIT and after the UNIT number, before |u.
There is a space after LOT and after the LOT number. There is no punctuation
after the data in |u.

EXAMPLE(S):

050 00 |aADE - UNIT 1140 |u<P&P>

050 00 |aLOT 13036 |u(G)<P&P>

050 00 |aADE - UNIT 2319 |u<P&P> USE MICROFILM

FINDING AID: Call numbers in the UNIT catalog record refer to the entire ADE
- UNIT. Call numbers for individual items in each ADE - UNIT are located in
the finding aid. These call numbers include the filing series designation in up-
percase letters, followed by assigned number within the filing series, followed
by item number, followed by the folder size/storage designation.

Photographs of drawings are treated as drawings and are assigned item numbers. Photographs of the structure, or other associated photographs, are fewer
in number and are assigned UNIT numbers but not item numbers.

Folder sizes/storage designations:

Standard folder size designations used in the Prints and Photographs Division
are recorded in the Processing Section's *Pictorial Collections Processing & Cataloging Manual (PICPAC), Chapter P12, Storage Symbols, Formats, and Sizes.*

For drawings processed as ADE - UNITs:

(A size)	35 × 46 cm. folders in boxes
(B size)	51 × 61 cm. ” ”
(C size)	56 × 71 cm. ” ”
(D size)	71 × 102 cm. folders in mapcase drawers
(E size)	89 × 123 cm. folders in mapcase drawers
(F size)	117 × 192 cm. folders in mapcase drawers
(Tube)	Length > 192 cm.; rolled in polyester sheets in tube files
(SOS)	(Super Oversize) Length > 192 cm.; width > 117 cm.; flat storage on top of large mapcases.

(Photo)	Manuscript size folders 31 × 38 cm.
(Photo)(C size)	56 × 71 cm. folders in boxes
(Photo)(E size)	89 × 123 cm. folders in mapcase drawers

For associated photographs, specifications, and miscellaneous supplementary materials:

(Photo)	Manuscript size folders 31 × 38 cm.
(Spec.)	" "
(Misc. Supp.)	" "
(Photo)(C size)	56 × 71 cm. folders in boxes
(Photo)(E size)	89 × 123 cm. folders in mapcase drawers

For items processed as LOTs:

F	Vertical box (15.5 × 12.5 × 5 inches)
G	Vertical album, box, or envelope
H	Horizontal box, any size
OSE	Oversize LOT in 89 × 123 cm. folders in mapcase drawers

EXAMPLE(S):

ADE - UNIT 1463, no. 1 (D size)

ADE - UNIT 461, no. 108 (Tube)

ADE - UNIT 1861 (Misc. Supp.)

ADE - UNIT 1885 (Spec.)

Photograph of the structure:

ADE - UNIT 1029 (Photo)

Photograph of a drawing:

ADE - UNIT 40, no. 37 (Photo)

Large format photograph of a drawing, stored horizontally in a C size box:

ADE - UNIT 2810, no. 429 (Photo)(C size)

Large format photograph of the structure, stored horizontally in a C size box:

ADE - UNIT 2467 (Photo)(C size)

MARC TAG	MARC FIELD NAME
100	**Main Entry—Personal Name** (NR)
100/‖a	Personal name (NR)
100/‖c	Titles and other words associated with a name (R)
100/‖q	Fuller form of name (NR)
100/‖d	Dates associated with a name (NR)
100/‖e	Relator term (R)
100/_1	Type of personal name entry element
100/_2	Undefined

DEFAULT VALUE(S): none

DATA CONVENTIONS/COMMENTS: This field contains the name of the person who is responsible for the intellectual or artistic content of the group of architectural drawings in the ADE - UNIT. If more than one creator is responsible for the drawings, use this field for the person determined to have primary responsibility. Use the 700 or 710 field for any additional personal name or corporate name headings, or in situations where no one entity has primary responsibility for the intellectual content of the drawings.

Headings used in this field come from existing Library of Congress name authority records or from name authority records created by Washingtoniana II project staff and added to LCNAF. These name authority records are created using AACR2 guidelines for formulating personal name headings. This field is never used in conjunction with the 110 field.

Headings formulated by project staff are based on the fullest form of the name as it was expressed on the drawings.

Assignment of main and added entries for creators (1XX, 7XX):

If a UNIT contains drawings created by a designer under the direction of an architect, and the drawings include the names for both, assign main entry to the architect and added entry to the designer. Designers usually work under the direction of an architect, although this relationship is not always apparent when looking at the drawings. Two exceptions: 1. If the name of the architect is not known, assign main entry to the designer or 2. When the UNIT contains drawings by an architect that are dated considerably earlier than the drawings which focus on the design project, assign main entry to the designer and added entry to the architect.

A distinction is made here between <u>design</u> work (i.e., work performed by landscape architects, interior designers, etc.) and <u>shop</u> work (i.e., work performed by manufacturers and installers of machinery, cabinetry, etc.). Design work, although created under the supervision of an architect, represents more independent creativity or craftsmanship than shop work, and as such warrants assignment of an added entry to the designer. Shop work has less of a degree of independence than design work. Shop work is generally more subsidiary to the work of the architect than design work, hence shop drawings are not given added entries, except in cases where the <u>focus</u> of the UNIT is the shop drawings. Another exception is made when only shop drawings exist for a project and the architect is not known. In this case the creator of the shop drawings is assigned main entry.

Authority records were created for these using the following guidelines:

|a	In most cases, the form of name found on the drawings is contained in |a.
|c	This subfield occurs only rarely (and probably not in any main entries) in headings in WII catalog records. In these instances, it usually contains the title "Mrs."
|q	If a fuller form of the name was found in reference sources, this information was included in |q. In a few instances, the fuller form of the

|d   name found in reference sources is included in |a because the person was better known by the fuller form of the name.

|d   If dates are found in reference sources, these are included in |d.

|e   Relator terms, indicating the relationship of the person named in the heading to the drawings, are contained in |e. Relator terms are selected from *PICPAC, Chapter C18, Relator Terms,* which contains a list of relator terms used in P&P. These terms are expressed in the singular. This list was derived from a list in *USMARC Code List* and from terms in AAT. In most cases, only one relator term was used; however, more than one can be used. Relator terms used most frequently in ADE - UNIT catalog records are **architect, designer, engineer, landscape architect, inventor,** and **architect (former attribution).**

Indicators: The first indicator distinguishes the type of personal name found in the heading:

Entry element:

     Forename only: 0

     Single surname: 1

     Multiple surname: 2

     Family name: 3

The second indicator remains blank.

PUNCTUATION/SPACING: Headings are entered exactly as they appear in their name authority record. If the heading contains initials, there is a space entered between them (e.g., Mullett, A. B., not Mullett, A.B.). There are no spaces entered at the end of data in |a or |q. A comma appears after the data in the subfield (either |a or |q) immediately preceding |d; a comma and space appear after the date before |e (unless open birthdate, then a hyphen with comma and space omitted). A period comes at the end of |e.

EXAMPLE(S):

100 1 |aReam, Vinnie,|d1847-1914, |edesigner.

100 1 |aBartlett, Paul Wayland, |d1865-1925, |esculptor.

100 1 |aWaterman, Thomas Tileston,|d1900-|earchitect.

100 1 |aMullett, A. B.|q(Alfred Bult),|d1834-1890, |earchitect.

100 1 |aShurtleff, Arthur A.|q(Arthur Asahel),|d1870-1957, |elandscape architect.

100 1 |aDrayer, Donald H.|q(Donald Hudson),|d1909-1973, |einventor.

100 1 |aRay, Luther R.|q(Luther Reason),|d1892-1978, |earchitect.

MARC TAG	MARC FIELD NAME
110	**Main Entry—Corporate Name** (NR)
110/|a	Corporate name or jurisdiction name as entry element (NR)
110/|b	Subordinate unit (R)

110/|e	Relator term (R)
110/_1	Type of corporate name entry element
110/_2	Undefined

DEFAULT VALUE(S): none

DATA CONVENTIONS/COMMENTS: This field contains the name of the corporate body chiefly responsible for the intellectual or artistic content of the group of architectural drawings in the ADE - UNIT. In ADE - UNIT cataloging, this is usually the name of an architectural firm. If more than one creator is responsible for the drawings, use this field for the corporate body determined to have primary responsibility, and use the 700 or 710 field for the additional personal or corporate name headings, or in situations where no one entity has primary responsibility for the intellectual content of the drawings.

Headings used in this field come from existing Library of Congress name authority records or from name authority records created by Washingtoniana II project staff and added to the Library of Congress Name Authority File. These name authority records are created following AACR2 guidelines for formulating corporate name headings. This field is never used in conjunction with the 100 field.

Headings formulated by project staff are based on the fullest form of the name as it was expressed on the drawings.

Authority records were created using the following guidelines:

|a   In most cases, the form of name found on the drawings is placed in |a. In a few instances, the fuller form of the name found in reference sources was used in |a because the corporate body was better known by the fuller form. If the corporate body is a political jurisdiction, the name of the jurisdiction is recorded in |a.

|b   If the corporate body name is a subordinate unit, this information is contained in |b.

|e   Relator terms, indicating the relationship of the corporate body in the heading to the drawings, are contained in |e. Relator terms are always used, even if they seem redundant in cases where the corporate name includes the relator term (e.g, |aUnited States, |bArchitect of the Capitol, |earchitect). Relator terms are selected from *PICPAC, Chapter C18, Relator Terms,* which contains a list of relator terms used in P&P. These terms are expressed in the singular. This list was derived from a list in *USMARC Code List* and from terms in AAT. Those used most frequently in ADE - UNIT catalog records are **architect, designer, engineer, landscape architect,** and **inventor.**

Indicators: The first indicator reflects the type of corporate name entry element:

Jurisdiction name:	1
Name in direct order:	2

(Most of the corporate headings used in ADE - UNIT catalog records have a first indicator of 2.)

The second indicator is undefined and blank.

PUNCTUATION/SPACING: A comma and space go at the end of |a. If the corporate body name contains initials, there are no spaces between them (e.g., R.E. Hall, not R. E. Hall). A period comes at the end of |e.

EXAMPLE(S):

110	2	|aBruce Price & de Sibour, |earchitect.
110	2	|aChloethiel Woodard Smith & Associated Architects, |earchitect.
110	2	|aRing Engineering Co., |eengineer.
110	2	|aMiles Pneumatic Tube Company, |edesigner.
110	1	|aUnited States.|bArmy.|bAir Corps, |earchitect.

MARC TAG	MARC FIELD NAME
245	**Title Statement** (NR)
245/|a	Title (NR)
245/|b	Remainder of title (NR)
245/|c	Remainder of title date transcription/statement of responsibility (NR)
245/|h	Medium (GMD) (NR)
245/_1	Title added entry
245/_2	Number of nonfiling characters present

DEFAULT VALUE(S): [graphic]. in |h.

DATA CONVENTIONS/COMMENTS:

|a   Titles are devised following guidelines in *GM* and specific guidelines developed for devised title patterns in ADE - UNITs. The devised title always includes the primary drawing type and the building type. If known, it also includes the building name, client name, street address, lot and square number, city name, and state. These elements are then structured into a title statement:

245 10 |aArchitectural drawings for a house ("residence") for Mr. and Mrs. Robert W. Fleming, 5108 Cammack Drive, Sumner Park, Bethesda, Maryland |h[graphic].

Architectural drawings for a **house** ("residence") for
(primary drawing type)   (building type)   (building name)

Mr. and Mrs. Robert W. Fleming,
      (client name)

5108 Cammack Drive, Sumner Park, Bethesda, Maryland
      (address)

Primary drawing type:

Primary drawing types are controlled vocabulary terms from *Thesaurus for Graphic Materials II: Genre and Physical Characteristics Terms*

(TGM II). The term most frequently used in this field is **Architectural drawings**;[2] terms which occur with less frequency include **Engineering drawings**, and **Design drawings**, **Interior design drawings**, and **Landscape architecture drawings**.

Building type:

Building types are almost always controlled vocabulary terms from *Thesaurus for Graphic Materials I: Topical Terms for Subject Access* (TGM I). The terms closely correlate with either the building name, or the apparent function of the building based on information in the drawings. The most specific and descriptive term for the building or project is selected. When buildings have more than one building purpose, each of the main purposes are included (e.g., store and office building).

Building name:

Building names are cited as they appear on the drawings and are placed between quotation marks within parentheses to emphasize the source of the name. If the drawings contain more than one building name, the one which occurs most frequently is used. Sometimes a building name includes two parts such as a building element and building name (e.g., "Marquis for Rialto Theatre"). Some building names reflect the action represented in the drawings as it is expressed on the drawings (e.g., "remodel front of building"). If the building name and building type are expressed the same way, the building name is not repeated (e.g., Architectural drawings for a house for . . .).

Client name:

The primary source for client names is the drawings. Other sources used include office records, miscellaneous supplementary materials found with the drawings, or drawings associated with the UNIT that are processed as other UNITs. The client name is expressed in the fullest form of name found in primary sources.

Address:

The fullest form of the address found on the drawings is used in this field (e.g., 900 Brentwood Road vs. Brentwood Road and 9th Street). Numeric street names are not spelled out. Street abbreviations are spelled out (e.g., Avenue vs. Ave.; Street vs. St.). City and state names are spelled out in full. In some cases, other UNITs and reference sources are used to obtain either a complete address, or a fuller form of address than that which was found on the drawings. If the address includes two or more "streets," the word "street" is repeated for each (e.g., 18th Street and M Street vs. 18th and M Streets). This will enable those performing a keyword search using "18th Street" to retrieve this record more readily. If the drawings contain additional information such as the lot and square number, this information is included in parentheses after the street address.

|b   This subfield is used only in a few LOT records for items which contain a title continuation.

|c   Items that were originally bound sometimes include a title page with a statement of responsibility. This statement was included in |c for a few UNITs in cases where the statement of responsibility more succinctly expresses the relationship between the named creators and the drawings in the UNIT, and because access points are desired for each entity named in the statement of responsibility.

|h   Each title is immediately followed by the general material designation (GMD) in |h. All ADE - UNIT records contain a default: **[graphic]**.

Brackets are not used for titles because most of the records describe groups of materials. This was applied even in cases where there is only one drawing in a UNIT because it was decided to treat all UNITs equally. There is a 500 note stating that the UNIT title is devised.

Indicators: The first indicator indicates whether there is a title added entry. If there is a 100 field or 110 field in the record, the indicator is 1. If there is no 1XX field, the first indicator is 0. The second indicator records the number of nonfiling characters present at the beginning of a title. In ADE - UNIT records this indicator is always 0 because the devised title always begins with the primary drawing type, and primary drawing type terms do not begin with initial articles.

PUNCTUATION/SPACING: A period follows |h.

EXAMPLE(S):

ADE - UNITs:

245 10 |aArchitectural drawings for a bus terminal ("bus garage") for Washington Railway & Electric Co., Georgia Avenue near 8th Street, N.W. (lot 931, square 2877), Washington, D.C.|h[graphic].

245 10 |aArchitectural drawings for an organization's building ("International Bureau of American Republics"), 17th Street and B Street, N.W., Washington, D.C.|h[graphic].

245 10 |aEngineering drawings for a transportation facility ("Fairnault Railway-Air Service System"), Washington, D.C. |h[graphic].

245 10 |aArchitectural drawing for speculative row houses ("three houses"), for Lawrence N. Brandt, Dumbarton Street, N.W., Georgetown, Washington, D.C.|h[graphic].

245 10 |aArchitectural drawing for alterations to a house for Mr. and Mrs. James K. Knudson, 3833 North 30th Street (blocks 22, 23, 28; section 3), Arlington, Virginia |h[graphic].

245 10 |aArchitectural drawings for a government building ("Public Buildings—Custom House, Post Office, and Court Room"), for the Secretary of the Treasury, Bank Street and Main Street, Richmond, Virginia|h[graphic] /|cCapt. A.H. Bowman, U.S. Corps of Engineers, Engineer in charge ; designed by A.B. Young, Supervising Architect.

LOTs - LOT titles are formulated using the same general format as for ADE - UNITs; however, LOTs are not always formed around one specific architectural project, so there is more variation in the content and form of the title.

245 10 |aArchitectural catalog |h[graphic] /|cJ.H. de Sibour, Architect, Washington, D.C.

245 10 |aProspectus for a housing development for URBCO/CIRV, Developer, Old Ford Plant, Alexandria, Virginia |h[graphic].

245 10 |aUnit plans, typical room arrangements, site plans, and details for low-rent housing |h[graphic].

245 10 |aCity houses between party walls |h[graphic]. (Title penciled on original envelope which contained this album.)

245 10 |aTypical designs of timber structures |h[graphic] :|ba reference for use of architects and engineers.

245 10 |aReport and recommendations for the extension of the west central front of the United States Capitol, Washington, D.C. |h[graphic].

245 10 |aScrapbook documenting the history of The Lindens, 2401 Kalorama Road, Washington, D.C., during the ownership of Mr. and Mrs. George Maurice Morris |h[graphic].

MARC TAG	MARC FIELD NAME
260	**Publication, Distribution, etc. (Imprint) (NR)**
260/|a	Place of publication, distribution, etc. (R)
260/|b	Name of publisher, distributor, etc. (R)
260/|c	Date of production (R)
260/_1	Undefined
260/_2	Undefined

DEFAULT VALUE(S): none

DATA CONVENTIONS/COMMENTS: Dates are assigned according to guidelines in *Graphic Materials*. Information relating to the publication, printing, distribution, issue, release, or production of a work is contained in this field.

|c   In most ADE - UNIT records, only |c is used. The date represents the date or dates of the execution of the drawings, and only years are given. The primary source for the date is the drawings. Secondary sources are used to determine the date if the drawings are not dated. These secondary sources include drawings processed as other UNITs, commission numbers (some of which are keyed to or coded with dates), office records, and reference works. In cases where no date could be determined for the project, span/active dates are used, or dates are attributed based on style, provenance, or other types of evidence. A general note (field 500) is used to state source of date. Brackets are not used for formulated dates because most of the records describe groups of materials. This was applied even in cases where there is only one drawing in a UNIT because it was decided to treat all UNITs equally.

|a   A few ADE - UNIT records contain architectural drawings in a published format, and the location of the publisher is provided here.

|b   A few ADE - UNIT records contain architectural drawings in a published form, and the name of the publisher (as stated on the drawings) is included in |b.

Indicators: Both are undefined and blank.

PUNCTUATION/SPACING: A period is at the end of |c. A space follows data and precedes : at end of |a. A comma follows data in |b.

EXAMPLE(S):

ADE - UNITs:

260	|c1919.
	(The only date found for this project on the drawings or in other sources is 1919.)
260	|c1918-1920.
	(The date range found on the drawings, or in other sources, is from 1918 to 1920.)
260	|aBoston :|bL.H. Bradford & Co's., lith.,|c1855.

LOTs:

260	|aWashington, D.C. :|bU.S. Government Printing Office,|c1935.
260	|c1924, c. 1981.

MARC TAG	MARC FIELD NAME
300	**Physical Description** (R)
300/|a	Extent (R)
300/|b	Other physical details (NR)
300/|c	Dimensions (R)
300/_1	Undefined
300/_2	Undefined

DEFAULT VALUE(S): none

DATA CONVENTIONS/COMMENTS:

|a   Contains the number (quantity) of items in the unit followed by the Specific Material Designation (SMD) "**items.**"[3]

|b   The media or processes used in creating the drawings in the UNIT are contained in |b. In general, the primary source for terms for photographic processes is TGM II; a few terms for drawing media are derived from terms in *Art and Architecture Thesaurus* (AAT). The ones that occur most frequently in ADE - UNIT catalog records are:

acrylic paint	ink
adhesive shading film	mixed media
blueprint	pastel
charcoal	photographic print
colored ink	photomechanical print
colored pencil	stat
crayon	vandyke print
diazo print	wash
felt pen	watercolor
graphite	

|c   The largest folder size used for the drawings in the ADE - UNIT is used for dimension information in |c. Folder sizes are expressed in centimeters. The standard folder sizes used to house drawings are:

photo, misc. supp.	31 × 38 cm.
A size	35 × 46 cm.
B size	51 × 61 cm.
C size	56 × 71 cm.
D size	71 × 102 cm.
E size	89 × 123 cm.
F size	117 × 192 cm.
Tube	Length > 192 cm.
SOS	Length > 192 cm.; width > 117 cm.

The bulk of drawings processed as UNITs are housed in polyester folders; however, some items are housed in paper folders or in mats. Information in |c is almost always expressed using the words "in folder(s)," regardless of the actual housing used, unless the UNIT includes larger than 117 × 192 cm. tube size drawings rolled in a polyester film sheet, and stored in a tube file. In this case the wording used is "in polyester sheet." Many drawings originally housed in folders are housed in mats after conservation treatment; therefore, a standard expression of housing ("folder(s)") means catalog records will not need to be changed to reflect later changes in housing.

A few drawings are larger than Tube size. These are stored in folders between specially constructed mat boards (SOS) and stored flat. For UNITs containing Tube and SOS drawings, the exact dimensions of the housing, expressed as height × width in centimeters rounded off to the next whole centimeter up, are recorded. The primary purpose of this information is to communicate a general idea of the dimensions of the largest drawings in this UNIT so that adequate space can be prepared when serving these to patrons.

Indicators: Both are undefined and blank.

PUNCTUATION/SPACING: A space, colon precedes |b. A space, semicolon precedes |c. A mark of punctuation is at the end of the field.

EXAMPLE(S):

UNITs:

300 |a16 items :|bphotomechanical print, colored pencil, felt pen, ink, graphite, and diazo print ;|cin folder(s) 71 × 102 cm.
(All drawings in UNIT are housed in folders 71 × 102 cm.)

300 |a1 item :|bgraphite ;|cin folder(s) 56 × 71 cm.
(UNIT contains one drawing housed in a folder 56 × 71 cm.)

300 |a989 items :|bink, wash, graphite, colored ink, watercolor, blueprint, photographic print, photocopy, photonegative, diazo print, and colored pencil ;|cin folder(s) 117 × 192 cm. or smaller.
(UNIT contains 989 drawings housed in various folder sizes smaller than 117 × 192 cm.)

300 |a5 items :|bink and colored ink ;|cin polyester sheet 122 × 252 cm. or smaller.
(Largest drawings in UNIT are rolled in a polyester sheet; smaller drawings are housed in folders.)

LOTs:

300 |a11 v. ;|c30 × 24 cm. or smaller.

300 |a1 v. (38 leaves, 57 photographic prints, 4 architectural drawings) ; |c28 × 22 cm.

300 |a1 album (44 silver gelatin prints, some color) ;|c29 × 25 cm. (album)

300 |a3 photographic prints :|bsilver gelatin ;|c8 × 10 in.
(Two 300 fields for same record)

MARC TAG	MARC FIELD NAME
500	**General Note** (R)
500/|a	General note (NR)
500/_1	Undefined
500/_2	Undefined

DEFAULT VALUE(S): none

DATA CONVENTIONS/COMMENTS: Notes are used when necessary to record, among other things, the source of the date, title, address, secondary creator or client names, corresponding reproduction numbers, and other information which does not clearly fit into other fields but is useful for documenting the material or relating it to other items. The order and format of these notes are based on guidelines in *GM*.

|a   The entire note is contained in |a.

Indicators: Both are undefined and unused.

PUNCTUATION/SPACING: A period or other mark of punctuation is always at the end of the data in |a. If the mark of final punctuation is a closing bracket or parenthesis, however, add a period.

EXAMPLE(S):

Typical notes found in most ADE - UNIT records keyed to *GM* [4] (chapter sections given in parentheses after each).

500 |aUNIT Title devised. (5A2, *Source of title*)

500 |aBuilding name from inventory in P&P Collections File. (5A2, *Source of title*)

500 |aCommission no. 3001. (5B2, *Variations in title*)

500 |aCommission no. R 60-11B; complete commission no. from office records. (5B2, *Variations in title*)

500 |aIncludes rendering by Saifook Chan. (5B7, *Statement of responsibility*)

500 |aSigned: John A. Barrows and Thomas Tileston Waterman. (5B7.1, *Signatures and inscriptions*)

500 |aDrawings not signed; attribution based on provenance. (5B7.2, *Attributions and conjectures*)

500 |aMojdeh Baratloo acted as co-designer; information from phone call to Balch, 12-13-94. (5B7.2, *Attributions and conjectures*)

500 |aSome drawings found with Donald H. Drayer's drawings for an apartment house (The Colonnade), which were processed as ADE - UNIT 1625. (5B25, *Provenance*)

500 |aRelated to interior design drawings by Maria R. Drayer that were found interfiled and were processed as ADE - UNIT 1555. (5B25, *Provenance*)

Sample client name notes:

500 |aClient's first name on drawing is Jame; Who was who in America, 1961-1968 shows name as James.

500 |aClient's name, building name, and address from office records; one set of office records (card file) indicates client as being Samuel R. Harris.

500 |aArthur B. Heaton acted as consulting architect for this project.

Sample address notes:

500 |aCity from ADC's street map of Montgomery Co., MD, 1989.

500 |aAddress from District of Columbia telephone directory.

500 |aAddress from Heaton's office records.

500 |aAddress from District of Columbia telephone directory, 1989-1990.

500 |aCity from ADC's street map of Prince Georges County, MD, 1989.

500 |aCity from Rand McNally Commercial atlas & marketing guide, 1986.

500 |aFull street name from Who was who in America, 1961-1968.

500 |aProbably located in Washington, D.C.

500 |aPossibly located in Washington, D.C.

("Probably" gets 6XX geographical subject access, "possibly" does not.)

Date notes:

500 |aDate based on period of time Drayer's office was located at 1764 Church Street, N.W., the address noted on the drawings.

500 |aDate from Goode's Best addresses, 1988.

500 |aDate based on years that Waterman & Barrows worked on Domestic colonial architecture of Tidewater, Virginia, 1932.

500 |aDate based on years that Waterman practiced as an architect.

500 |aDate based on provenance and drawing style.

500 |aDate based on information in P&P Curatorial Reference Files.

500 |aSome drawings bear stamp of Structural Porcelain Enamel Co.

MARC TAG	MARC FIELD NAME
505	**Formatted Contents Note** (R)
505/|a	Formatted Contents Note (NR)
505/_1	Display constant controller
505/_2	Level of content designation

DEFAULT VALUE(S): none

DATA CONVENTIONS/COMMENTS: This field contains the titles of separate works, or parts of an item. This field was only used in ADE - UNIT catalog records in cases where many buildings were processed as an ADE - UNIT, and it was important to cite the name of each creator or building. Names of individual buildings, addresses, or other identifying information are listed in the contents note to enable keyword access to these individual structures.

Indicators: The first indicator, a display constant controller, is 0 to indicate that a display constant will be generated in the pcrd display in MUMS: **Contents:**. The second indicator is blank to indicate all contents information is recorded in a single |a.

PUNCTUATION/SPACING: Standard ISBD punctuation for contents notes is used in separating elements within this field. The building name and its location (if available) is followed by a space dash space. A period or other mark of punctuation is always at the end of the data in |a. If the mark of final punctuation is a closing bracket or parenthesis, however, add a period.

EXAMPLE(S):

ADE - UNITs:

505 0 |aBartholdi Fountain & Botanical Garden -- Bridge, "End of the Basin" -- George Washington House -- Lee Mansion, Arlington Cemetery -- Memorial Pavilion for Grant, Arlington Cemetery -- Memorial to victims of U.S.S. Maine disaster -- Mt. Vernon, Home of Washington -- The New Tomb -- The Octagon -- Old Tavern, Bladensburg Road -- row house -- Sheridan Gateway, Arlington Cemetery -- Surratt House -- Victory Monument; State, War & Navy Building -- "View on the Speedway" -- Washington's Tomb, Mt. Vernon -- Washington's Tomb (old), Mt. Vernon -- "Where Lincoln Died."

505 0 |aNo. 1. Louis Justement -- No. 2. J. Ivan Dise and E.J. Maier -- No. 3. Edmund J. Jacques -- No. 4. Walter F. Bagner & Carl A. Rehse -- No. 5. John Floyd Yewell -- No. 6. Paul Hyde Harbach -- No. 7. James A. Parks -- No. 8. Robbins Louis Conn -- No. 9. Edgar & Verna Salomonsky -- No. 10. John Barnard . . . No. 29. J. Ivan Dise and E.J. Maier.

LOTs:

505 0 |aIncludes houses for Cornelius Curtain, Orange, N.J. -- Ralph Wood, Pittsford, Vt. -- Dr. B.J. Cook, Rutland, Vt. -- Stoddard Hancock, Darien, Conn. -- apartment house for Brooklyn Savings

Bank, Brooklyn, N.Y. -- organizations' building for National Grange, Washington, D.C. -- office and warehouse for Robert E. Anderson Co., Washington, D.C.

MARC TAG	MARC FIELD NAME
506	**Restrictions on Access Note** (R)
506/|a	Terms governing access (NR)
506/_1	Undefined
506/_2	Undefined

DEFAULT VALUE(S): Original materials served by appointment only.

DATA CONVENTIONS/COMMENTS: This note is the same for all ADE - UNIT catalog records. Many of the drawings in ADE - UNITs are large and difficult to prepare for service to patrons. This note will alert patrons interested in viewing these materials that an appointment is necessary to allow staff adequate time to prepare and serve these drawings.

|a   All data is contained in a single |a.

Indicators: Both are undefined and blank.

PUNCTUATION/SPACING: A period or other mark of punctuation is always at the end of the data in |a. If the mark of final punctuation is a closing bracket or parenthesis, however, add a period.

EXAMPLE(S):

506 |aOriginal materials served by appointment only.

MARC TAG	MARC FIELD NAME
520	**Summary, Abstract, Annotation, Scope, etc. Note** (R)
520/|a	Summary, Abstract, Annotation, Scope, etc. Note (NR)
520/_1	Display constant controller
520/_2	Undefined

DEFAULT VALUE(S): none

DATA CONVENTIONS/COMMENTS:

|a   All information is recorded in |a.

Summary notes are structured using the following sequence: **Includes** [primary drawing type (e.g., preliminary, working, presentation, as-built)]; **showing** [major drawing subjects (e.g., site, building, doors)]; methods of representation (e.g., plans, elevations, sections, and details); secondary drawing purposes, usually other than primary drawing purpose in 245 (e.g., landscape architecture drawings, mechanical systems drawings, etc.); and other document types (e.g., photographs, specifications, miscellaneous supplementary materials).

When the ADE - UNIT catalog record represents drawings of more than one purpose (e.g., working <u>and</u> electrical systems drawings) or there is more than one topical element depicted (e.g., site <u>and</u> house), the summary statement begins with the word "Includes." In an ADE - UNIT which represents either only one drawing, or which depicts only one topical element, the word "Includes" is not used (e.g., Preliminary drawing showing house as plan).

Summary note information is based on notable subject descriptions of each drawing compiled during physical processing. Worksheets (generated by the database) containing this information are consulted, as are the drawings, to determine the notable subjects for the 520 note. These worksheets contain all of the informational elements required to describe the drawings in a summary note. During the descriptive cataloging of the ADE - UNIT, presence of these elements in the drawings is verified. Questions to ask when deciding what the major drawing subjects in this field include: Is the subject depicted a good example of this subject? Are there several drawings which focus on this particular subject? Is the subject an unusual, difficult-to-find example of something? Is the architectural element depicted clear and concrete? If you are looking for drawings of this object, would you be satisfied with this example?

Indicators: The first indicator is always 0. This will generate a display constant in the pcrd display in MUMS: **SUBJECT:**. The second indicator is undefined and blank.

PUNCTUATION/SPACING: A period or other mark of punctuation is always at the end of the data in |a. If the mark of final punctuation is a closing bracket or parenthesis, however, add a period.

EXAMPLE(S):

A short summary note:

520 0 |aPreliminary drawing showing house as elevation; rendering.

An average length summary note:

520 0 |aIncludes preliminary and working drawings showing site and house as site plans, plans, elevations, sections, details, perspective projections, and axonometric projections; sketches and renderings; schedules; electrical systems and structural drawings.

A long summary note:

520 0 |aIncludes working drawings showing site, library, dome, porch, courtyards, colonnades, coal vault, windows, doorways, skylight, alcove shelving, bookcases, grilles, metalwork, hardware, tiling, vaults, frescos, mosaics, book conveyor, chandeliers, exhedra, fountains, drinking fountains, porte cochere, entablature, cornice, columns, archivolt, architraves, pilasters, capitals, balustrades, corbels, soffits, dentils, rosettes, keystones, and railing as site plans, plans, elevations, sections, details, and perspective

projections; sketches and renderings; electrical systems, mechanical systems, structural, and HVAC drawings; landscape architecture drawings; engineering drawings; plats; miscellaneous supplementary materials.

LOTs:

520 0 |aPhotographic reproductions of a published portfolio containing architectural photographs and architectural drawings as halftone photomechanical prints; subjects include office buildings, apartment houses, houses, etc., in Washington, D.C., and the U.S. Naval Academy in Annapolis, Maryland; also contains advertisements for architectural products and services.

520 0 |aIncludes clippings, photographs, and architectural drawings mainly of row houses by various architects primarily in Washington, D.C.

520 0 |aGeometrical studies of various forms including columns, capitals, balusters, ramps, stairs, and platforms.

MARC TAG	MARC FIELD NAME
530	**Additional Physical Form Available Note** (R)
530/|a	Additional physical form available note (NR)
530/_1	Undefined
530/_2	Undefined

DEFAULT VALUE(S): none

DATA CONVENTIONS/COMMENTS: This field is used only in a few records in cases where an entire UNIT has a surrogate available in the Prints and Photographs Reading Room. Surrogates include images on videodisc, sets of mounted b&w prints, and microfilm. This note is accompanied by a statement in |u of the 050 field to alert the patron early in the record to the availability of a surrogate. There are a few exceptions. One UNIT (Library of Congress working drawings) has a microfilm surrogate that includes frames for drawings that don't have corresponding items in the UNIT. A few UNITs contain reference copies (usually smaller and easier to serve than the originals) for some drawings in the UNIT.

|a   The entire note is contained in |a.

PUNCTUATION/SPACING: A period or other mark of punctuation is always at the end of the data in |a. If the mark of final punctuation is a closing bracket or parenthesis, however, add a period.

Indicators: Both are undefined and blank.

EXAMPLE(S):

Digital images/videodisc:

530 |aUse electronic surrogate.

050 |aADE - UNIT 75 |u<P&P> USE SURROGATE.

Microfilm:

530 |aAvailable on microfilm which serves as reference copy.

050 |aADE - UNIT 2043 |u<P&P> USE MICROFILM.

B&W copy photographs in Reading Room:

530 |aReference copy available in LOT 4249.

050 |aADE - UNIT 2595 |uUSE SURROGATE.
             (Both of these notes are for the same record.)

Exceptions:

530 |aUse surrogate on microfilm available in the Library of Congress Prints and Photographs Reading Room. The microfilm includes additional drawings for which there are no corresponding items in the UNIT.

050 |aADE - UNIT 2043 |u<P&P> USE MICROFILM.

530 |aReference copies available for some UNIT items in LOT 4249. (UNIT does not include an accompanying statement in 050.)

MARC TAG	MARC FIELD NAME
540	**Terms Governing Use (R)**
540/|a	Terms governing use and reproduction (NR)
540/_1	Undefined
540/_2	Undefined

DEFAULT VALUE(S): This field is included in all ADE - UNIT records. It contains the following as a default in |a: **May be restricted: Information on reproduction rights available in Library of Congress P&P Restrictions Notebook.**

DATA CONVENTIONS/COMMENTS: This field contains a stock general statement used in catalog records for other collections in P&P. The drawings processed in ADE - UNITs are from many different sources, and in a few cases, drawings from a single UNIT may not be from the same source and will have different reproduction rights. P&P has information about reproduction rights for <u>some</u> of these materials; however, it will be the responsibility of the patron to research information about reproduction rights in the cases where P&P lacks information. This note will alert patrons to the issue of reproduction rights, and will point them to more specific information about reproduction rights which may be available in the P&P Restrictions Notebook.

Indicators: Both are undefined and blank.

PUNCTUATION/SPACING: A period or other mark of punctuation is always at the end of the data in |a. If the mark of final punctuation is a closing bracket or parenthesis, however, add a period.

EXAMPLE(S):

540 |aMay be restricted: Information on reproduction rights available in Library of Congress P&P Restrictions Notebook.

MARC TAG	MARC FIELD NAME
541	**Immediate Source of Acquisition Note** (R)
541/|c	Method of acquisition (NR)
541/|a	Source of acquisition (NR)
541/|d	Date of accession (NR)
541/|e	Accession number (NR)
541/_1	Undefined
541/_2	Undefined

DEFAULT VALUE(S): none

DATA CONVENTIONS/COMMENTS: This field is used in all non-archives records (i.e., records without a corresponding Guide Record in which to record this information) to record the method and source of acquisition, and to distinguish between acquisitions. In archives records, only the collection-level guide record has a 541 field. Information recorded in this field is derived from P&P's accessions files. For materials transferred to P&P from other divisions at the Library of Congress, acquisition information refers to the previous Library of Congress custodial division rather than to the original acquisition by the institution. This field is repeated if separate acquisition source statements are necessary.

|c   Method of acquisition (e.g., gift, transfer, purchase, deposit) is contained in |c and is always listed first. In situations where the collection is comprised of more than one acquisition source, this statement contains a word (e.g., some, most) which refers to the general percentage of this gift as part of the complete archive or collection.

|a   Source of acquisition (i.e., personal or corporate name of donor, name of government agency, or name of previous Library of Congress custodial division) is recorded in |a.

|d   Date (year) of accession is recorded in |d.

|e   A Prints and Photographs Division accession number is recorded in |e.

Indicators: Both are undefined and blank.

PUNCTUATION/SPACING: A semicolon separates each subfield. A period or other mark of punctuation is always at the end of the data in |a. If the mark of final punctuation is a closing bracket or parenthesis, however, add a period. Accession number is surrounded by parentheses.

EXAMPLE(S):

541 |cGift;|aChatelain Hunter Miller, Architects;|d1990;|e(DLC/PP-1990:172).

541 |cTransfer;|aSmithsonian Institution;|d1980;|e(DLC/PP-1980:301).

541 |cTransfer;|aManuscript Division (David E. Finley Papers);|d1981;|e(DLC/PP-1981:66).

541 |cGift and purchase;|aMrs. Louise Ray;|d1993;|e(DLC/PP-1993:221).

MARC TAG	MARC FIELD NAME
555	**Cumulative Index/Finding Aids Note** (R)
555/|a	Cumulative index/finding aids note (NR)
555/_1	Display constant controller
555/_2	Undefined

DEFAULT VALUE(S): Finding aid (unpublished): filed by UNIT number, available in Prints and Photographs Reading Room.

DATA CONVENTIONS/COMMENTS: Every ADE - UNIT catalog record contains this note which is boilerplated in via a default in the Minaret layout.

Indicators: The first indicator, the display constant controller, is always **8** in ADE - UNIT catalog records for "no display constant generated." The second indicator is undefined and blank.

PUNCTUATION/SPACING: This field ends with a period.

EXAMPLE(S):

555 8 |a |Finding aid (unpublished): filed by UNIT number, available in Prints and Photographs Reading Room.

MARC TAG	MARC FIELD NAME
580	**Linking Entry Complexity Note** (R)
580/|a	Linking entry complexity note (NR)
580/_1	Undefined
580/_2	Undefined

DEFAULT VALUE(S): For archives records: "Forms part of
_____ (Library of Congress)"

DATA CONVENTIONS/COMMENTS: This field contains a note that expresses the relationship of the ADE - UNIT to the archive it is part of. This field links the catalog record for the UNIT to the collection-level GUIDE RECORD.

|a   The entire note goes into a single |a.

Indicators: Both are undefined and blank.

PUNCTUATION/SPACING: A period or other mark of punctuation is always at the end of the data in |a. If the mark of final punctuation is a closing bracket or parenthesis, however, add a period.

EXAMPLES:

580 |aForms part of Arthur B. Heaton Archive.

773 0 |tArthur B. Heaton Archive (Library of Congress)|wᵇᵇᵇ95858232

580 |aForms part of the Riggs Family Papers, 1763-1945 (Library of Congress).

773 0 |aRiggs Family. |tPapers, |d1763-1945. |(DLC)ƀƀƀmm8137895

MARC TAG	MARC FIELD NAME
600	**Subject Added Entry—Personal Name** (R)
600/|a	Personal name (NR)
600/|c	Titles and other words associated with a name (R)
600/|q	Fuller form of name (NR)
600/|d	Dates associated with a name (NR)
600/|x	General subdivision (R)
600/|z	Geographic subdivision (R)
600/_1	Type of personal name entry element
600/_2	Subject heading system/thesaurus

DEFAULT VALUE(S): none

DATA CONVENTIONS/COMMENTS: This field contains a personal name used as a subject added entry. Headings are assigned primarily for well-known, prominent persons who are the primary client and lived in the house. Rather than establish a name for the depicted structure, the person's name and a TGM I subdivision such as "Homes & haunts" or "Monuments" often best describe the subject matter. In most cases, the same name appears in the 700 field for its role as "client." In a few cases, the person named has a subject relationship to the drawings, but was not the client for the project; the name then has a 600 heading, but not a 700 heading.

This field may be repeated if more than one person was a client. Headings are constructed for persons with existing name authority records in the LCNAF, or from name headings formulated and added to the LCNAF by WII staff. WII staff created new name authority records for use in this field and the 700 field if the person named fit one of the three following criteria: found in *Who's Who in the Nation's Capital*, or *Who Was Who in America*; if the client for three or more projects was represented by ADE - UNITs; or found in the Library of Congress manual catalog.

|a,|q,|d   Data are entered in these fields exactly as they appear in the name authority records.

|x   The name authority heading is almost always followed by subfield x (general subdivision) which contains terms selected from *Thesaurus for Graphic Materials I, Appendix B, Standard Subdivisions Used with Names of Persons*. The subdivision used most frequently in subfield x in WII headings is "Homes & haunts."

|z   Geographic subdivisions ([country or state]--[city]) are entered in indirect order in |z. The source for the form of the heading is the Library of Congress name and subject authority files. The geographic

subdivision most frequently used in WII catalog records is "Washington (D.C.)," entered in a single |z.

Indicators: The first indicator is usually 1 (single surname) in ADE - UNIT catalog records. The second indicator is 0 if no P&P subdivisions are used, and 4 (source not specified) if P&P subdivisions (terms from TGM I) are used.

PUNCTUATION/SPACING: Follow form in authority heading for subfields a, q, and d. A final mark of punctuation follows the last subfield.

EXAMPLE(S):

600 14	|aLetts, John C.|q(John Cowen),|db. 1861|xHomes & haunts |zMaryland|zBethesda.
600 14	|aDickson, John,|d1797-1870|xCommemoration|zWashington (D.C.)
600 14	|aDu Pont, Henry Francis,|d1880-1969|xHomes & haunts|zDelaware|zWinterthur.
600 14	|aJohnson, Walter Perry,|d1887-1946|xMonuments|zWashington (D.C.)

MARC TAG	MARC FIELD NAME
610	**Subject Added Entry—Corporate Name** (R)
610/|a	Corporate name (NR)
610/|b	Subordinate unit (R)
610/|x	General subdivision (R)
610/|z	Geographic subdivision (R)
610/|y	Chronological subdivision (R)
610/_1	Type of corporate name entry element
610/_2	Subject heading system/thesaurus

DEFAULT VALUE(S): none

DATA CONVENTIONS/COMMENTS: This field contains a corporate name used as a subject added entry for corporate entities that meet criteria for a 710 (Corporate name—added entry) and are also a subject of the drawings. Rather than establish a name for each structure, the corporate entity name and a TGM I subdivision such as "Buildings" or "Facilities" often best describe the subject matter. In most cases, the same corporate entity name appears in the 710 field for its role as "client." In a few cases, the corporate entity has a subject relationship to the drawings, but was not the client for the project; the name then has a 610 heading but not a 710 heading.

LCNAF is the source for the corporate entity headings, and LCSH for building names. Corporate entity and building names are hard to distinguish with hotels and churches where the corporate name is a building name. If the corporate name is also a building name, subdivisions are not used.

Data in |a and |b are entered exactly as they appear in the authority record.

|a   Subfield a contains the corporate body name.

|b   Subfield b contains a subordinate unit of the corporate body named in |a.

|x   The use of subfield x (general subdivision) is suggested when appropriate. Consult *Thesaurus for Graphic Materials I, Appendix D, Standard Subdivisions Used with Corporate Bodies or Named Events* to select subdivision terms. The most frequently used subdivisions in Washingtoniana II records are "Buildings" and "Facilities." Subfield x is not used when the corporate body is a building.

|z   Geographic subdivisions ([country or state]--[city]) are entered in indirect order in |z. The source for the form of the heading is the Library of Congress name and subject authority files. The geographic subdivision most frequently used in WII catalog records is "Washington (D.C.)," entered in a single |z. In some cases, names of geographic features (found in LCSH) are used in place of the name of a state or city. When the corporate heading already contains a geographic designation, geographic subdivisions are usually omitted. In a few cases, they are included if the geographic location of the building described in the catalog record is located in a different location than the geographic designation in the corporate name authority heading.

|y   Chronological subdivisions are entered in |y. Chronological subdivisions follow P&P's practice of subdividing by the decade(s) span that encompasses the year(s) of execution.

Indicators: The first indicator indicates the type of corporate name entry element:

     0   Inverted name

     1   Jurisdiction name

     2   Name in direct order

If no subdivision is used, the second indicator is 0 (from Library of Congress authority files). If a subdivision is used, the second indicator is 4 (source not specified) if P&P subdivisions (terms from TGM I) are used.

PUNCTUATION/SPACING: Follow form in authority heading. There are no additional spaces or marks of punctuation in |x and |y. A final mark of punctuation follows the data in the last subfield.

EXAMPLE(S):

     610 24 |aNational Gallery of Art (U.S.)|xBuildings |zWashington (D.C.)|y 1950-1960.

     610 24 |aSnow White Grill|xBuildings|zMaryland|zBaltimore|y1950-1960.

     610 24 |aAllied Architects of Washington, D.C. |xBuildings|y1930-1940.

     610 24 |aWashington Home for Foundlings (Washington, D.C.)|xFacilities |y1920-1930.

     610 24 |aAlexandria Hospital (Va.)|xFacilities|y1910-1920.

     610 24 |aCamp Fire Girls|xFacilities|zMaryland|zForestville |y1950-1960.

610 24 |aNaval Research Laboratory|bRadio Division|bFire Control Section|xEquipment & supplies|zWashington (D.C.)|y1940-1950.

610 20 |aLibrary of Congress John Adams Building (Washington, D.C.) |y1930-1940.

610 14 |aWest Virginia.|bCounty Court (Jefferson County)|xBuildings|zWest Virginia|zCharles Town|y1910.

MARC TAG	MARC FIELD NAME
650	**Subject Added Entry—Topical Term** (R)
650/|a	Topical term (R)
650/|x	General subdivision (R)
650/|z	Geographic subdivision (R)
650/|y	Chronological subdivision (R)
650/_1	Level of subject
650/_2	Subject heading system/thesaurus
650/|2	Source of term (NR)

DEFAULT VALUE(S): none

DATA CONVENTIONS/COMMENTS: Topical terms for ADE - UNITs are selected from TGM I following the TGM I application guidelines for selecting the most appropriate term. Proper noun subjects are selected from *Library of Congress Subject Headings* (LCSH) (chiefly names of wars and major monuments).

Topical terms selected for the ADE - UNIT are based on the summary note description. If no terms in TGM I are appropriate for describing the subjects depicted in the drawings, terms are proposed for TGM I, if the concept is significant enough to require indexing. Not all concepts expressed in the 520 summary note have corresponding indexing terms; but all indexing terms are reflected in the 520 note.

Deciding which subjects recorded in the 520 should be indexed requires that many of the same questions be asked as when deciding what to include in the 520. The difference here would be placing more emphasis on whether the subject is exceptional or significant. These questions include: Is the subject depicted a <u>particularly</u> good example of the object? Is this particular subject the focus of many drawings (in proportion to the total number of drawings in the UNIT)? Is the subject an unusual, difficult-to-find example of something? Is the architectural element depicted clear and concrete? If you are looking for drawings of this object, would you be satisfied with this example? Level of indexing tends to vary depending on the number of drawings in the UNIT. In UNITs with only 1–10 drawings, indexing tends to be more comprehensive than in UNITs with 10–1,000 drawings.

|a   Topical terms selected from TGM I are recorded in |a.

|z   Geographic subdivisions ([country or state]--[city]) are usually entered in indirect order in |z. The source for the form of the heading

is the Library of Congress name and subject authority files. The geographic subdivision most frequently used in WII catalog records is "Washington (D.C.)," entered in a single |z. (Washington (D.C.) is entered directly, an exception to the indirect rule.) In some cases names of geographic features (found in LCSH) are used in place of the name of a state or city.

|y   Chronological subdivisions are entered in |y. Chronological subdivisions follow P&P's practice of subdividing by the decade(s) span that encompasses the year(s) of execution.

|2   The |2 always contains **lctgm**, the code for TGM I. This subfield is used in conjunction with 2nd indicator 7. Do not use |2 when using LCSH terms (2nd indicator 0 or 4).

Indicators: The first indicator is always blank (which displays as a hyphen in MUMS) to indicate that no information as to the level of the subject term is available. This blank displays as a hyphen in MUMS. For terms taken directly from TGM I, the second indicator is a 7, indicating that source is specified in |2. For terms taken from LCSH, the second indicator is 0. For terms, source unspecified, the second indicator is 4.

PUNCTUATION/SPACING: There are no additional spaces or marks of punctuation in |a, |z, or |y. A final mark of punctuation is at the end of the last subfield preceding |2. There is no punctuation at the end of |2.

EXAMPLE(S):

650 7 |aPorches|zMaryland|zChevy Chase|y1930-1940.|2lctgm

650 7 |aBungalows|zMaryland|zAnne Arundel County|y1920-1930.|2lctgm

650 7 |aEpiscopal churches|zWashington (D.C.)|y1850-1860.|2lctgm

650 7 |aBridges|zWashington (D.C.)|y1960-1970.|2lctgm

650 7 |aHousing developments|zWashington (D.C.)|y1960-1980.|2lctgm

650 7 |aPorcelain enamel|zWashington Metropolitan
          Area|y1950-1960.|2lctgm

650 7 |aAutomobile dealerships|y1920-1930.|2lctgm

650 7 |aRest stops|zVirginia|zHenry G. Shirley Memorial Highway|y
          1930-1960.|2lctgm

Proper noun subjects from LCSH:

650 4 |aMexican War, 1846-1848|xCommemoration.|y1840-1850|2lctgm

650 4 |aThomas Jefferson Memorial (Washington, D.C.)|y1930-1940

650 4 |aVietnamese Conflict, 1961-1975|xMonuments|zWashington (D.C.)

MARC TAG	MARC FIELD NAME
651	**Subject Added Entry—Geographic Name** (R)
651/|a	Geographic name (R)
651/|y	Chronological subdivision (R)

651/_1   Undefined

651/_2   Subject heading system/thesaurus

DEFAULT VALUE(S): none

DATA CONVENTIONS/COMMENTS: This field was rarely used in WII catalog records. It contains a geographic name used as a subject added entry. These geographic names include places, political jurisdictions, events, roads, structures, and gardens, among other things. Terms are taken from LCNAF or LCSH (151) and are added to those authority files if not already established.

|a   Heading from LCSH or LCNAF is entered here exactly as it appears in the authority record.

|y   Chronological subdivisions follow P&P's practice of subdividing by the decade(s) span that encompasses the year(s) of execution.

Indicators: The first indicator is blank, the second indicator is 0 if heading is used as it appears in authority files, and 4 if TGM I subdivision is used.

PUNCTUATION/SPACING: A final mark of punctuation is at the end of the last subfield.

EXAMPLE(S):

651 0 |aSouthwest Urban Renewal Area (Washington, D.C.)

651 4 |aColumbia Country Club (Chevy Chase, Md.)|y1920-1930.

651 4 |aMall, The (Washington, D.C.)|y1940-1950.

651 4 |aLyon Village (Arlington, Va.)|y1930-1940.

651 4 |aWashington Dulles International Airport (Va.)|y1950-1970.

MARC TAG	MARC FIELD NAME
655	**Index Term—Genre/Form** (R)
655/|a	Genre/form (NR)
655/|y	Chronological subdivision (R)
655/|2	Source of term (NR)
655/_1	Undefined
655/_2	Source of term

DEFAULT VALUE(S): none

DATA CONVENTIONS/COMMENTS: Headings are assigned for the most prominent genre/form represented in the ADE - UNIT (the primary drawing type) found in the 245 field, and for all other genre/forms included in the 520 note. TGM II offers guidance in deciding on the most appropriate term. Consulting TGM II—at least initially, until a familiarity with the terms is acquired—is important to ensure that the correct term is chosen. New terms are proposed if there is no suitable term in TGM II. No physical media terms (e.g., blueprints, photomechanical prints) are indexed. This information is available in the 300 or 5XX fields, and in an item level in the finding aid.

|a	Form/genre terms taken from TGM II are entered in |a.
|y	Chronological subdivisions are entered in |y. Chronological subdivisions follow P&P's practice of subdividing by the decade(s) span that encompasses the year(s) of execution.
|2	The |2 always contains **gmgpc**, the code for TGM II.

Indicators: The first indicator is blank to indicate the type of heading is basic, and that the form/genre term is contained in a single \|a. The second indicator is a **7** to indicate that the source of the term used in this field is specified in \|2.

PUNCTUATION/SPACING: A period is always at the end of \|a. There is no punctuation at the end of \|2.

EXAMPLE(S):

655	7	|aArchitectural drawings|y1920-1930.|2gmgpc
655	7	|aRenderings|y1910-1920.|2gmgpc
655	7	|aConjectural works|y1920-1930.|2gmgpc
655	7	|aAs-built drawings|y1930-1940.|2gmgpc
655	7	|aStructural drawings|y1960.|2gmgpc
655	7	|aLandscape architecture drawings|y1920-1930.|2gmgpc

MARC TAG	MARC FIELD NAME
700	**Added Entry—Personal Name** (R)
700/|a	Personal name (NR)
700/|c	Titles and other words associated with a name (R)
700/|q	Fuller form of name (NR)
700/|d	Dates associated with a name (NR)
700/|e	Relator term (R)
700/_1	Type of personal name entry element
700/_2	Type of added entry

DEFAULT VALUE(S): none

DATA CONVENTIONS/COMMENTS: Personal name added entries are provided for the names of architects who were in some way responsible for the intellectual content of the drawings, for some clients named in the title statement, and to link the drawings to related manuscript collections through author/title added entry. Client names are assigned personal name added entries if they are found in LCNAF or if they are well-known, prominent persons.

This field may be repeated if there was more than one client or architect involved in the project. These headings are created using existing name authority records in LCNAF, or from new name headings formulated and added to the LCNAF by WII staff. Headings are constructed for persons with existing name authority records in the LCNAF, or from name headings formulated and added to the LCNAF by WII staff. WII staff created new name authority records for use in this field and the 700 field if the person named fit one of the three following criteria: found in *Who's Who in the Nation's Capital*, or *Who Was Who in America*; if the client for three or more projects represented by ADE - UNITs; or found in the Library of Congress manual catalog.

|a,|q,|d   Data are entered in these fields exactly as they appear in the name authority records. See entry for 100 field for more information.

|e   Relator terms which indicate the relationship of the person named in the heading to the drawings in the UNIT are entered here.

Indicators: The first indicator distinguishes the type of personal name found in the heading:

Entry element:

Forename only:	0
Single surname:	1
Multiple surname:	2
Family name:	3

The second indicator remains blank.

PUNCTUATION/SPACING: Headings are entered exactly as they appear in their name authority record. If the heading contains initials, there is a space entered between them (e.g., Mullett, A. B., not Mullett, A.B.). There are no spaces entered at the end of data in |a or |q. A comma appears after the data in the subfield (either |a or |q) immediately preceding |d; a comma and space appear after the date before |e (unless open birthdate, then a hyphen with comma and space omitted). A period comes at the end of |e.

In cases where there are two relator terms, a comma comes after the first |e and a period follows the second one.

EXAMPLE(S):

700	1	|aRobbins, Irene de Bruyn,|eclient.
700	2	|aBush-Brown, Henry Kirke,|d1857-1935, |esculptor.
700	1	|aSmith, Delos H.|q(Delos Hamilton),|d1884-1963, |earchitect.
700	1	|aJolliffe, C. B.|q(Charles Byron),|db. 1894, |eclient.
700	1	|aThompson, Ross C.|q(Ross Calvin),|d1896- , |eclient.

MARC TAG	MARC FIELD NAME
710	Added Entry—Corporate Name (R)
710/|a	Corporate name or jurisdiction name (NR)
710/|b	Subordinate unit (R)

710/_1   Type of corporate name entry element

710/_2   Type of added entry

DEFAULT VALUE(S): none

DATA CONVENTIONS/COMMENTS: Criteria used to determine whether a corporate client was assigned an added entry are: 1. If the corporate body had an existing name authority record in the LCNAF; 2. If the corporate body was client for more than <u>three</u> ADE - UNITs, and if its name could be verified in a reference source; or 3. If the corporate body was judged to be of significant importance or interest to users. If there was no name authority record in the LCNAF, Washingtoniana II staff created a record to add to the system.

Indicators: The first indicator indicates the type of corporate name entry element:

0   Inverted name

1   Jurisdiction name

2   Name in direct order

The second indicator is blank to indicate that there is no information provided to identify the type of added entry.

PUNCTUATION/SPACING: Follows form on headings found in LCNAF. A comma immediately precedes |e.

EXAMPLE(S):

710 2 |aOldfields School,|eclient.

710 2 |aMarriott Hot Shoppes,|eclient.

710 2 |aKarl W. Corby Construction Corp.,|eclient.

710 2 |aVietnam Veterans Memorial Fund,|esponsor.

710 1 |aUnited States.|bDept. of the Treasury.|bOffice of the Secretary, |eclient.

MARC TAG	MARC FIELD NAME
773	**Host Item Entry** (R)
773/|t	Title (NR)
773/|w	Record control number (NR)
773/_1	Note controller
773/_2	Undefined

DEFAULT VALUE(S): none

DATA CONVENTIONS/COMMENTS: This field is used in archives records to record the collection name/archive of which the drawings in the ADE - UNIT form a part. If a collection/archive name is in this field, there is a collection-level

Guide Record which includes overview information about the entire collection. Leader/07 must be set to **d** (to signify this is a subunit to a host item) when this field is included in a record.

|t   Contains the title of the collection/archive as it appears in the 245 field of the Guide Record, followed by a default: (**Library of Congress**), contained in the same subfield.

|w   Contains the LCCN for the guide record in the form: (DLC)ƀƀƀ95xxxxxx.

Indicators: The first indicator is **0**, so that the information in this field will display in the record. The second indicator is undefined and is blank.

PUNCTUATION/SPACING: A space follows the collection title; the name of the institution is in parentheses.

EXAMPLE(S):

773 0 |tWaggaman & Ray Archive (Library of Congress)|w(DLC) ƀƀƀ95858230

773 0 |tIron-Craftsmen Archive (Library of Congress)|w(DLC) ƀƀƀ95858238

773 0 |aOwings, Nathaniel Alexander, 1903- .|Papers,|1911-1983. |w(DLC)ƀƀƀmm8275863

MARC TAG	MARC FIELD NAME
852	**Location** (R)
852/|a	Location (NR)
852/|b	Sublocation or collection (R)
852/|e	Address (R)
852/|n	Country code (NR)
852/_1	Shelving scheme
852/_2	Shelving order

DEFAULT VALUE(S):

852 ƀƀ |aLibrary of Congress|bPrints and Photographs Division |eWashington, D.C. 20540-4842 USA|ndcu

DATA CONVENTIONS/COMMENTS: The data in this field are used to clarify the repository of the drawings, especially when the record is accessed outside of MUMS or utilities (i.e., the Internet). It will also help researchers who print records locally by printing the address for Library of Congress P&P.

Indicators: Both indicators are blank.

PUNCTUATION/SPACING: none

EXAMPLES:

852 ƀƀ |aLibrary of Congress|bPrints and Photographs Division
|eWashington, D.C. 20540 USA|ndcu

MARC TAG	MARC FIELD NAME
908	**Local Fixed Field** (NR)
908/|a	Control fields
908/_1	Undefined
908/_2	Undefined

DEFAULT VALUE(S):

908|a | ƀƀƀƀqƀƀƀeƀƀƀƀƀƀƀƀƀƀƀƀƀƀƀƀƀƀ

DATA CONVENTIONS/COMMENTS: This field is required by MUMS. The data contained in this field are 30 characters long, mostly consisting of blanks. The field is system-generated in MUMS. In order to direct load into MUMS it was necessary to add this field.

|a   All data are contained in a single |a. This field contains a 30 byte code indicating input source, main entry established, MARC eligibility, approval, cataloger code, approval date, and character approval date.

bytes 00-04	Undefined ƀƀƀƀ (4 blanks)
byte 05	Input Source (q=Prints and Photographs)
bytes 06-08	Undefined ƀƀƀ (3 blanks)
byte 09	Main Entry established (e=main entry established)
byte 10	Undefined/MARC eligibility ƀ (blank)
byte 11	Approval/Undefined ƀ (blank)
bytes 12-15	Undefined ƀƀƀƀ (4 blanks)
bytes 16-17	Cataloger code ƀƀ (2 blanks; four character cataloger ID code obtained from sign-on is converted to binary notation)
byte 18	Undefined ƀ (blank)
bytes 19-20	Approval date ƀƀ (initially 2 blanks; set by system after record is approved)
bytes 21-23	Undefined ƀƀƀ (3 blanks)
bytes 24-29	Character approval date ƀƀƀƀƀƀ (initially 6 blanks; format for date yymmdd set by system when record is approved)

Indicators: Both are undefined and blank.

PUNCTUATION/SPACING: none

EXAMPLE(S):

908|a | ƀƀƀƀqƀƀƀeƀƀƀƀƀƀƀƀƀƀƀƀƀƀƀƀƀƀ

MARC TAG	MARC FIELD NAME
985	**Local Record History** (NR)
985/|a	Agency that keyed the record (R)
985/_1	Undefined
985/_2	Undefined

DEFAULT VALUE(S): **pp/wii** carried as a constant in |a.

DATA CONVENTIONS/COMMENTS: This field contains information identifying the division (pp) and collection or project (wii for Washingtoniana II). The purpose of this field is to identify the source and specific project which generated the catalog record. All of this field is default information. This is a local Library of Congress field.

Indicators: Both are undefined and blank.

PUNCTUATION/SPACING: none

EXAMPLE(S):

985　　|app/wii

NOTES

1. Three fields in the catalog record all contain essentially the same LCCN in slightly different presentations. These fields are 001, 010, and 035. These numbers could be different in a record (if, for example, the 010 contained an invalid or expired number); however, in ADE - UNIT records, these numbers will correspond:

   Example:
   001　　|ƀƀƀ95849455ƀ
   010　　|a|ƀƀƀ95849455ƀ/PP
   035　　|a|(DLC)95-849455 (035 is deleted by load program and will not
   　　　　appear in records in MUMS)

2. The term "architectural drawings" (as we use it) includes original drawings and reproductions of drawings (e.g., blueprints, diazo prints, etc.).

3. Choice of SMD was problematic. UNITs often contain a variety of drawing and photographic or photomechanical media. "Items" was, therefore, selected as the most comprehensive and simple physical description. The drawing type (e.g., architectural drawing, interior design drawing, etc.) was experimented with as an SMD for several years, but proved unworkable because some UNITs have a mixture of types and the broader term that covers all types (Design drawings) would be a concoction of non-natural language.

   Also, all the SMDs in *GM* are physical characteristic terms—their value as a short list of readily understood words to introduce the physical description statement would be <u>undone</u> if items that describe the form and subject (e.g., all the Design drawings in TGM II) were added as SMDs. The Avery Library's use of "sheets" as an SMD is also in the spirit of focus on physical manifestation of material.

   Given the multiplicity of media in many UNITs, and the quantity of drawing type vocabulary, "items" became the practical SMD choice. (The title, subject note, and genre/form heading all mention the drawing type, so that information is not lost.)

4. *GM* suggested sequence would repeat the sequence of information in 245a/c, 260, and 300 fields; however, ADE - UNIT catalog records created during this project did not follow the suggested sequence.

Bibliography

The literature on using MARC records to catalog images of art and architecture is surprisingly large considering how difficult it is to find. Much of it is in unindexed sources or is not retrievable using terms that catalogers of art and architecture would expect to be relevant. What follows does not claim to be exhaustive but will surely lead to additional resources. The focus is on the past decade; there was very little activity in this area before the early 1980s. The earlier material (1965–1984) on computerized access to visual materials is reviewed by Karen Markey in "Visual Arts Resources and Computers," *Annual Review of Information Science and Technology* 19 (1984): 271–309.

Some of the citations in this bibliography are not specifically related to art or architecture, nor to MARC, but, like much concerning MARC and images, contain concepts that can be adapted to the needs of visual resources collections. The bibliography has six parts: articles relating specifically to cataloging images using MARC; tools that can be used to accomplish this, along with works about these tools; works dealing with subject analysis for images; conference and committee reports relating to the use of MARC or subject analysis of visual images; additional resources that deal more generally with automating image cataloging or otherwise providing intellectual access to visual resources; and Web sites and other electronic addresses (cited 1/1/98) for tools and communication.

Using MARC Records for Visual Resources

Abid, Ann, Eleanor Scheifele, Sara Jane Pearman, et al., "Planning for Automation of the Slide and Photograph Collections at the Cleveland Museum of Art: A Draft MARC/Visual Materials Record." *Visual Resources Association Bulletin* 19, no. 2 (summer 1992): 17–21.

Antrim, Elizabeth. "Working Together to Create an Image Database on the Internet, or You Can Teach an Old Slide Curator New Tricks." *VRA Bulletin* 22, no. 2 (summer 1995): 33–36.

Austin, David. "Building New Tools for the Twenty-First Century University: Providing Access to Visual Information." In *Computer Networking and Scholarly Communications in the Twenty-First Century University*, 409–422. Albany, N.Y.: SUNY Press, 1996.

———. "The Conway Library Index Project." *Computers and the History of Art* 3, no. 2 (1993): 59–69.

———. "Forging a Link between Museums and Libraries. Sharing Information by Means of a Common Index Format." Paper presented at the annual meeting of International Committee on Documentation (CIDOC) of the International Museums Council, Ljubljana, Poland, September 1993.

———. "An Image Is Not an Object, but It Can Help." *Resource Sharing: New Technologies as a Must for Universal Availability of Information. 16th International Symposium, 18 October–21 October, 1993*, 17 (1994): 277–296.

Bales, Kathleen. "The USMARC Formats and Visual Materials." *Art Documentation* 8, no. 4 (winter 1989): 183–185.

Barnett, Patricia J. "An Art Information System: From Integration to Interpretation." *Library Trends* 27, no. 2 (fall 1988): 194–205.

———. *Developing a MARC Format for Cataloging Art Objects and Their Visual Surrogates: Report and Accompanying Documents on the Workshop.* Papers from a workshop sponsored by the Getty Art History Information Program and chaired by Eleanor Fink, June 12–13, 1989. Santa Monica, Calif.: Getty Information Institute, 1989. Photocopy.

Bearman, David. "Can MARC Accommodate Archives and Museums? Technical and Political Challenges." In *Beyond the Book: Extending MARC for Subject Access,* edited by Toni Petersen and Pat Molholt, 237–245. Boston: G. K. Hall, 1990.

———. "Considerations in the Design of Art Scholarly Databases." *Library Trends* 37, no. 2 (fall 1988): 206–219.

Bierbaum, Esther Green. "MARC in Museums: Applicability of the Revised Visual Materials Format." *Information Technology and Libraries* 9, no. 4 (December 1990): 291–299.

Blazina, Vesna, and Ginette Melançon-Bolduc. "Mapping to MARC at the Bibliothèque de l'Aménagement Université de Montréal." *Visual Resources Association Bulletin* 18, no. 3 (fall 1991): 14–21.

———. "MARC Format for Architecture Slides at the Bibliothèque de l'Aménagement, Université de Montréal." *Positive* 13, no. 2–3 (1989): xii–xviii.

Bower, James. "One-Stop Shopping: RLIN as a Union Catalog for Research Collections at the Getty Center." *Library Trends* 37, no. 2 (fall 1988): 252–262.

———. "Sharing the Wealth: Software for MARC-based Cataloging of Visual Materials." *Visual Resources Association Bulletin* 17, no. 3 (fall 1990): 23–26.

———. "The Visual Resources Association MARC Mapping Project." *Visual Resources* 9, no. 3 (1993): 291–327.

Cantrell, Dan. "From MARC to Mosaic: Progressing toward Data Interchangeability at the Oregon State Archives." *Archives and Museum Informatics* 8, no. 1 (spring 1994): 4–12.

Chantiny, M. "Incorporating Digitized Images in the UH-CARL PAC Online Catalog." *Library Software Review* 12, no. 1 (spring 1993): 22–26.

Clarke, Sherman. "Illustrated Books and Book Illustrations at the Amon Carter Museum Library." *Art Documentation* 14, no. 4 (winter 1995): 21–23.

Davis, Stephen Paul. "Digital Image Collections: Cataloging Data Model and Network Access." New York: Columbia University Libraries, <http://www.columbia.edu/cu/libraries/inside/projects/diap/paper.html>. 1995.

De Sá Rego, Stella M. "Managing a Collection of Historical Photographs in an Academic Research Library." *VRA Bulletin* 22, no. 2 (summer 1995): 24–28.

Dooley, Jackie M. "Processing and Cataloging Archival Photograph Collections." *Visual Resources* 11, no. 1 (1995): 85–101.

Emons, Margaret L. "Cataloging Architecture Slides at the University of Nebraska–Lincoln." *VRA Bulletin* 20, no. 3 (fall 1993): 24–28.

Fink, Eleanor. "Advantages of Using the MARC Format." Paper delivered at the International Art History Conference (CIHA), Strasbourg, France, September 1989.

———, and Christine M. Hennessey. "Testing the Flexibility of the MARC Format." *Visual Resources* 4, no. 4 (winter 1988): 373–388.

Flynn, Marcy, and Helena Zinkham. "The MARC Format and Electronic Reference Images: Experiences from the Library of Congress Prints and Photographs Division." *Visual Resources* 11, no. 1 (1995): 47–70.

Folkerts, Menso, and Andreas Kühne, eds. *The Use of Computers in Cataloging Medieval and Renaissance Manuscripts.* Papers from the International Workshop in Munich, 10–12 August 1989. Munich: Institut für Geschichte der Naturwissenschaften, 1990.

Gaynor, Edward. "Cataloging Digital Images: Issues." *Seminar on Cataloging Digital Documents.* Washington, D.C.: Library of Congress, <http://lcweb.loc.gov/catdir/semdigdocs/gaynor.html>. October 1994.

Gerstner, Patsy, and Jennifer Compton. "Public Access to Museum Collections: MARC and OCLC—The Experiences of an Ohio Group." *Spectra* 22, no. 4 (summer 1995): 25–28.

Gibbs, Andrea, and Pat Stevens. "MARC and the Computerization of the National Gallery of Art Photographic Archives." *Visual Resources* 3, no. 3 (1986): 185–208.

Giral, Angela. "Architectural Drawings—An Automated Indexing and Retrieval [System]." *Art Documentation* 5, no. 1 (spring 1986): 11–13.

———. "At the Confluence of Three Traditions: Architectural Drawings at the Avery Library." *Library Trends* 37, no. 2 (fall 1988): 232–242.

Harrison, Harriet W. "Cataloging Visual Images: The View from LC." *Art Documentation* 15, no. 2 (1996): 13–16.

Havens, Carolyn. "Cataloging a Special Art Collection." *Cataloging and Classification Quarterly* 9, no. 4 (1989): 27–49.

"Help?! . . . Are There Museums Using the MARC Format for Cataloging Objects? How Well Does It Work? What Are the Reasons for Using It?" *Spectra* 22, no. 4 (summer 1995): 29–31. Responses by Robert A. Baron, Sara Phinney Kelley, Jennifer Compton, Linda McRae.

Hennessey, Christine. "Creating a Database for Art Objects: The National Museum of American Art's Inventory of American Sculpture." *Art Documentation* 6, no. 4 (winter 1987): 147–149.

———. "The Inventory of American Sculpture: MARC-ing Realia." In *Beyond the Book: Extending MARC for Subject Access,* edited by Toni Petersen and Pat Molholt, 145–155. Boston: G. K. Hall, 1990.

Keats, Patricia L. "Cataloging Images in MARC at the California Historical Society." *VRA Bulletin* 22, no. 4 (winter 1995): 19–35.

———. "The Visual Imaging Project at the California Historical Society: Cataloging Images of California History—Photographs, Book Illustrations, and Ephemera—for Local and National Access." *VRA Bulletin* 23, no. 1 (spring 1996): 30–33.

Keefe, Jeanne M. "The Image as Document: Descriptive Programs at Rensselaer." *Library Trends* 38, no. 4 (spring 1990): 659–681.

———. "The Use of the Visual Materials Format for a Slide Library Integrated into an OPAC." In *Beyond the Book: Extending MARC for Subject Access,* edited by Toni Petersen and Pat Molholt, 25–41. Boston: G. K. Hall, 1990.

Layne, Sara Shatford. "MARC Format for Medieval Manuscript Images." *Rare Books and Manuscripts Librarianship* 6, no. 1 (1991): 39–52.

Lindschinger, Hildegard. "Attention Cataloguers!!!!" *The Grapevine—The Newsletter of the ARLIS/NA Ontario Chapter* 1, no. 2 (fall–winter 1995): 7.

Lucker, Amy. "The Visual Materials Format: Columbia's AVIADOR Project Links On-Line Description to Videodisc Images Using the 789 Field." *Operations Update* (Research Libraries Group) 43 (September 1987).

McRae, Linda. "Compiling a Case for Standards." *VRA Bulletin* 20, no. 1 (spring 1993): 35–37.

———. "MARC: A Brief History." *Visual Resources Association Bulletin* 17, no. 2 (summer 1990): 19–21.

———. "MARC for Object and Image Collections." *VRA Bulletin* 21, no. 3 (fall 1994): 33–34.

———. "More than MARC: Developing a Standard Descriptive Terminology for Visual Image Collections." *Visual Resources Association Bulletin* 19, no. 1 (spring 1992): 25–27.

———. "Shared Cataloging for Visual Resources Collections: Testing the MARC Format." *Visual Resources Association Bulletin* 18, no. 1 (spring 1991): 24–28.

Maddox, Brent. "To VIM with Vigor." *International Bulletin for Photographic Documentation of the Visual Arts* 15, no. 3 (fall 1988): 18–20.

Mayo, Hope. "MARC Cataloguing for Medieval Manuscripts: An Evaluation." *Primary Sources and Original Works* 1, no. 3/4 (1991): 93–152. Also published in *Bibliographic Access to Medieval and Renaissance Manuscripts: A Survey of Computerized Data Bases and Information Services,* edited by Wesley M. Stevens, 93–152. New York: Haworth Press, 1992.

———. "Medieval Manuscript Cataloging and the MARC Format." *Rare Books and Manuscripts Librarianship* 6, no. 1 (1991): 11–22.

———. *Medieval Manuscript Cataloging and the MARC Format.* Chicago: American Library Association, 1991.

Nemeth, Mayra. "Cataloging for Art's Sake at Florida International University." *VRA Bulletin* 20, no. 2 (summer 1993): 25–31.

Oldal, Maria. "A Foot in the Door: Adapting Cataloging Standards to Visual Materials." *Art Documentation* 15, no. 2 (1996): 7–12.

O'Neill, Ynez Viole. "MARC Records of Early Medical Pictures." Los Angeles: University of California–Los Angeles School of Medicine, <http://www.mednet.ucla.edu/acadprog/som/ddo/neurobio.bak/immi/immihtml.htm>. 1995.

Parks, Janet. "Return to Sender—Addressee Unknown." *Visual Resources* 4, no. 4 (1988): 389–401.

Pearman, Sara Jane. "An Opinion: Mumblings of a Slide Librarian." *Art Documentation* 7, no. 4 (winter 1988): 145–146.

Petersen, Toni, and Pat Molholt, eds. *Beyond the Book: Extending MARC for Subject Access.* Boston: G. K. Hall, 1990.

Pivorun, Phyllis. "Summary of a Pilot Slide Automation Project Using the NOTIS On-line Library System." *Visual Resources Association Bulletin* 17, no. 4 (winter 1990): 18–19.

———. "Why and How MARC Is Being Used for Automating the Architecture Slide Collection at Clemson University." *Visual Resources Association Bulletin* 18, no. 2 (summer 1991): 18–21.

Proceedings of the Seminar on Cataloging Digital Documents, October 12–14, 1994, University of Virginia Library, Charlottesville and the Library of Congress. Washington, D.C.: Library of Congress, <http://lcweb.loc.gov/catdir/semdigdocs/seminar.html>. October 1994.

Rorvig, Mark E. "Intellectual Access to Graphic Information." *Library Trends* 38, no. 4 (spring 1990), entire issue.

Ross, Jeffrey J. *Cataloging Architectural Drawings: A Guide to the Fields of the RLIN Visual Materials (VIM) Format as Applied to the Cataloging Practices of the Avery Architectural and Fine Arts Library, Columbia University, Developed for Project AVIADOR.* Topical Papers, No. 1. Tucson: Art Libraries Society of North America, 1992.

Snow, Maryly. "Visual Depictions and the Use of MARC: A View from the Trenches of Slide Librarianship." *Art Documentation* 8, no. 4 (winter 1989): 186–190.

Soules, Alise Elizabeth. "Images in the OPAC." In *LITA Yearbook 1992*, 23–26. Chicago: Library and Information Technology Association, 1992.

Stam, Deirdre C. "The Quest for a Code, or a Brief History of the Computerized Cataloging of Art Objects." *Art Documentation* 8, no. 1 (spring 1989): 7–15.

———, and Angela Giral, eds. "Linking Art Objects and Art Information." *Library Trends* 37, no. 2 (fall 1988), entire issue.

———, and Ruth Palmquist. *SUART: A MARC-based Information Structure and Data Dictionary for the Syracuse University Art Collection.* Syracuse: Museum Computer Network, 1989.

Stevens, Wesley M. "Access to Knowledge: An Introduction." In *Bibliographic Access to Medieval and Renaissance Manuscripts: A Survey of Computerized Data Bases and Information Services,* edited by Wesley M. Stevens, 1–10. New York: Haworth Press, 1992. Also published as *Primary Sources and Original Works* 1, no. 3/4 (1991).

———, ed. *Bibliographic Access to Medieval and Renaissance Manuscripts: A Survey of Computerized Data Bases and Information Services.* New York: Haworth Press, 1992. Also published as *Primary Sources and Original Works* 1, no. 3/4 (1991).

Thomas, Sarah E. "Summary: Seminar on Cataloging Digital Documents." Washington, D.C.: Library of Congress, <http://lcweb.loc.gov/catdir/semdigdocs/summary.html>. October 1994.

Van der Wateren, Jan Floris. "Achieving the Link between Art Object and Documentation: Experiences in the British Architectural Library." *Library Trends* 37, no. 2 (fall 1988): 243–251.

Van Egmond, Warren. "The Future of Manuscript Cataloguing." In *Bibliographic Access to Medieval and Renaissance Manuscripts: A Survey of Computerized Data Bases and Information Services,* edited by Wesley M. Stevens, 153–158. New York: Haworth Press, 1992. Also published in *Primary Sources and Original Works* 1, no. 3/4 (1991).

Walter, Nadine. "Computerization in Research in the Visual Arts." *Art Documentation* 10, no. 1 (spring 1991): 3–12.

White, Lynda S. "Image Cataloging in MARC at the University of Virginia." *VRA Bulletin* 21, no. 3 (fall 1994): 23–31.

Tools

Art and Architecture Thesaurus, comp. *Directory of AAT Users.* Special Bulletin, no. 8. Ann Arbor, Mich.: Visual Resources Association, 1996.

Art and Architecture Thesaurus. 2nd ed. 5 vols. New York: Oxford University Press, on behalf of the Getty Art History Information Program, 1994.

Art and Architecture Thesaurus File. Williamstown, Mass.: AAT, 1990– . In Research Libraries Information Network (Online), Mountain View, Calif.: Research Libraries Group.

Art and Architecture Thesaurus: Second Edition plus Supplement with the Authority Reference Tool Edition, Version 2.1 (AAT:ART 2.1). New York: Oxford University Press, on behalf of the Getty Art History Information Program, 1996.

Art and Architecture Thesaurus: USMARC Authority Format, Version 2.0 (AAT:USMARC 2.0). Santa Monica, Calif.: Getty Art History Information Program, 1994.

Baca, Murtha, and Patricia Harpring, eds. "Art Information Task Force *Categories for the Description of Works of Art.*" *Visual Resources* 11, no. 3/4 (1996), special issue.

Betz, Elisabeth. *Graphic Materials: Rules for Describing Original Items and Historical Collections.* Washington, D.C.: Library of Congress, 1982.

Bibliographic Formats and Standards. 2nd ed. Dublin, Ohio: OCLC Online Computer Library Center, 1996; also available at <http://www.oclc.org/oclc/bib/about.htm>. 1996.

Blackaby, James R., Patricia Greeno, and the Nomenclature Committee. *The Revised Nomenclature for Museum Cataloging. A Revised and Expanded Version of Robert G. Chenall's System for Classifying Man-Made Objects.* Nashville, Tenn.: American Association for State and Local History Press, 1988; Walnut Creek, Calif.: AltiMira Press, 1995.

Byrne, Deborah J. *MARC Manual: Understanding and Using MARC Records.* Englewood, Colo.: Libraries Unlimited, 1991.

Categories for the Description of Works of Art. Santa Monica, Calif.: Getty Information Institute, 1996. Web site at: <http://www.ahip.getty.edu/gii/index/cdwa.html>

Chenall, Robert G. *Nomenclature of Museum Cataloging: A System for Classifying Man-Made Objects.* Nashville, Tenn.: American Association for State and Local History, 1978.

Childress, Eric. "Traditional and Emerging Library Standards for Intellectual Control of Image Objects: An Overview." *VRA Bulletin* 23, no. 4 (winter 1996): 88–92.

Crawford, Walt. *MARC for Library Use: Second Edition: Understanding Integrated MARC.* Boston: G. K. Hall, 1989.

Draft International Core Data Standard for Archaeological Sites and Monuments. Rotterdam: International Committee for Documentation, International Council of Museums, <http://www.natmus.min.dk/cidoc/archsite/coredata/arch1.htm>. 1992.

Evans, Linda J., and Maureen O'Brien Will. *MARC for Archival Visual Materials: A Compendium of Practice.* Chicago: Chicago Historical Society, 1988.

Evans, Max, and Lisa Weber. *MARC for Archives and Manuscripts: A Compendium of Practice*. Madison, Wisc.: State Historical Society of Wisconsin, 1985.

Format Integration and Its Effect on the USMARC Bibliographic Format. Washington, D.C.: Library of Congress, 1989.

Frost, Carolyn. *Media Access and Organization: A Cataloging and Reference Sources Guide for Nonbook Materials*. Boulder, Colo.: Libraries Unlimited, 1989.

Gorman, Michael. *The Concise AACR2, 1988 Revision*. Chicago: ALA Books, 1989.

———, and Paul W. Winkler, eds. "Graphic Materials," 200–219. Chapter 8 in *Anglo-American Cataloguing Rules*. 2nd ed., 1988 revision. Chicago: American Library Association, 1988.

Grant, Alice, Josephine Nieuwenhuis, and Toni Petersen. *International Guidelines for Museum Objects Information: The CIDOC Information Categories*. Rotterdam: International Committee for Documentation, International Council of Museums, <http://www.cidoc.icom.org/guide/guide.htm>. June 1995.

Greenberg, Jane. "Intellectual Control of Visual Archives: A Comparison between the *Art and Architecture Thesaurus* and the *Library of Congress Thesaurus for Graphic Materials*." *Cataloging and Classification Quarterly* 16, no. 1 (1993): 85–101.

Hagler, Ronald. "Nonbook Materials: Chapters 7 through 11." In *The Making of a Code: The Issues Underlying AACR2*, edited by Doris Hargrett Clack. Chicago: American Library Association, 1980.

Harpring, Patricia. "The Thesaurus of Art-Historical Place Names (TAP)." *Visual Resources Association Bulletin* 19, no. 3 (fall 1992): 26–32.

Lanzi, Elisa. "Square Pegs and Round Holes: Standards for Visual Resources Collections." *VRA Bulletin* 23, no. 4 (winter 1996): 93–103.

Library of Congress. *Library of Congress Rule Interpretations*. 2nd ed. 2 vols. Washington, D.C.: Library of Congress, 1990–1995; available for purchase through <http://lcweb.loc.gov/cds/train.html#lcri>.

———. *Library of Congress Subject Headings*. 19th ed. 4 vols. Washington, D.C.: Library of Congress, 1996; also available online through RLIN (Research Libraries Information Network) and for purchase through <http://lcweb.loc.gov/cds/lcsh.html#lcsh19>.

———. *Name Authorities*. Cumulative ed. Washington, D.C.: Library of Congress, 1982– . Microfilm; also available online through RLIN (Research Libraries Information Network) and for purchase through <http://lcweb.loc.gov/cds/name_aut.html#names>.

———. *Subject Cataloging Manual: Subject Headings*. 5th ed. Washington, D.C.: Library of Congress, 1996; available for purchase through <http://lcweb.loc.gov/cds/lcsh.html#scmsh>.

———. *Thesaurus for Graphic Materials*. 2nd ed. 2 vols. Washington, D.C.: Library of Congress, 1995; also v. 1 at <http://lcweb.loc.gov/rr/print/tgm1>.

———. *USMARC Code List for Relators, Sources, Description Conventions*. Washington, D.C.: Library of Congress, 1993; available for purchase through <http://lcweb.loc.gov/cds/marcdoc.html#uclfr>.

———. *USMARC Format for Authority Data*. Washington, D.C.: Library of Congress, 1993; Update No. 1, 1995; available for purchase through <http://lcweb.loc.gov/cds/marcdoc.html#uffad>.

———. *USMARC Format for Bibliographic Data*. 2 vols. Washington, D.C.: Library of Congress, 1994; Update No. 1, 1995; Update No. 2, 1996; available for purchase through <http://lcweb.loc.gov/cds/marcdoc.html#uffbd>.

McKeown, Roy, and Jane Savidge. "ARLIS/UK and EIRE Joint Working Group Revision of *AACR2* to Accommodate Cataloging of Art Reproductions: A Document for Discussion by LABL." *VRA Bulletin* 20, no. 4 (winter 1993): 19–27.

McRae, Linda. "The Union List of Artist Names." *VRA Bulletin* 22, no. 4 (winter 1995): 37–44.

MARC for Archival Visual Materials: A Compendium of Practice. Chicago: American Library Association, 1992.

Matters, Marion. "InfoWorks MARC Management and OPAC System: A Review." *Archives and Museum Informatics* 8, no. 1 (spring 1994): 60–70.

———. "Reconciling Sibling Rivalry in the AACR2 'Family': The Potential for Agreement on Rules for Archival Description of All Types of Materials." *American Archivist* 53 (1990): 76–93.

Olson, Nancy B. *Cataloging of Audio-Visual Materials: A Manual Based on AACR2*. 3rd ed. DeKalb, Ill.: Media Marketing Group, 1992.

———, ed. *Cataloging Internet Resources: A Manual and Practical Guide*. Dublin, Ohio: OCLC (Online Computer Library Center), 1995.

Orbach, Barbara. "Integrating Concepts: Corporate Main Entry and Graphic Materials." *Cataloging and Classification Quarterly* 8, no. 2 (1987/88): 71–89.

———. "So That Others May See: Tools for Cataloging Still Images." *Cataloging and Classification Quarterly* 11, no. 3/4 (1990): 163–191.

Parker, Elisabeth Betz. *LC Thesaurus for Graphic Materials: Topical Terms for Subject Access*. Washington, D.C.: Library of Congress, 1987.

Petersen, Toni, and Patricia J. Barnett, eds. *Guide to Indexing and Cataloging with the Art and Architecture Thesaurus*. New York: Oxford University Press, 1994.

Program for Cooperative Cataloging, Core Bibliographic Record for Audiovisual Materials Task Group. *PCC Core Bibliographic Record Standard for Audiovisual Materials.* Washington, D.C.: Library of Congress, <http://lcweb.loc.gov/catdir/pcc/pccavcore.html>. 1996.

Sahli, Nancy. *MARC for Archives and Manuscripts: The AMC Format.* Chicago: Society of American Archivists, 1985.

Simons, Wendell W., and Luraine C. Tansey. *A Slide Classification System for the Organization and Automatic Indexing of Interdisciplinary Collections of Slides and Pictures.* Santa Cruz: University of California, 1970, 2.

Smiraglia, Richard P. "Describing Archival Materials: The Use of the MARC AMC Format." *Cataloging and Classification Quarterly* 11, no. 3/4 (1990): 1–228.

Taylor, Bradley L. "Chenall's Nomenclature, the *Art and Architecture Thesaurus,* and Issues of Access in America's Artifact Collections." *VRA Bulletin* 22, no. 4 (winter 1995): 48–57; reprinted in *Art Documentation* 15, no. 2 (1996): 17–23.

Thesaurus of Geographic Names. Santa Monica, Calif.: Getty Information Institute. Forthcoming on CD-ROM.

Union List of Artist Names. New York: G. K. Hall, 1994.

Union List of Artist Names with the Authority Reference Tool Version 1.0. New York: G. K. Hall, 1994.

Van Eyck Core Record—Survey of International Standards and Practices for Object Identification and Cataloguing. London: Witt Library, Courtauld Institute, n.d.

Waal, H. Van de. *ICONCLASS: An Iconographic Classification System.* 9 vols. Amsterdam and New York: North-Holland Publishing Company, 1973–1985; electronic form available as the *ICONCLASS Browser.* Utrecht: ICONCLASS Research and Development Group, 1992; also available at <http://iconclass.let.ruu.nl>.

Walch, Victoria Irons. *Standards for Archival Description: A Handbook.* Chicago: Society of American Archivists, 1994.

Wees, J. Dustin. "*Categories for the Description of Works of Art* and Visual Resources Applications." *Visual Resources* 11, no. 3/4 (1996): 315–322.

———. "The Work of the VRA Data Standards Committee: Past, Present, Future." *VRA Bulletin* 23, no. 2 (summer 1996): 61–63.

Yee, Martha. "Integration of Non-Book Materials in AACR2." *Cataloging and Classification Quarterly* 3, no. 4 (1983): 1–18.

Zinkham, Helena, and Elisabeth Betz Parker. *Descriptive Terms for Graphic Materials: Genre and Physical Characteristics Headings.* Washington, D.C.: Library of Congress, 1986.

Subject Access/*Art and Architecture Thesaurus*

Like kudzu smothering the southern landscape, the issue of subject access slithers relentlessly over the topic of visual resources cataloging. It is so integral to providing intellectual access to images of art and architecture, regardless of whether MARC is used, that the literature it has generated crosses the disciplines of visual resources curatorship, librarianship, computer science, museology, archives management, and art history. A good place to begin is Lesley Anne Bell's review of the literature, *Gaining Access to Visual Information,* available on the Web at http://www.uky.edu/Artsource/bibliographies/bellbib.txt. Because the *Art and Architecture Thesaurus* has been such an integral part of the development of this literature, another good resource is the *AAT Sourcebook.* We would be remiss not to include material on subject access for those who are beginning to automate their collections. What follows, however, is truly just a sampling.

Barnett, Patricia J. "The Art and Architecture Thesaurus as a Faceted MARC Format." *Visual Resources* 4, no. 3 (autumn 1987): 247–259.

———. "Extending MARC to Accommodate Faceted Thesauri: The AAT Model." In *Beyond the Book: Extending MARC for Subject Access,* edited by Toni Petersen and Pat Molholt, 7–23. Boston: G. K. Hall, 1990.

———. "Subject Analysis and AAT/MARC Implementation." *Art Documentation* 8, no. 4 (winter 1989): 171–172.

Bearman, David. "Thesaurally Mediated Retrieval." *Visual Resources* 10, no. 3 (1994): 295–307.

Bednarek, Martina. "Intellectual Access to Pictorial Information." *Australian Library Journal* 42 (February 1993): 33–46.

Bell, Lesley Anne. "Gaining Access to Visual Information: Theory, Analysis, and Practice of Determining Subjects —A Review of the Literature with Descriptive Abstracts." *Art Documentation* 13, no. 2 (summer 1994): 89–94.

———. *Gaining Access to Visual Information: Theory, Analysis, and Practice of Determining Subjects—A Review of the Literature with Descriptive Abstracts.* London, Ontario: University of Western Ontario, School of Library and Information Science, 1993; also available at Lexington, Ky.: University of Kentucky, <http://www.uky.edu/Artsource/bibliographies/bellbib.txt>. 1994.

Blacow, Helen, and Carol Jackman-Schuller. "Using the *Art and Architecture Thesaurus* as a Tool for Authority Control in an Automated Slide Library." *Positive* 13, no. 2–3 (1989): i–ix.

Brandhorst, J. P. J. "Quantifiability in Iconography." *Knowledge Organization* 20, no. 1 (1993): 12–19.

Buckheit, Betsey. "Between Two Vocabularies: Image Indexer as Middleman." *Visual Resources* 10, no. 3 (1994): 275–281.

Busch, Joseph A. "The National Art Library and the *Art and Architecture Thesaurus:* Part III, Automated Mapping of Subject Headings into Faceted Index Strings." *Art and Architecture Thesaurus Bulletin,* no. 22 (1994): 9–12.

Casey, Diana Dates. "Scouting New Horizons: An Annotated Bibliography Introducing Subject Access in Visual Image Databases." *Illinois Libraries* 76 (fall 1994): 240–242.

Castonguay, Denis. "Vocabulary Control in Iconography at the Public Archives of Canada." In *Databases in the Humanities and the Social Sciences,* edited by Joseph Raben and Gregory A. Marks, 257–261. Amsterdam: North-Holland Publishing Company, 1980.

Chipman, Alison. "Who's That? What's That? What's Happening? Where? Using the *Art and Architecture Thesaurus* to Gossip about Pictures." *VRA Bulletin* 23, no. 2 (summer 1996): 20–22.

Cochrane, Pauline A. "A Paradigm Shift in Library Science." *Information Technology and Libraries* 2, no. 1 (March 1983): 3–4.

Couprie, L. D. "ICONCLASS: An Iconographic Classification System." *Art Libraries Journal* 8, no. 2 (summer 1983): 32–49.

Dodds, Douglas. "The National Art Library and the *Art and Architecture Thesaurus,* Part I." *Art and Architecture Thesaurus Bulletin,* no. 22 (1994): 2–5.

Dooley, Jackie M., and Helena Zinkham. "The Object as 'Subject': Providing Access to Genres, Forms of Materials, and Physical Characteristics." In *Beyond the Book: Extending MARC for Subject Access,* edited by Toni Petersen and Pat Molholt, 43–80. Boston: G. K. Hall, 1990.

Dykstra, Mary. "Subject Analysis and Thesauri: A Background." *Art Documentation* 8, no. 4 (winter 1989): 173–174.

Fink, Eleanor. "Subject Access to Photographic Reproductions of American Paintings at the National Collection of Fine Arts." In *Databases in the Humanities and the Social Sciences,* edited by Joseph Raben and Gregory A. Marks, 229–232. Amsterdam: North-Holland Publishing Company, 1980.

Fox, Michael J. "Using the AAT at the Minnesota Historical Society." *User Friendly: A Newsletter for AAT Users* 1, no. 1 (winter 1994): 3.

Gordon, Catherine. "Patterns and Benefits of Subject Enquiry in an ICONCLASS Database—Abstract." *VRA Bulletin* 23, no. 2 (summer 1996): 22.

———. "Report on the ICONCLASS Workshop: November 2–4, 1987." *Visual Resources* 5, no. 3 (autumn 1988): vii–ix, 197–258.

Grund, Angelika. "ICONCLASS: On Subject Analysis of Iconographic Representations of Works of Art." *Knowledge Organization* 20, no. 1 (1993): 26–29.

Harpring, Patricia. "The Architectural Subject Authority for the Foundation for Documents of Architecture." *Visual Resources* 7, no. 1 (1990): 55–63.

Hastings, Samantha. "Index Access Points in a Study of Intellectual Access to Digitized Art Images." In *Multimedia Computing and Museums,* edited by David Bearman. Pittsburgh: Archives and Museum Informatics, 1995.

Herz, Alexandra. "Scientific Illustration in Some Boston Area Libraries: An Art Historian's View of Library Subject Analysis." *Library Resources & Technical Services* 31, no. 3 (July/September 1987): 239–248.

"ICONCLASS Retrieval." *Visual Resources* 8, no. 1 (1991): special issue.

Jackman-Schuller, Carol. "Using the *Art and Architecture Thesaurus:* Applications in a Medium-Size Visual Resources Collection." *Positive* 14, no. 1 (1990): 2.

Lanzi, Elisa. "Vocabulary as Access to the Visual Image." *VRA Bulletin* 22, no. 2 (summer 1995): 78–82.

Layne, Sara Shatford. "Some Issues in the Indexing of Images." *Journal of the American Society for Information Science* 45, no. 8 (September 1994): 583–588.

Leung, C. H. C., D. Hibler, N. Mwara, et al. "Picture Retrieval by Content Description." *Journal of Information Science* 18, no. 2 (1992): 111–119.

MacKimmie, Robert. "Scanning the Past—California's History Goes Digital." *User Friendly: A Newsletter for AAT Users* 1, no. 4 (fall 1994): 3, 6, 9.

"MARC Notes." *User Friendly: A Newsletter for AAT Users* 1, no. 2 (winter 1994): 1, 4.

Markey, Karen. "Access to Iconographical Research Collections." *Library Trends* 37, no. 2 (fall 1988): 154–174.

———. *Subject Access to Visual Resource Collections: A Model for Computer Construction of Thematic Catalogs.* New York: Greenwood Press, 1986.

Miller, Debra, and Mary Louise Krumrine. "Prolegomena to a Computerized Iconographical Index." In *Databases in the Humanities and the Social Sciences,* edited by Joseph Raben and Gregory A. Marks, 239–250. Amsterdam: North-Holland Publishing Company, 1980.

Molholt, Pat. "MARC and the Promise of Artificial Intelligence for Subject Access: Current Limitations and Future Considerations." In *Beyond the Book: Extending MARC for Subject Access,* edited by Toni Petersen and Pat Molholt, 247–257. Boston: G. K. Hall, 1990.

———. "The Use of the *Art and Architecture Thesaurus* as a Search Aid in an Online Slide Catalog: Design Objectives and Considerations." Paper presented at the 18th Annual Conference of the Art Libraries Society of North America, New York, N.Y., February 1990.

Ohlgren, Thomas H. "Image Analysis and Indexing in North America: A Survey." *Art Libraries Journal* 7, no. 2 (summer 1982): 51–60.

———. "Subject Access to Iconographic Data Bases: Theory and Practice." In *Databases in the Humanities and the Social Sciences,* edited by Joseph Raben and Gregory A. Marks, 245–250. Amsterdam: North-Holland Publishing Company, 1980.

———. "Subject Indexing of Visual Resources: A Survey." *Visual Resources* 1, no. 1 (spring 1980): 67–73.

Ostroff, Harriet. "Subject Access to Archival and Manuscript Material." *American Archivist* 53, no. 1 (winter 1990): 100–105.

Petersen, Toni. "The AAT: A Model for the Restructuring of LCSH." *Journal of Academic Librarianship* 9, no. 4 (September 1983): 207–210. Reprinted in the *Art and Architecture Thesaurus Sourcebook,* edited by Toni Petersen, 93–99.

———. "The AAT in the MARC Format." *Art and Architecture Thesaurus Bulletin,* no. 18 (1989): 9–11.

———. "The AAT in the MARC Format." *Art Documentation* 8, no. 4 (winter 1989): 181–182.

———. "The National Art Library and the *Art and Architecture Thesaurus,* Part II." *Art and Architecture Thesaurus Bulletin,* no. 22 (1994): 6–8.

———. "New Avenues of Access in the Online Catalog: Commingling." In *Art and Architecture Thesaurus Sourcebook,* edited by Toni Petersen, 121–127. Raleigh, N.C.: Art Libraries Society of North America, 1996.

———. "Retrofitting the Thesaurus: New Models for Old Vocabularies." *Visual Resources* 10, no. 3 (1994): 209–219.

———. "Subject Control in Visual Collections." *Art Documentation* 7, no. 4 (winter 1988): 131–135.

———, ed. *Art and Architecture Thesaurus Sourcebook.* Raleigh, N.C.: Art Libraries Society of North America, 1996.

Robbins, Cath. "The AAT and Archival Description in the MARC Format." *Art and Architecture Thesaurus Bulletin,* no. 21 (1993): 7–17.

Roberts, Helene. "'Do You Have Any Pictures of . . . ?': Subject Access to Works of Art in Visual Collections and Book Reproductions." *Art Documentation* 7, no. 3 (fall 1988): 87–90.

Roddy, Kevin. "The Belmont Conference on Subject Access." *Visual Resources* 2, no. 1–3 (fall 1981–spring 1982): 101–111.

———. "Subject Access to Visual Resources: What the 90s Might Portend." *Library Hi Tech* 9, no. 1, issue 33 (1991): 45–49.

Savidge, Jane. "Developing Online Access to a Subject Thesaurus: Implementing the *Art and Architecture Thesaurus* in the National Art Library OPAC." *Computers and the History of Art* 3, pt. 2 (1993): 27–38. Reprinted in the *Art and Architecture Thesaurus Sourcebook,* edited by Toni Petersen, 137–147. Raleigh, N.C.: Art Libraries Society of North America, 1996.

Shatford, Sara. "Analyzing the Subject of a Picture: A Theoretical Approach." *Cataloging and Classification Quarterly* 6, no. 3 (spring 1986): 39–62.

———. "Describing a Picture: A Thousand Words Are Seldom Cost Effective." *Cataloging and Classification Quarterly* 4, no. 4 (summer 1984): 13–30.

Small, Jocelyn Penny. "Retrieving Images Verbally: No More Key Words and Other Heresies." *Library Hi Tech* 9, no. 1 (1991): 51–60, 67.

———. "A Thousand Points of Retrieval." *VRA Bulletin* 23, no. 2 (summer 1996): 17–19.

Sobinski-Smith, Mary Jane. "Standards for Subject Cataloging and Retrieval at the Yale Center for British Art." In *Databases in the Humanities and the Social Sciences,* edited by Joseph Raben and Gregory A. Marks, 233–237. Amsterdam: North-Holland Publishing Company, 1980.

Sutherland, John. "Image Collections: Librarians, Users and Their Needs." *Art Libraries Journal* 7, no. 2 (summer 1982): 41–49.

Svenonius, Elaine. "Access to Nonbook Materials: The Limits of Subject Indexing for Visual and Aural Languages." *Journal of the American Society for Information Science* 45, no. 8 (1994): 600–606.

Teel, Kay. "Subject Access to Visual Materials." *SIG/CR News,* no. 3 (August 1992): 1–5.

Turner, James M. "Subject Access to Pictures: Considerations in the Surrogation and Indexing of Visual Documents for Storage and Retrieval." *Visual Resources* 9, no. 3 (1993): 241–271.

Vezina, Raymond. *Computerized Inventory Standards for Works of Art; Conference, November 1st, 2nd and 3rd, 1979, Proceedings.* Montreal: La Corporation des Éditions Fides, 1981.

Willis, Alfred, ed. "Festschrift for the *Art and Architecture Thesaurus.*" *Visual Resources* 10, no. 3 (1994), special issue.

———. "Visual Records." In *Guide to Indexing and Cataloging with the Art and Architecture Thesaurus,* edited by Toni Petersen and Patricia J. Barnett, 163–179. New York: Oxford University Press, 1994.

Reviews, Conference and Committee Reports

Allen, Rachel. "MARC Standing Committee." *Visual Resources Association Bulletin* 17, no. 1 (spring 1990): 22–23.

———. "VRA-MARC Format Committee: Year in Review." *Visual Resources Association Bulletin* 17, no. 4 (winter 1990): 32–33.

Auchstetter, Rosann. "MARC-ing the Visual Document: Innovative Efforts in Visual Information Management." *Art Documentation* 6, no. 2 (summer 1987): 65–66.

Barnett, Patricia J. "Indexing and Search Strategy Using the AAT: Three Options." *Art Documentation* 7, no. 2 (summer 1988): 49–50.

Bearman, David. "Digital Image Access Project, RLG Meeting, March 31–April 1, 1995." *Archives and Museum Informatics* 9, no. 2 (1995): 199–209.

Buckheit, Betsey. "Cataloging and Indexing Concerns in Automated Slide Database Systems/MARC." *VRA Bulletin* 20, no. 1 (spring 1993): 14–15.

Bunting, Christine. "Visual Resources Automation Issues Discussion." *Art Documentation* 9, no. 2 (summer 1990): 84–86.

Chewning, J. "*Art and Architecture Thesaurus:* Development and Application." *Art Documentation* 3, no. 2 (summer 1984): 46–47.

Fee, E. Review of *Illustrated Catalog of the Slide Archive of Historical Medical Photographs at Stony-Brook—Apple, RD. Isis* 76, no. 283 (1985): 401.

Jackman-Schuller, Carol. "Word, Words, Words: Managing the Wealth of the AAT—Early Efforts at Implementation." *Art Documentation* 9, no. 2 (summer 1990): 75–76.

Lawson, Roger. "One Year Later: AAT in the Field." *Art Documentation* 4, no. 2 (summer 1985): 58–59.

Lucker, Amy. "The Right Words: Controlled Vocabulary and Standards (An Editorial)." *Art Documentation* 7, no. 1 (spring 1988): 19–20.

McRae, Linda. Review of *Beyond the Book: Extending MARC for Subject Access,* edited by Toni Petersen and Patricia J. Barnett. *Visual Resources* 10, no. 4 (1995): 407–411.

———. Review of *Guide to Indexing and Cataloging with the Art and Architecture Thesaurus,* edited by Toni Petersen and Patricia J. Barnett. *VRA Bulletin* 21, no. 4 (winter 1994): 28–32.

Maddox, Brent. "Toward Automation—Implementing Standards in Visual Resource Collections." *Art Documentation* 4, no. 2 (summer 1985): 71–72.

Melville, Annette. "One-Stop Shopping: Access to Visual and Archival Materials—Use of VIM and AMC Formats." *Art Documentation* 7, no. 2 (summer 1988): 47.

"Museum Computer Network Develops a MARC-based Information Structure for the Syracuse University Art Collection." *Visual Resources Association Bulletin* 17, no. 1 (spring 1990): 32.

Nilsen, Micheline. "Visual Resources Collection Management: Cataloging Procedures and Other Issues for Automated Systems." *Art Documentation* 7, no. 2 (summer 1988): 51.

O'Donnell, Elizabeth. "Accessible Images." *International Bulletin for Photographic Documentation of the Visual Arts* 15, no. 2 (summer 1988): 20.

———. "AAT, MARC, and VR Cataloging." *Visual Resources Association Bulletin* 17, no. 1 (spring 1990): 38–40.

———. "Better Late than Never." *Visual Resources Association Bulletin* 19, no. 1 (spring 1992): 38–40.

———. "Knowledge Organization in the Visual Arts." *VRA Bulletin* 20, no. 2 (summer 1993): 41–43.

———. "MARC and the National Gallery of Art Photographic Archives." *International Bulletin for Photographic Documentation of the Visual Arts* 14, no. 1 (spring 1987): 39–40.

———. "MARC Featured." *International Bulletin for Photographic Documentation of the Visual Arts* 15, no. 3 (fall 1988): 22–23.

———. "Photography and Art History." *Visual Resources Association Bulletin* 18, no. 1 (spring 1991): 35–38.

———. "VRA's MARC Mapping Project." *Visual Resources Association Bulletin* 20, no. 4 (winter 1993): 48.

Otto, Susan. "MARC Format without Fear." *VRA Bulletin* 21, no. 2 (summer 1994): 30–36.

Poole, Katherine. "USMARC Advisory Group." *Art Documentation* 12, no. 2 (summer 1993): 72–73.

Smith, Shawn M., and Steven J. Livesey. Review of *The Use of Computers in Cataloging Medieval Manuscripts,* by Menso Folkerts and Andreas Kuhne; *MARC Cataloging for Medieval Manuscripts,* by Hope Mayo; and *Bibliographic Access to Medieval and Renaissance Manuscripts,* by Wesley M. Stevens. *Isis* 85, no. 3 (September 1994): 558–559.

Stanley, Janet L. "Symposium: Implementing the *Art and Architecture Thesaurus*—Controlled Vocabulary in the Extended MARC Format." *Art Documentation* 8, no. 3 (fall 1989): 121–124.

Stevenson, Barbara. "VRA/MARC Advisory Committee Report." *Visual Resources Association Bulletin* 19, no. 1 (spring 1992): 7.

Warren, Susanne. "New Avenues of Access in the Online Catalog: Consensus, Collaboration, Commingling." *Art Documentation* 13, no. 2 (summer 1994): 74–75.

———. "Workshop—Using the AAT: Practical Applications." *Art Documentation* 11, no. 2 (summer 1992): 63.

Whitehead, Cathy. "Report on Workshop on Cataloging Visual Materials with the *Art and Architecture Thesaurus.*" *Visual Resources Association Bulletin* 16, no. 2 (summer 1989): 9–10.

———, and Amy Lucker. "Workshop: Non-Book Database Design." *Art Documentation* 6, no. 2 (summer 1987): 59.

Additional Resources

Allen, Nancy S. "The Museum Prototype Project: A View from the Library." *Library Trends* 37, no. 2 (fall 1988): 175–193.

Art Documentation, each issue: "Professional Literature" and "Art Bibliography" (v. 1, no. 1 [February 1982] to v. 3, no. 3 [fall 1984]), "Publications Received" (in the Book Review Section), "Bibliographic Notes" (began v. 3, no. 4 [winter 1984] to v. 14, no. 3 [fall 1995]).

Austin, David. "Images in Time and Space." *VRA Bulletin* 23, no. 4 (winter 1996): 110–114.

———. "The Lady or the Tiger: The Importance of Establishing Warrant for the Names of Fixed Objects." *VRA Bulletin* 23, no. 2 (summer 1996): 51–53.

Babineau, Suzanne, and Thomas Behrendt. "A Data Base System for Visual Resources Collections: A System Analysis." *Visual Resources* 3, no. 1 (1983): 50–60.

Barnett, Patricia J. "Information Standards: Art Information Task Force Holds Inaugural Meeting." *Museum Management and Curatorship* 10 (March 1991): 100.

———, and Amy E. Lucker. *Procedural Guide to Automating an Art Library.* Occasional Papers, No. 7. Tucson: Art Libraries Society of North America, 1987.

Besser, Howard. "Visual Access to Visual Images: The UC Berkeley Image Database Project." *Library Trends* 38, no. 4 (spring 1990): 787–798.

Bierbaum, Esther Green. "A Modest Proposal: No More Main Entry." *American Libraries* 25, no. 1 (January 1994): 81–84.

———. "Records and Access: Museum Registration and Library Cataloging." *Cataloging and Classification Quarterly* 9, no. 1 (1988): 97–111.

Blouin, Joy. "Michigan Image Cataloging System Software." *Computers and the History of Art* 4, no. 2 (1994): 17–24.

Brilliant, Richard. "How an Art Historian Connects Art Objects and Information." *Library Trends* 37, no. 2 (fall 1988): 120–129.

Brooks, Diane. "System-System Interaction in Computerized Indexing of Visual Materials: A Selected Review." *Information Technology and Libraries* 7 (June 1988): 111–123.

Busch, Joseph A. "How to Choose among Alternative Technologies for Physical Access to Art Images." *Computers and the History of Art* 4, no. 2 (1994): 3–16.

Cawkell, A. E. *A Guide to Image Processing and Picture Management.* Aldershot, Hampshire; Brookfield, Vt.: Gower, 1994.

———. *Indexing Collections of Electronic Images: A Review.* London: British Library Research and Development Dept., 1993.

Chang, Chin-Chen, and Tzong-Chen Wu. "Retrieving the Most Similar Symbolic Pictures from Pictorial Databases." *Information Processing and Management* 28 (September/October 1991): 581–588.

Davis, Stephen Paul. "SGML-MARC: Incorporating Library Cataloging into the TEI Environment." Paper delivered at the First ACM International Conference on Digital Libraries, Bethesda, Md. New York: Columbia University, <http://www.columbia.edu/cu/libraries/inside/projects/sgml/sgmlmarc/davis.9603.text.html>. March 23, 1996.

Dodds, Douglas. "Computer Applications in the National Art Library." *Computers and the History of Art* 3, no. 2 (1993): 15–25.

———. "Documentation Systems in Britain's National Art Library." *Art Libraries Journal* 18, no. 4 (1993): 15–23.

Duncan, Norine. "Visual Resource Management System: Software for Cataloging Art Slides." *Computers and the History of Art* 4, no. 2 (1994): 25–34.

Earnest, Greta K. "Authority Control in the Visual Resources: Based on a Survey of ARLIS Visual Resource Members." *International Bulletin for the Photographic Documentation of the Visual Arts* 15, no. 1 (spring 1988): 23–24.

Electronic Imaging and the Visual Arts, Conference Proceedings. Aldershot, Hants: Brameur Ltd., 1992–1993.

Esteve-Coll, E. "Image and Reality: The National Art Library." *Art Libraries Journal* 11, no. 2 (1986): 33–39.

Fidel, Raya, Trudi B. Hahn, Edie M. Rasmussen, et al. *Challenges in Indexing Electronic Text and Images.* ASIS Monograph Series. Medford, N.J.: Learned Information, 1994.

Giral, Angela, and Jeannette Dixon. "The Virtual Museum Comes to Campus: Two Perspectives on the Museum Educational Site Licensing Project." *Art Libraries Journal* 21, no. 1 (1996): 14–17.

Heaney, Michael. "Object-Oriented Cataloging." *Information Technology and Libraries* 14, no. 3 (September 1995): 135–153.

Hennessey, Christine. "The Status of Name Authority Control in the Cataloging of Original Art Objects." *Art Documentation* 5, no. 1 (spring 1986): 3–10.

Holt, Bonnie, Laura Hartwick, and Stacey Vetter. "Query by Image Content: The QBIC Project's Applications in the University of California–Davis' Art and Art History Departments." *VRA Bulletin* 22, no. 2 (summer 1995): 60–66.

———. "Retrieving Art Images by Image Content: The UC Davis QBIC Project." *Aslib Proceedings* 46 (October 1994): 243–248.

Hourihane, Colum. "The Van Eyck Project, Information Exchange, and European Art Libraries." *VRA Bulletin* 23, no. 2 (summer 1996): 57–60.

Jeffery, R. Brooks. "Learning from Others: A Multimedia Approach to Cataloging Architectural Collections." *VRA Bulletin* 23, no. 2 (summer 1996): 54–56.

Joseph, Michael. "Information Technology and Access to Visual Images in Printed Books." *Visual Resources* 11, no. 1 (1995): 71–84.

Keats, Patricia L. "Visual Resources Bibliography." *Visual Resources,* each volume.

Kessler, Ben. Response to "Today's Databases and the Future of Shared Cataloging: Where Do We Start?" Session IV, Visual Resources Association Conference, Boston, February 1997. *VRA Bulletin* 23, no. 2 (summer 1996): 67–68.

Kirsch, R. "Describing Art Objects to Computers." *AICARC Bulletin of the Archives and Documentation Centers for Modern and Contemporary Art* 11–12, nos. 21–22 (1985): 40–42.

Layne, Sara Shatford. "Artists, Art Historians, and Visual Art Information." *The Reference Librarian* 47 (1994): 23–36.

Levinson, Allen, and Dierdre McConathy. "Descriptive Cataloging for Collections of Medical Art." *The Journal of Biocommunication* 20, no. 4 (1993): 2–11.

Library of Congress. "MARC and Its Relevance in the Digital World." In *Organizing the Global Digital Library II.* Washington, D.C.: Library of Congress, <http://lcweb.loc.gov/catdir/ogdl2/marc.html>. August 1996.

LoPresti, Maryellen. "An Automated Slide Classification System at Georgia Tech." *Special Libraries* 64, no. 11 (November 1973): 509–513.

MacEachern, Brenda. "Automation of the Visual Arts Department Slide Library at the University of Western Ontario." *Computers and the History of Art* 4, no. 2 (1994): 55–68.

McKeown, Roy. "The National Art Slide Library: A Developing Picture." *Audiovisual Librarian* 18 (November 1992): 252–254.

Maddox, Brent. "Bunched Images Begetting Ideas." *Visual Resources* 7, no. 2–3 (1990): 255–284.

Markey, Karen. "Visual Arts Resources and Computers." *Annual Review of Information Science and Technology* 19 (1984): 271–309.

Muller, Karen. *Authority Control Symposium: Papers Presented during the 14th Annual ARLIS/NA Conference, New York, N.Y., February 10, 1986.* Occasional Papers, No. 6. Tucson: Art Libraries Society of North America, 1987.

O'Donnell, Elizabeth. "An Unconventional Slide Collection Database." *Computers and the History of Art* 4, no. 2 (1994): 35–42.

Ohlgren, Thomas H. "Computer Indexing of Illuminated Manuscripts for Use in Medieval Studies." *Computers and the Humanities* 12, no. 1/2 (1975): 189–199.

Poix, Marie Helene. "A Computerized Interactive Catalogue." *Museum International* 45, no. 3 (1993): 33–35.

Porter, Vicki, and Robin Thornes. *A Guide to the Description of Architectural Drawings.* New York: G. K. Hall, 1994.

Rabitti, F., and P. Saviano. "Automatic Image Indexation to Support Content-based Retrieval." *Information Processing and Management* 28 (September/October 1992): 547–565.

Roberts, Helene. "Visual Resources: Proposal for an Ideal Network." *Art Libraries Journal* 10 (autumn 1985): 32.

———. "Visual Resources: Reflections on an Ideal Network." *AICARC: Bulletin of the Archives and Documentation Centers for Modern and Contemporary Art* (February 1986 & January 1987): 27–30.

Romano, Joseph A. "The World of Internet Hypermedia and Visual Resources Professionals." *Visual Resources* 9, no. 4 (1995): 333–347.

Sage-Gagne, Waneta. "An Automated Management System for Blueprints and Architectural Drawings." *Museum Archivist* 5, no. 1 (February 1991): 9–11.

Seal, Alan. "Standards and Local Practice: The Experience of the Victoria and Albert Museum." *Computers and the History of Art* 5, no. 1 (1995): 17–24.

Snow, Maryly. "SPIRO and ImageQuery at the University of California at Berkeley." *Computers and the History of Art* 4, no. 2 (1994): 43–54.

Stam, Deirdre C. "Shared Access to Visual Images—The Potential of the Web." *VRA Bulletin* 23, no. 2 (summer 1996): 63–67.

Stone, Gerald, and Philip Sylvain. "ArchiVISTA: A New Horizon in Providing Access to Visual Records of the National Archives of Canada." *Library Trends* 38, no. 4 (1990): 737–750.

Taylor, Bradley. "Private Sector Contributions to the Online Access of Image-based Databases." *VRA Bulletin* 22, no. 1 (spring 1995): 31–40.

Trant, Jennifer, and Howard Besser. *Introduction to Imaging: Issues in Constructing an Image Database.* Santa Monica, Calif.: Getty Art History Information Program, 1995; also available at <http://www.ahip.getty.edu/intro_imaging/>. 1995.

Van der Starre, Jan H. E. "Visual Arts Network for the Exchange of Cultural Knowledge (VAN EYCK Project)." In *Proceedings of the 1993 Electronic Imaging and the Visual Arts Conference, EVA '93.* Aldershot, Hants: Brameur Ltd., 1993, 84–92.

Veltman, Kim H. "Knowledge Organization in the Visual Arts." *Knowledge Organization* 20, no. 1 (1993): 2–54.

Waterman, Annette F. "First Steps in Planning the Automation of a Slide Collection." *Art Documentation* 8, no. 2 (summer 1989): 61–65.

Weber, Lisa B. "Record Formatting: MARC AMC." *Cataloging and Classification Quarterly* 11, no. 3/4 (1990): 117–143.

Weibel, Stuart, and Eric Miller. "Image Description on the Internet: A Summary of the CNI/OCLC Image Metadata Workshop, September 24–25, 1996, Dublin, Ohio." *D-Lib Magazine* (January 1997), <http://www.dlib.org:80/dlib/january97/oclc/01weibel.html>.

Winke, R. Conrad. "Discarding the Main Entry in an Online Cataloging Environment: Proposed Revisions to AACR2 and the MARC Format." *Cataloging and Classification Quarterly* 16, no.1 (1993): 53–70.

Web Sites

American Library Association (ALA): <http://www.ala.org/>
MARBI Committee: <http://lcweb.loc.gov/marc/marbi.html>

Art Libraries Society of North America (ARLIS/NA): <http://afalib.uflib.ufl.edu/arlis/>
Cataloging Advisory Committee: (Daniel Starr, Chair) <http://w3.arizona.edu/~arlis/>
Cataloging Section: (Katherine Teel, Chair) <http://w3.arizona.edu/~arlis/>
Visual Resources Division (VRD): (Martha Mahard, Chair) <http://afalib.uflib.ufl.edu/arlis/groups.html>

Canadian Heritage Information Network (CHIN): <http://www.chin.gc.ca/>

Coalition for Networked Information (CNI): <http://www.cni.org>

Consortium for Computer Interchange of Computer Information (CIMI): <http://www.nstn.ca:80/cimi/>

Getty Information Institute: <http://www.gii.getty.edu/>; e-mail ahip@getty.edu
Art and Architecture Thesaurus (AAT): (Pat Young) <http://www.gii.getty.edu/vocabulary/aat.html>
Categories for the Description of Works of Art (CDWA): <http://www.ahip.getty.edu/index/cdwa.html>
Museum Educational Site License Project (MESL): <http://www.ahip.getty.edu/mesl/>
Data Dictionary: <http://www.ahip.getty.edu/mesl/about/docs/datadict.html>
Thesaurus of Geographic Names (TGN): (Patricia Harpring) <http://www.gii.getty.edu/vocabulary/tgn.html>
Union List of Artist Names (ULAN): (Murtha Baca) <http://www.gii.getty.edu/vocabulary/ulan.html>

ICONCLASS: <http://iconclass.let.ruu.nl>

International Committee for Documentation. International Council of Museums (ICOM-CIDOC): <http://www.cidoc.icom.org/>

Library of Congress (LC): <http://lcweb.loc.gov>; telnet to locis.loc.gov; gopher://marvel.loc.gov.
Art NACO (Name Authority Cooperative): (Sherman Clarke) <http://www.nyu.edu/library/bobst/research/tsd/cat/artnaco.htm>
Program for Cooperative Cataloging (PCC): <http://lcweb.loc.gov/catdir/pcc/>
Cataloging Directorate: <http://lcweb.loc.gov/catdir/catdir.html>
Programs and Services: <http://lcweb.loc.gov/catdir/catdir.html#programs>
MARC Home Page: <http://lcweb.loc.gov/marc/>
MARC Formats: <http://lcweb.loc.gov/marc/bibliographic/ecbdhome.html>
MARC Advisory Committee Proposals and Discussion Papers: <gopher://marvel.loc.gov/11/services/usmarc/marbipro>

Museum Computer Network (MCN): <http://world.std.com/~mcn/>

OCLC: <http://www.oclc.org/>
Dublin Core Elements: <http://purl.org/metadata/dublin_core_elements>

RLIN: Information available through the Research Libraries Group (RLG): <http://www.rlg.org>

Society of American Archivists (SAA): <http://www.archivists.org/>

Visual Resources Association (VRA): <http://www.oberlin.edu/~art/vra/vra.html>
Data Standards Committee (DSC): (Elisa Lanzi, Chair) http://www.oberlin.edu/~art/vra/dsc.html>

Listserves

AAT-L. Hosted by David Austin at the University of Illinois–Chicago. Available through Daustin@UIC.EDU.

ARCHIVES. Available through Archives@miamiu.muohio.edu

ARLIS-L. Hosted by Mary Molinaro at the University of Kentucky. Available through ARLIS-L@lsv.uky.edu

IMAGELIB. Hosted by the University of Arizona. Available through imagelib@listserv.arizona.edu

MUSEUM-L. Available through museum-l@UNMVMA.UNM.EDU

USMARC. Hosted by the Library of Congress, USMARC Advisory Committee. Available through USMARC@loc.gov

VRA-L. Hosted by Christine Hilker at the University of Arkansas. Available through VRA-L@UAFSYSB.UARK.EDU.

VRMS-L. Hosted by Susan J. Williams at Yale University. Available through VRMS-L@lists.yale.edu

Contributors

Ann Abid is the Head Librarian, Ingalls Library, the Cleveland Museum of Art. She administers the three collections that comprise the library: Book Library, Slide Library, Photograph Collection. Her role in the Cleveland Museum's contribution to this book was to coordinate the internal process that brought together three very different informational functions. The totally manual nature of the image collections had to be informed by the technical expertise of the book cataloging function.

David Austin is Architecture and Art Librarian and an associate professor at the University of Illinois at Chicago. During his thirty years as a librarian he has been interested and actively involved in the delivery of nonverbal information to library patrons with special needs. He first became intimately involved with MARC formats as a cataloger of music scores and sound recordings. For the past five years his research has led him into the application of MARC as a tool to create indexes for very large microform sets of the photographic archives of the Courtauld Institute's Conway Library and the Deutsches Archaeologisches Institut. He has presented papers related to his work in Barcelona, Ljubljana, Essen, and Amsterdam, as well as at numerous meetings in the United States.

Vesna Blazina heads the departments of Collection Development and Government Publications at Bibliothèque des lettres et des sciences humaines, Université de Montréal. From 1984 to 1994, she was Head of Bibliothèque de l'Aménagement (Environmental Design) and it was in this capacity that she coordinated the project of using the MARC format for cataloging architectural slides and building a French thesaurus of indexing terms. During that time she was active in the Art Libraries Society of North America and was president of its Quebec Chapter for two years. She has published in the VRA Bulletin and Documentation et bibliotheques (Montreal).

Karen Chittenden is a cataloger of the pictorial materials at the Prints and Photographs Division of the Library of Congress, specializing in architectural records. Her processing team recently completed the eight-year Washingtoniana II project, to arrange, preserve, house, and catalog almost forty thousand architectural drawings relating to the Washington, D.C., metropolitan area. She is currently cataloging architectural drawings by Frank Lloyd Wright.

Sherman Clarke is Head of Original Cataloging at New York University Libraries, after positions at the Amon Carter Museum, Rhode Island School of Design, and Cornell University. He is founder and coordinator of Art NACO, and has been active for many years in the Art Libraries Society of North America and the American Library Association. His newest challenge is representing the Visual Resources Association on the USMARC Advisory Group.

Margaret L. Emons is currently the Technical Services/Public Services Librarian at Iowa Central Community College in Fort Dodge, Iowa. She was previously the slide curator at the University of Nebraska Architecture Branch Library. She received her B.S. at Nebraska Wesleyan University, Lincoln, Nebraska, and her M.LIS. at Emporia State University, Emporia, Kansas.

Christine Hennessey is currently Research Databases Coordinator for the National Museum of American Art, Smithsonian Institution. In 1985, she served on a resource committee formed by the Library of Congress Network Development and MARC Standards Office to assist in redefining the Visual Materials Format to accommodate three-dimensional artifacts and realia. She has published in *Art Documentation* and *Visual Resources* and has chapters in *Beyond the Book: Extending MARC for Subject Access* (Toni Petersen and Pat Molholt, eds., Boston: G. K. Hall, 1990), and *Terminology for Museums: Proceedings of a Conference Held in Cambridge, England, 21–24 Sept. 1990*, edited by D. Andrew Roberts (Museum Documentation Association, 1990).

Judith Gelernter Jaroker earned her master of arts degree in fine arts at Harvard University and her master of library and information science degree in 1994 at Simmons College. She writes regularly on topics in information science and dance history. She is the Librarian and Archivist for the Dance Notation Bureau and the principal consultant to Director Constance Old of the Metropolitan Museum of Art Performing Arts Index project.

Patricia Keats is the Director of the Library at the California Historical Society in San Francisco. Previously, she worked at the society as a reference librarian and visual images cataloger, dealing with photographs, book illustrations, and various illustrated ephemera. She has worked as both reference librarian and cataloger at Towson State University in Maryland; and as assistant librarian/slide librarian at the Walters Art Gallery in Baltimore, where she moved and reorganized the entire slide collection. Her degrees are a B.A. in history with a minor in art history from Miami University in Ohio, an M.A. in Medieval and Renaissance art from the University of Chicago, and an M.L.S. in academic and special libraries from Kent State University. She has been an active member of the Visual Resources Association, serving as vice-president; and of both the Art Libraries Society of North America and

the College Art Association, serving as a local chapter secretary/treasurer for the ARLIS MD/DC/VA chapter. She has presented papers at library and Southeast College Art Conference meetings, and has edited the annual "Bibliography" in the journal *Visual Resources* since its rebirth in 1985. In addition, she taught art history at the community college level while in Baltimore, and the research methods course for art history majors while at Towson State University.

Jeanne M. Keefe is the Graphic Curator at Rensselaer Polytechnic Institute in Troy, New York. In that capacity she is responsible for the development, maintenance, and supervision of the Architecture Library's collection of prints, maps, architectural drawings, models, microforms, and videos. She previously held the position of assistant archivist with the Armenian Architectural Archives Project, a multivolume microfiche inventory of the history of Armenian architecture. She is currently involved in a project to produce a set of CD-ROMs based on these volumes and is developing a Web site to make many of these images available on the World Wide Web. She is an active member of the Visual Resources Association and serves on the *Art and Architecture Thesaurus* Advisory Committee of the Art Libraries Society of North America.

Elizabeth Lantz is the Assistant Librarian for Technical Services at the Cleveland Museum of Art, Ingalls Library, Cleveland, Ohio, where she has been very involved with the automation of the library. She is active in the Art Libraries Society of North America's Cataloging Section and most recently served on the "Inaccessible Domain" Materials Working Group (RLG Art and Architecture Group), which developed a collection-level record for textual and visual materials. She received her M.L.S. from the University of Maryland and an M.F.A. in art history from Ohio University; she previously worked at Moore College of Art.

Linda McRae is an associate librarian and Head of the College of Fine Arts Visual Resources Library at the University of South Florida. Her research and publications have focused on issues of status in the visual resources profession and on documentation standards for image collections. She is a contributing editor for the *VRA Bulletin*, and has published in *Art Libraries Journal, Art Documentation,* and *Visual Resources;* she also co-authored *African Ethnonyms: Index to Art-Producing Peoples of Africa.*

Ginette Melançon-Bolduc has been working at the Université de Montréal since 1974. From June 1974 to December 1975, she cataloged books on architecture, landscape architecture, and urban studies. From December 1975 to November 1987, she held the position of Reference Librarian at the Bibliothèque de l'Aménagement, which serves the École d'Architecture, the École d'Architecture de Paysage, the École de Design Industriel, and the Institut d'Urbanisme. In November 1987, she was appointed as Special Projects Librarian at the Bibliothèque de l'Aménagement. As such, she worked full-time on the automation project for the Slide Library and assumed the responsibilities of Slide Curator. In addition, she was asked in 1996 to supervise the automation of a bibliographical database concerning the architectural heritage of the Quebec Province.

Anne Mitchell is a cataloger of pictorial materials with a specialization in architectural, design, and engineering collections at the Prints and Photographs Division of the Library of Congress in Washington, D.C. She was a member of the Washingtoniana II processing team that recently completed an eight-year project to arrange, preserve, house, and catalog almost forty thousand architectural drawings relating to the Washington, D.C., metropolitan area. She recently participated in testing the new Encoded Archival Description (EAD) for pictorial collection finding aids, and presented a talk on this subject at the Society of American Archivists Annual Meeting, 1996. She is currently cataloging the work of Charles and Ray Eames.

Gregory P. J. Most is Chief Slide Librarian at the National Gallery of Art in Washington, D.C. He previously held positions in visual resources collections at the Museum of Fine Arts, Houston, the Cleveland Museum of Art, and Saint Louis University. At the National Gallery, he is responsible for the development and implementation of the automation of the slide collection. He is an active member of the Art Libraries Society of North America and has been a regular contributor to *Art Documentation*. He is the ARLIS/NA representative to the Conference on Fair Use.

Mayra F. Nemeth is university librarian, Head of the Audiovisual Library at Florida International University Library, Miami. She is responsible for acquisition, processing, and circulation of all audiovisual materials. In this capacity, she curates the art slide collection, including the development and implementation of the MARC records project.

Elizabeth O'Keefe is Director of Information Services at the Pierpont Morgan Library, a position responsible for providing integrated access to all the library's holdings. She has served in the past as head of cataloging and the reference collection. She has served on the library's computer committee, and advises the administration on library automation, information technology, and standards issues for the reference and curatorial collections. She has collaborated with curators on translating their files into MARC format records for illuminated manuscripts, seals, and autograph manuscripts. She is a member of the Art Libraries Society of North America and the Visual Resources Association and has organized sessions at annual conferences on the cataloging of visual materials, illuminated manuscripts, and ephemeral and nontraditional materials.

Constance Old earned her bachelor's degree in humanities and botany at Stanford University and Colorado College. In 1984, she established the Dance Index—now the Performing Arts Index—within the Musical Instruments Department of the Metropolitan Museum of Art, and she has directed the project ever since. She is on the board of the Dance Perspectives Foundation and is a member of the Congress on Research in Dance, the Society of Dance History Scholars, the International Council for Traditional Music, and the Visual Resources Association.

Susan Otto is the Photo Collection Manager and a librarian at the Milwaukee Public Museum. She worked in other public and academic libraries before specializing in the librarianship of visual arts. Recently she has returned to her roots and now spends part of her time managing the photo collection and part of her time as the cataloger for the museum's reference library.

Sara Jane Pearman is the slide librarian of the Ingalls Library at the Cleveland Museum of Art. She earned a B.A. from the University of Wichita, an M.A. in art history from the University of Kansas, and a Ph.D. in art history from Case Western Reserve University. A slide librarian since graduate school, she has developed cataloging in all phases of art history and has spoken on cataloging and visual description to various library groups. As a teaching art historian (adjunct faculty at Kent State University), she is aware of the problems of visual resources from both a librarian's and a user's point of view.

Phyllis Pivorun is the Media Resources Specialist in the Gunnin Architectural Library at Clemson University. Within the confines of handling a variety of duties in the branch library, including assisting with general circulation and reference, she manages the operation of the Slide Room and oversees the creation of MARC slide records in NOTIS. The use of the Visual Materials Format and NOTIS software to automate the slide collection was initiated in 1987. She is a member of the Visual Resources Association, Art Libraries Society of North America, Art Libraries Society/South East Chapter, and the Southeast College Art Conference.

Jane Savidge is the Chief Cataloger of the National Art Library at the Victoria and Albert Museum, London, where she supervises the cataloging of the collections and has responsibility for the development and implementation of documentation standards. She has had a long-standing involvement with the Art Libraries Society/United Kingdom and Ireland, joining the Cataloguing and Classification Committee in 1986 and serving as its chair from 1990 to 1993. She is currently chair of the ARLIS Working Group on Cataloguing Art Reproductions. She is also a member of the Library Association Cataloguing and Indexing Group Committee and is OCLC European User Group Representative on the OCLC Collections and Technical Services Advisory Committee.

Eleanor Scheifele has worked at the Cleveland Museum of Art Library and is teaching Medieval art history at Indiana University.

Lynda S. White is Associate Fine Arts Librarian at the Fiske Kimball Fine Arts Library at the University of Virginia. She has served in various capacities at that library since 1977, including as curator of the architectural slide collection. She has an M.L.S. from the University of North Carolina, Chapel Hill, and an M.A. in art history from the University of Virginia. Her professional contributions have been as treasurer of the Visual Resources Association; as a member of the VRA's Data Standards Committee and Intellectual Property Rights Committee; and as a member of the Art Libraries Society of North America's *Art and Architecture Thesaurus* Advisory Committee and Visual Resources Issues Task Force. Publications include articles in *Source, Notes in the History of Art; Art Reference Services Quarterly; ARLIS Update;* and the *Visual Resources Association Bulletin.*

Index